Portraitography

Ink'd Artistry of the Female Figure

By
3ichael 7ambert

Introduction

Welcome to "Portraitography; Ink'd Artistry of the Female Form." In this collection, we embark on a journey into the heart of artistic expression, where ink'd drawings and black and white monochrome paintings serve as windows into the timeless beauty and grace of the female figure. Join me as we explore the intricacies of the human form and delve into the depths of the feminine spirit, captured through the masterful strokes of the artist's pen.

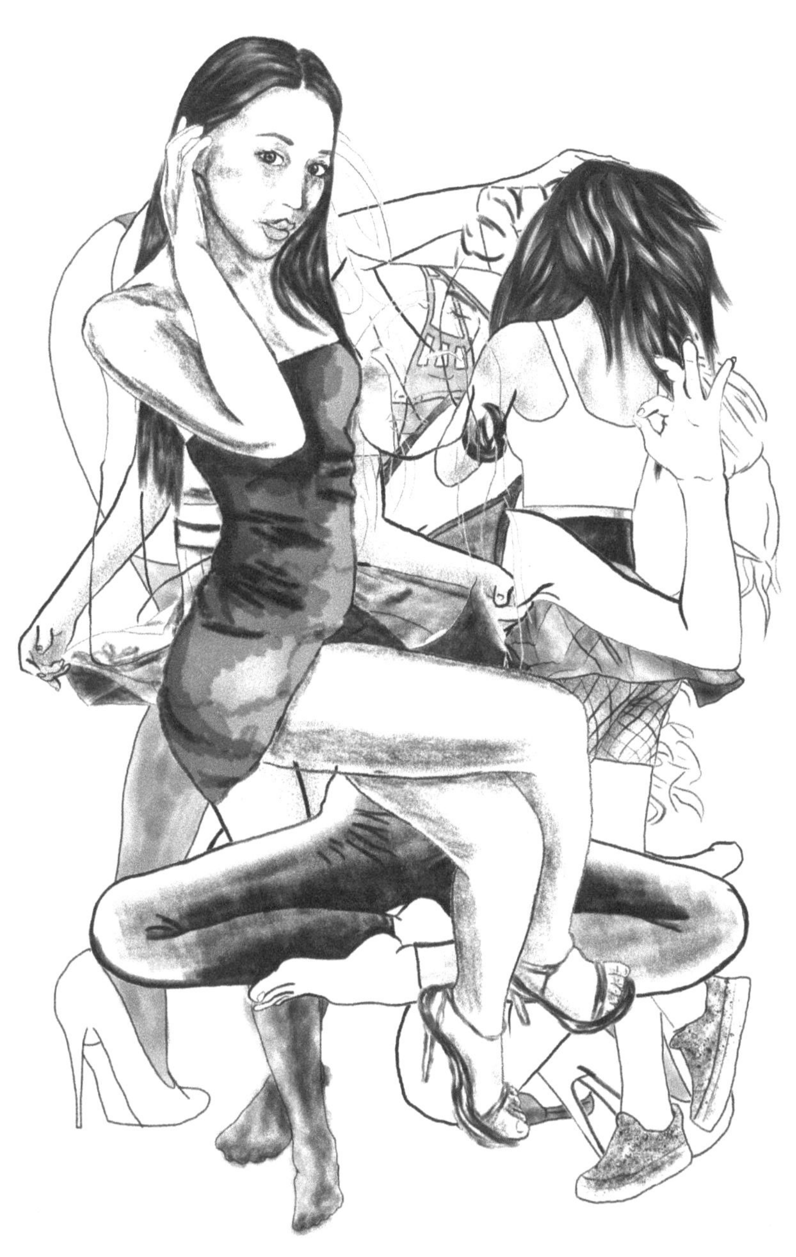

Dedication

To the wonderful people of my hometown, Aurora, whose unwavering support has been a constant source of inspiration on my artistic journey. To my fellow Coloradans, whose connections, friendship, and encouragement have fueled my passion for creativity. And to all the supporters I've encountered in the vast online community throughout the years, your belief in my work has lifted me higher than I could have imagined. This book is dedicated to you all.

Acknowledgment

I extend my heartfelt gratitude to everyone who has been a part of my artistic journey. Your support, whether near or far, has been instrumental in shaping my path as an artist. From the streets of Aurora to the corners of Colorado and beyond, your encouragement and belief in my work have been my guiding lights. I owe this moment to each one of you, for without your unwavering support, I wouldn't be where I am today. Thank you, from the bottom of my heart.

Special Thanks

I would like to express a heartfelt gratitude to my late grandmother, who played a pivotal role in shaping both my life and my artistic endeavors. From my earliest days, she stood by my side, offering unwavering support and encouragement. Whether it was attending school parties, cheering me on in Boy Scouts, or guiding me through the challenges of youth group, her belief in my dreams never wavered. Her love and presence continue to inspire me every day.

I also want to extend a special thanks to my late Uncle Johnboy. His awe and admiration for my skills were a constant source of motivation and validation. His unwavering belief in my abilities gave me the confidence to reach for the stars. Without his friendship and support, I would not be the person I am today. Though they may no longer be with us, their memories and influence will forever remain in my heart.

Author's Note

Art, to me, is more than just a hobby or a skill—it's a way of life. From the earliest moments of my childhood, I've been captivated by the endless possibilities that creativity offers. I believe that art is not confined to any single medium or genre; it transcends boundaries and manifests itself in myriad forms.

Throughout my journey as an artist, I've explored a wide array of mediums and genres, from traditional to digital, from ink to painting, from graphite to sculpture. Each medium presents its own unique challenges and rewards, yet they all share a common thread: the ability to evoke emotion, provoke thought, and inspire change.

Whether I'm sketching a portrait in graphite, crafting a poem that dances across the page, or designing a digital world that invites exploration, I approach each endeavor with the same passion and curiosity. Art, for me, is a lifelong journey of discovery—a journey that knows no bounds and holds endless possibilities.

In this book, I invite you to join me on this journey as we explore the diverse tapestry of artistic expression. From the intricate lines of ink drawings to the vibrant hues of digital paintings, from the sculpted forms of three-dimensional art to the evocative verses of poetry, we'll journey together through the vast landscape of creativity.

I believe that art has the power to transcend language and culture, to bridge gaps and foster connections. It is my hope that through these pages, you'll discover the transformative power of art and perhaps find inspiration to embark on your own creative journey.

So let us embark on this adventure together, guided by the boundless spirit of creativity and fueled by the belief that art has the power to change the world.

Michael Lambert Jr

Preface

In the pages that follow, I invite you to immerse yourself in the captivating world of ink'd elegance. As an artist, I have long been fascinated by the power of monochrome to convey emotion and evoke thought. In this collection, I seek to pay homage to the beauty and strength of women, exploring the subtle interplay of light and shadow, form and expression.

Each piece in this collection is a testament to my belief in the transformative power of art and its ability to transcend boundaries and connect us on a deeper level. Whether you are a seasoned art enthusiast or simply curious to explore the beauty of the feminine form, I hope that you will find inspiration and solace within these pages.

So join me as we embark on this artistic journey together, guided by the timeless allure of ink'd elegance and the enduring spirit of the feminine.

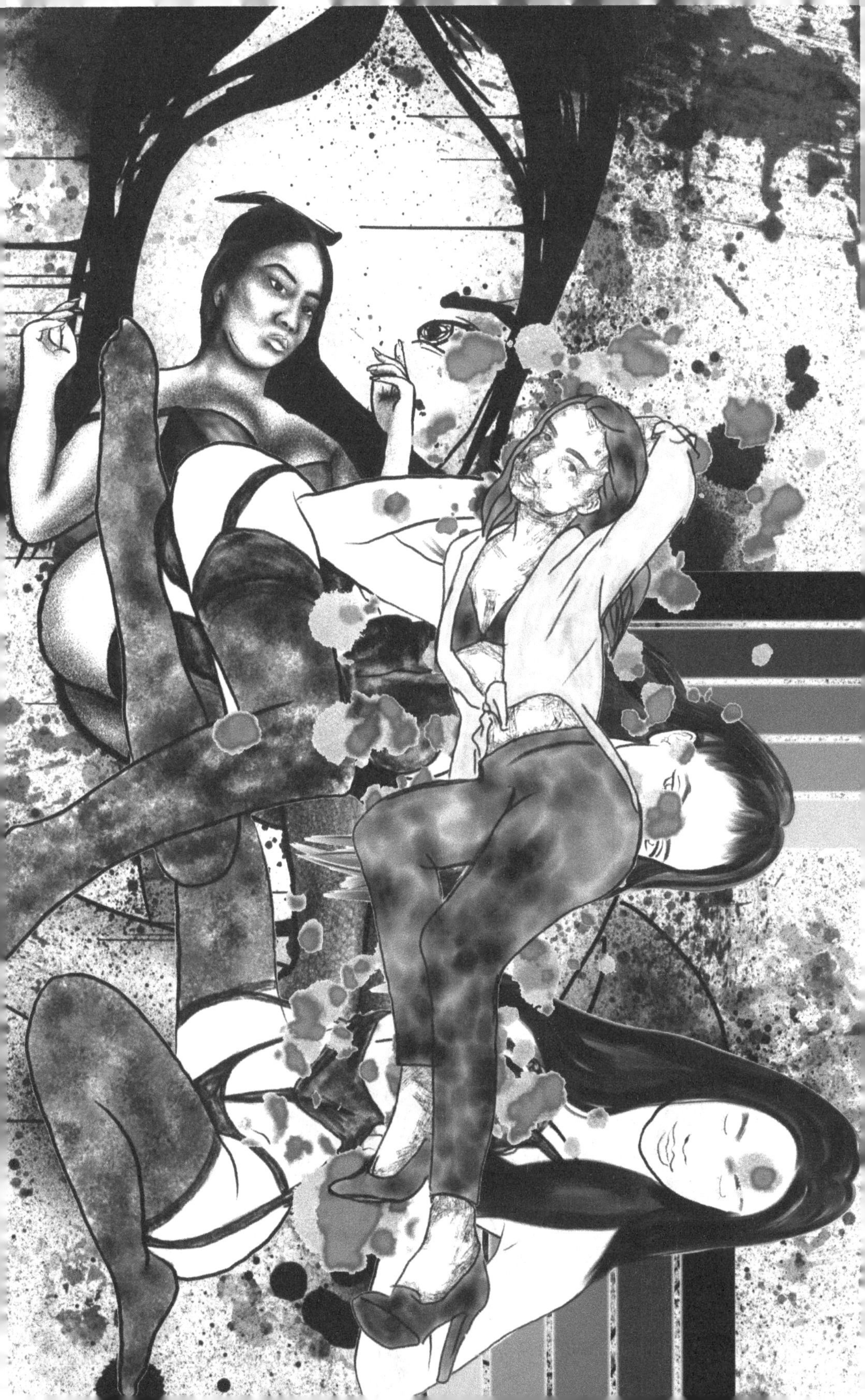

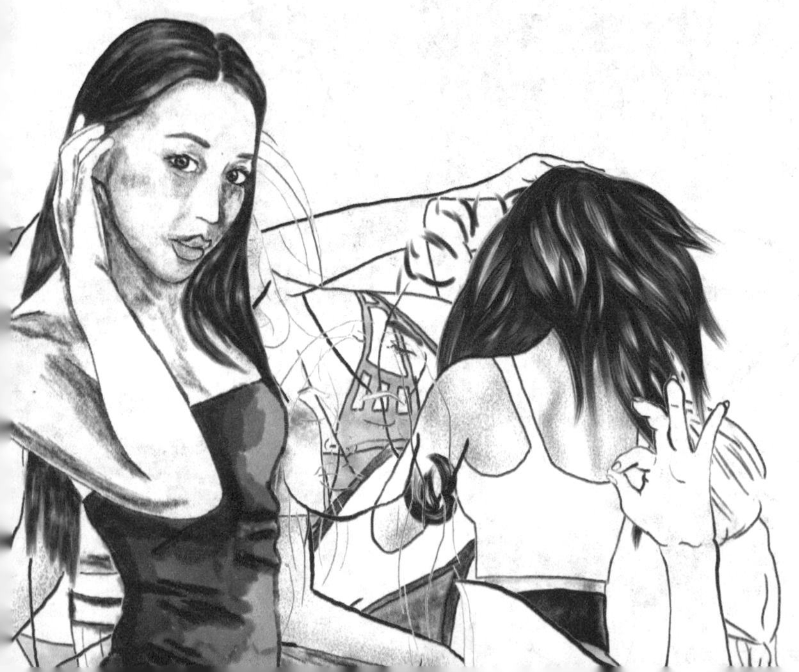

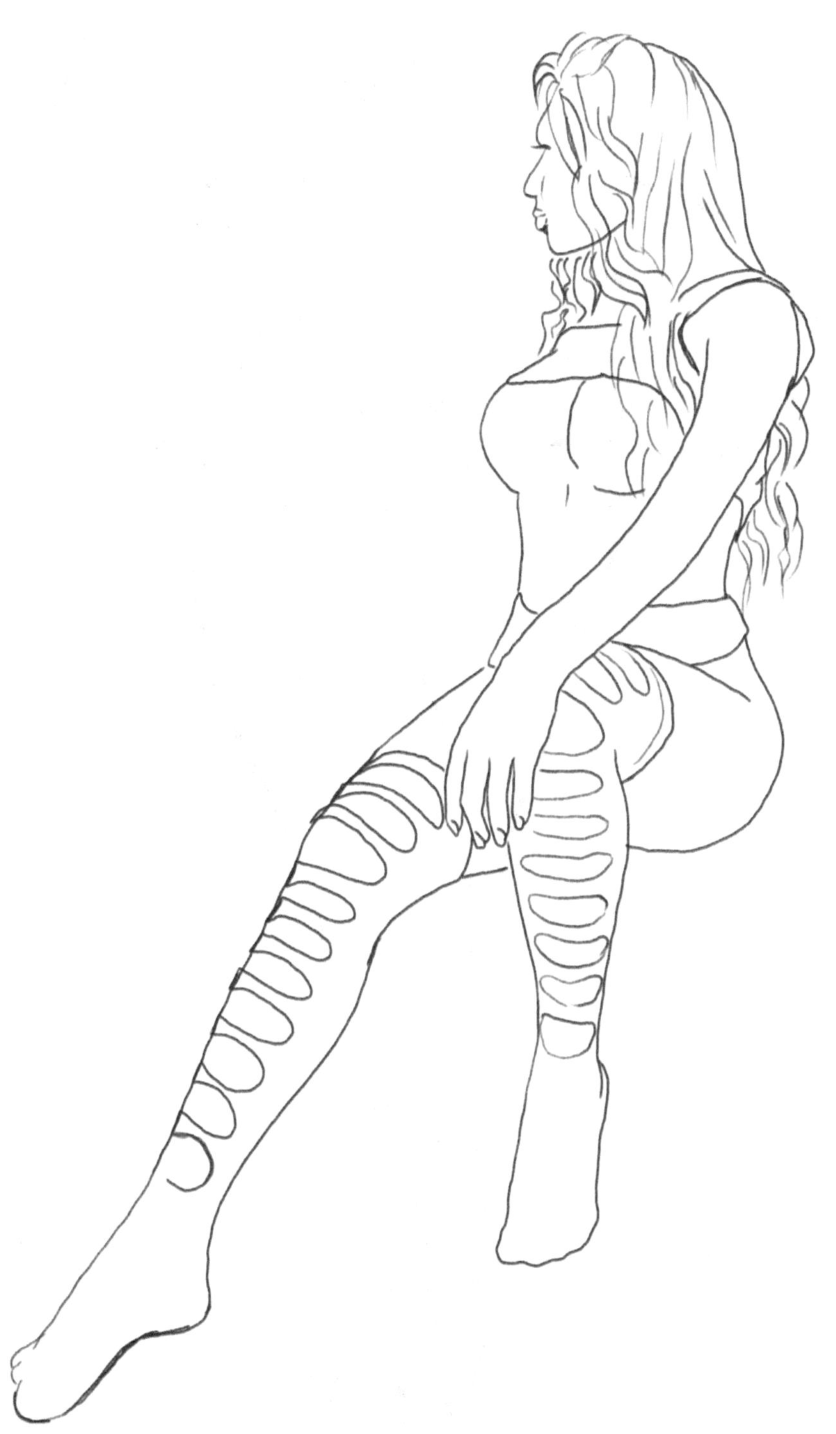

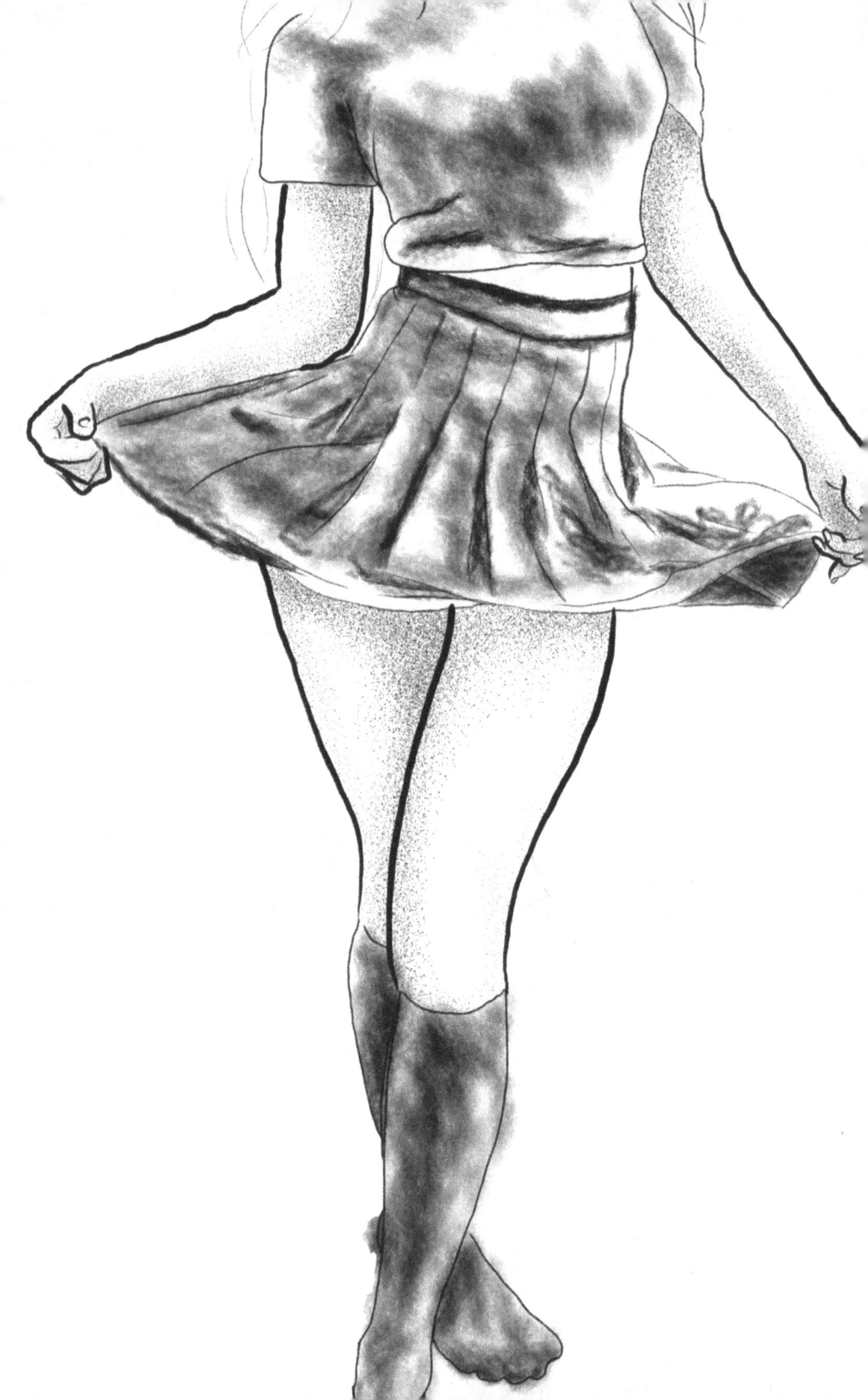

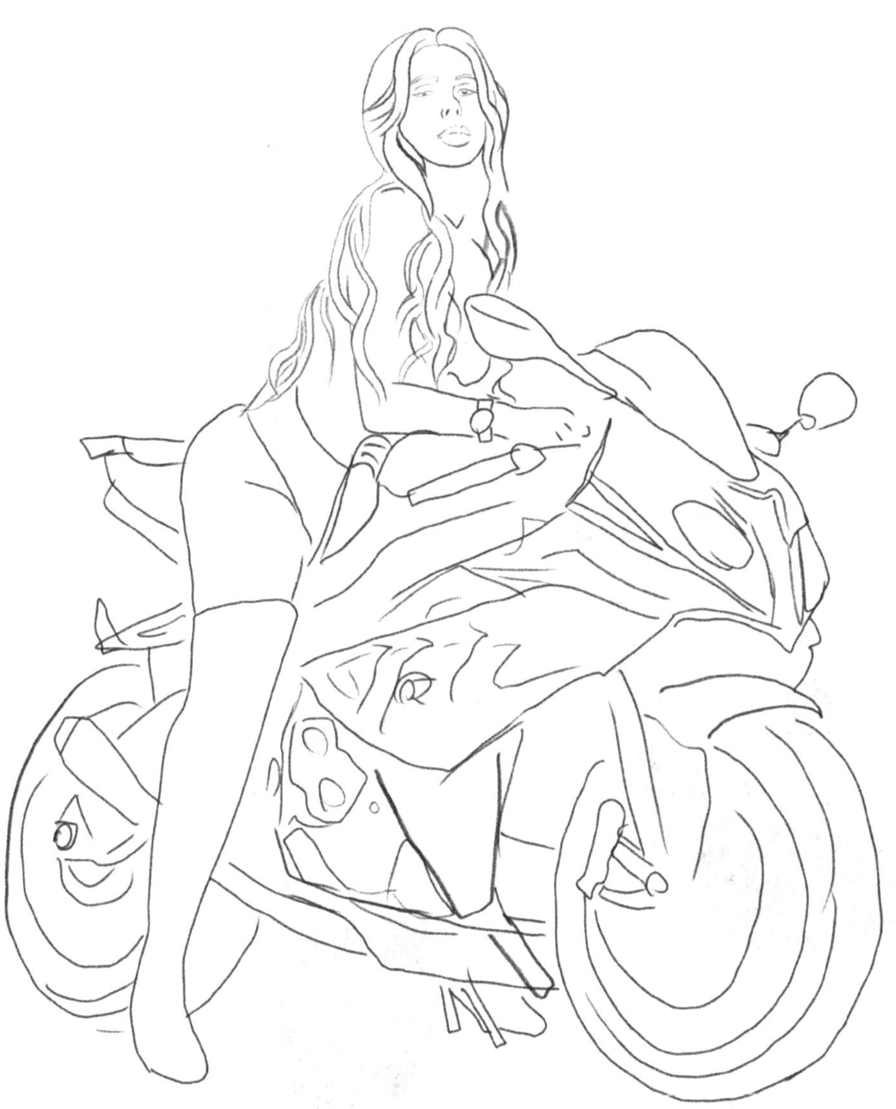

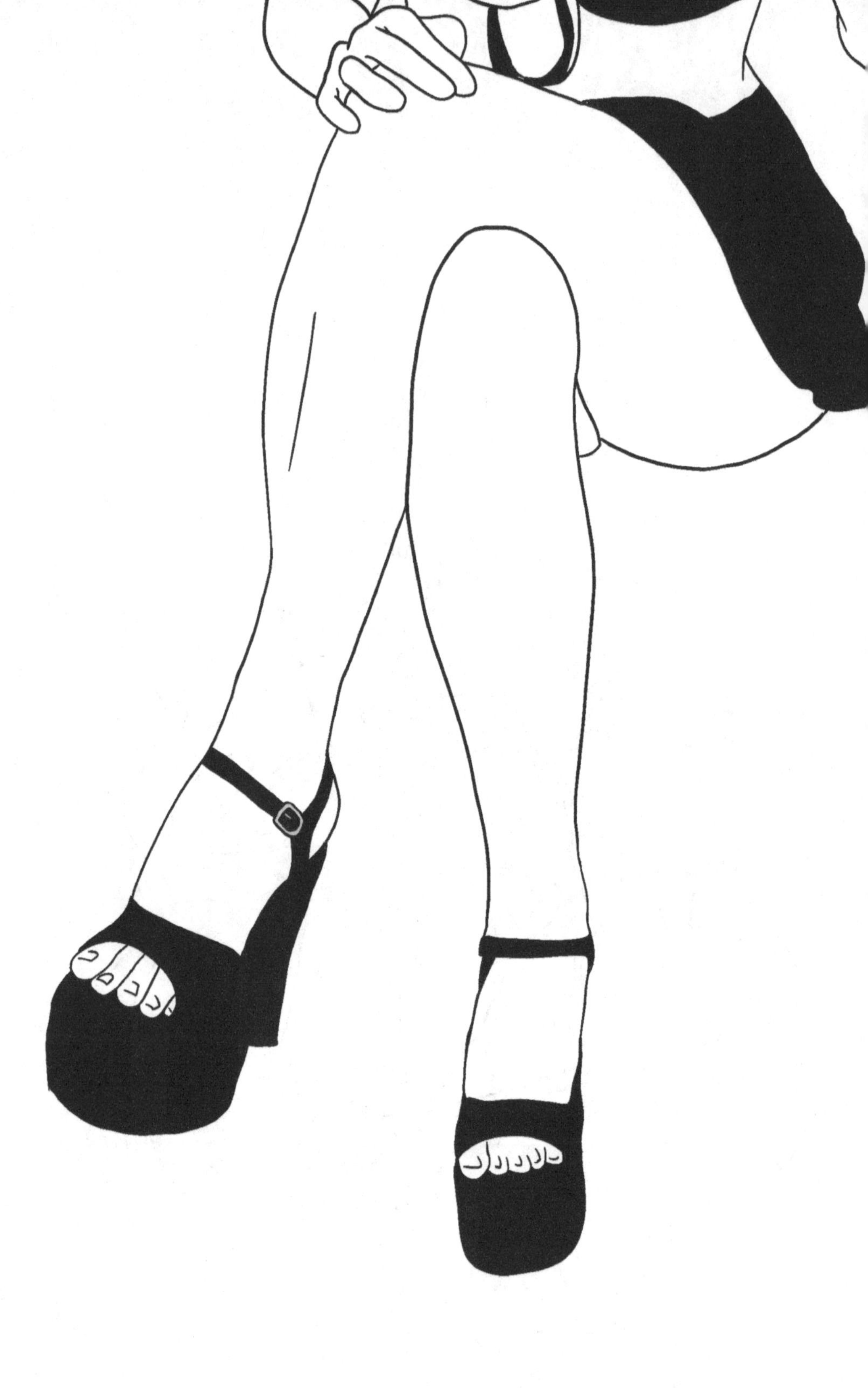

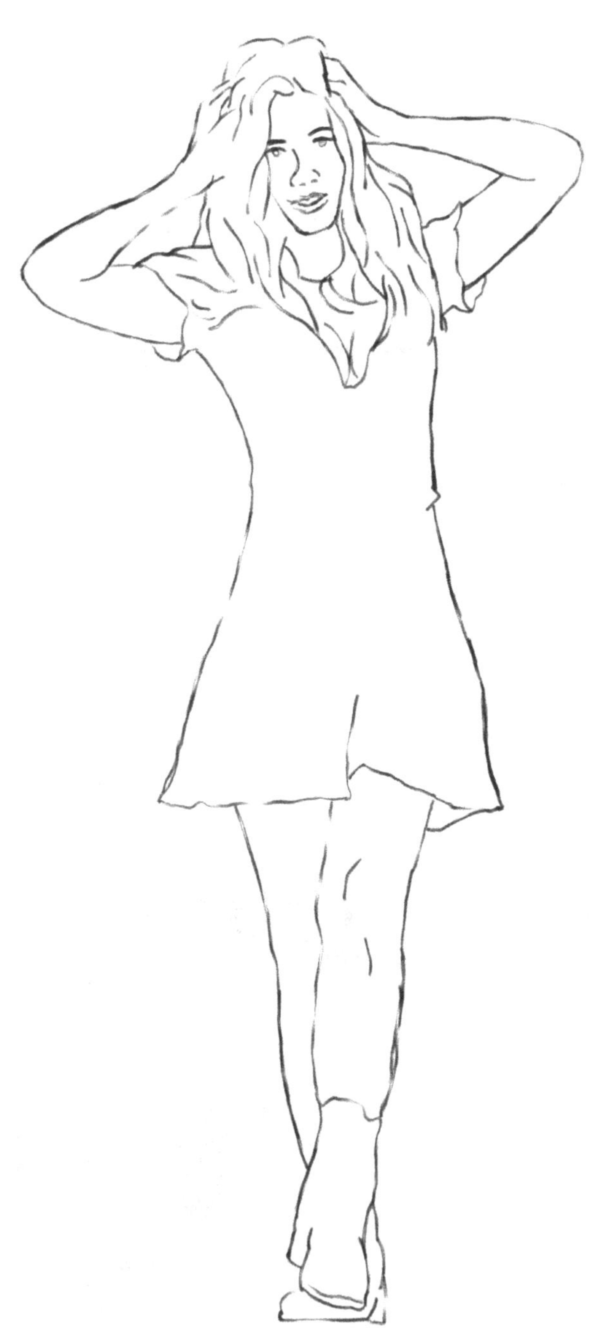

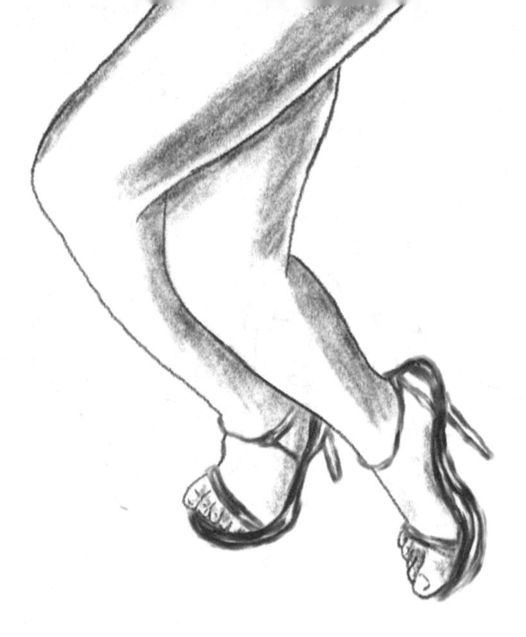

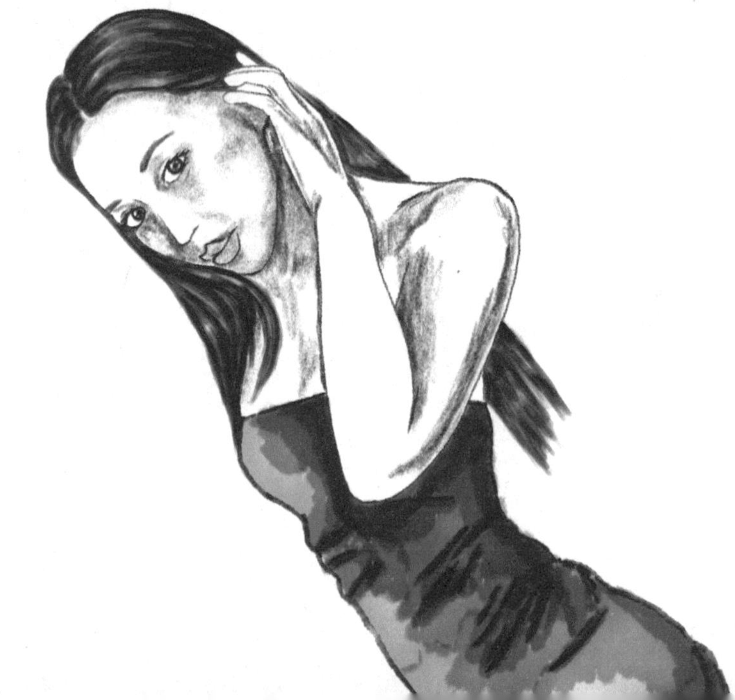

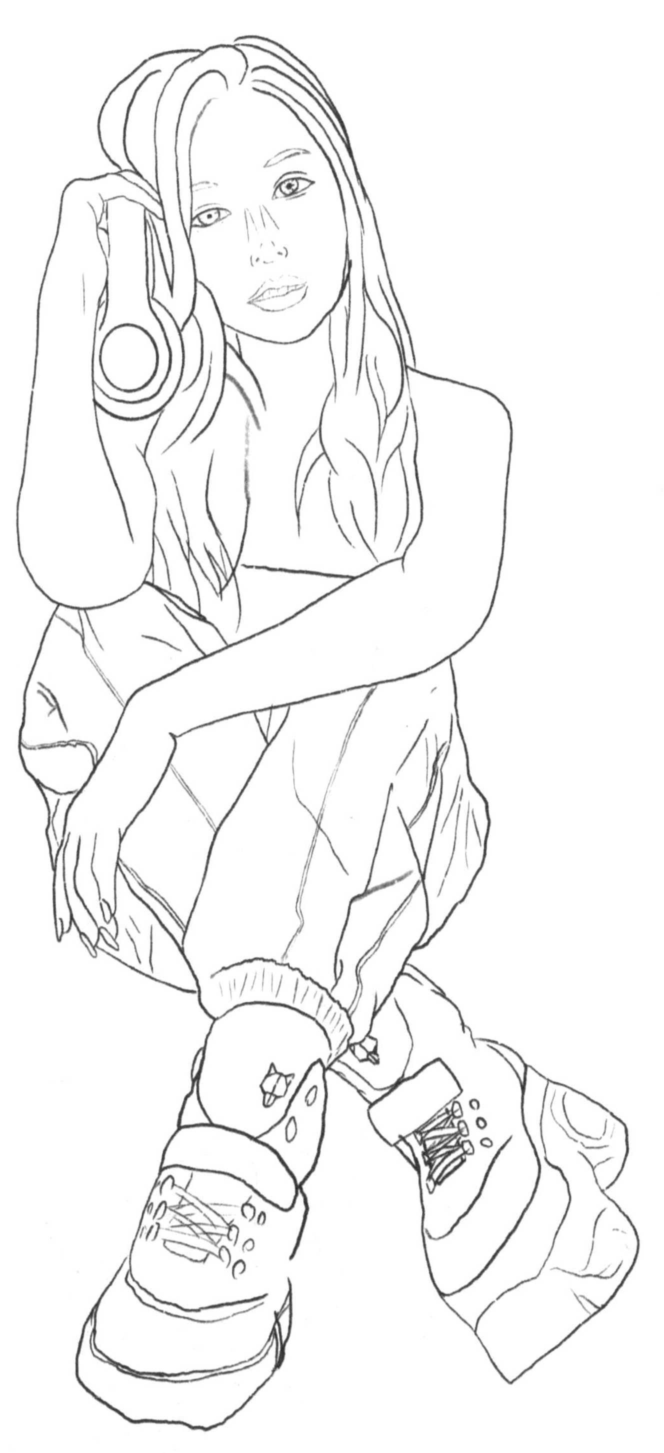

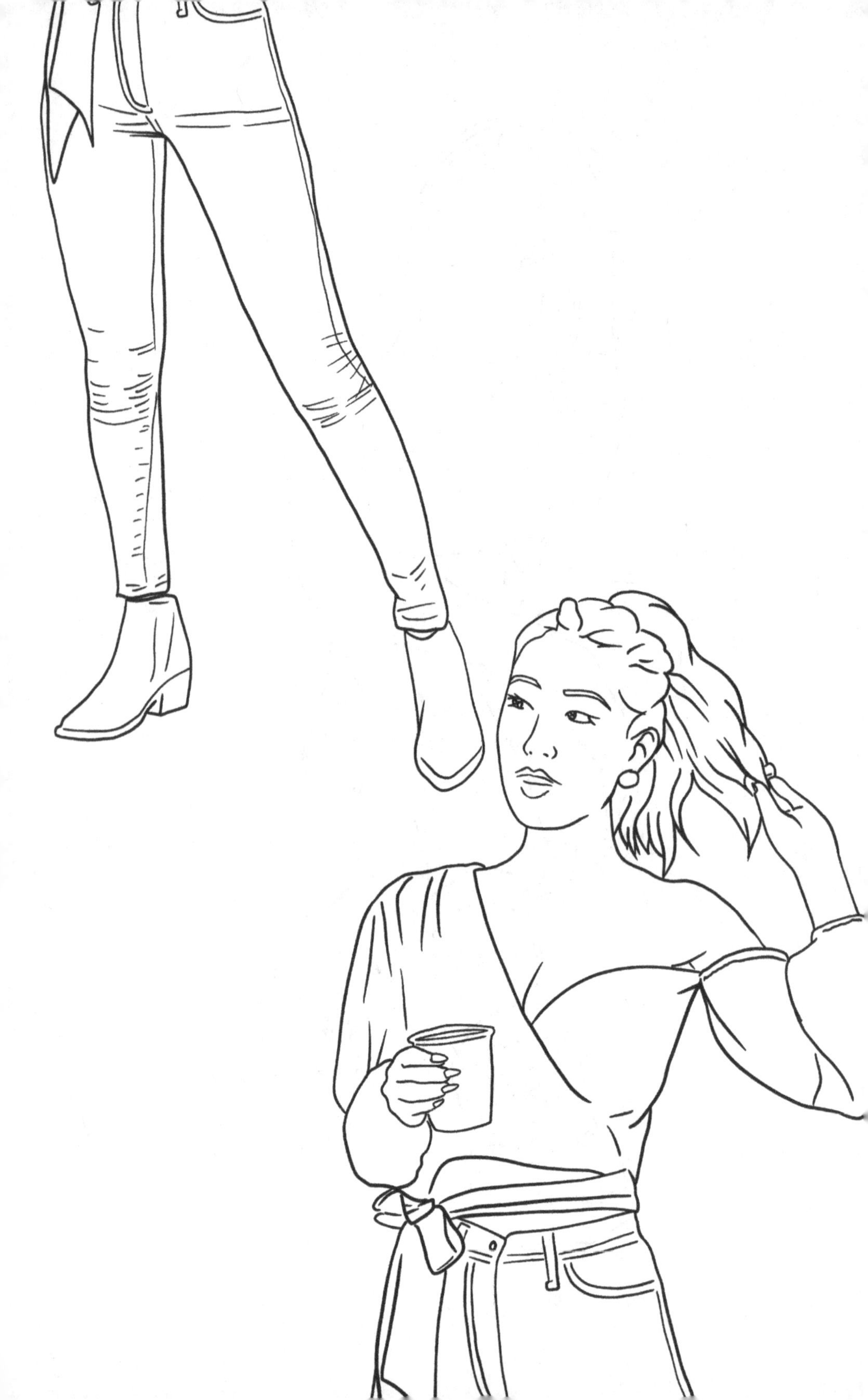

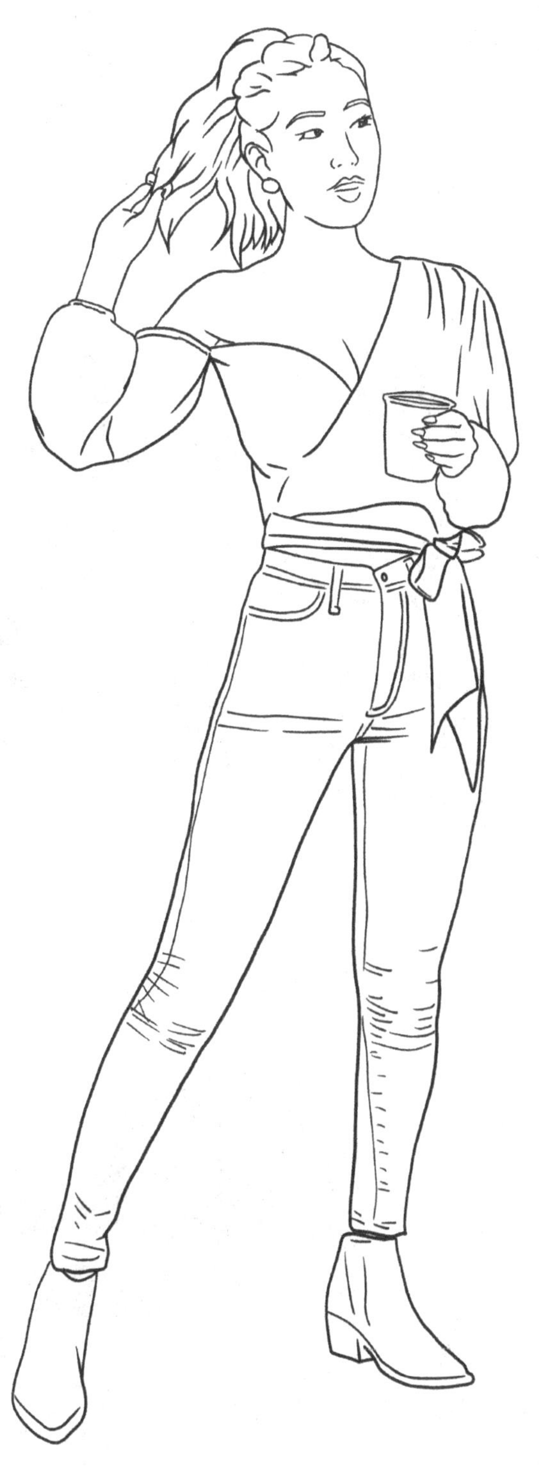

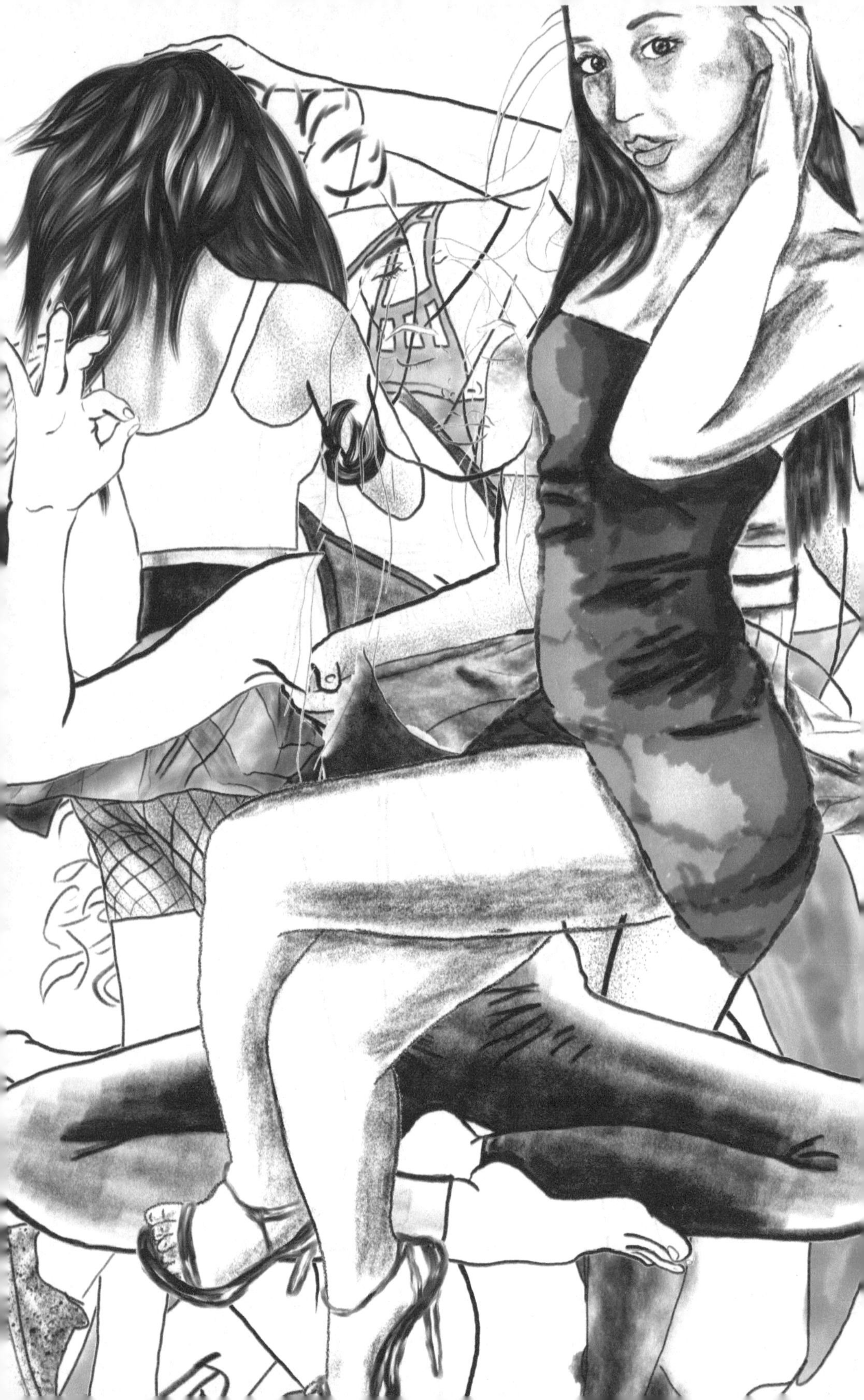

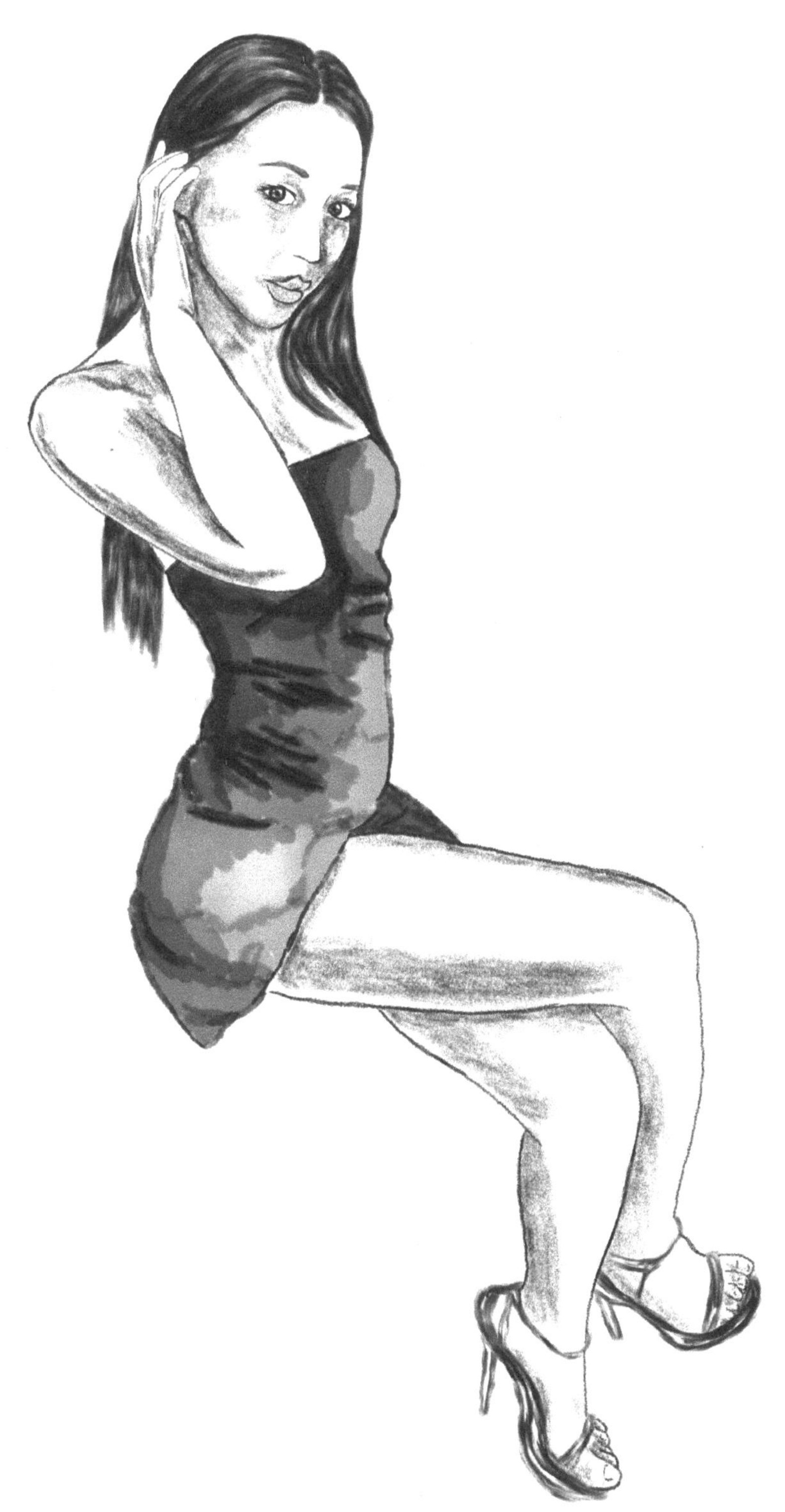

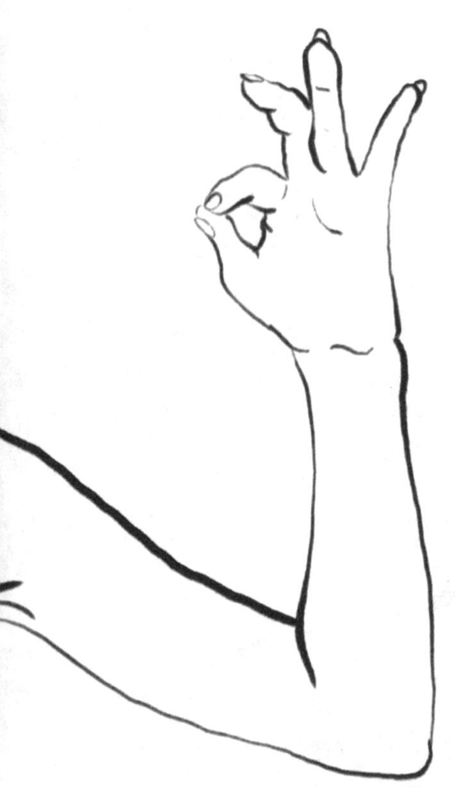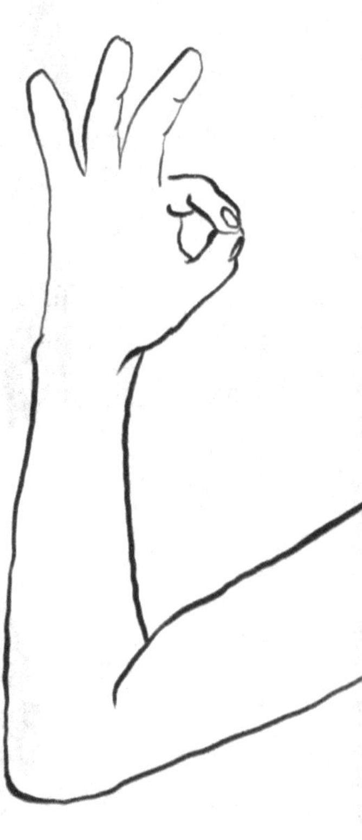

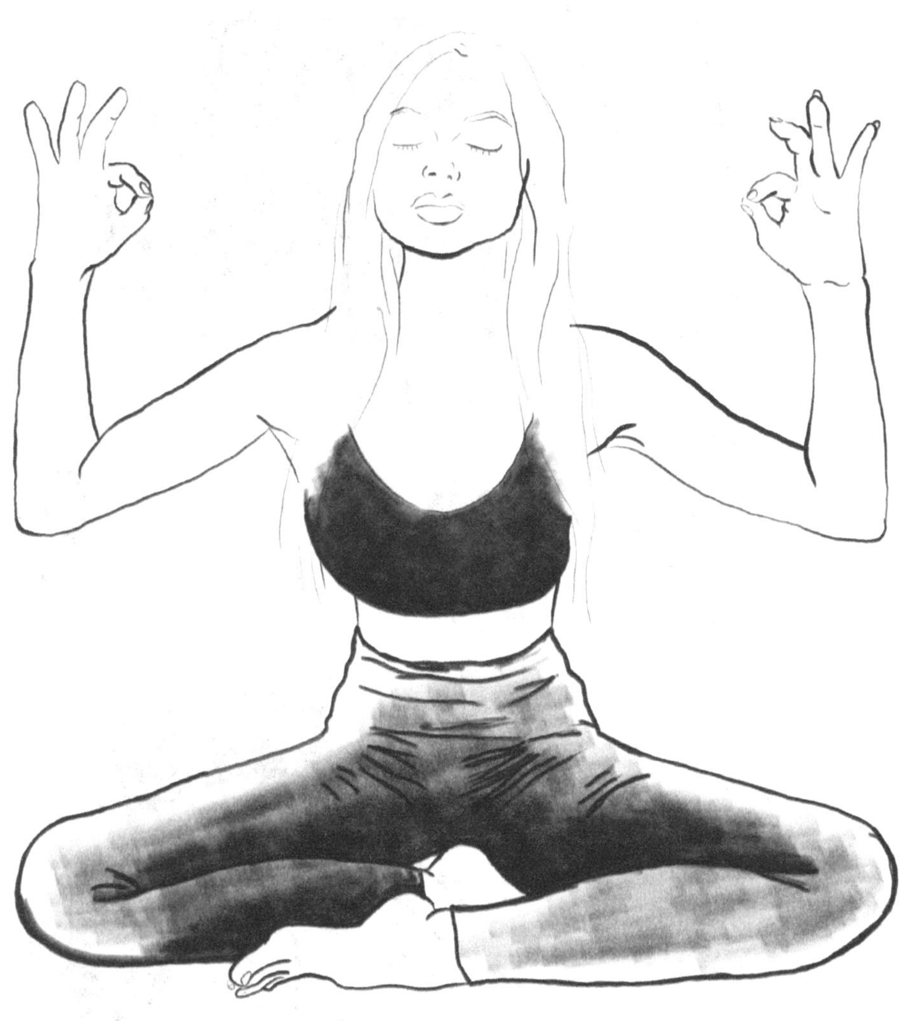

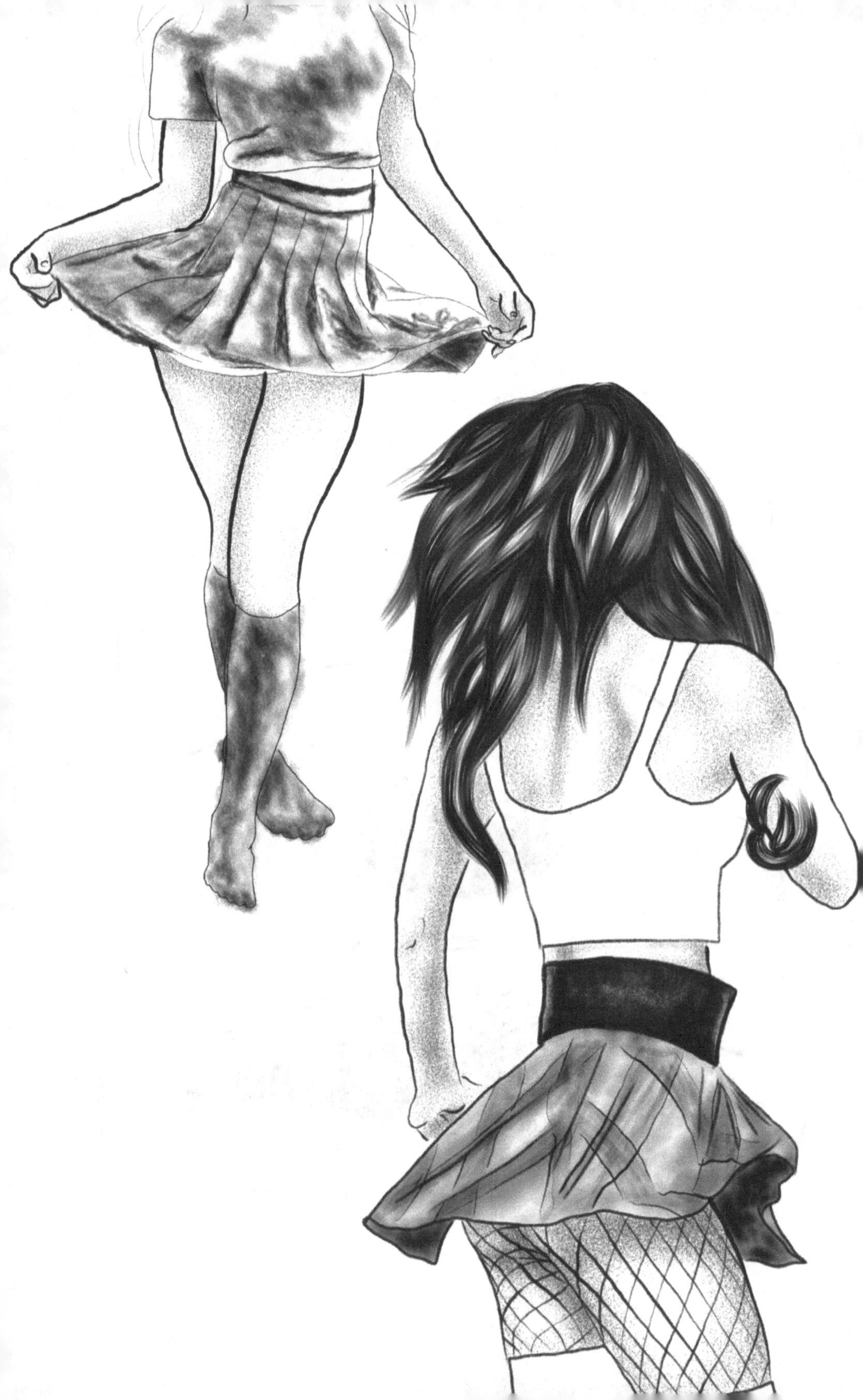

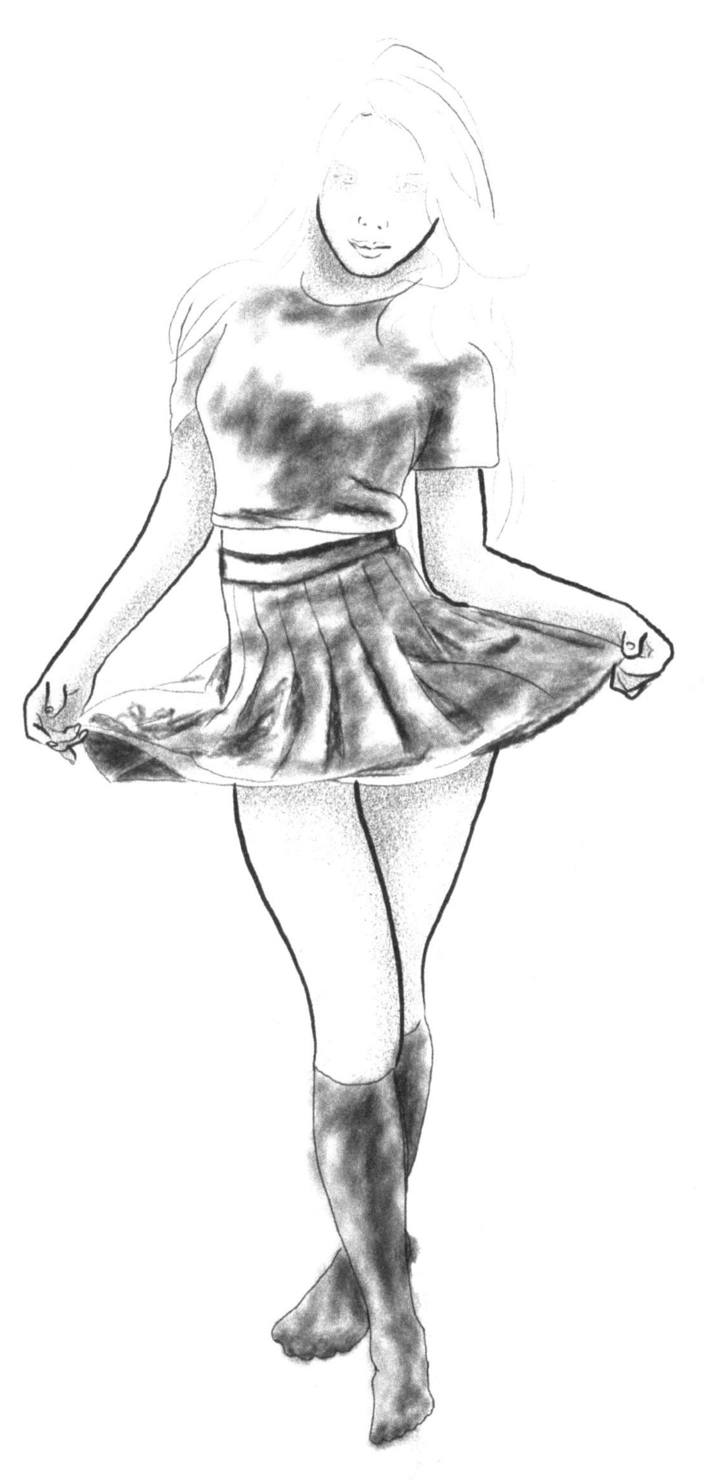

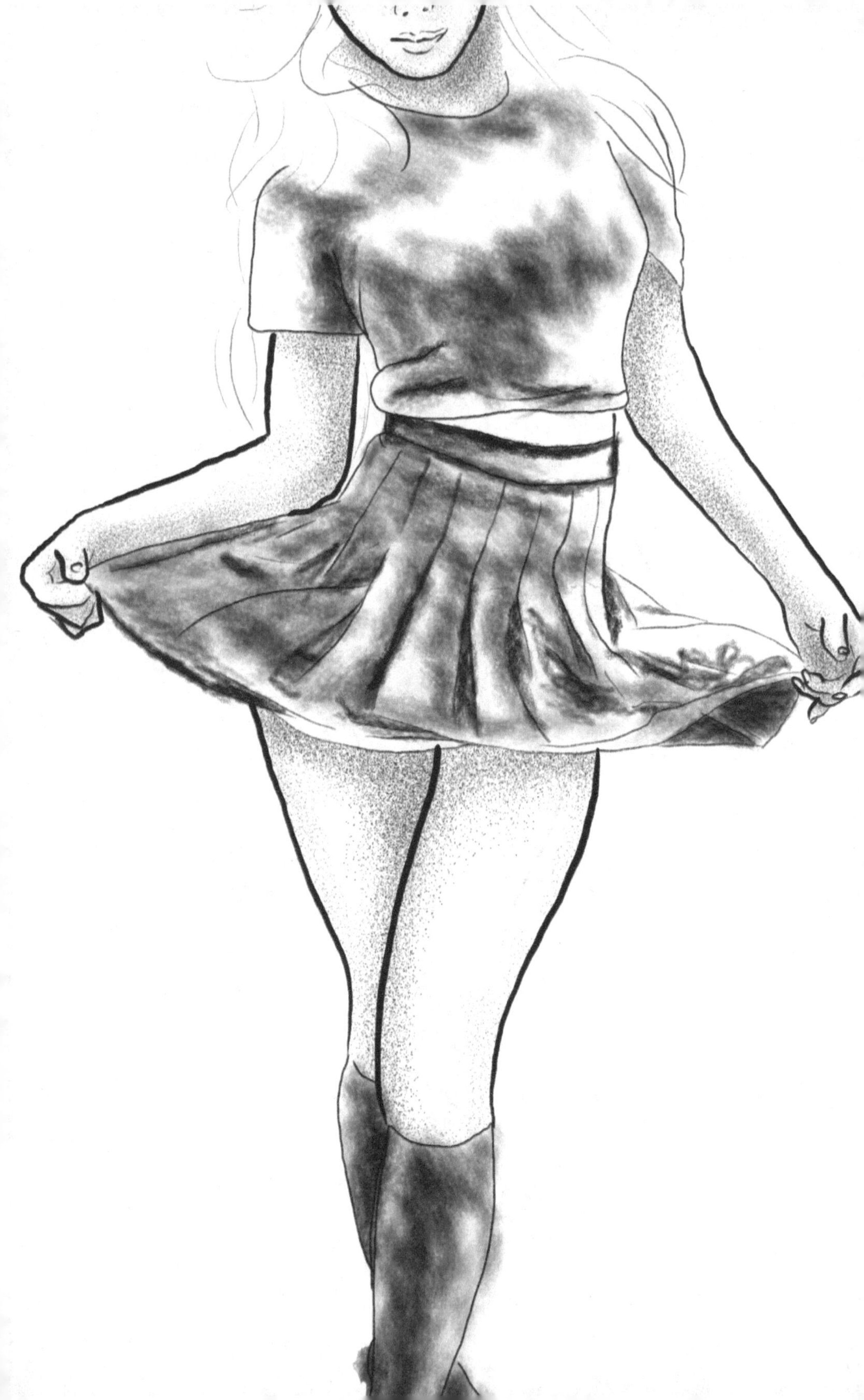

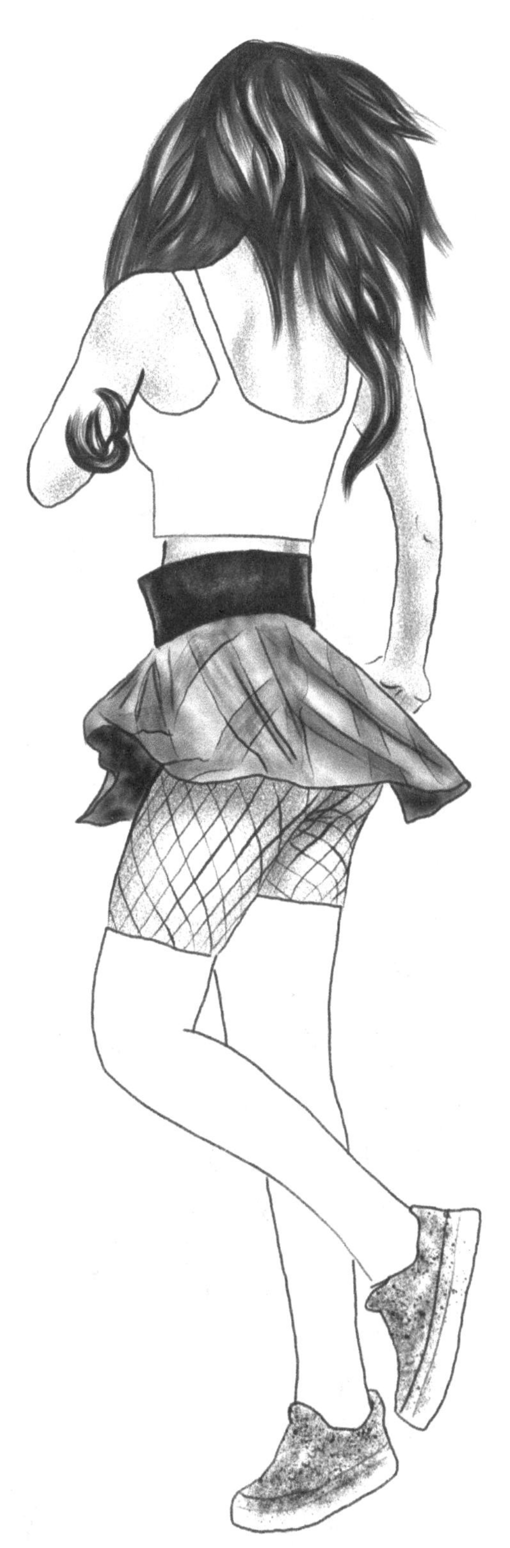

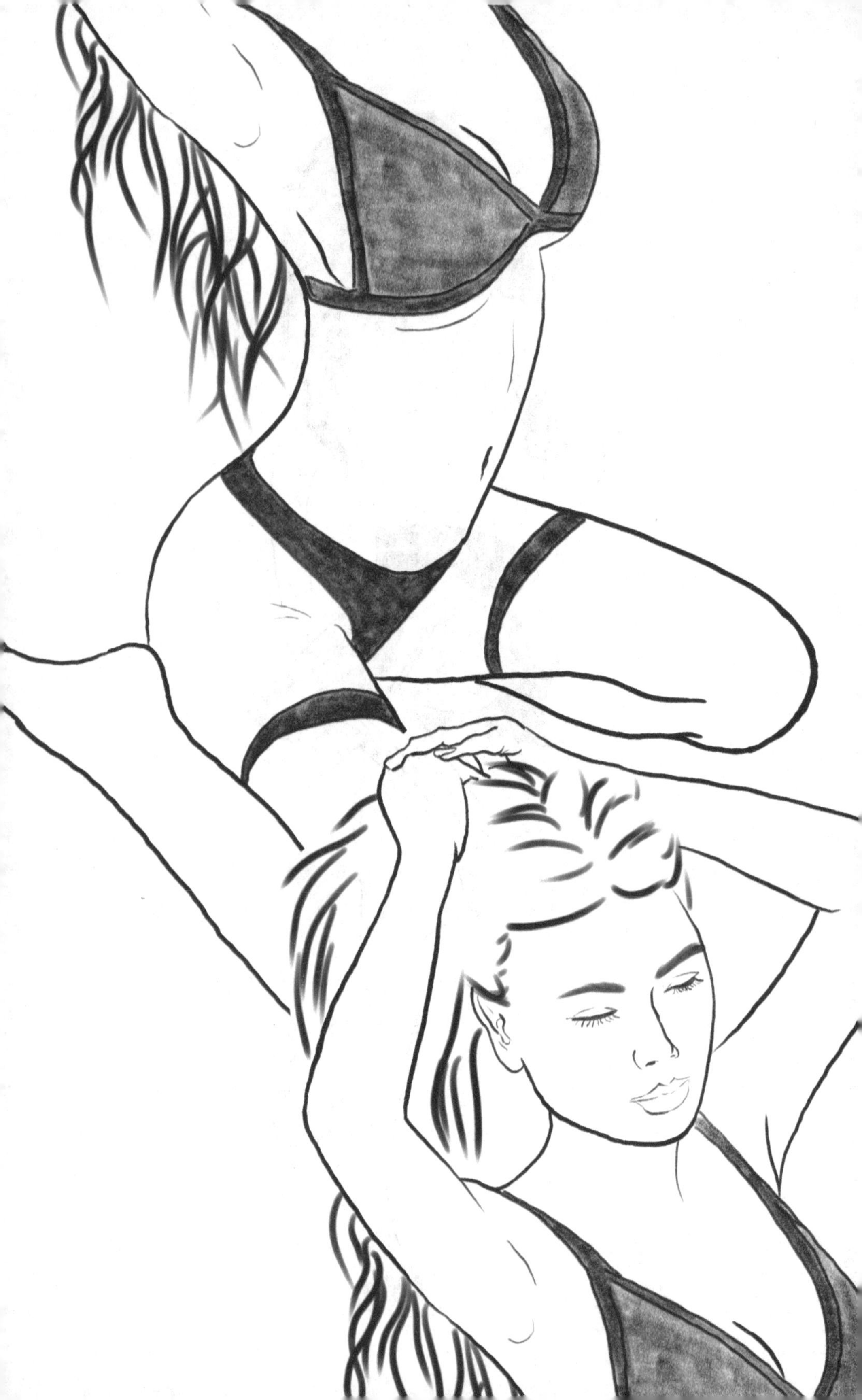

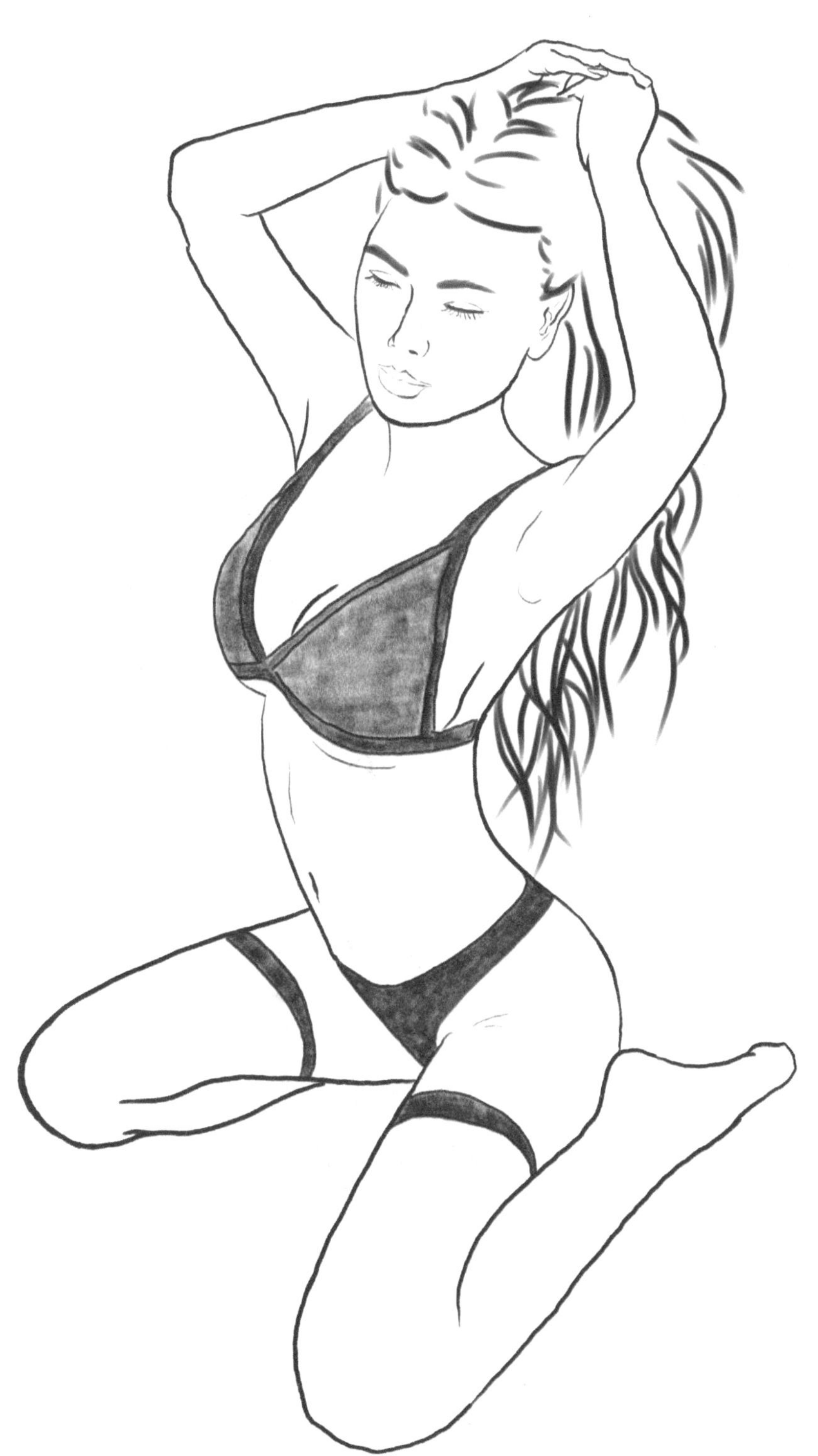

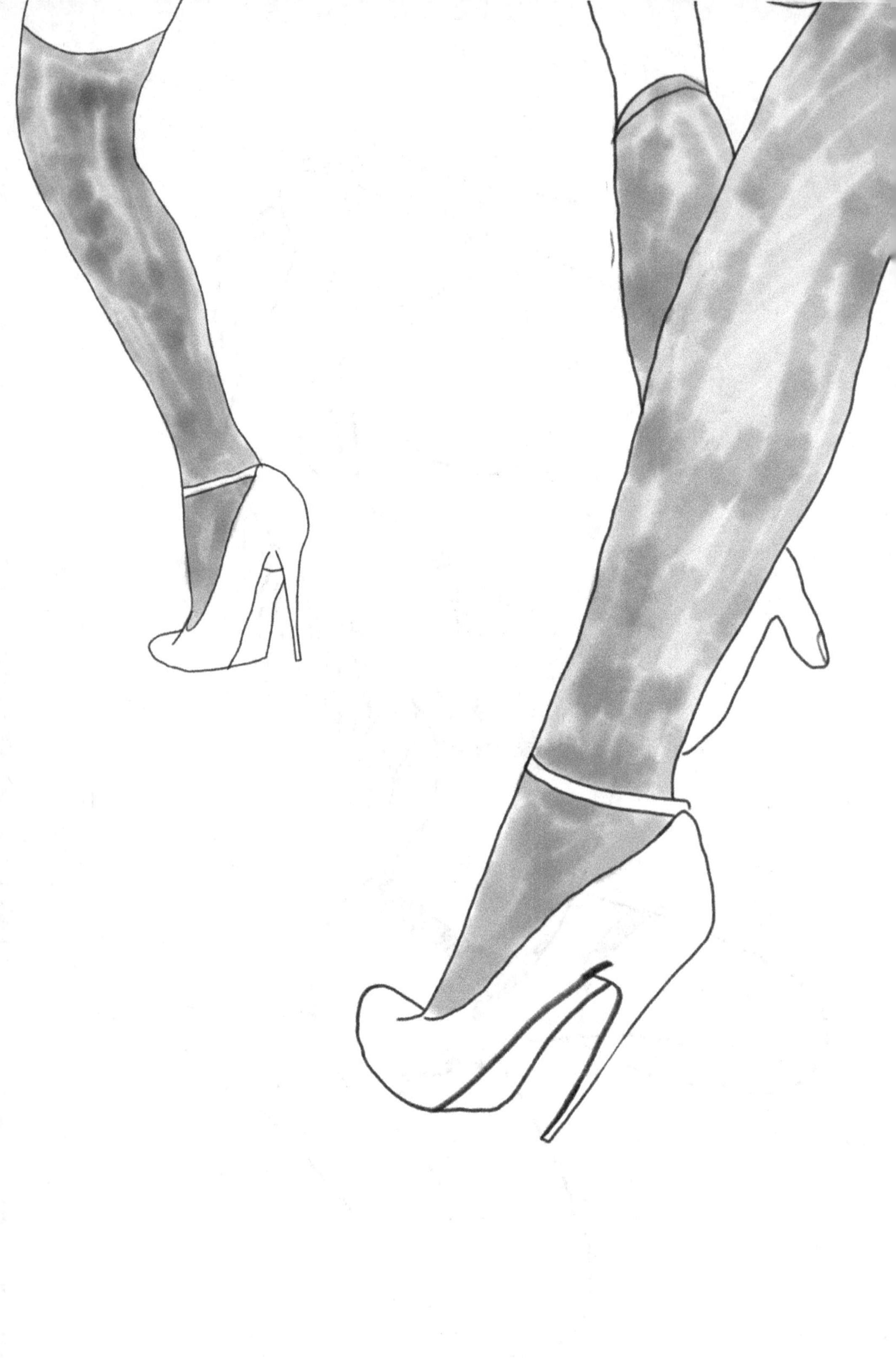

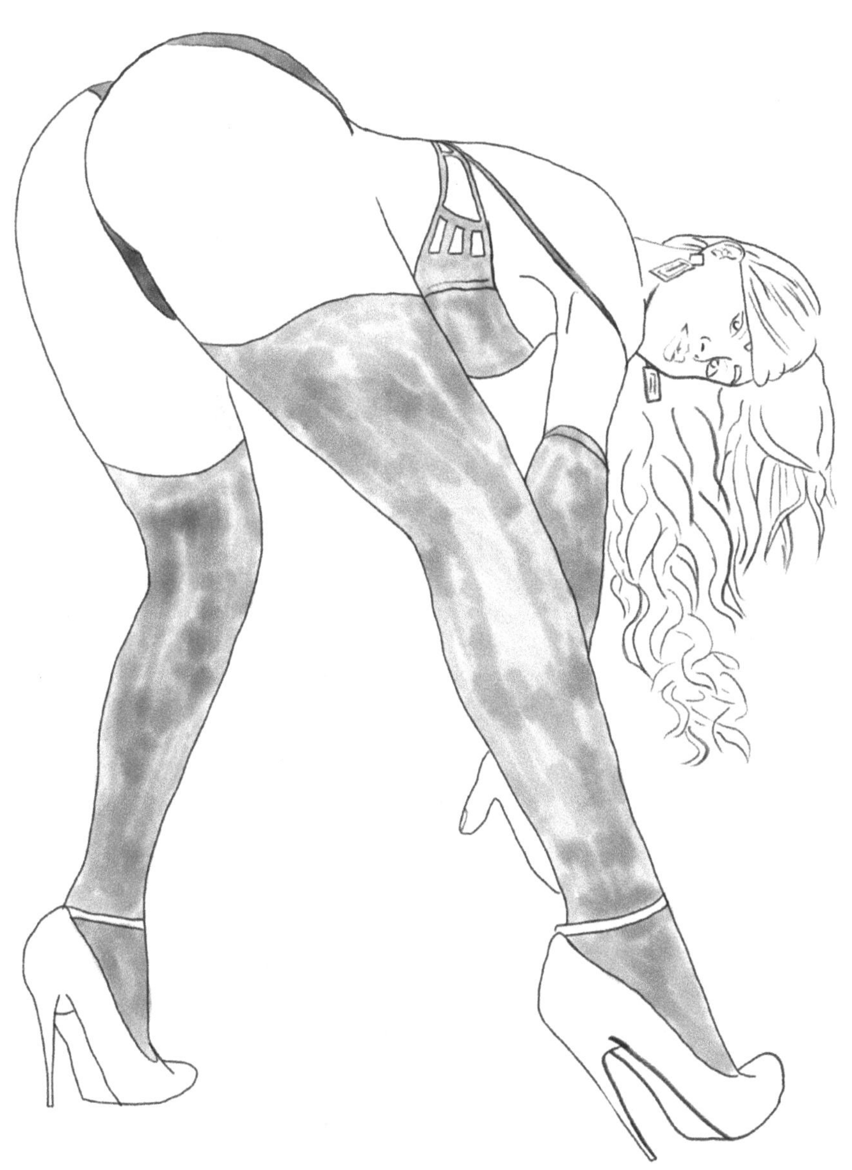

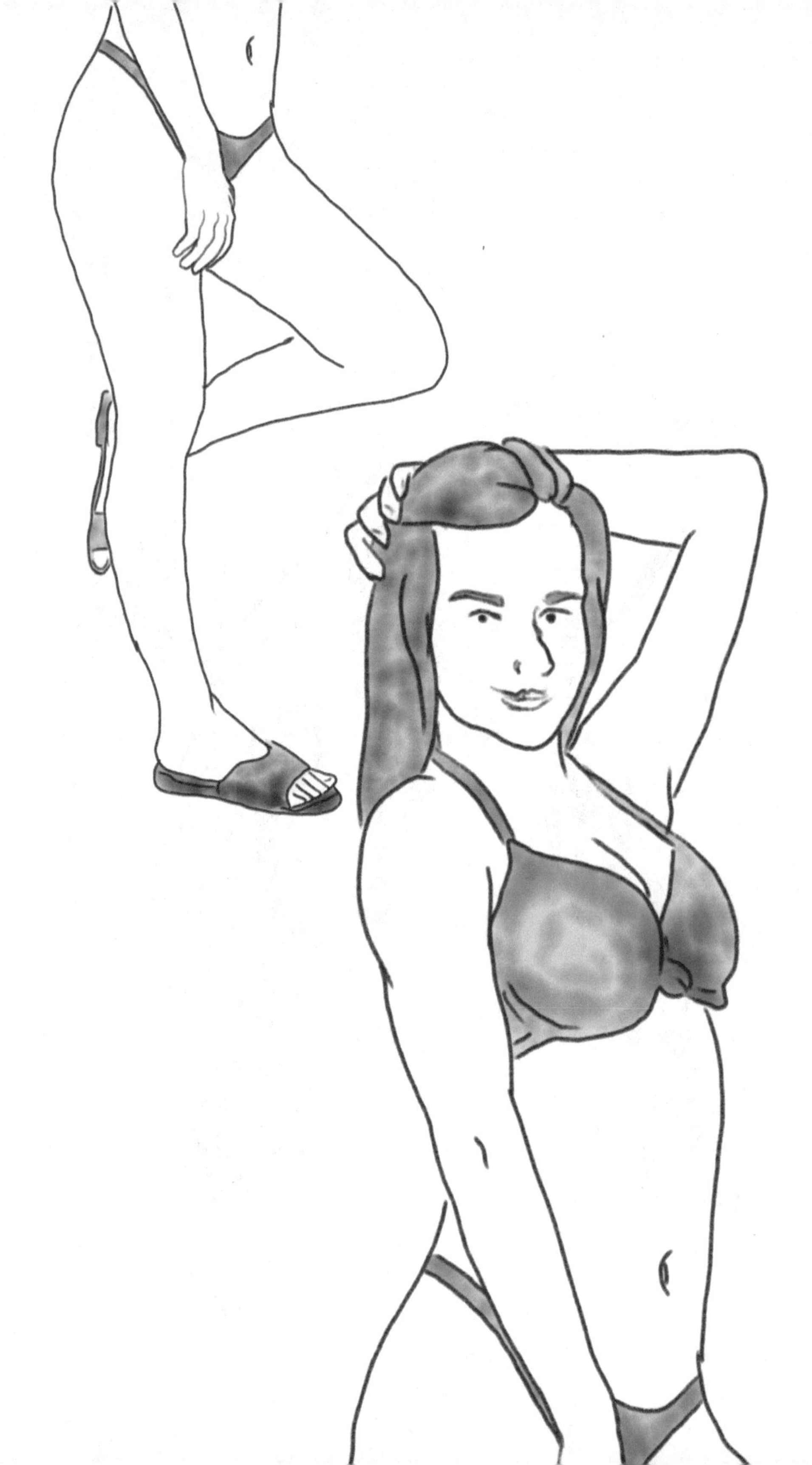

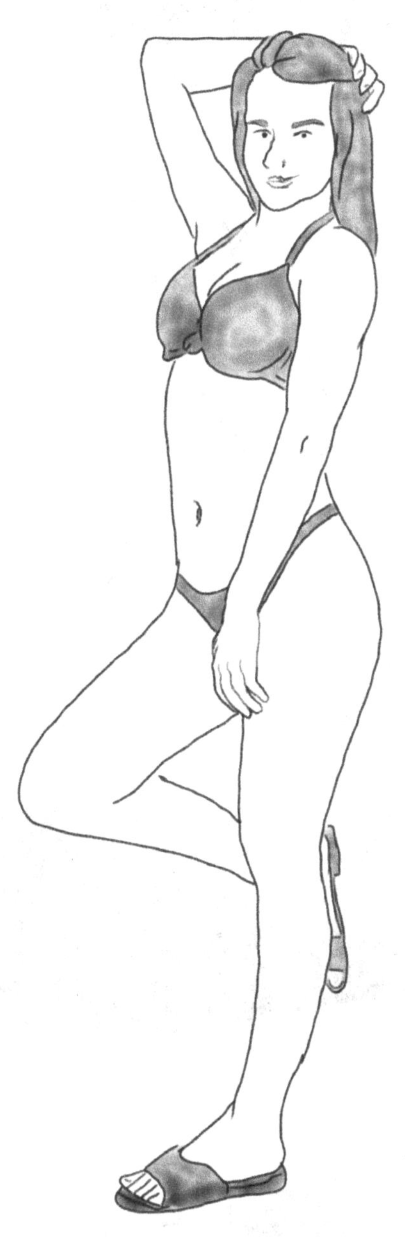

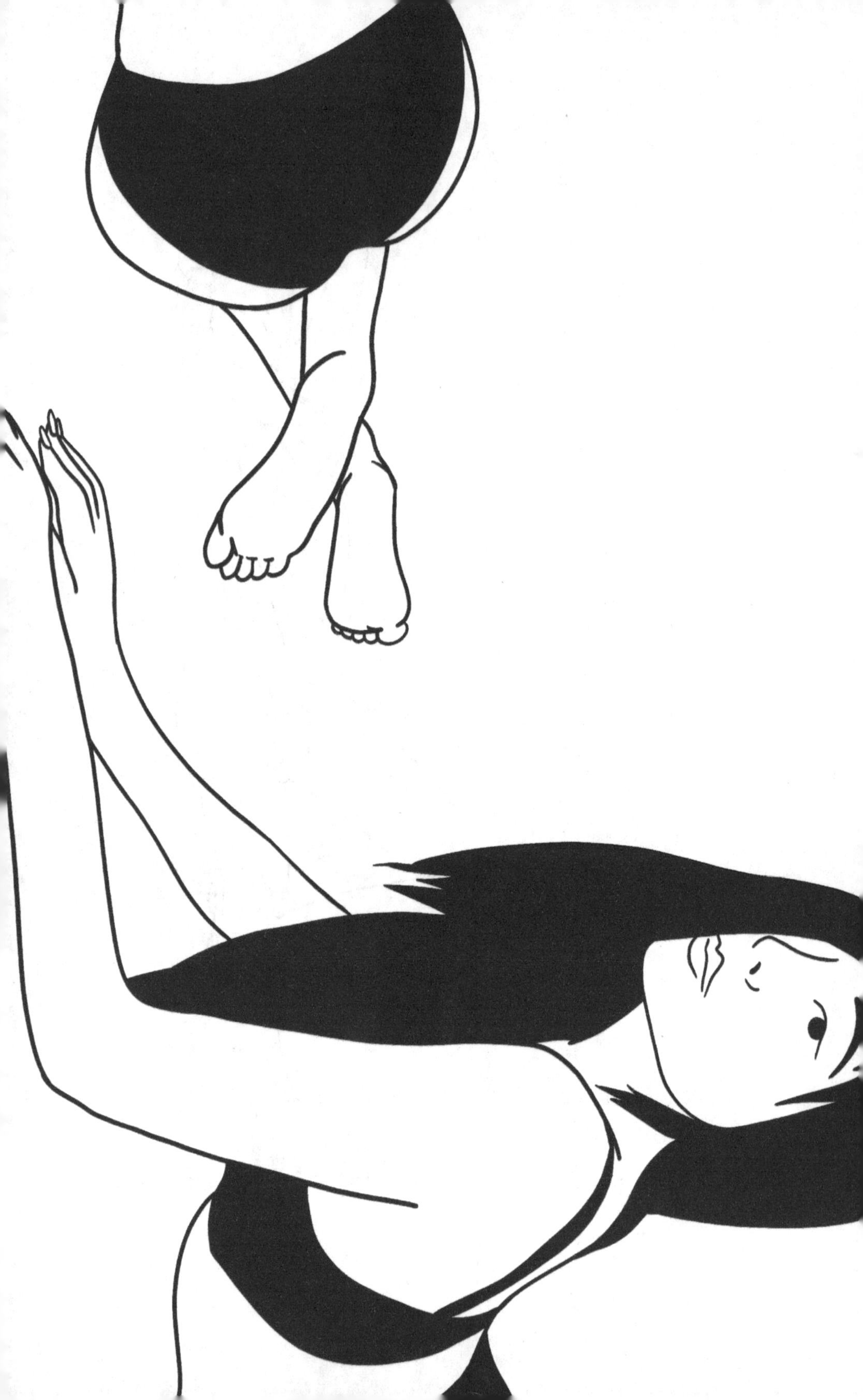

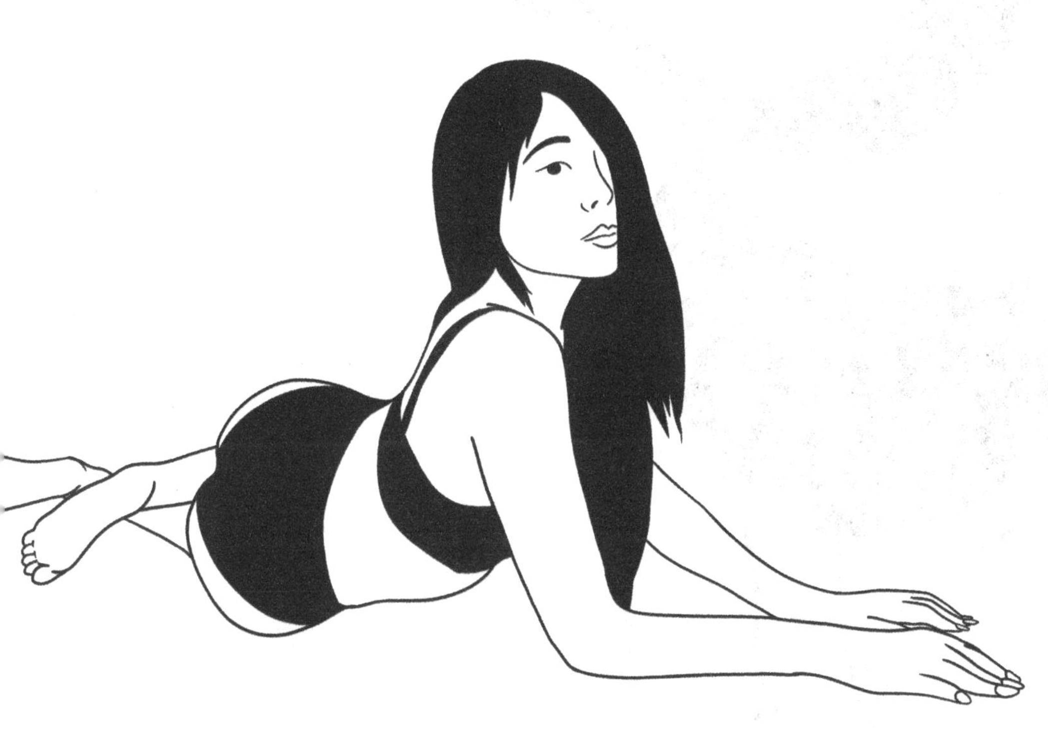

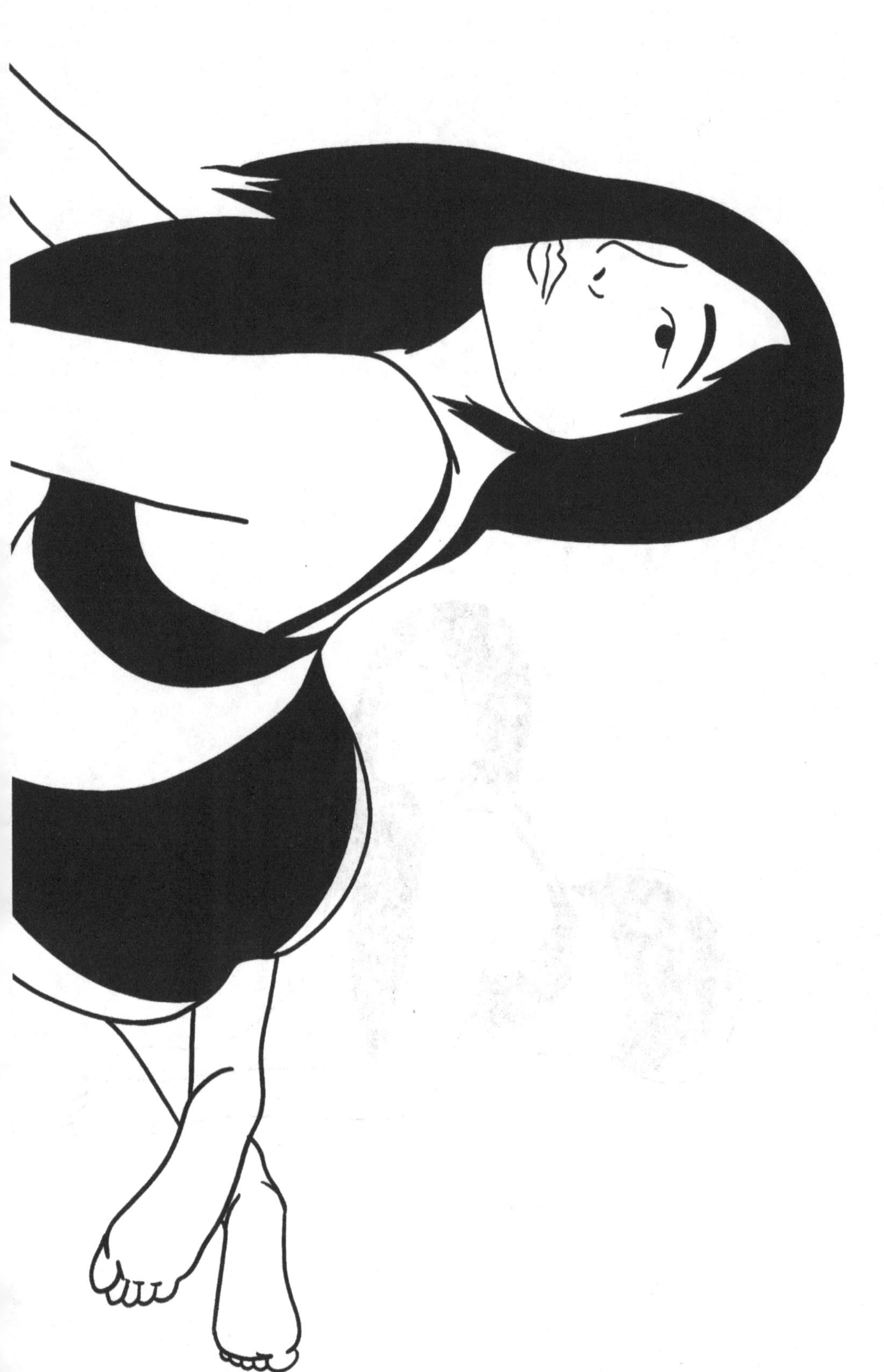

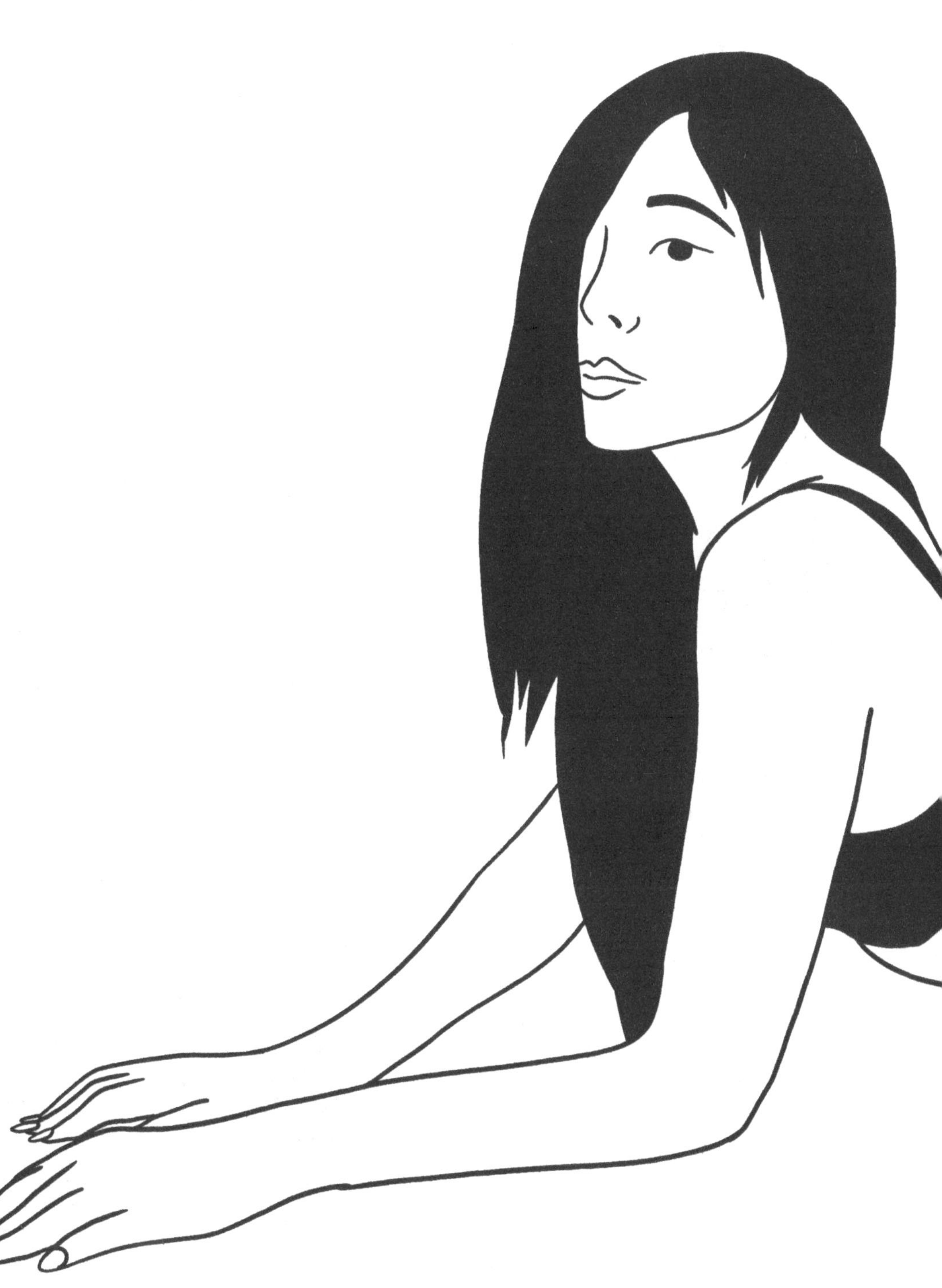

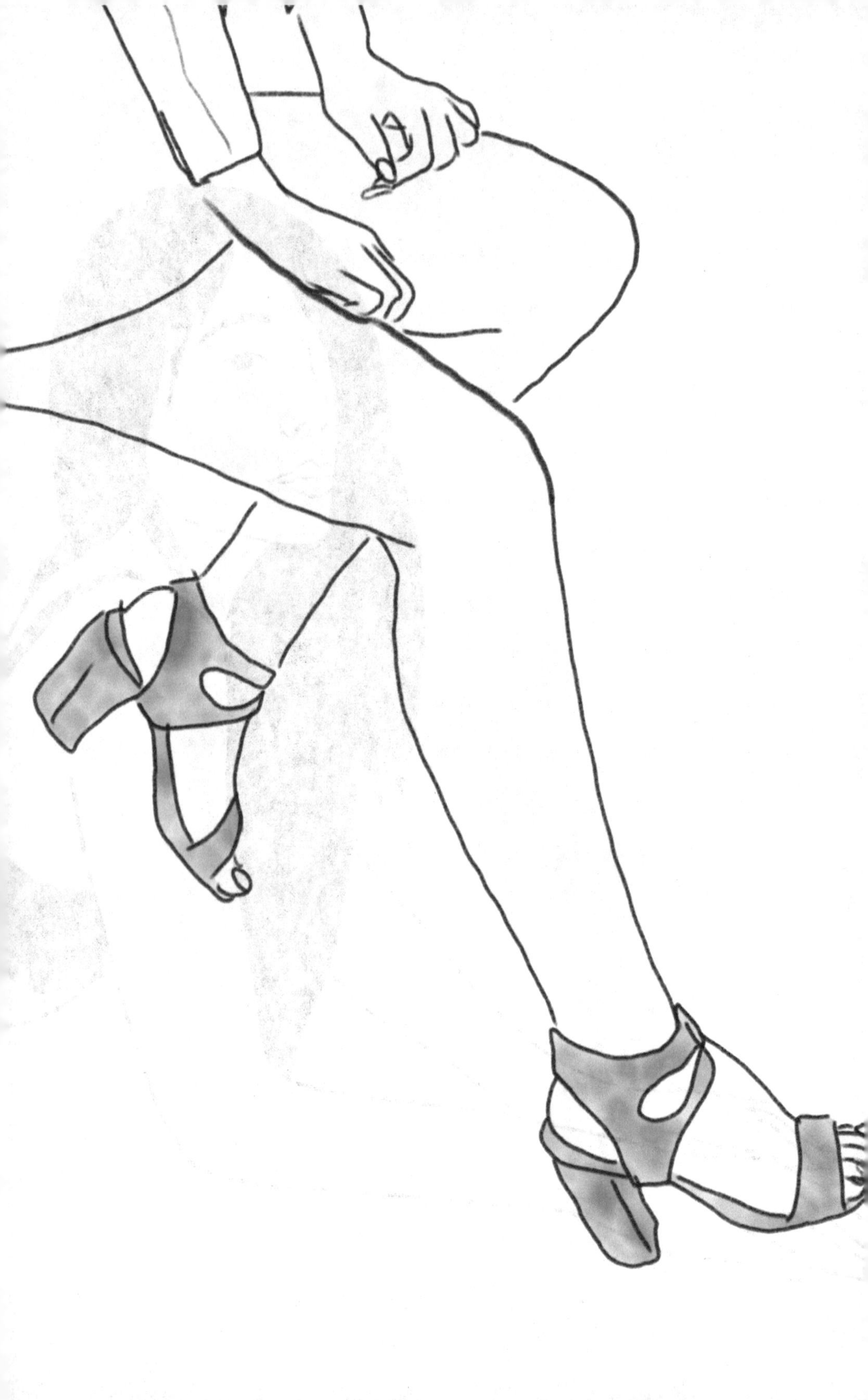

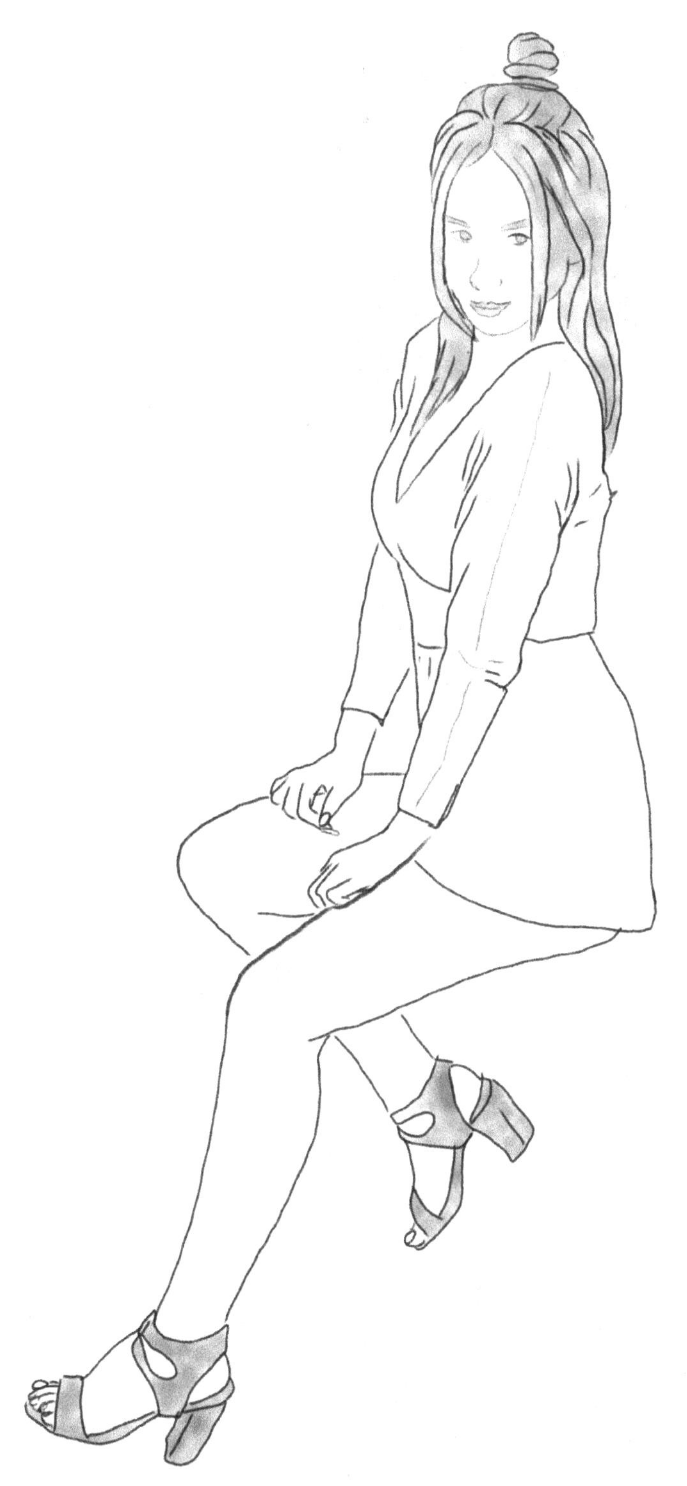

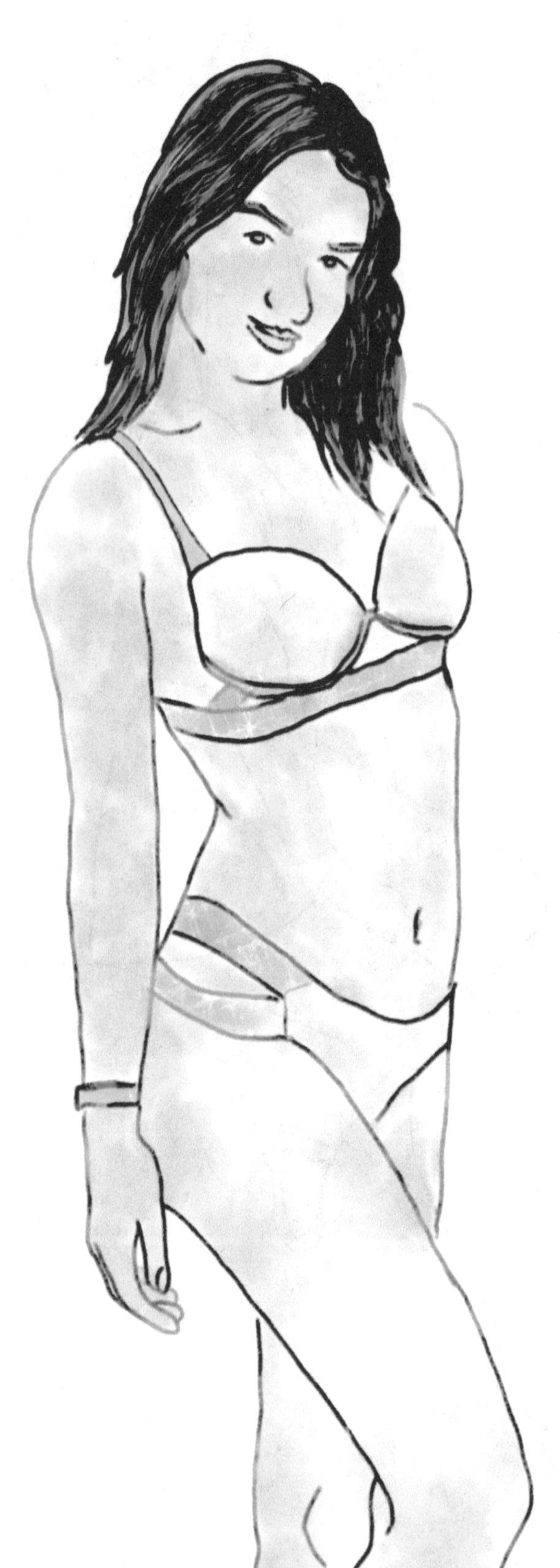

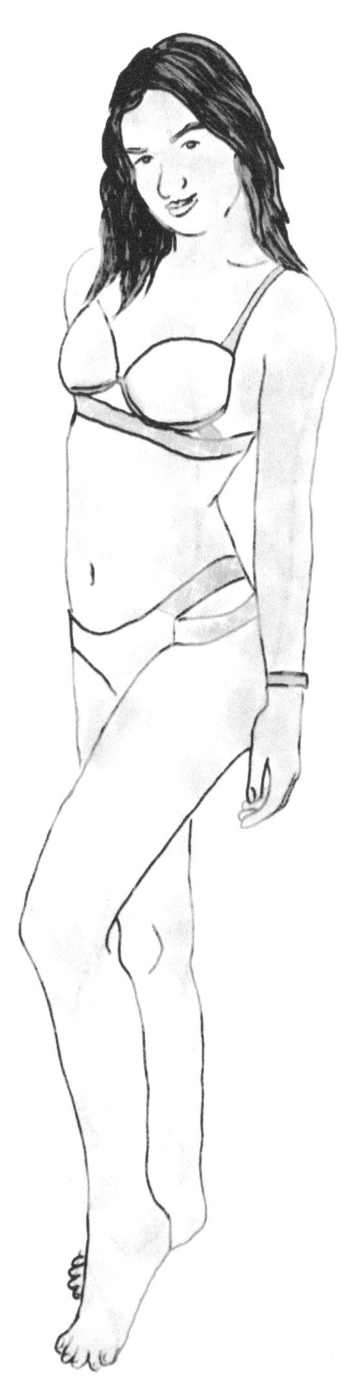

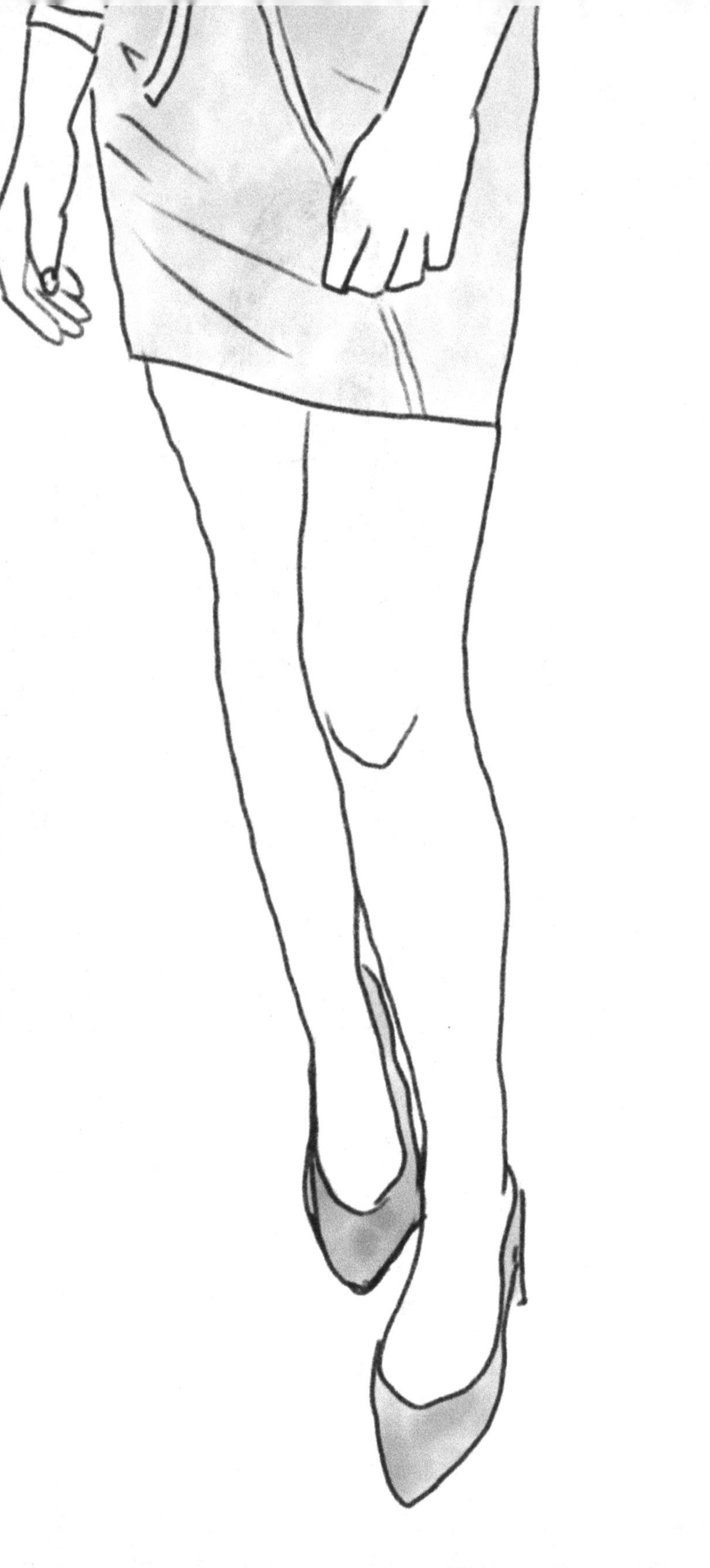

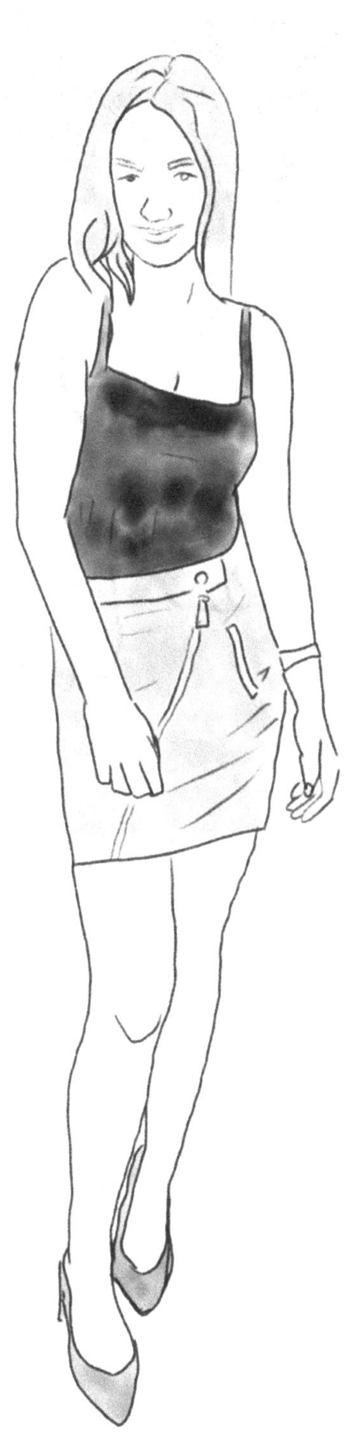

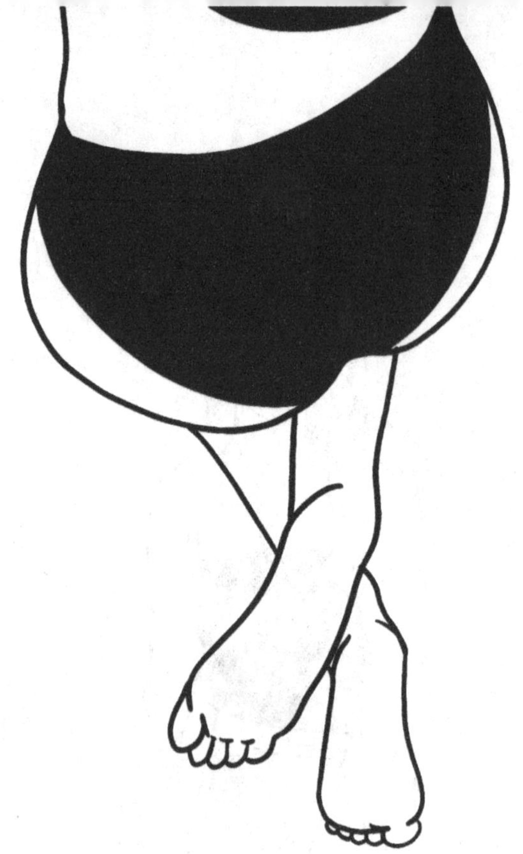

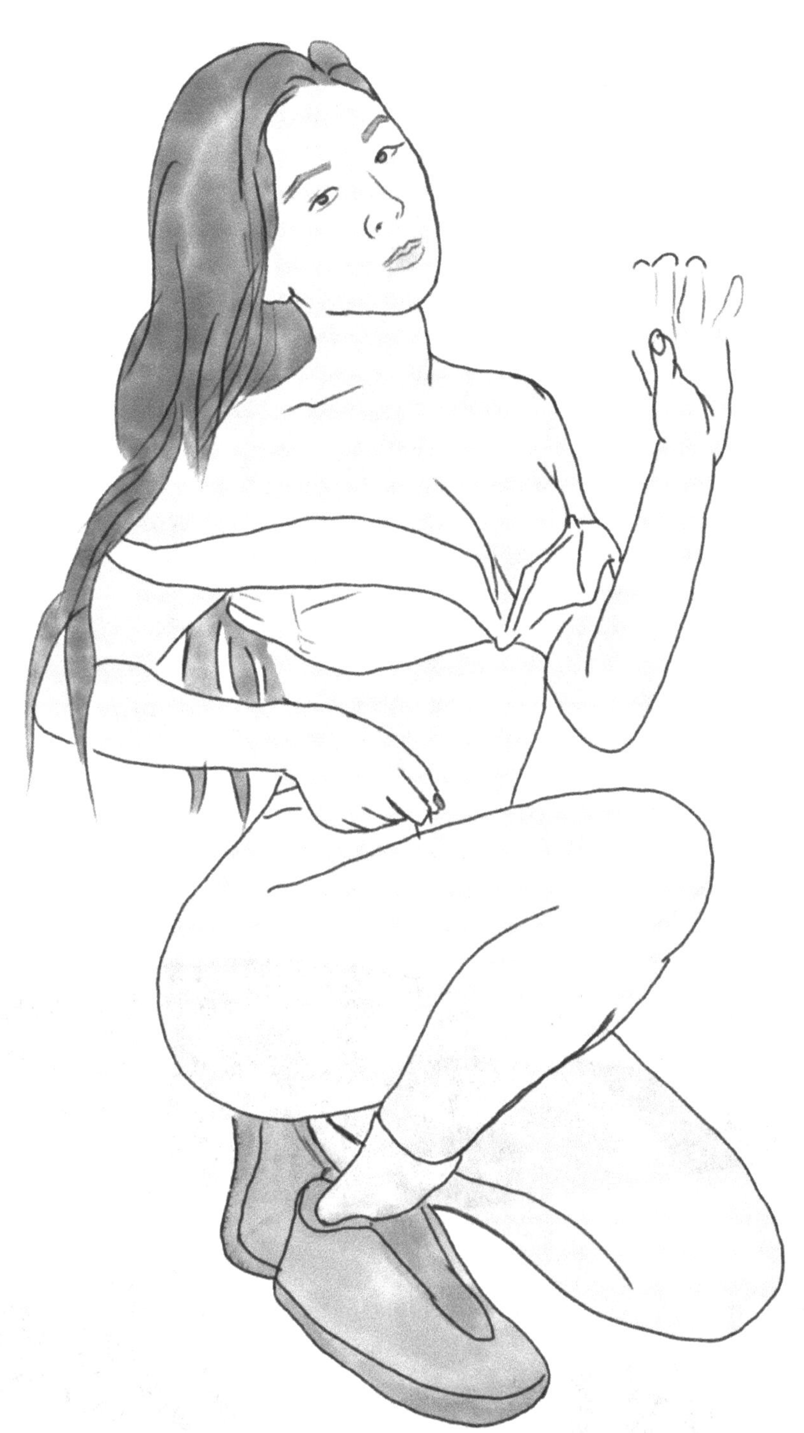

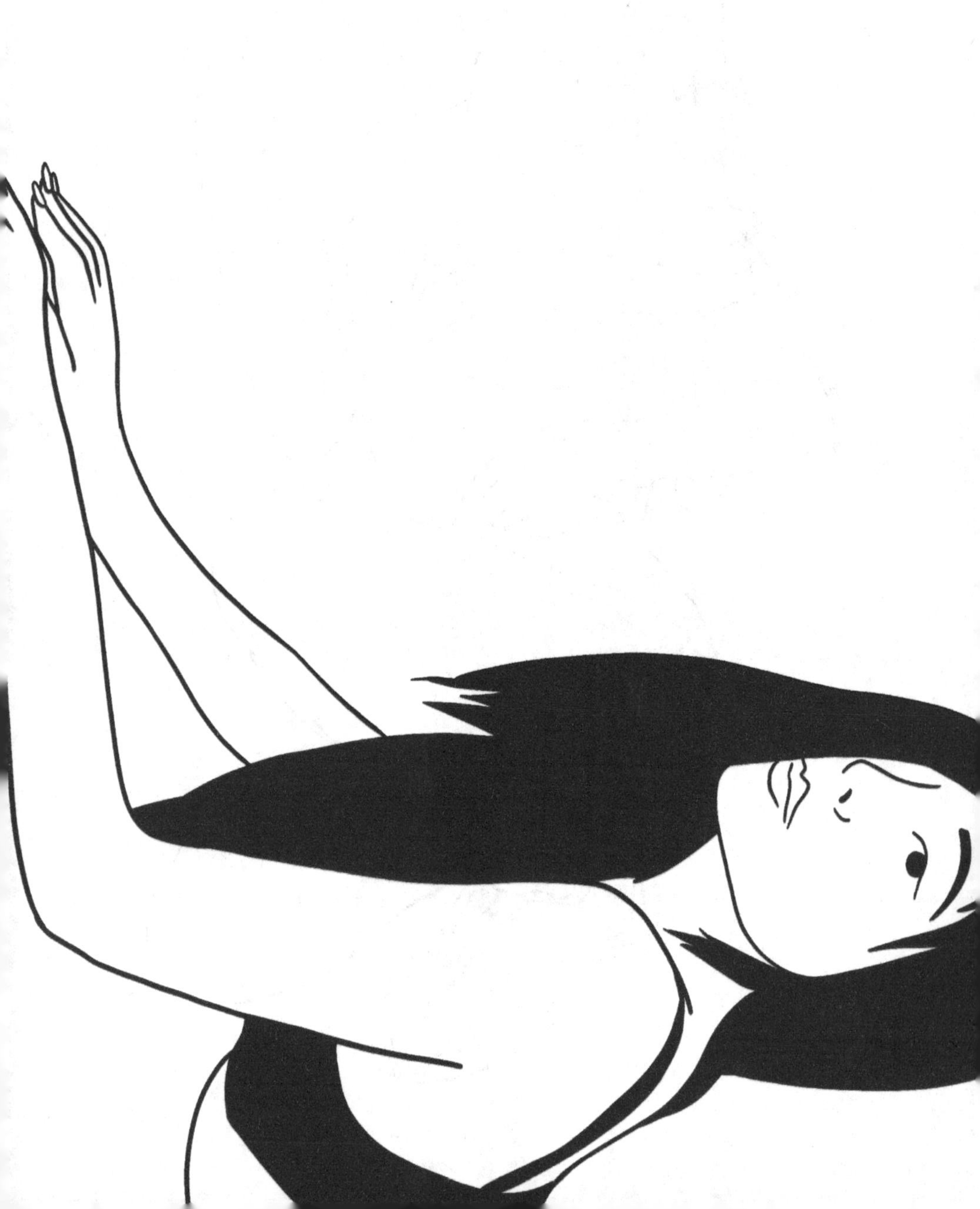

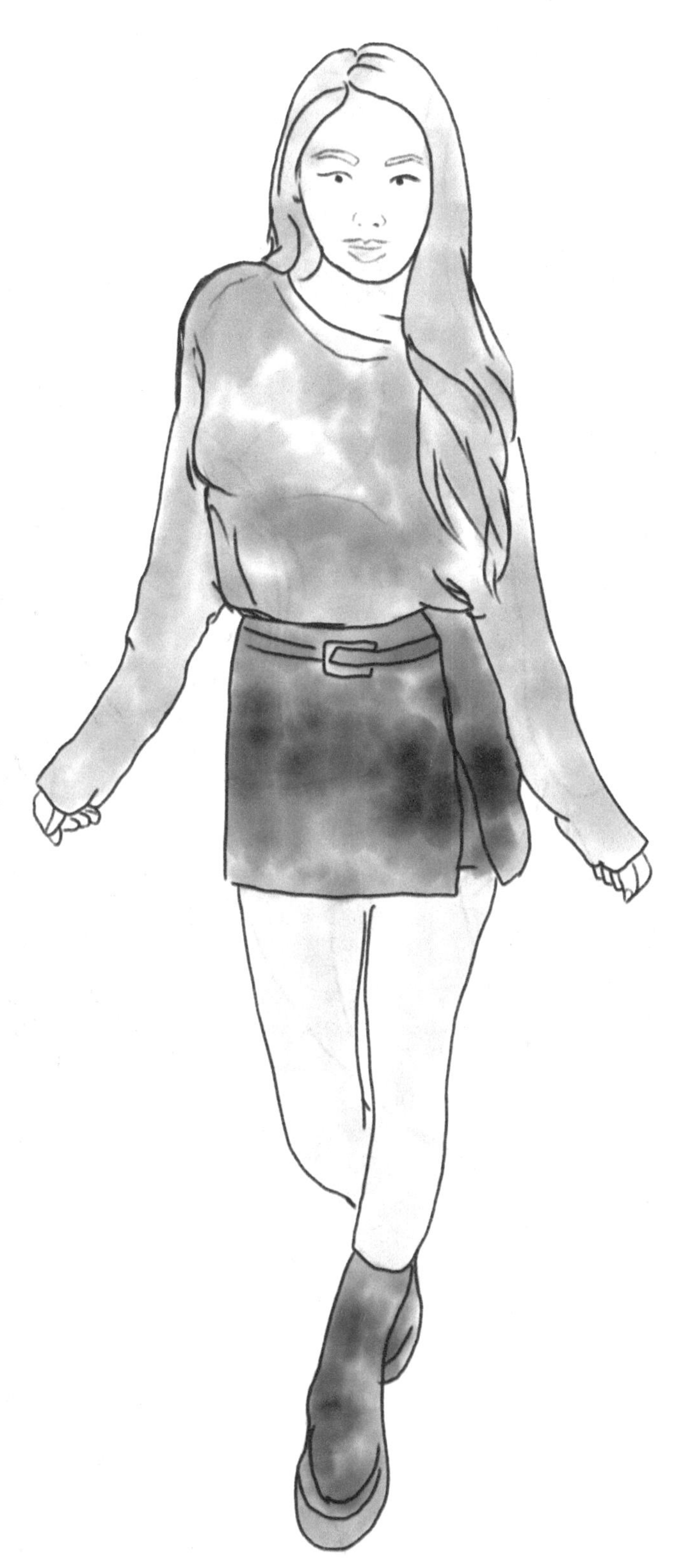

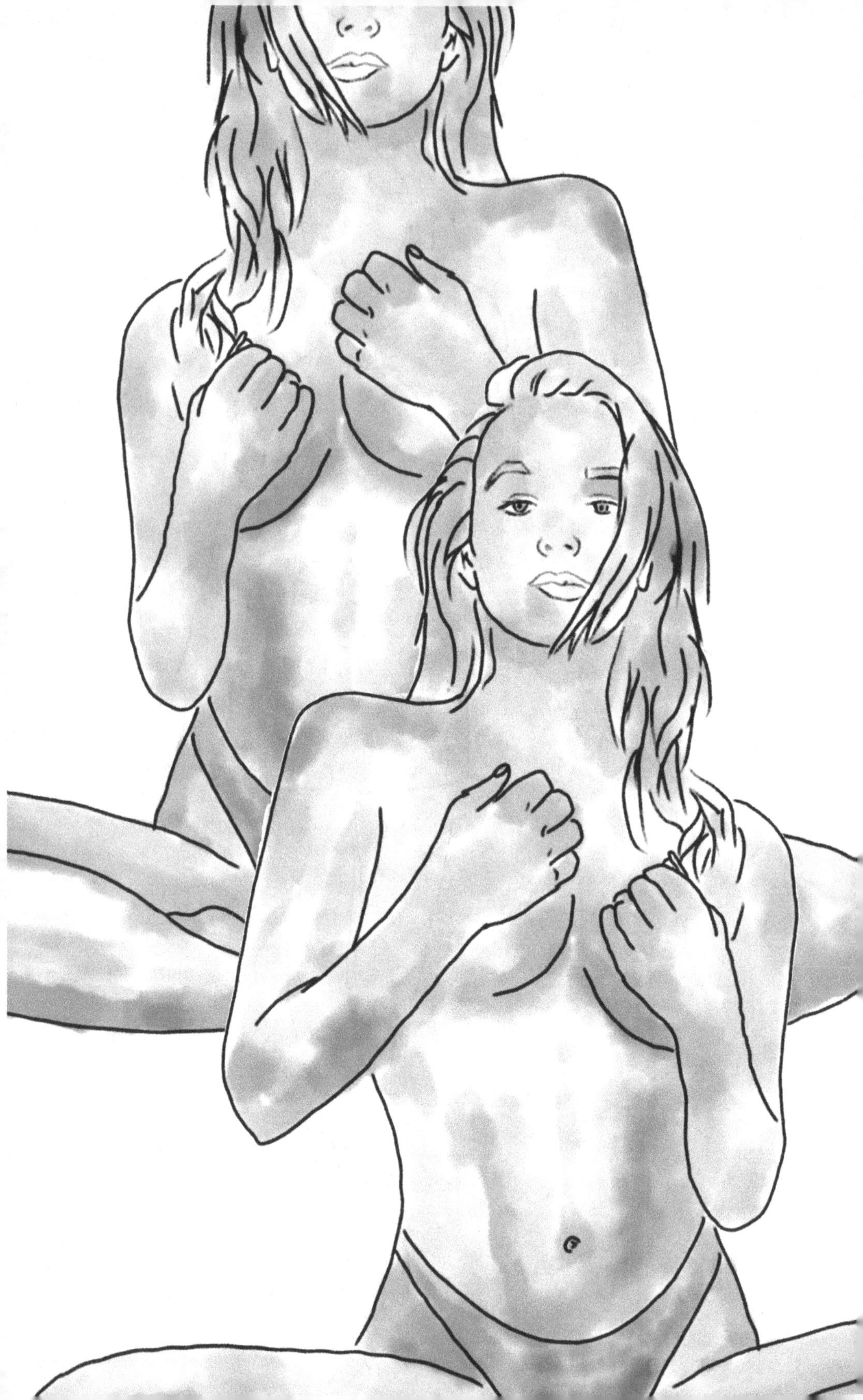

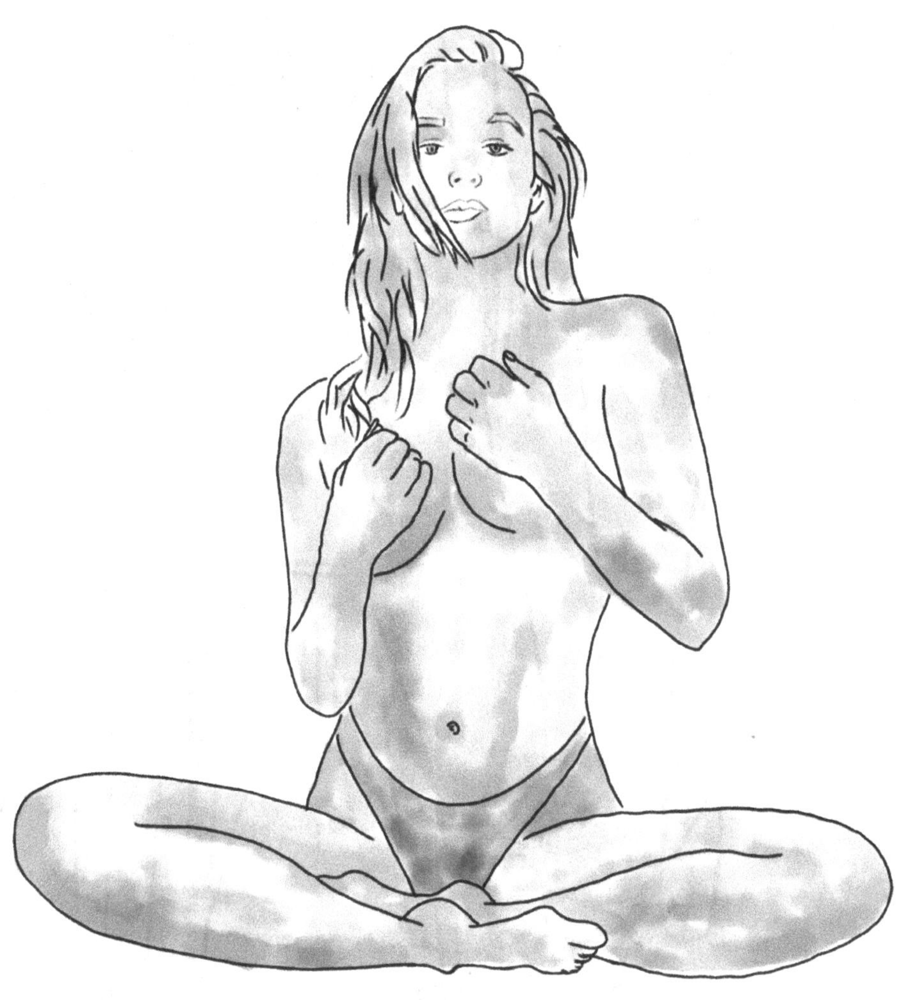

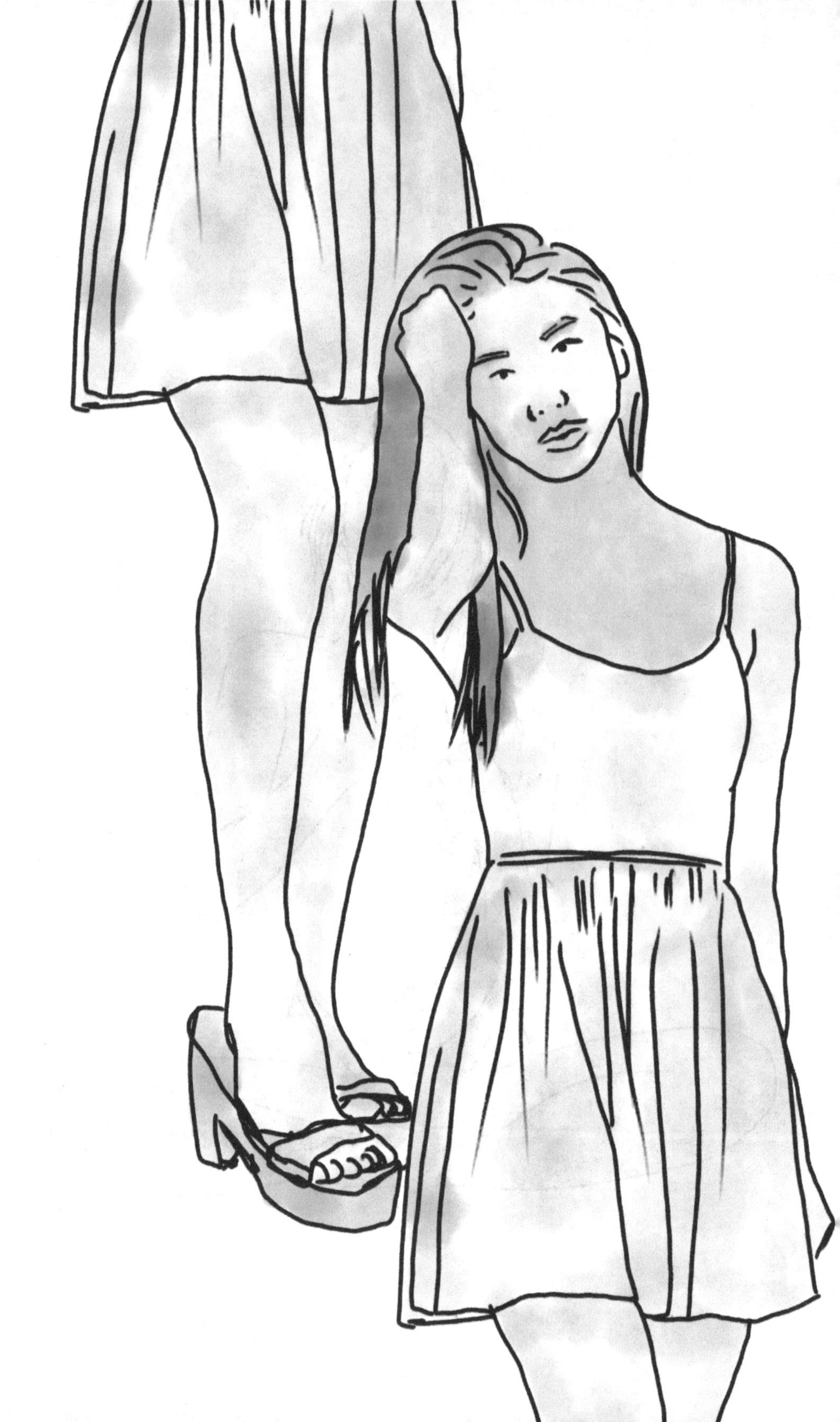

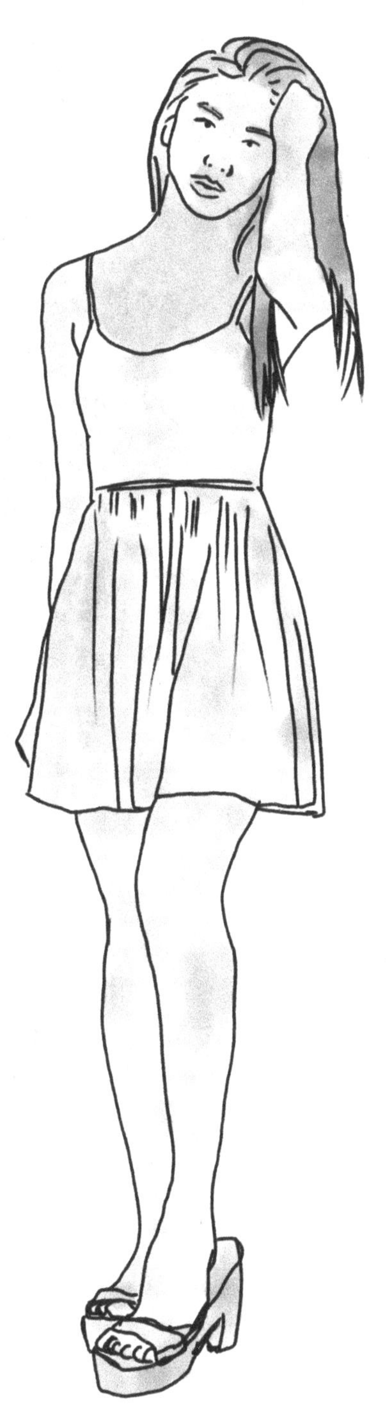

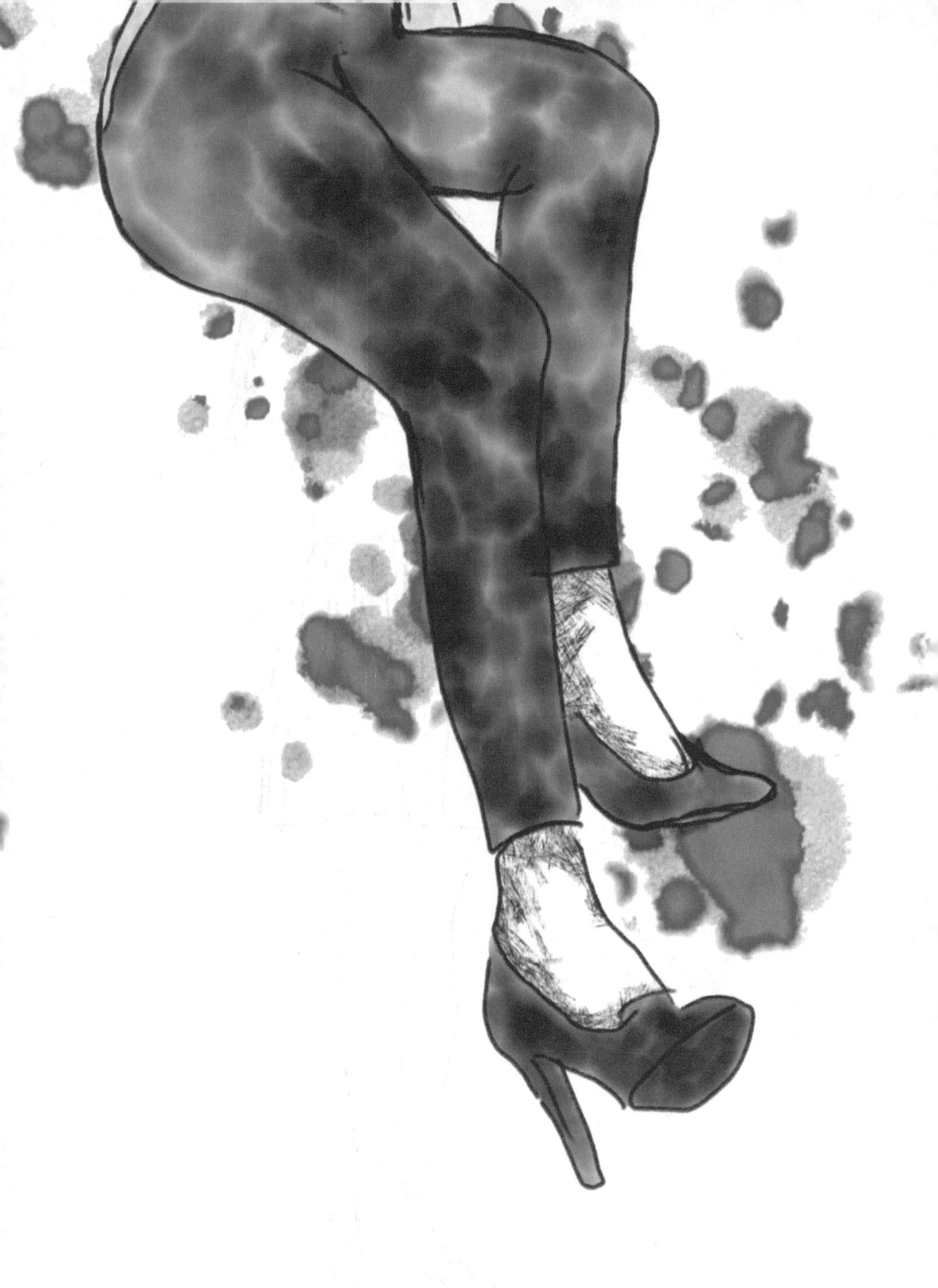

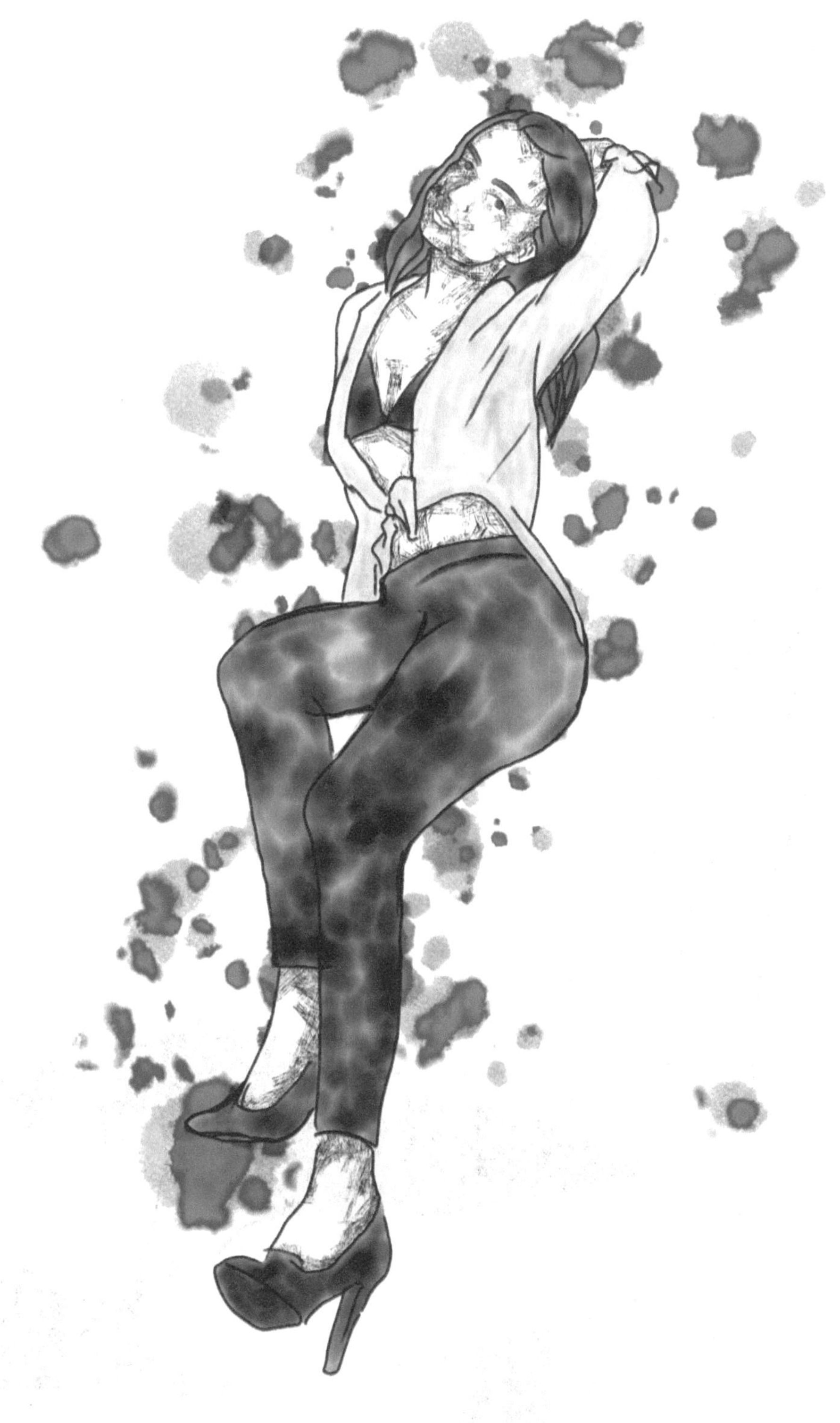

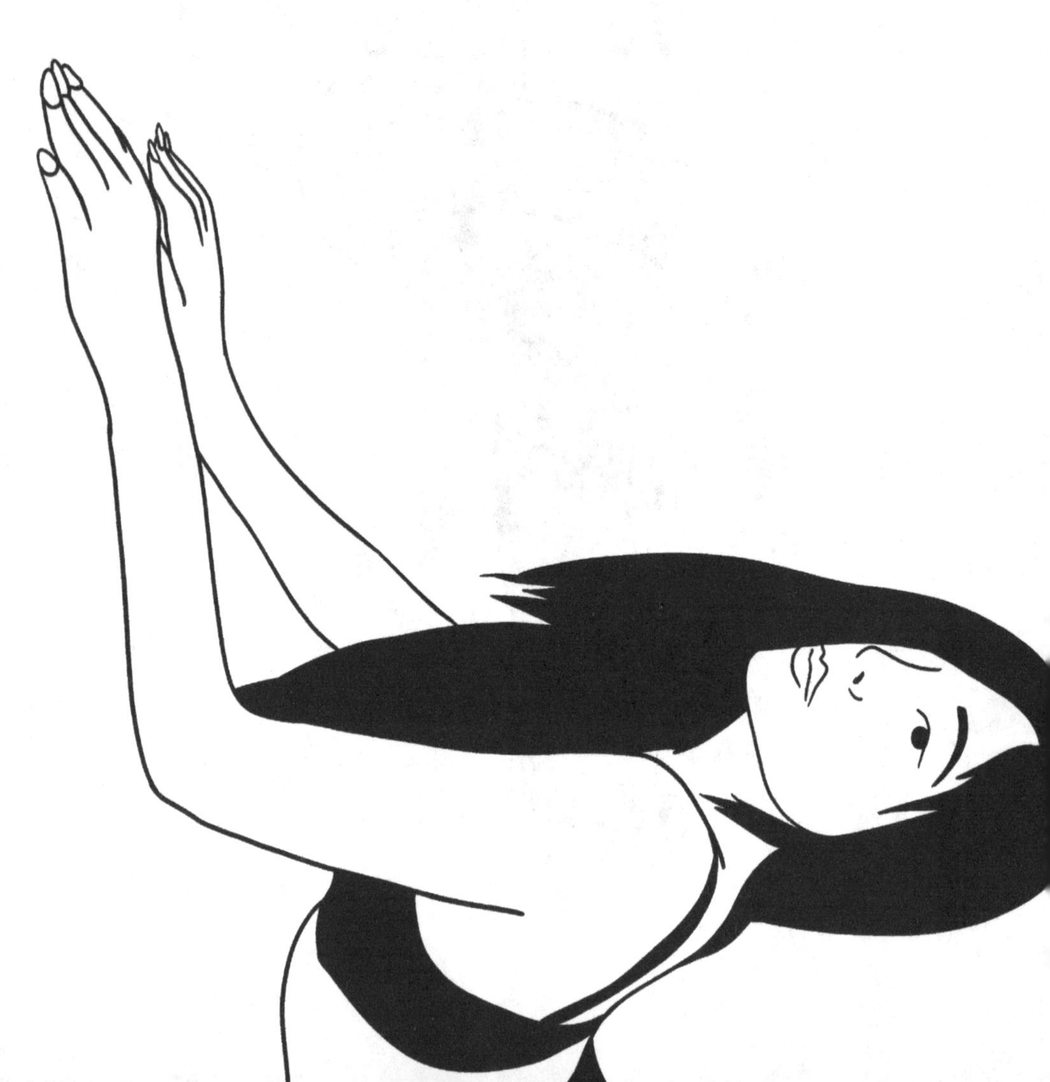

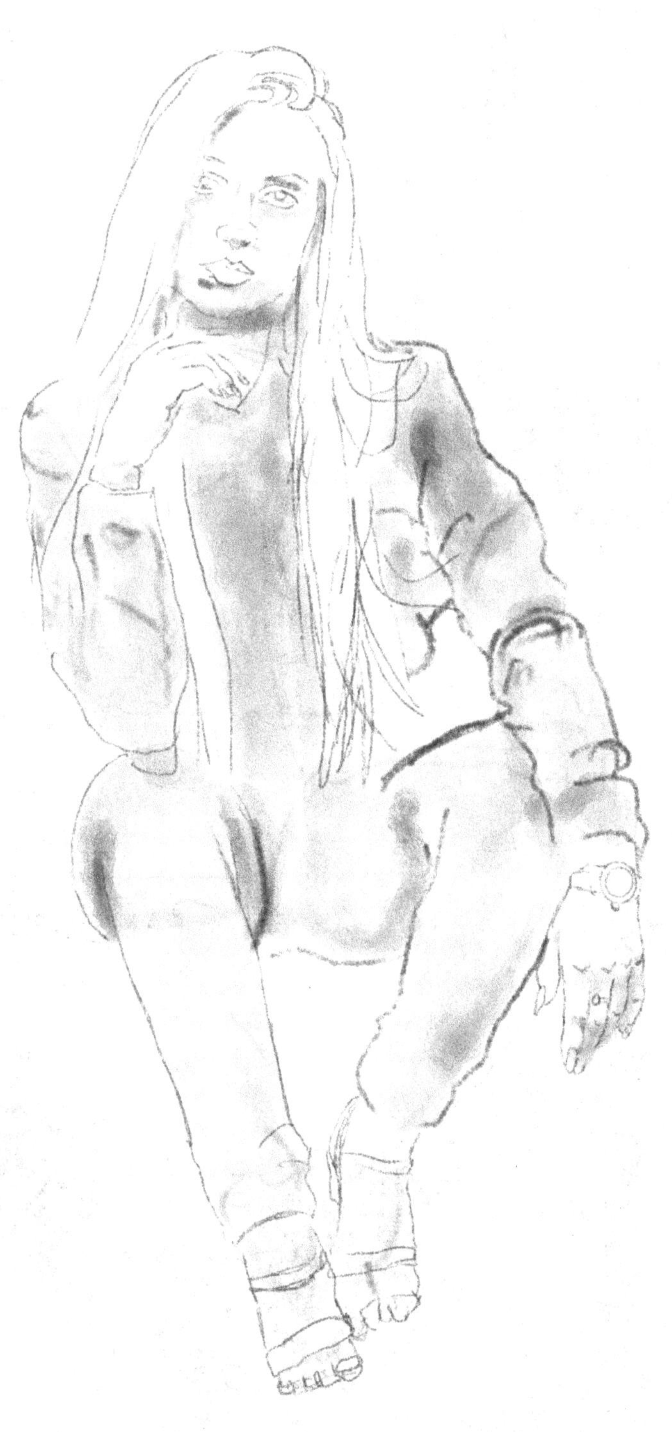

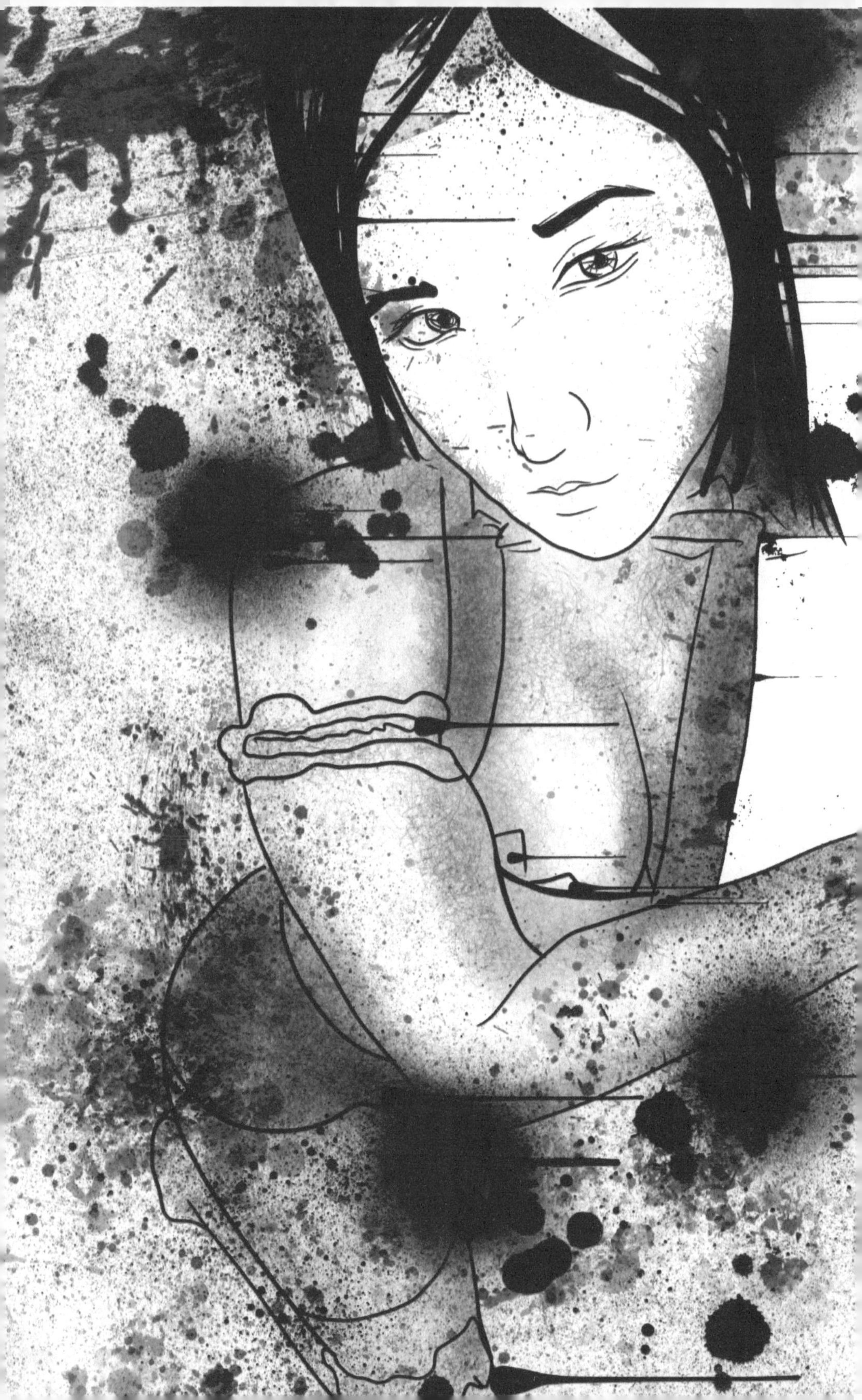

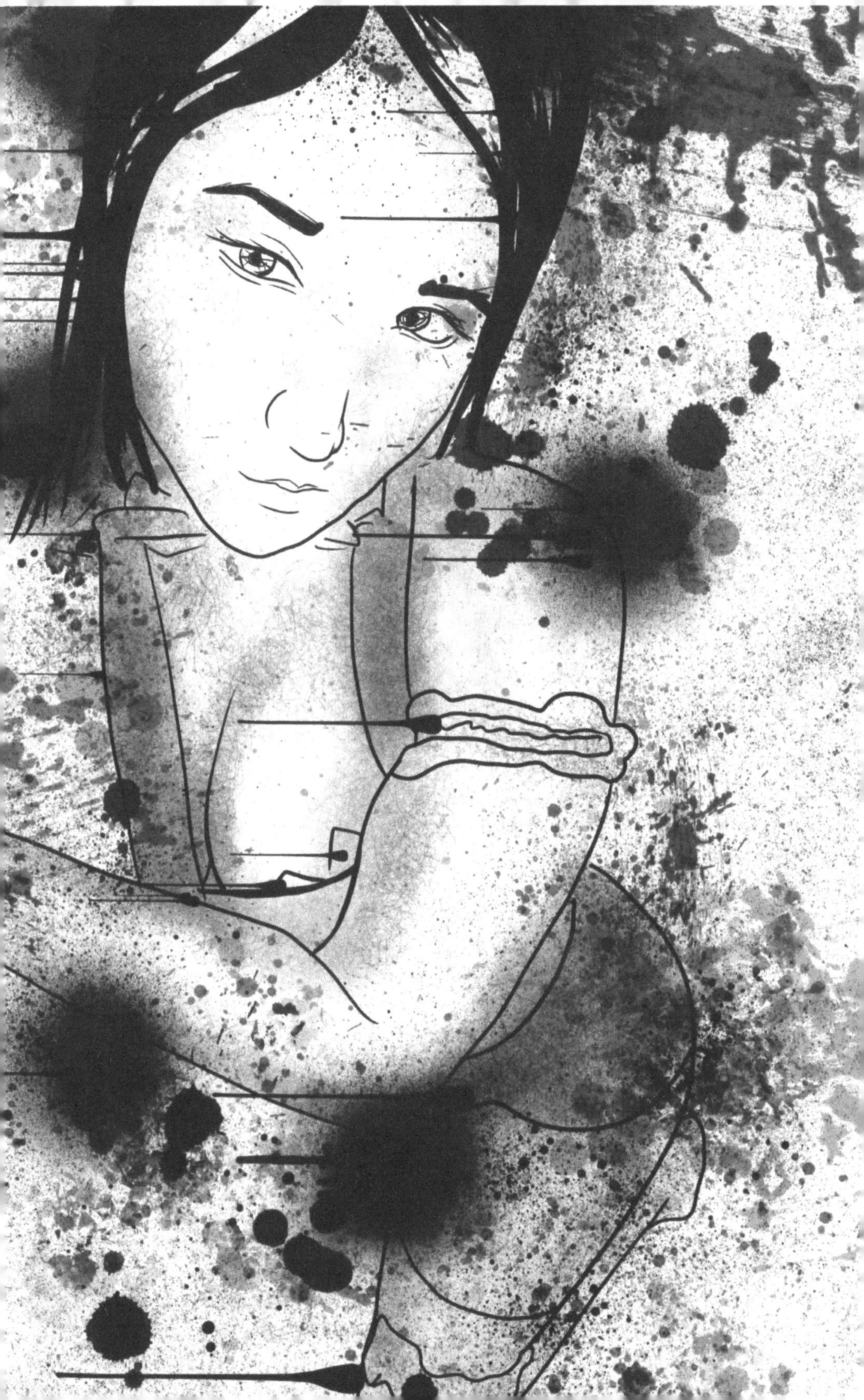

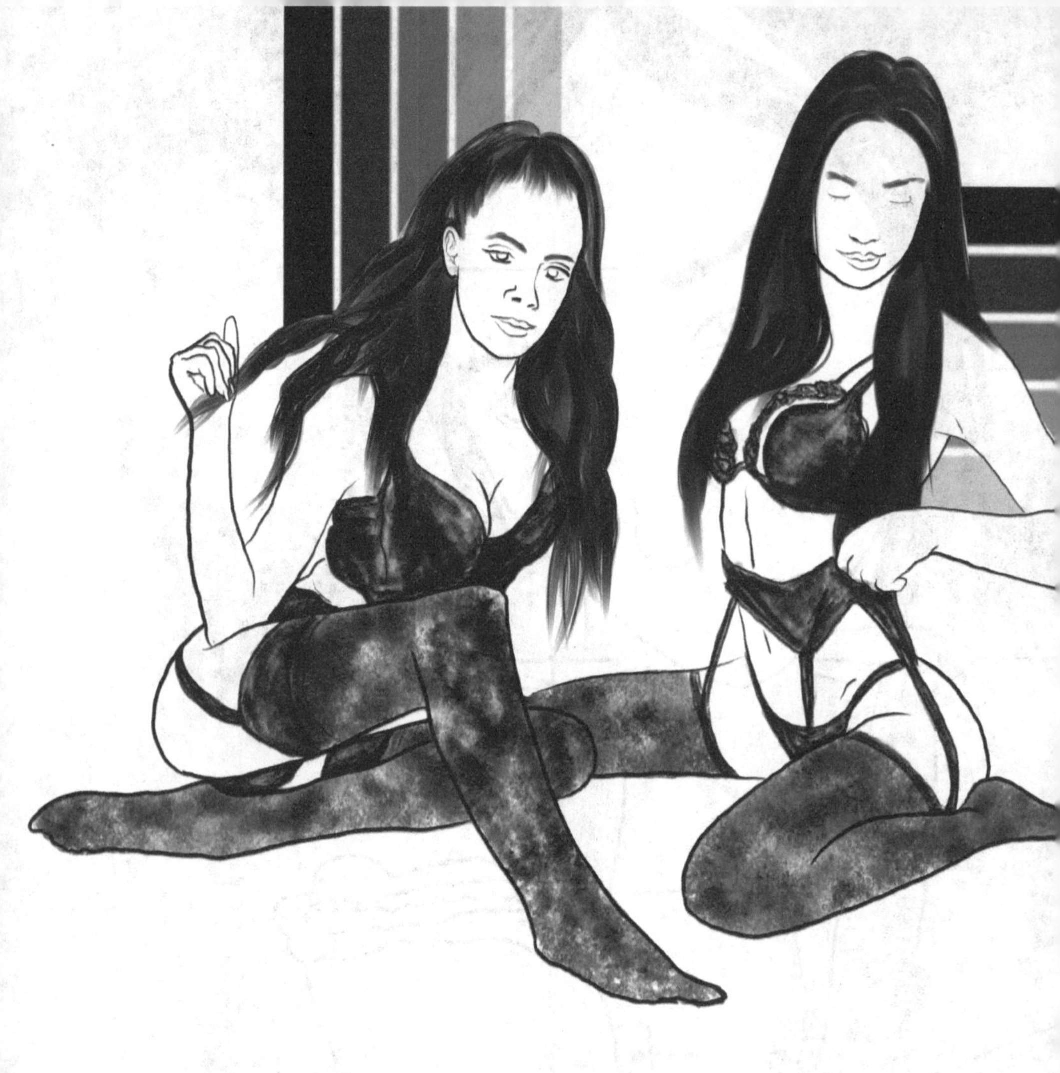

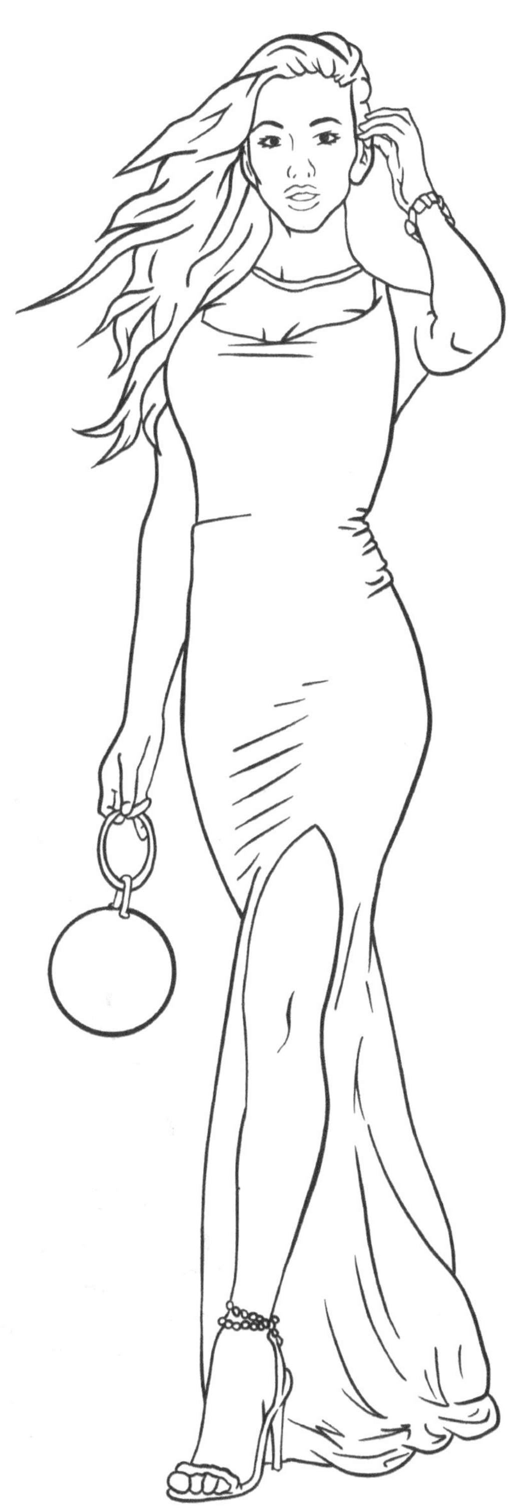

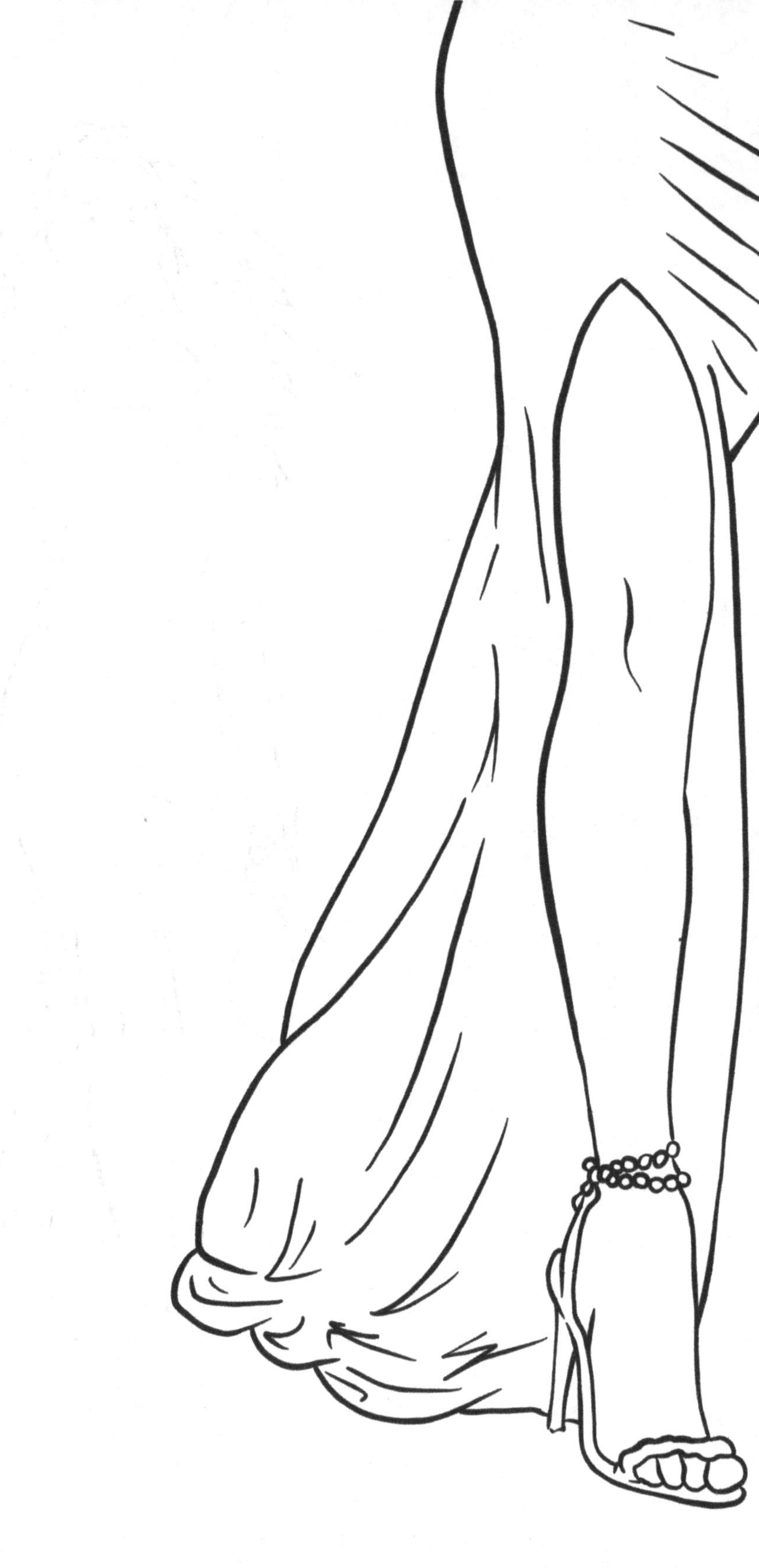

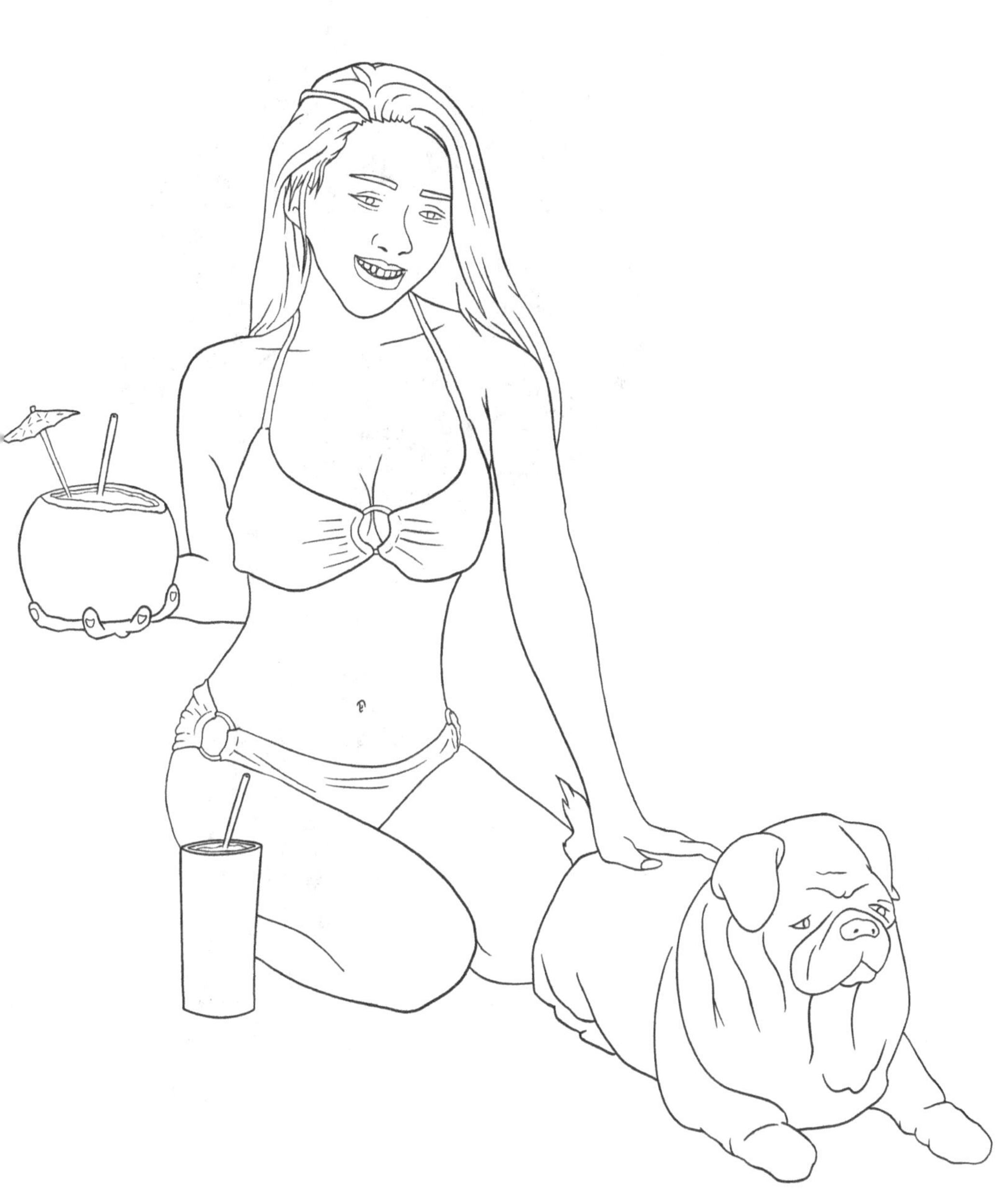

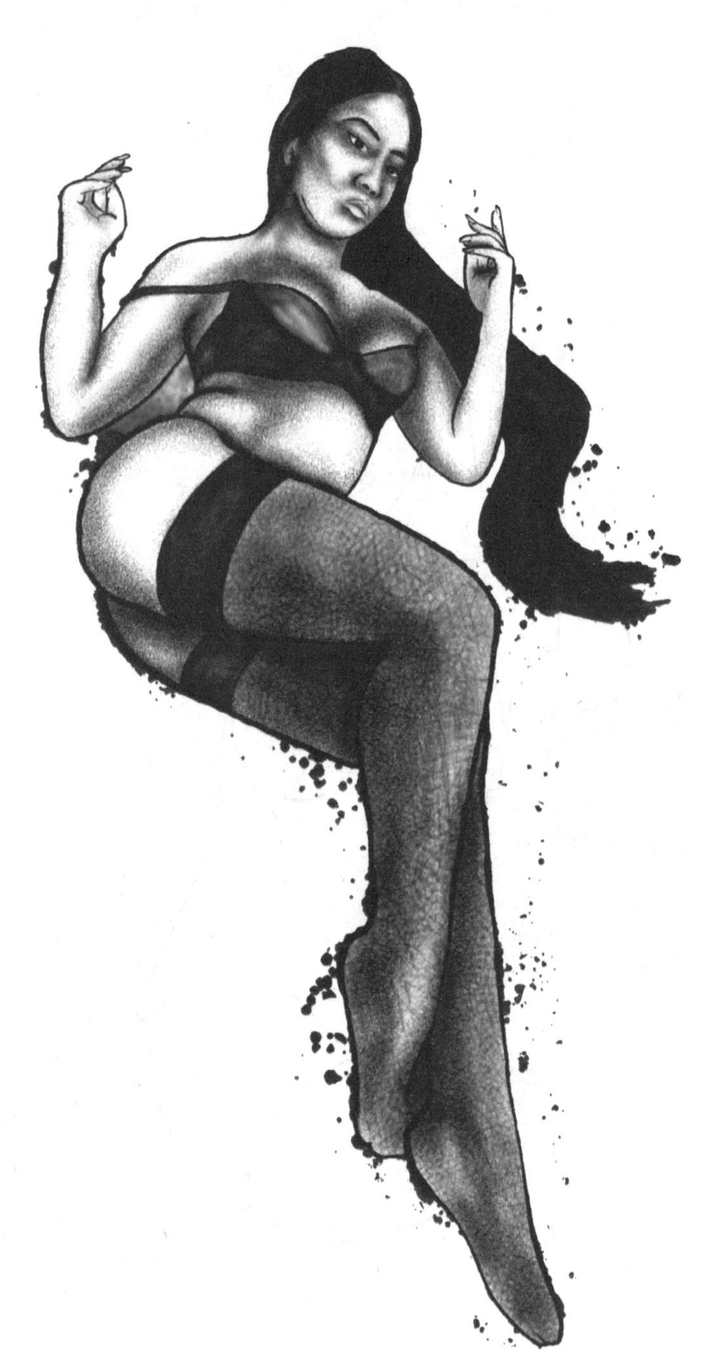

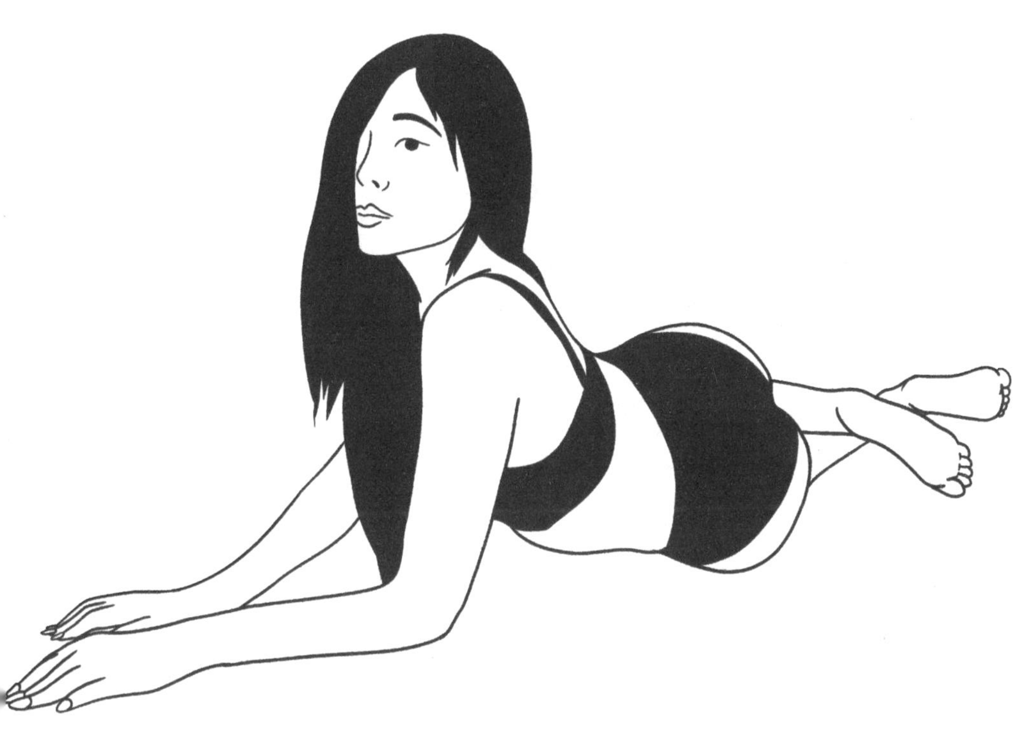

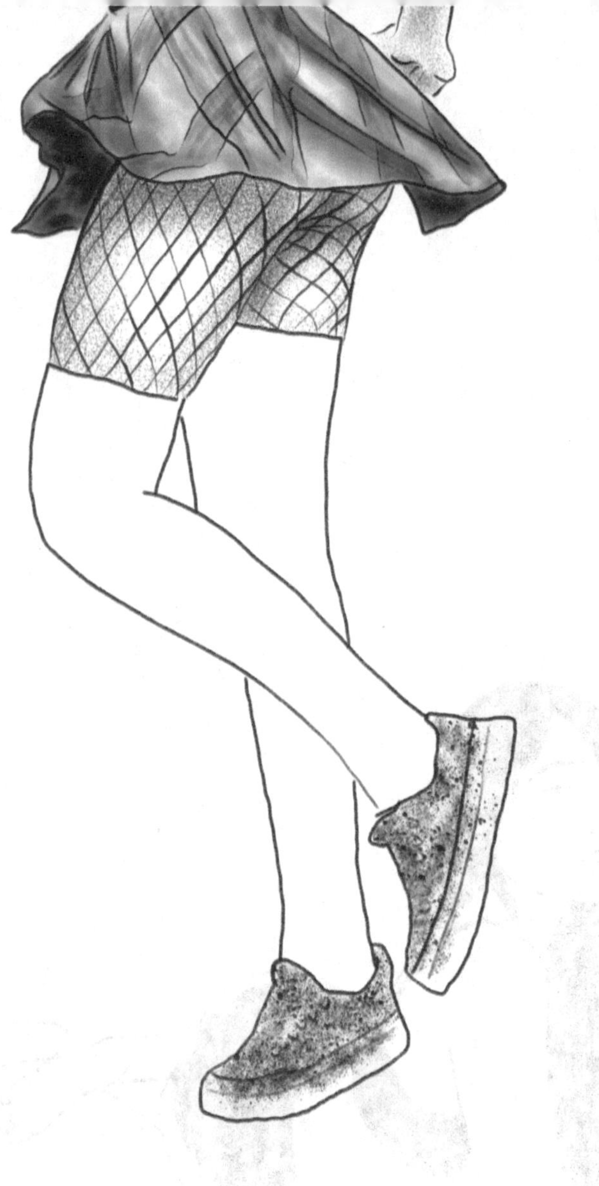

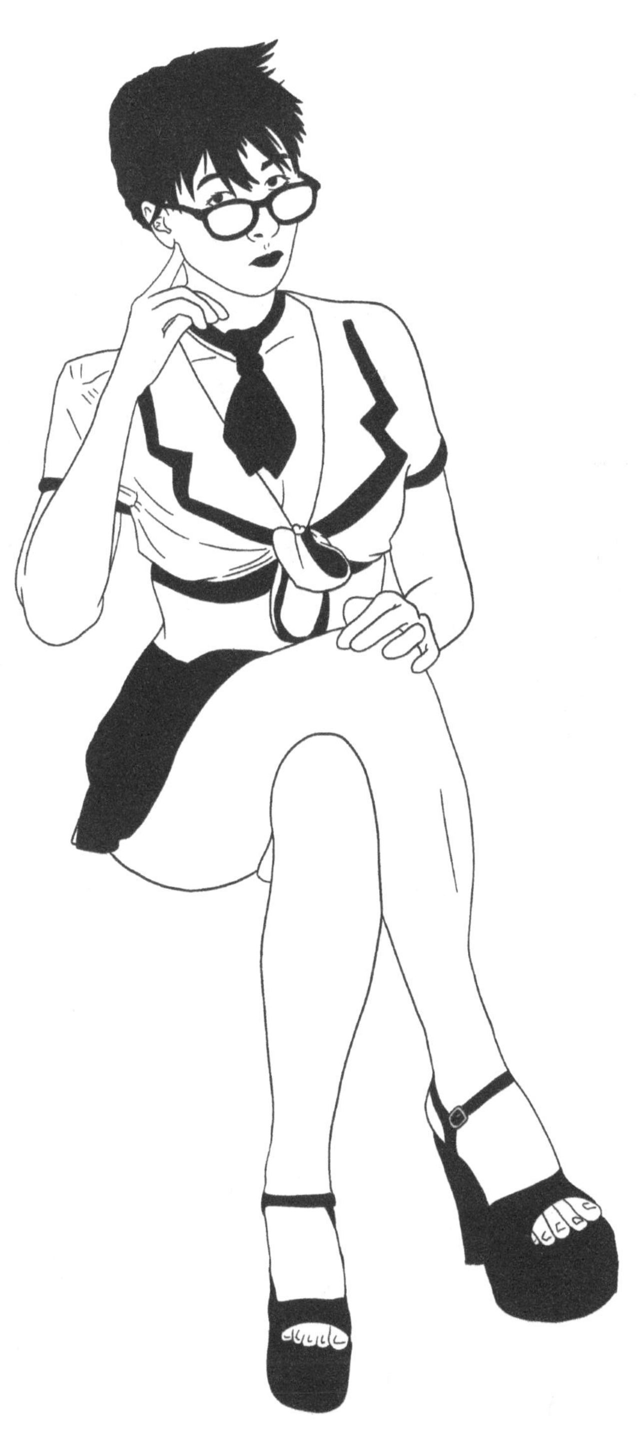

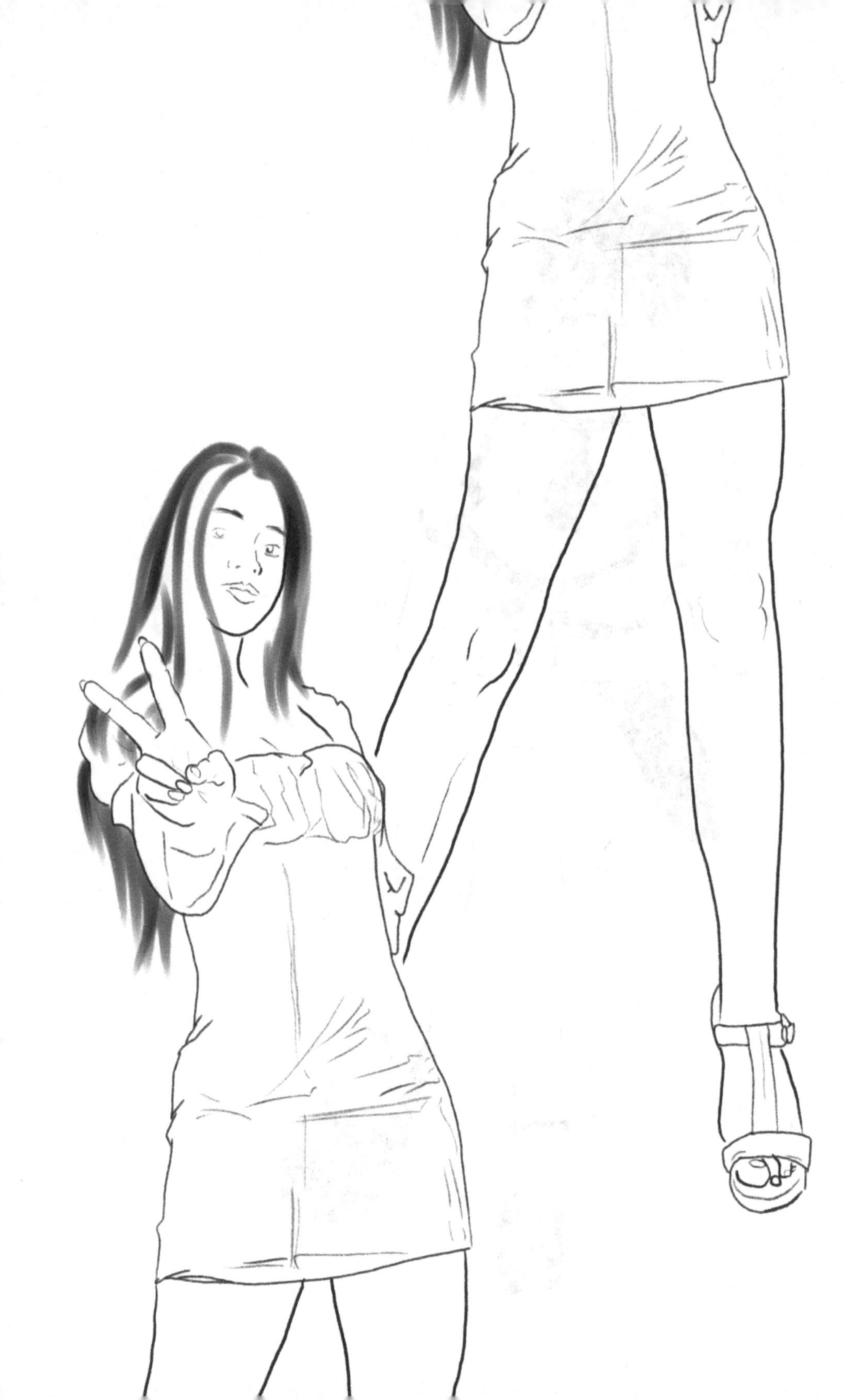

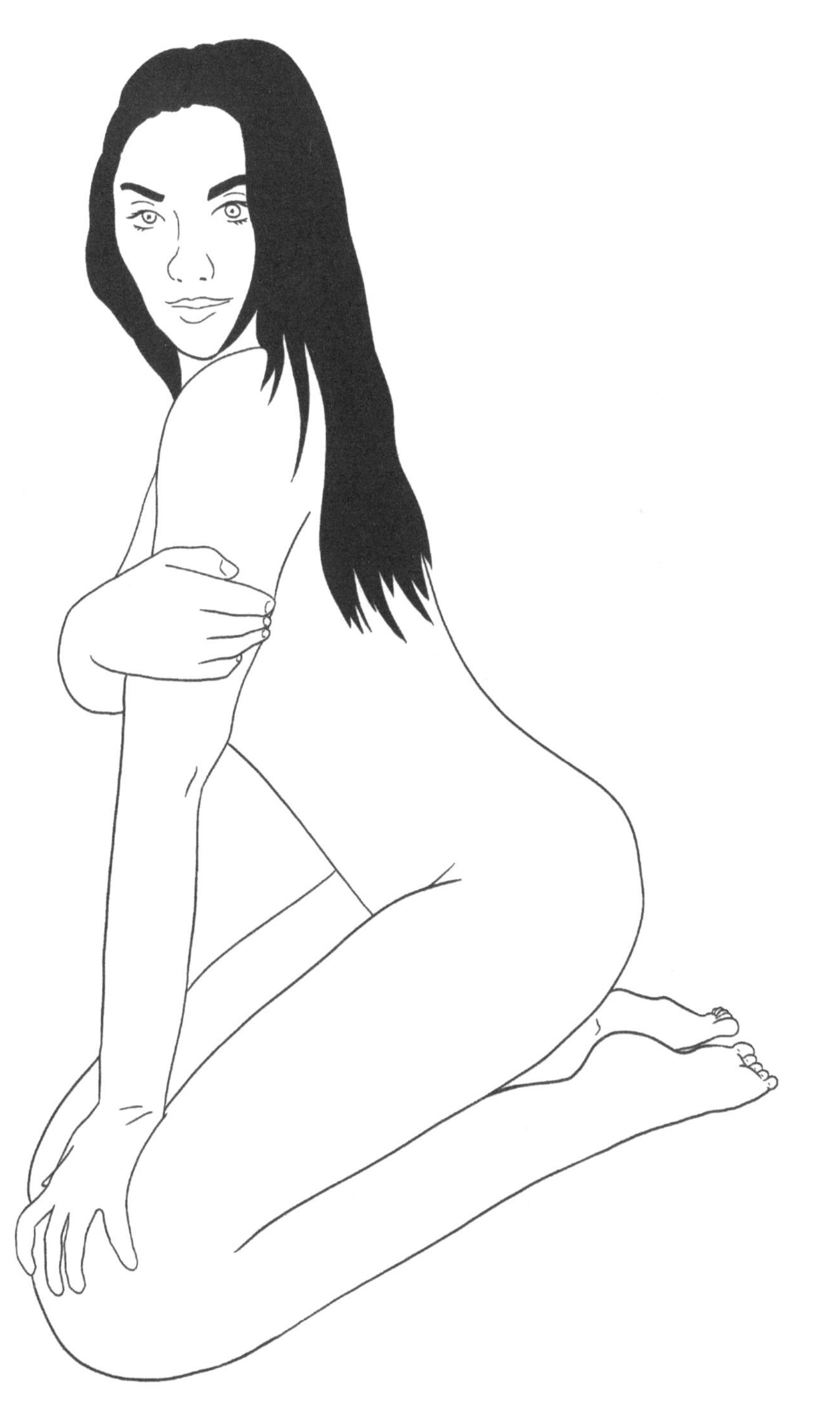

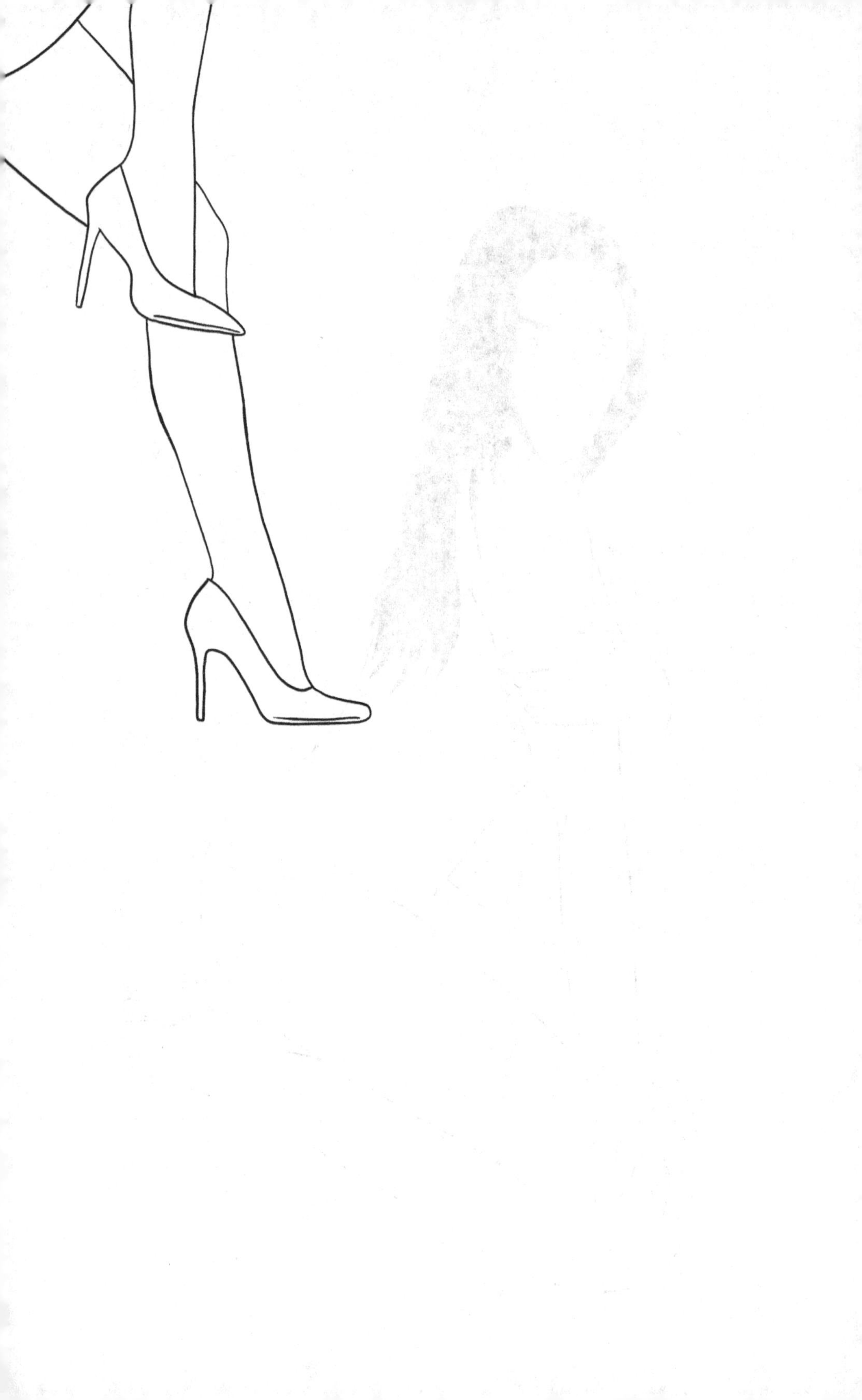

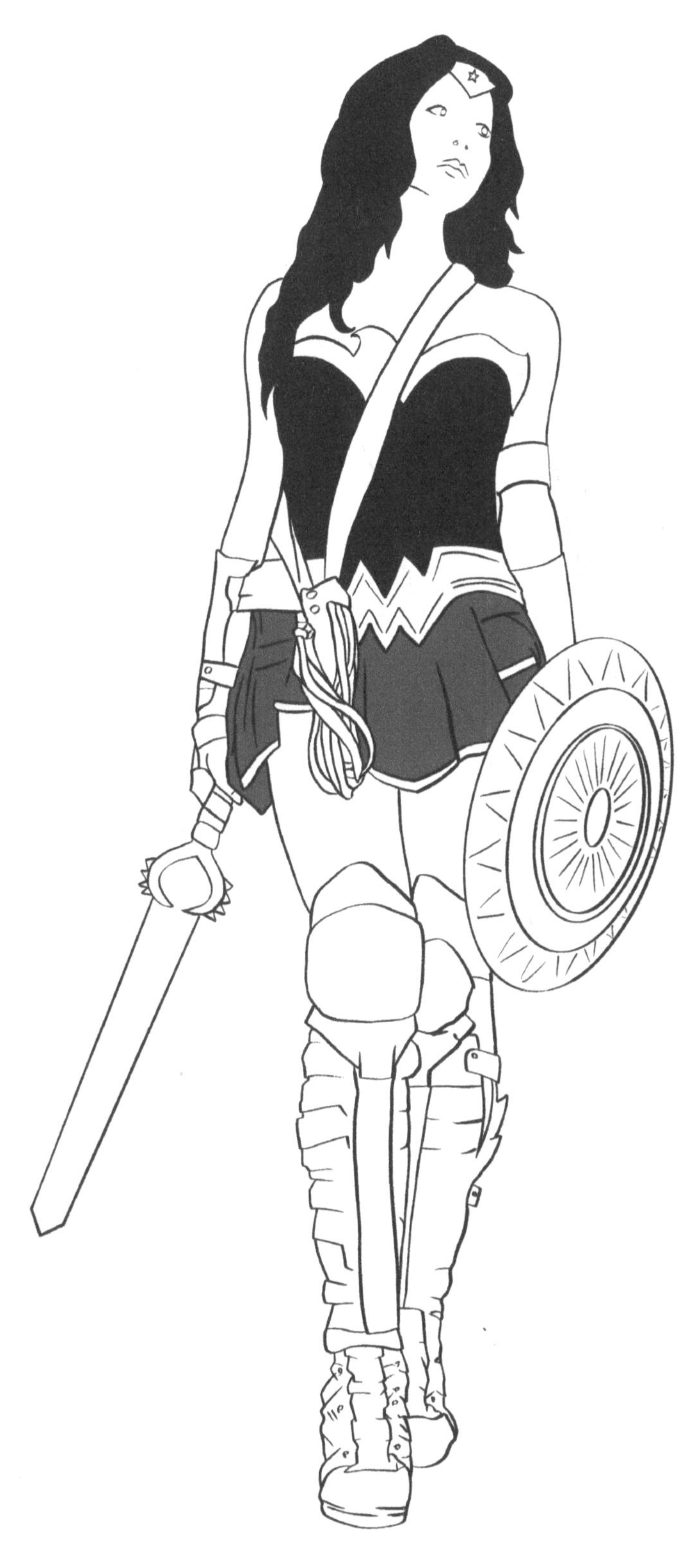

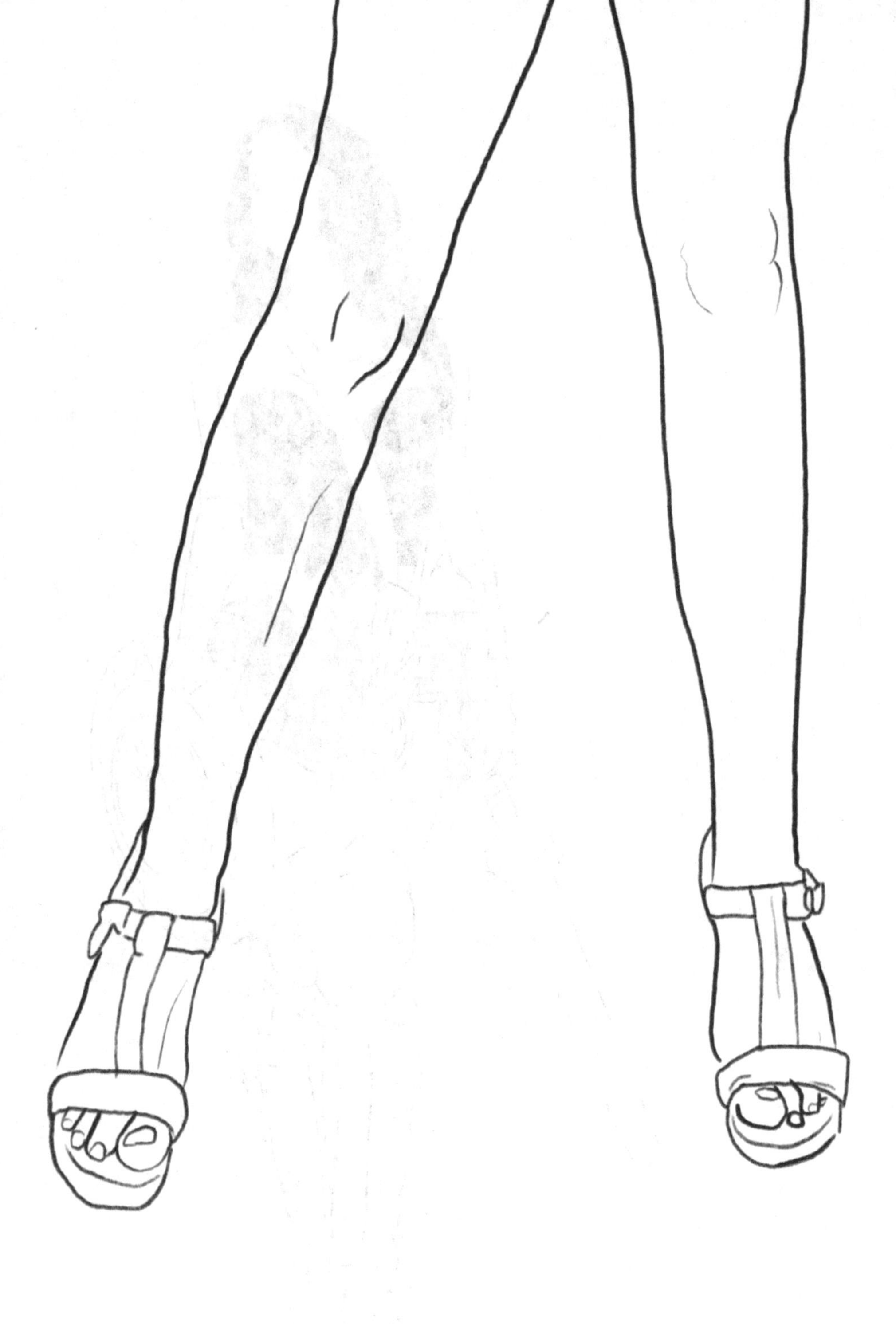

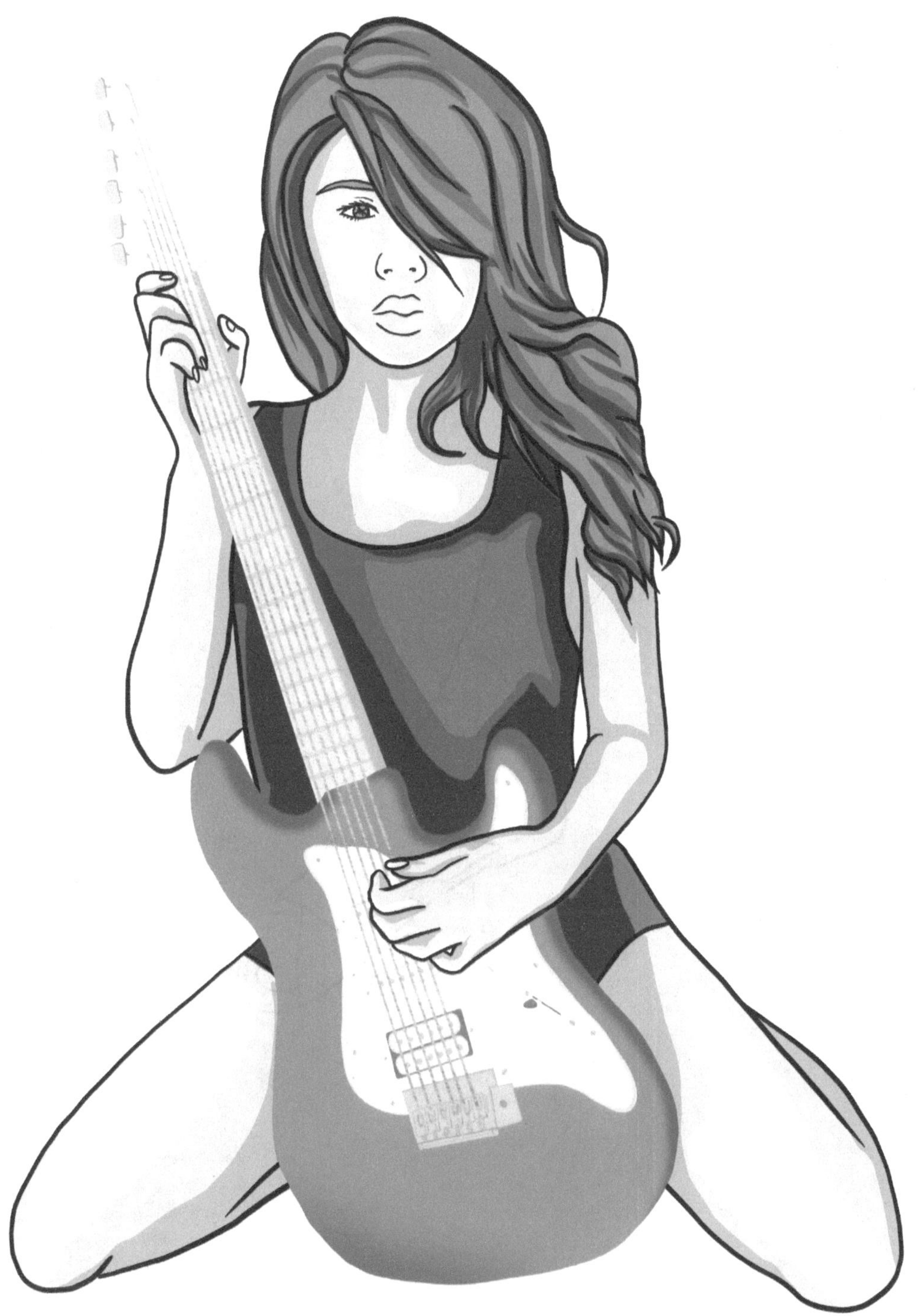

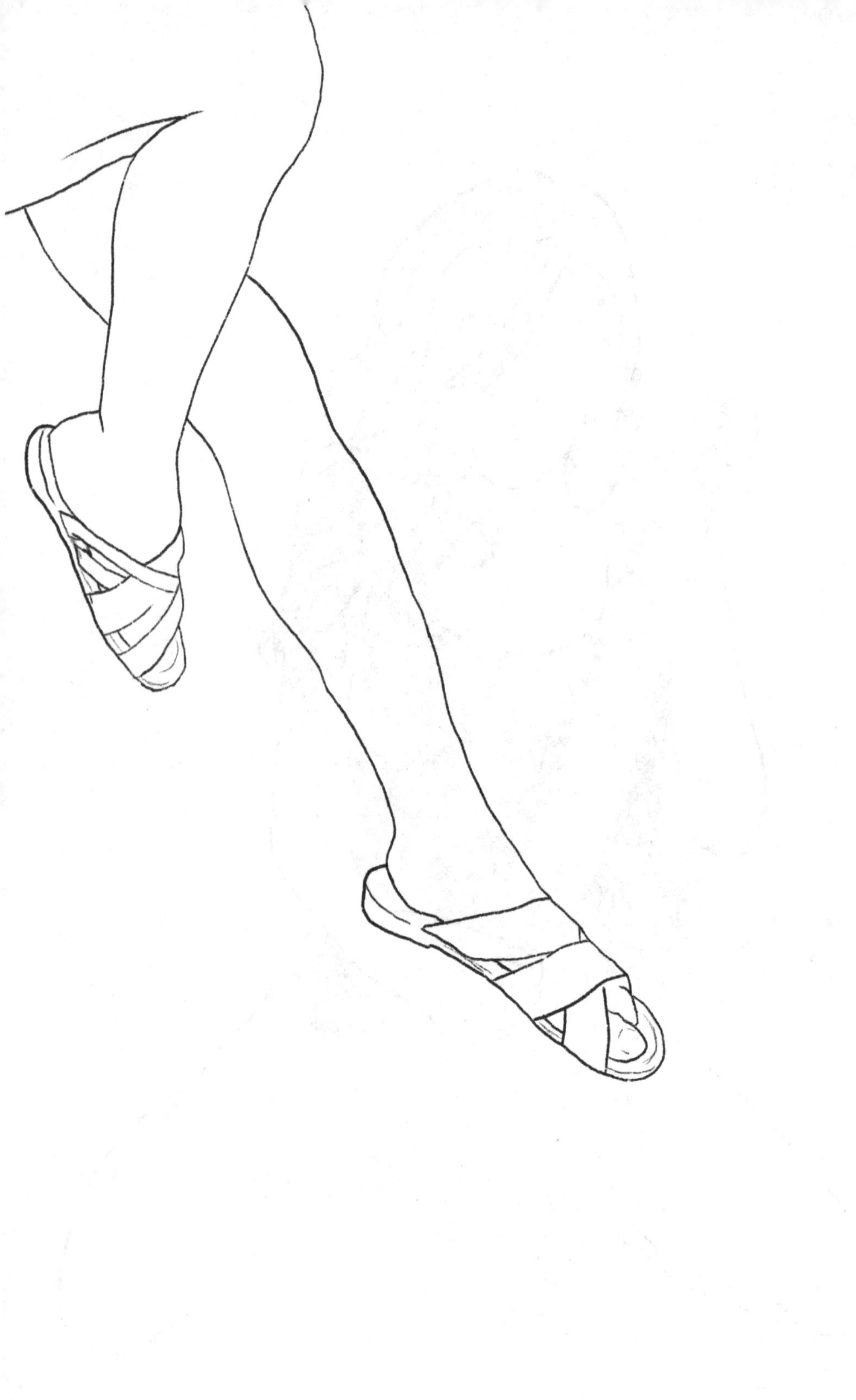

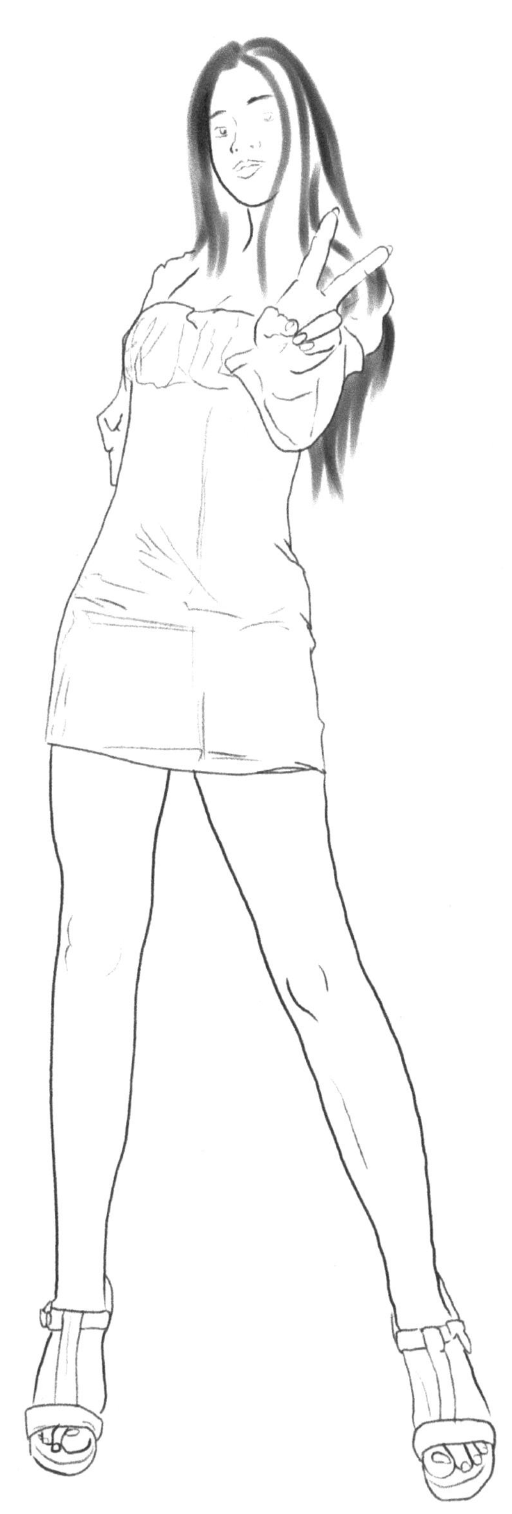

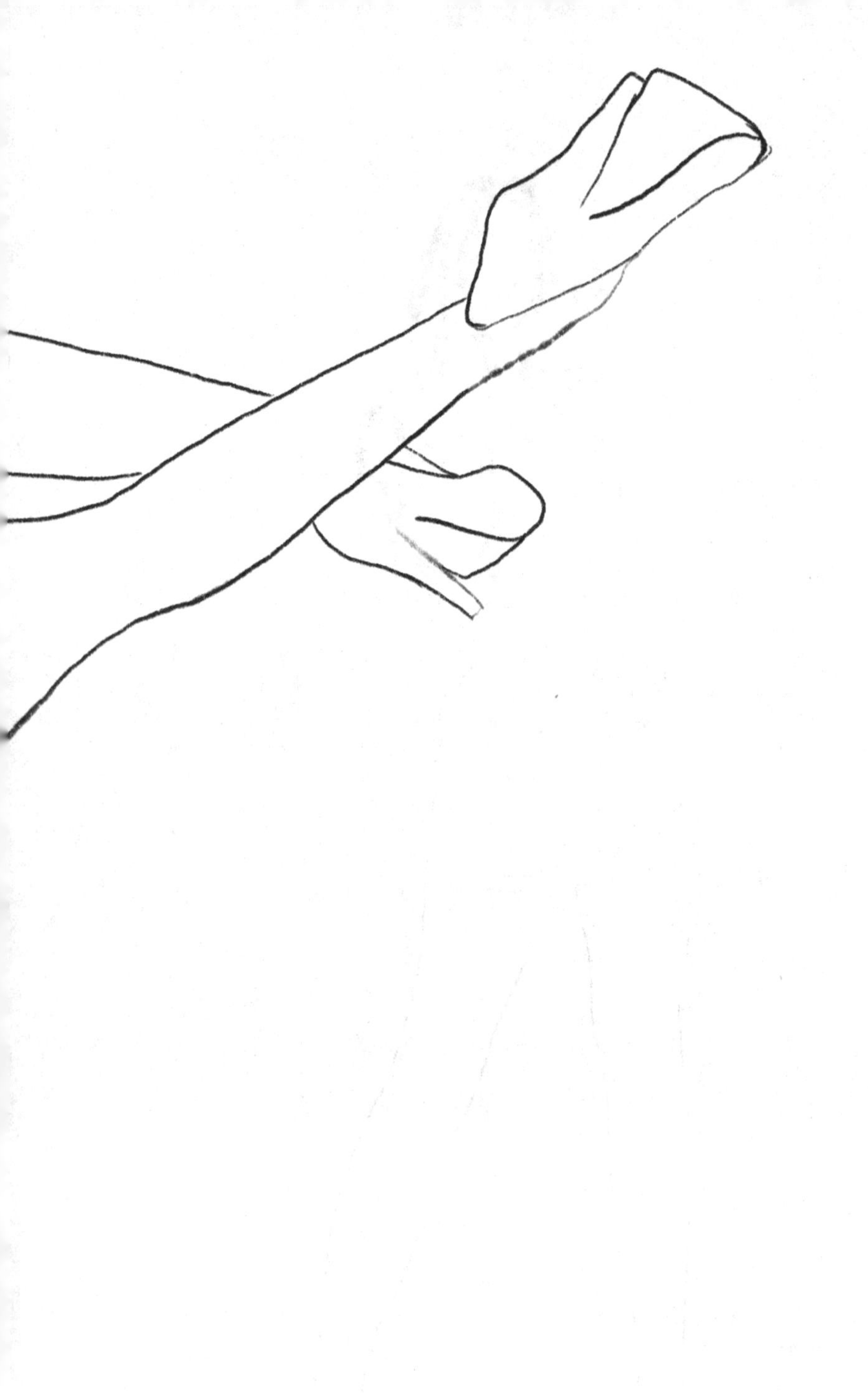

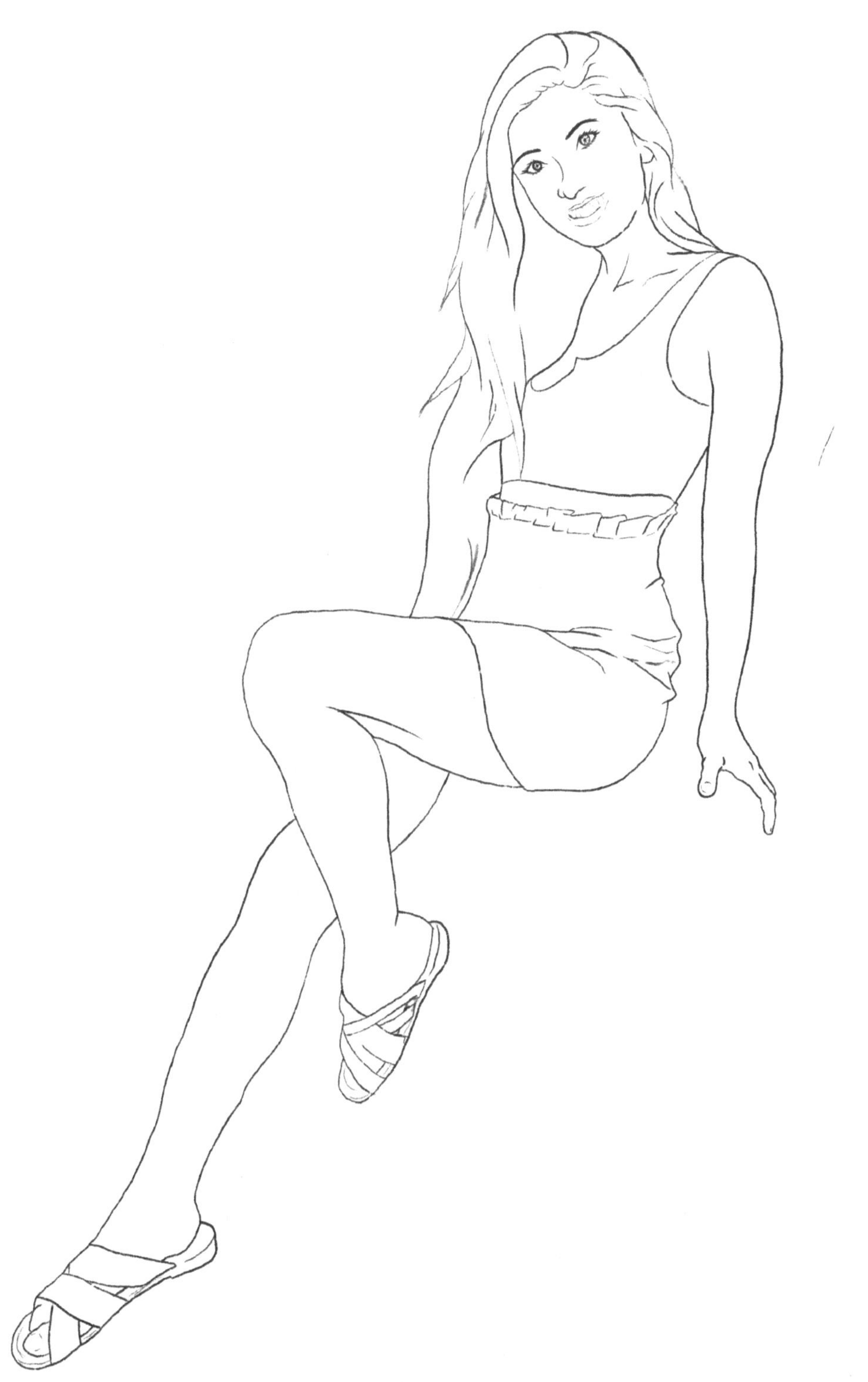

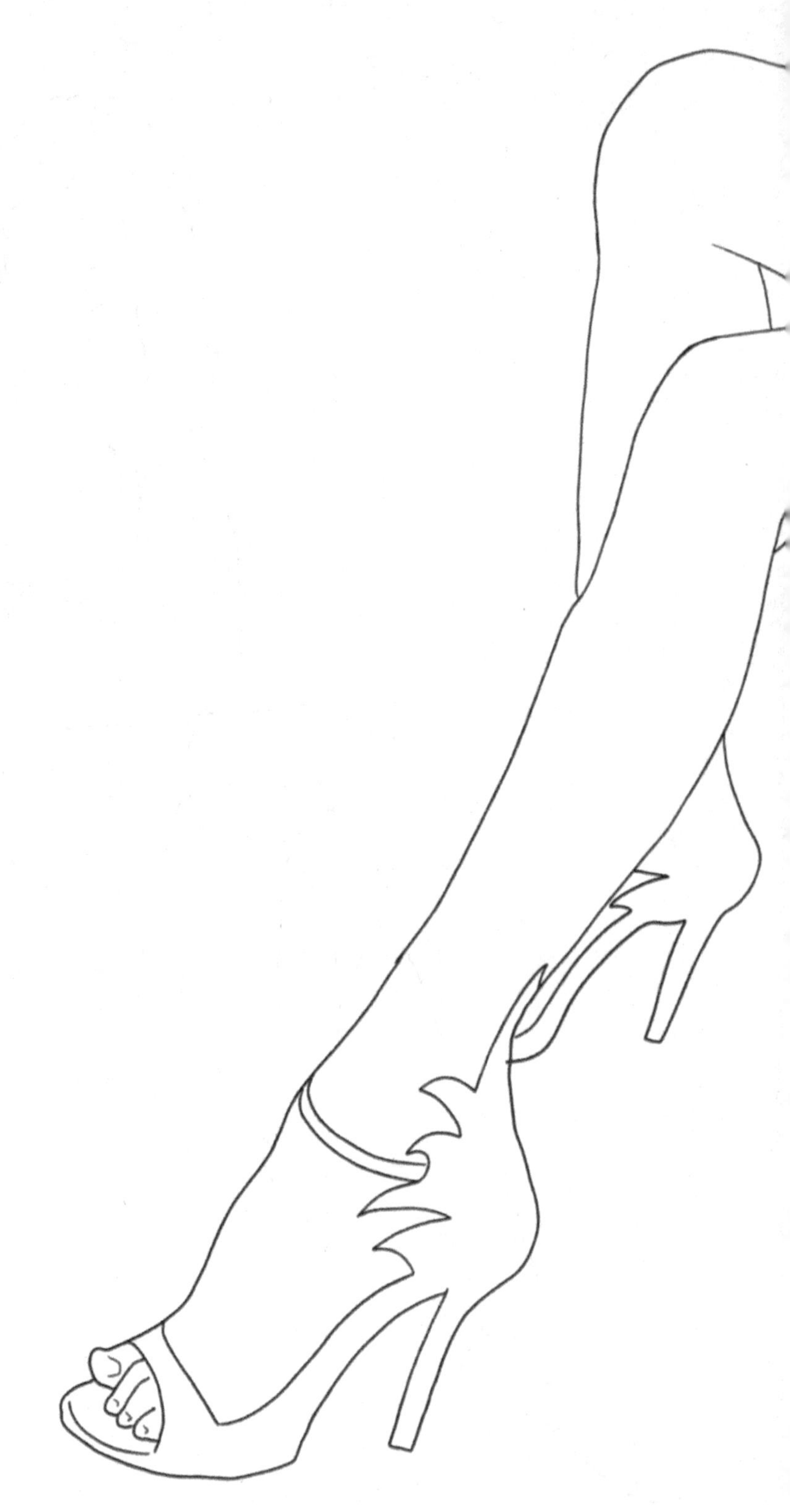

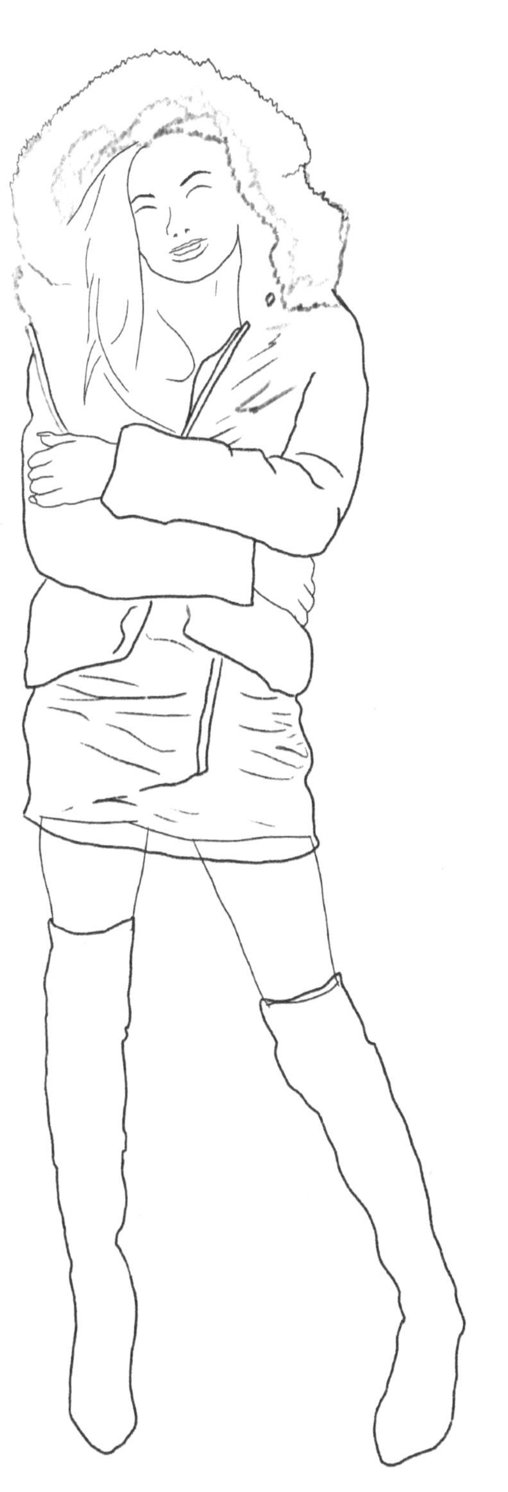

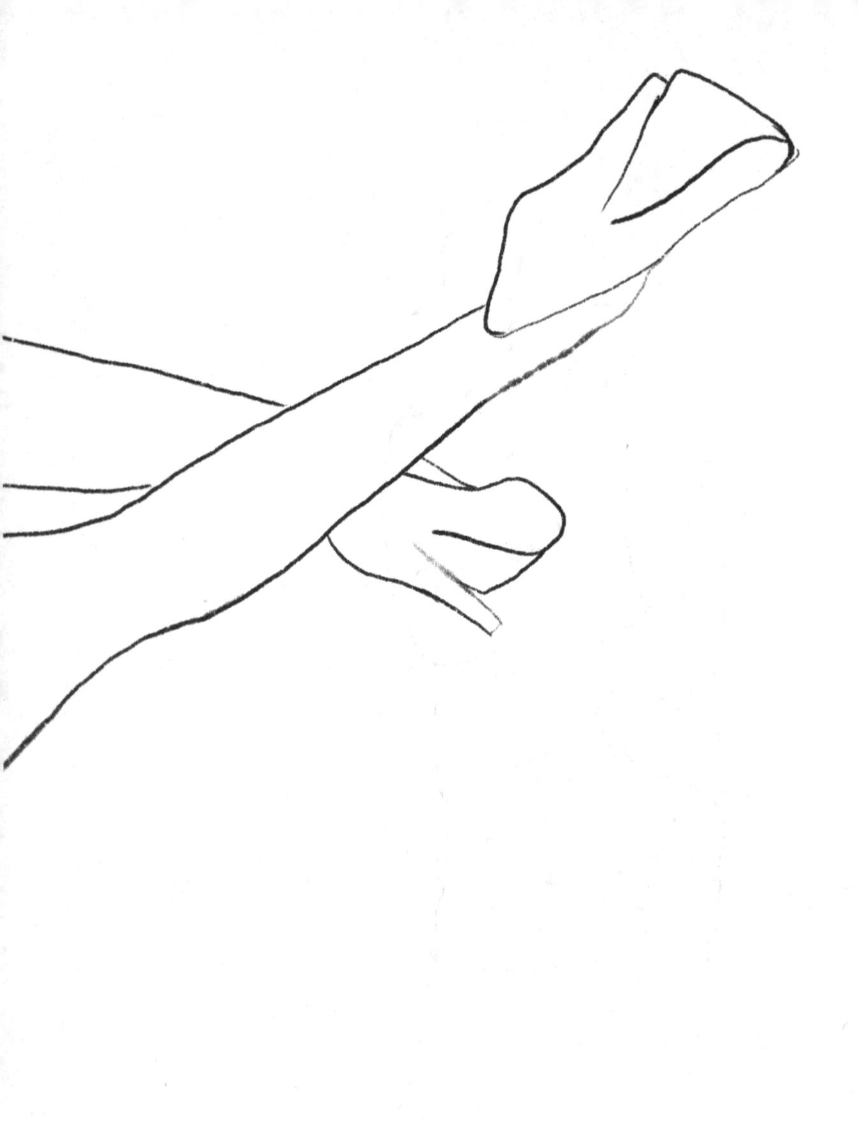

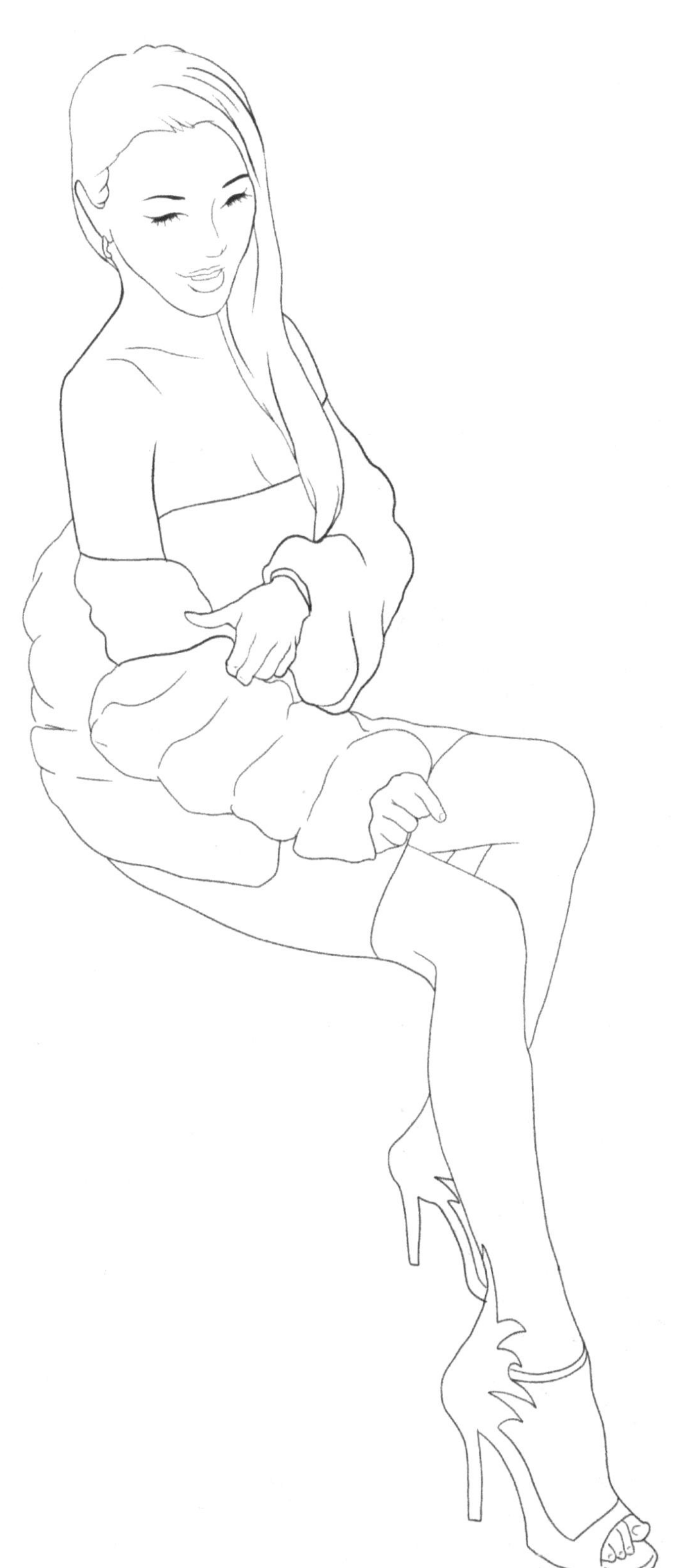

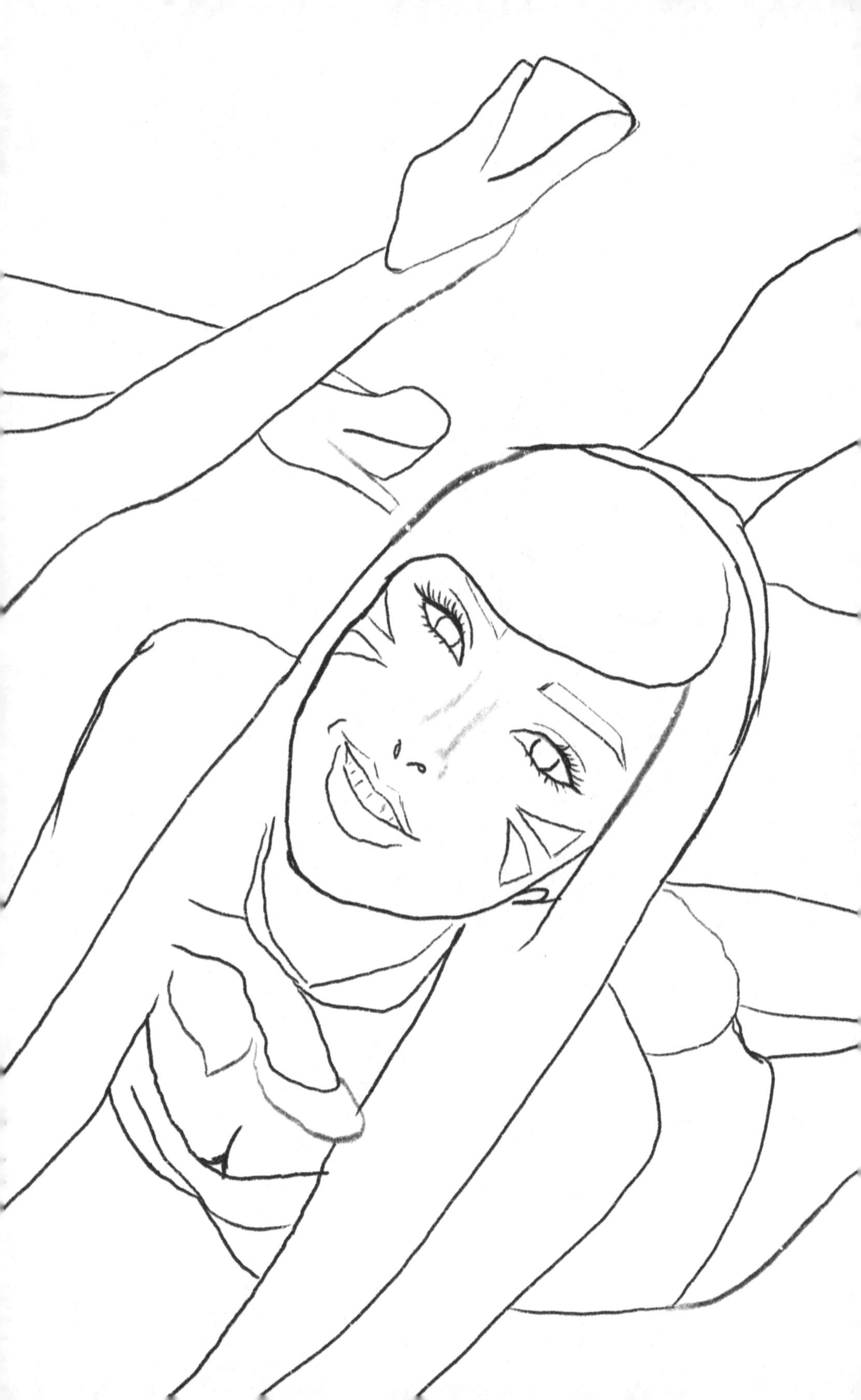

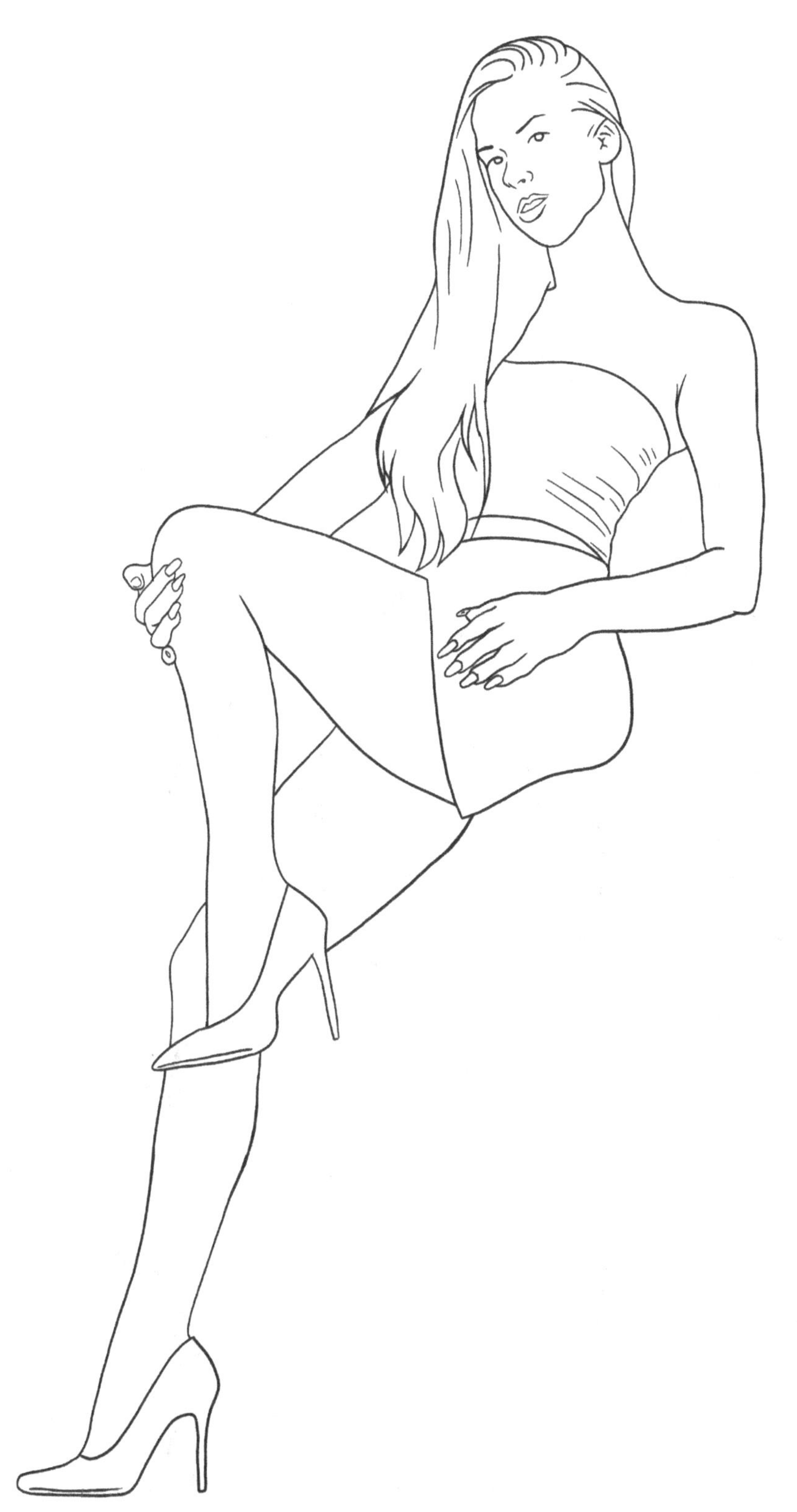

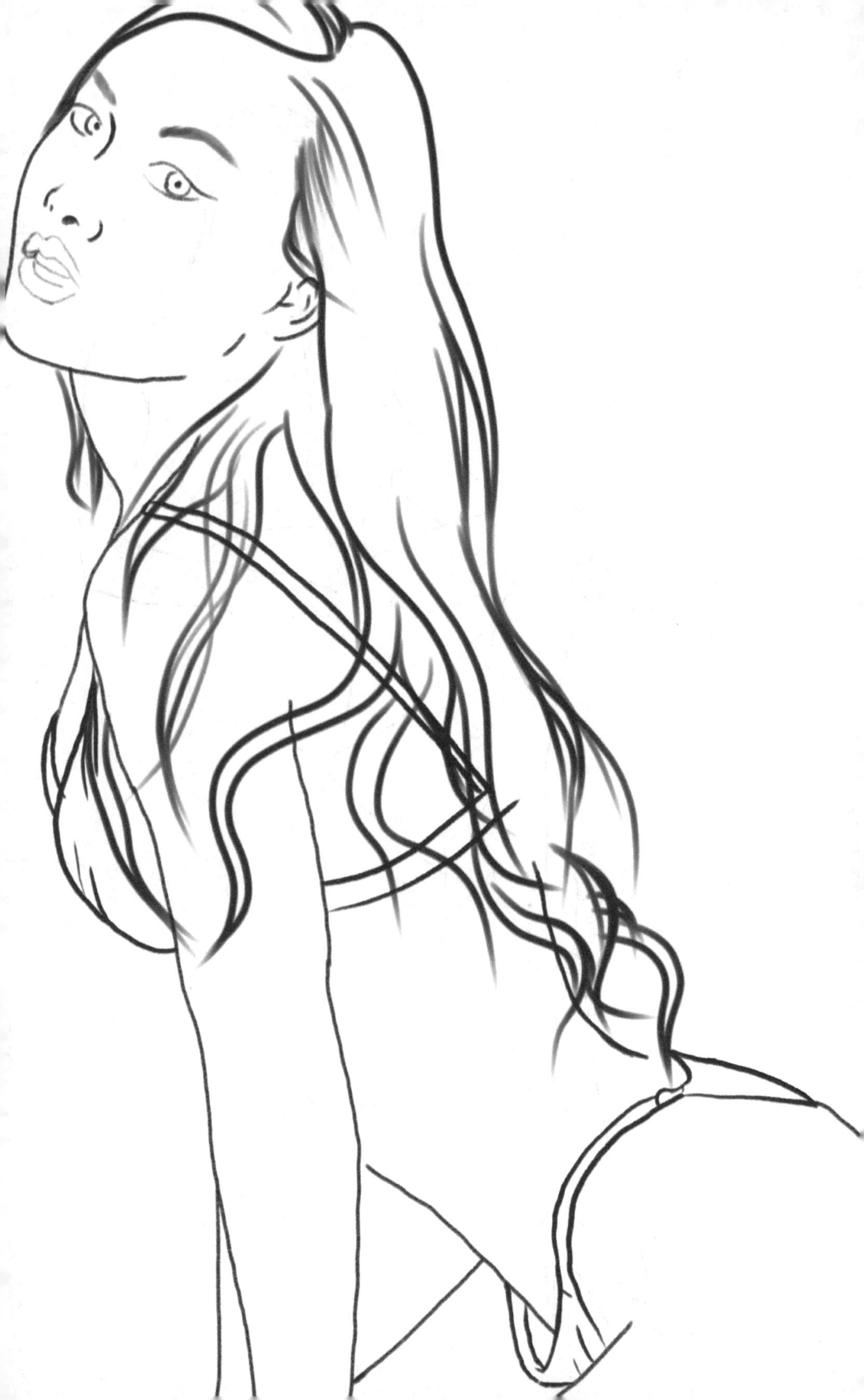

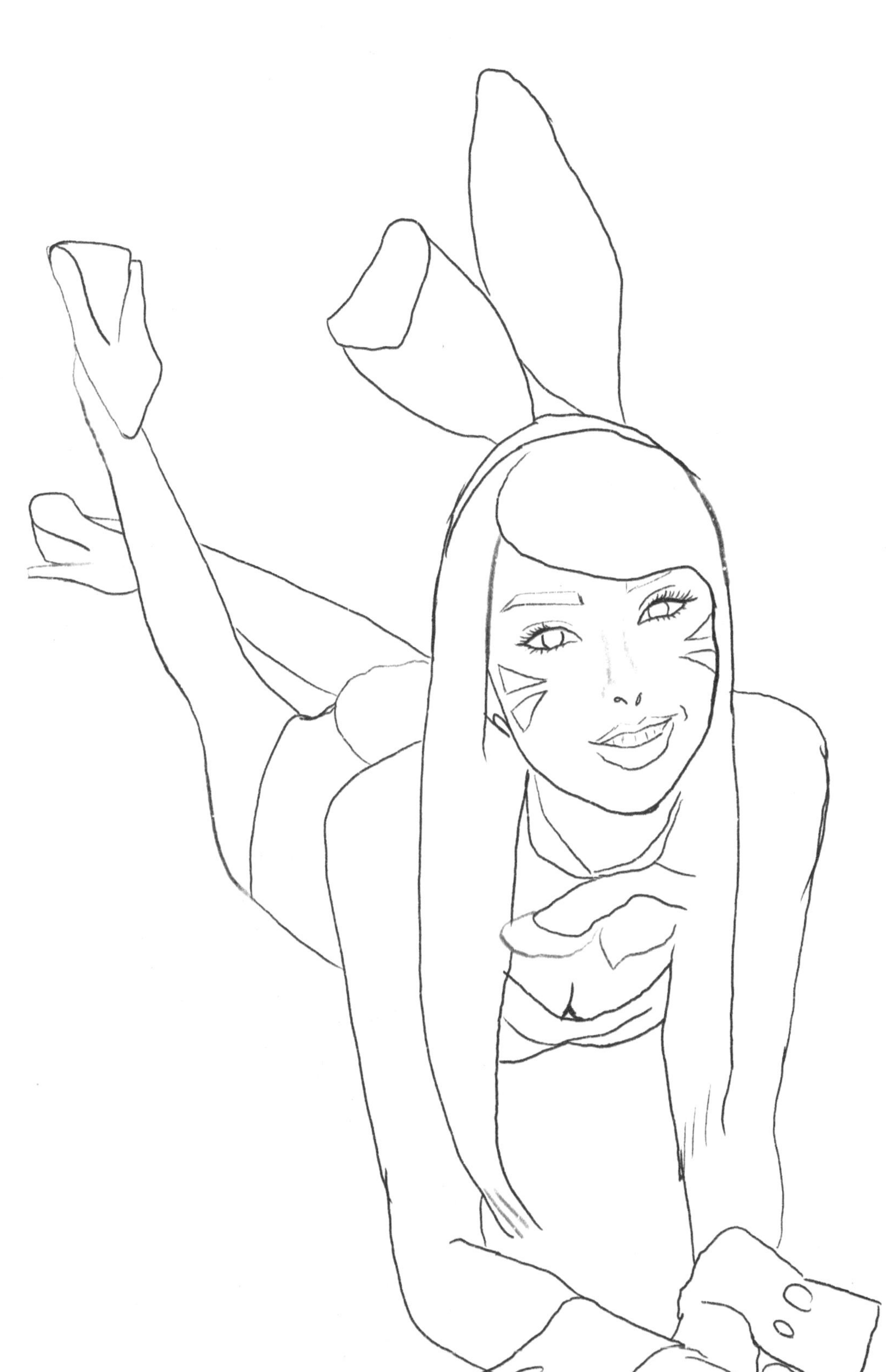

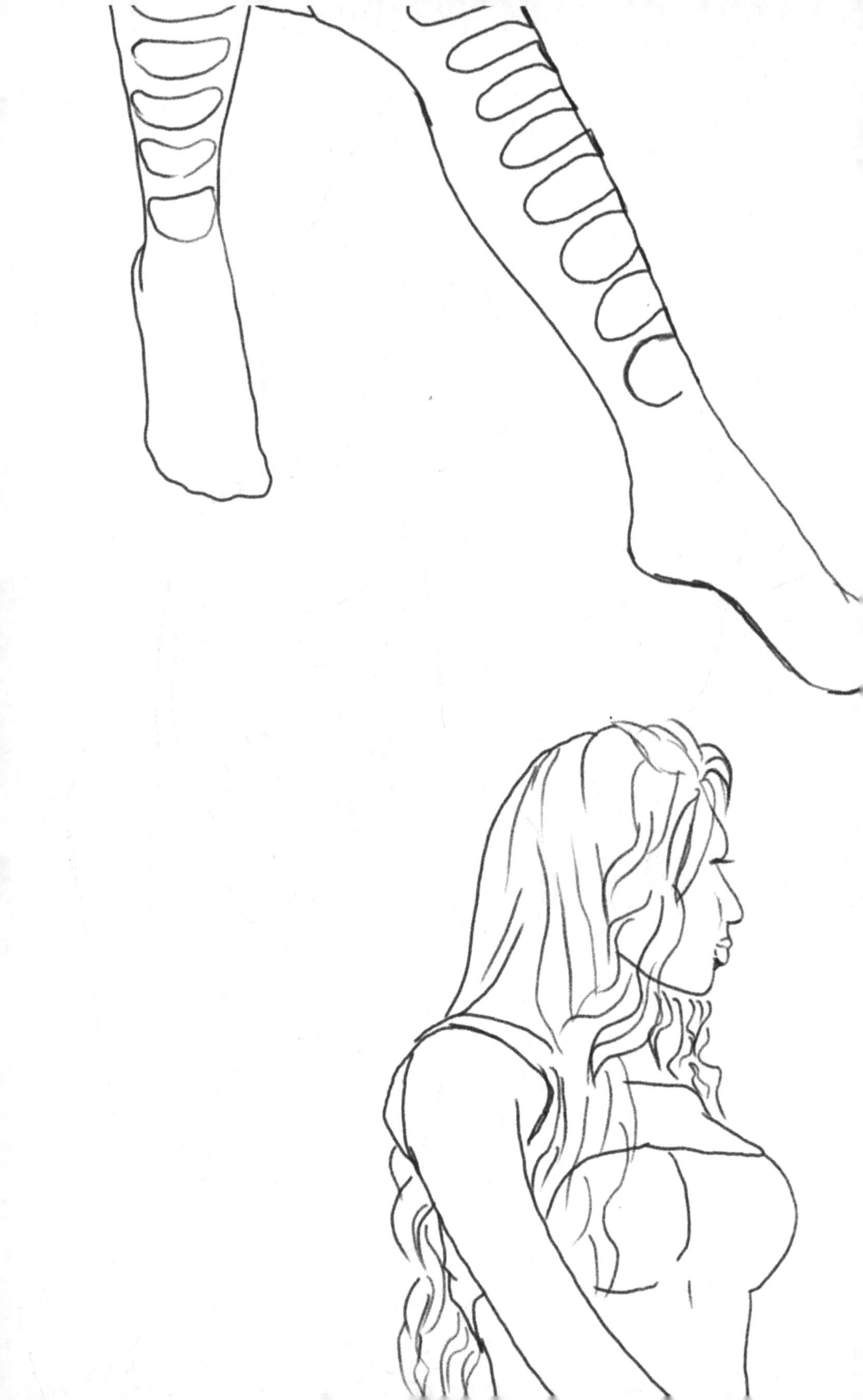

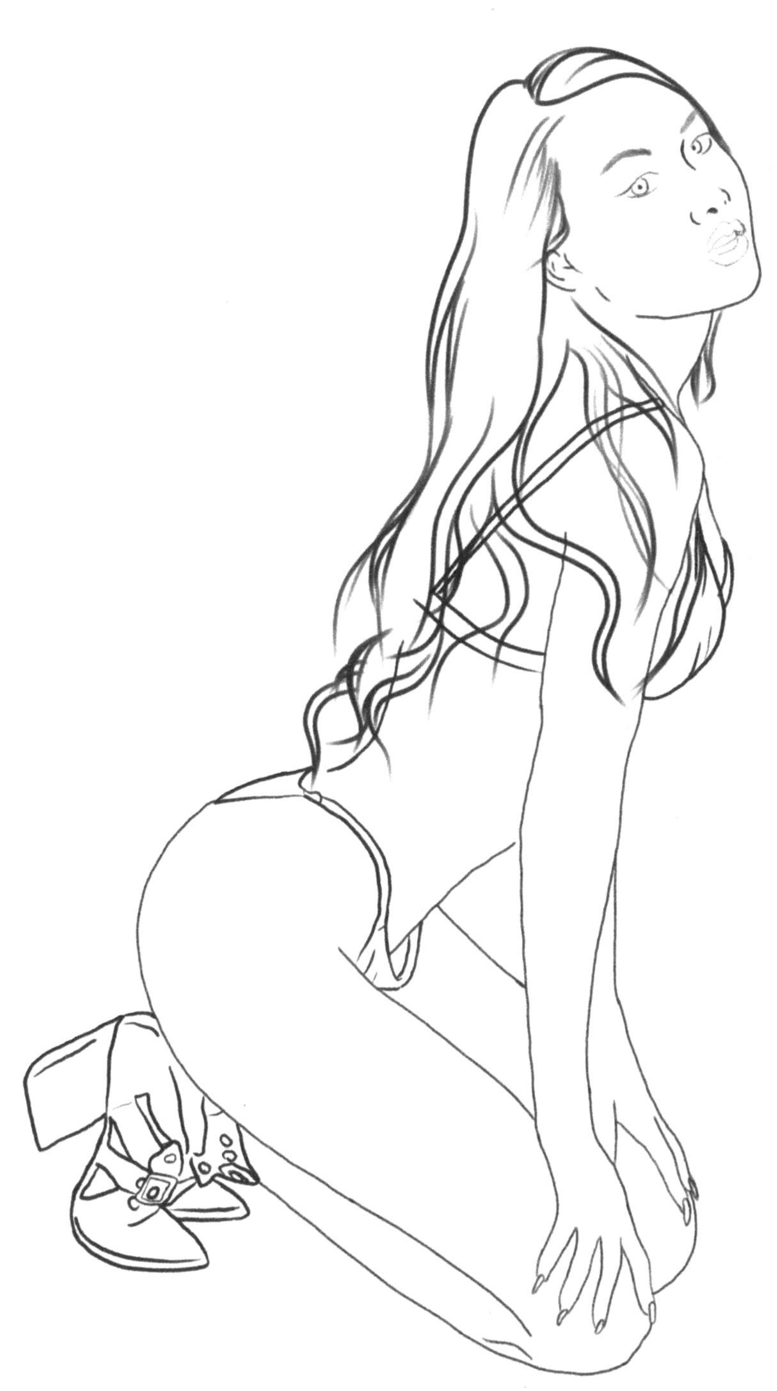

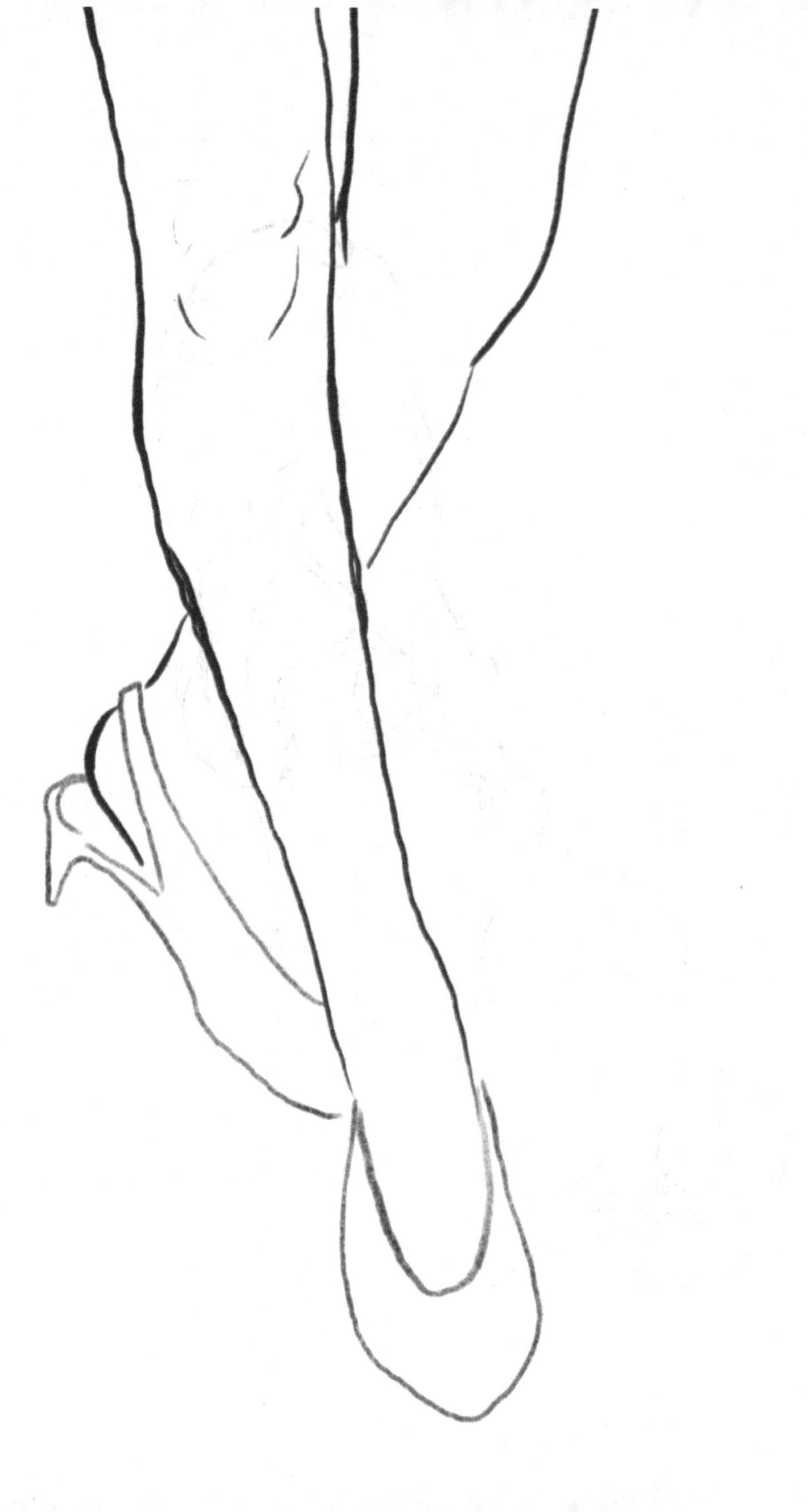

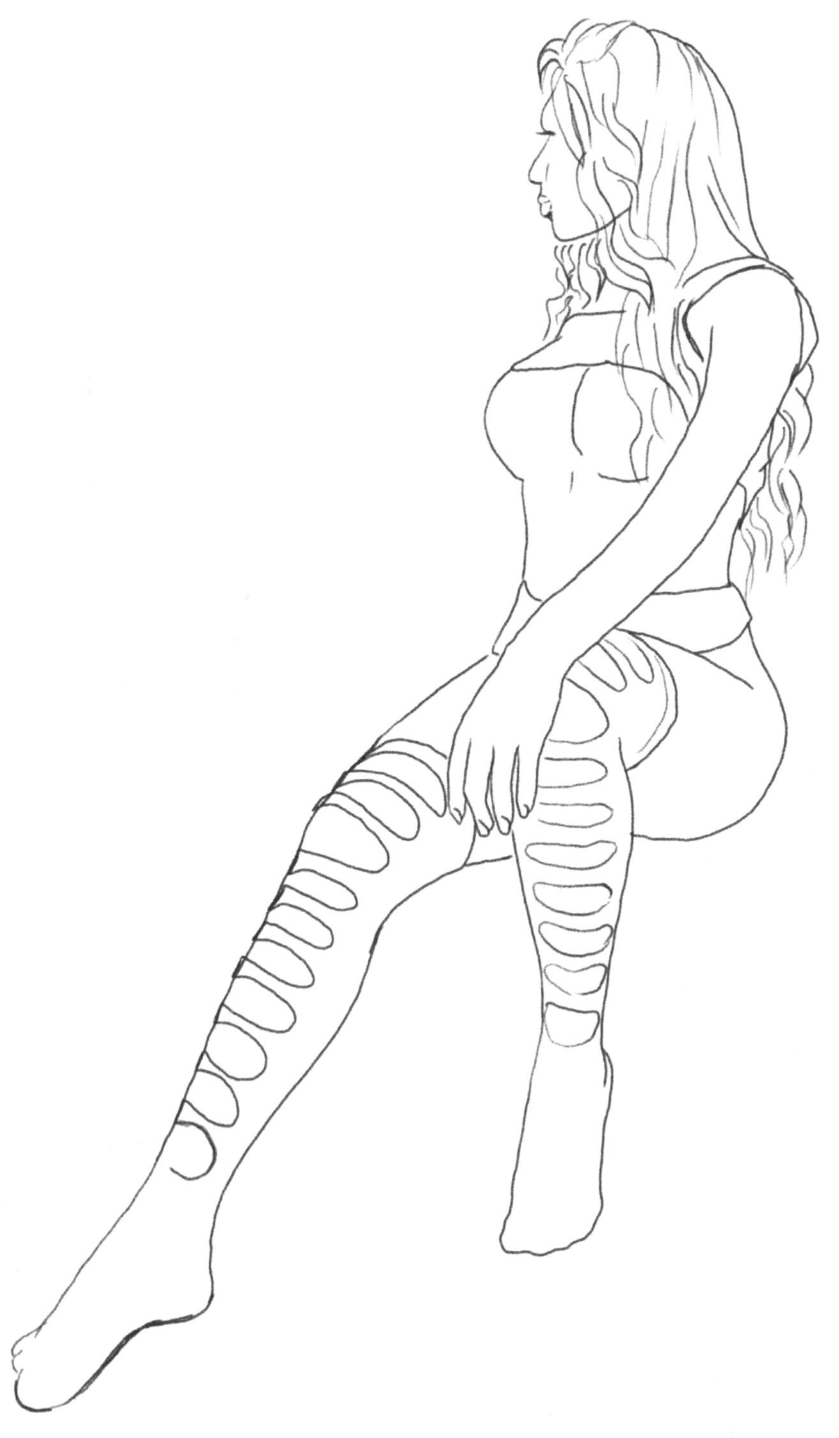

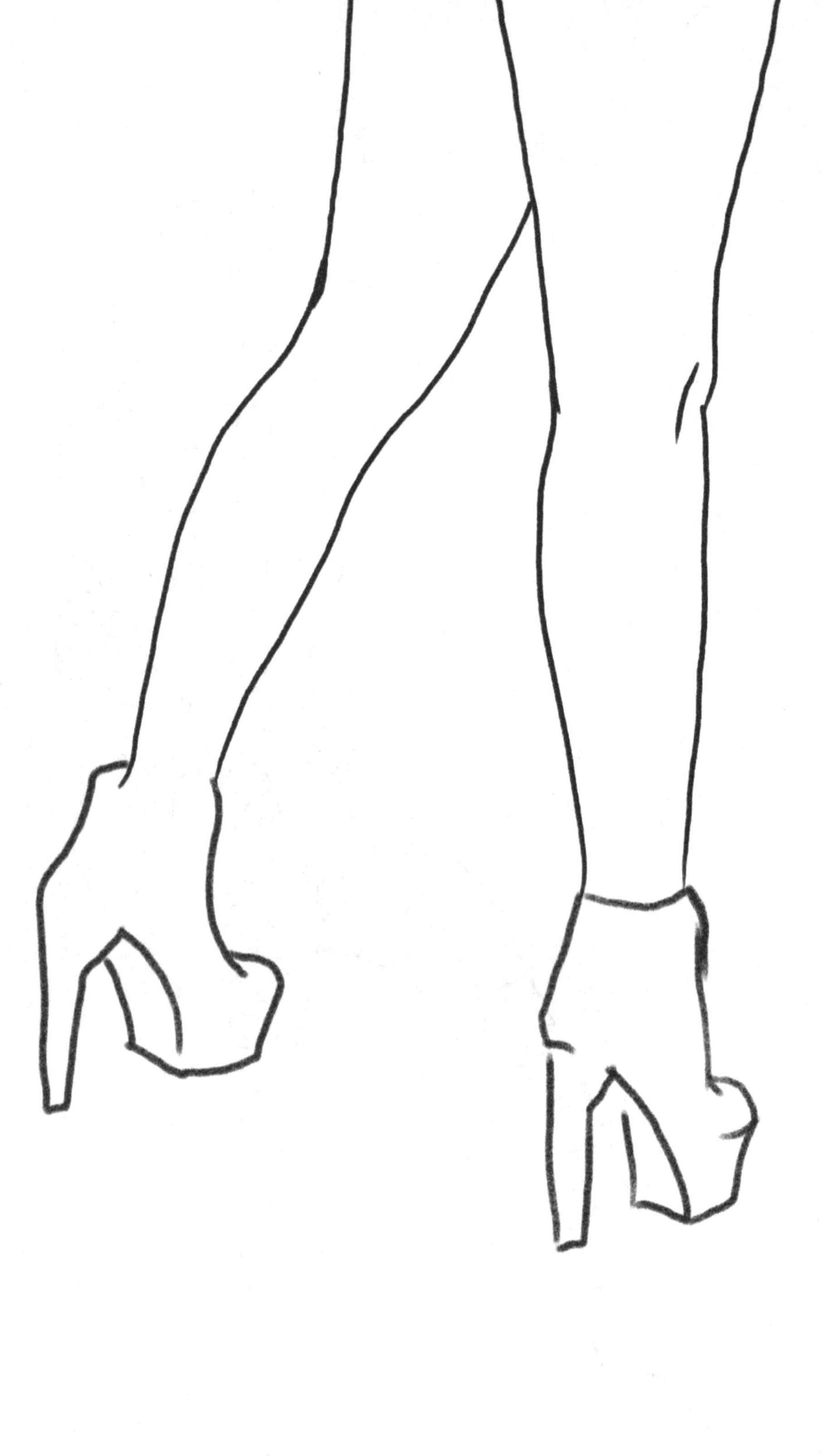

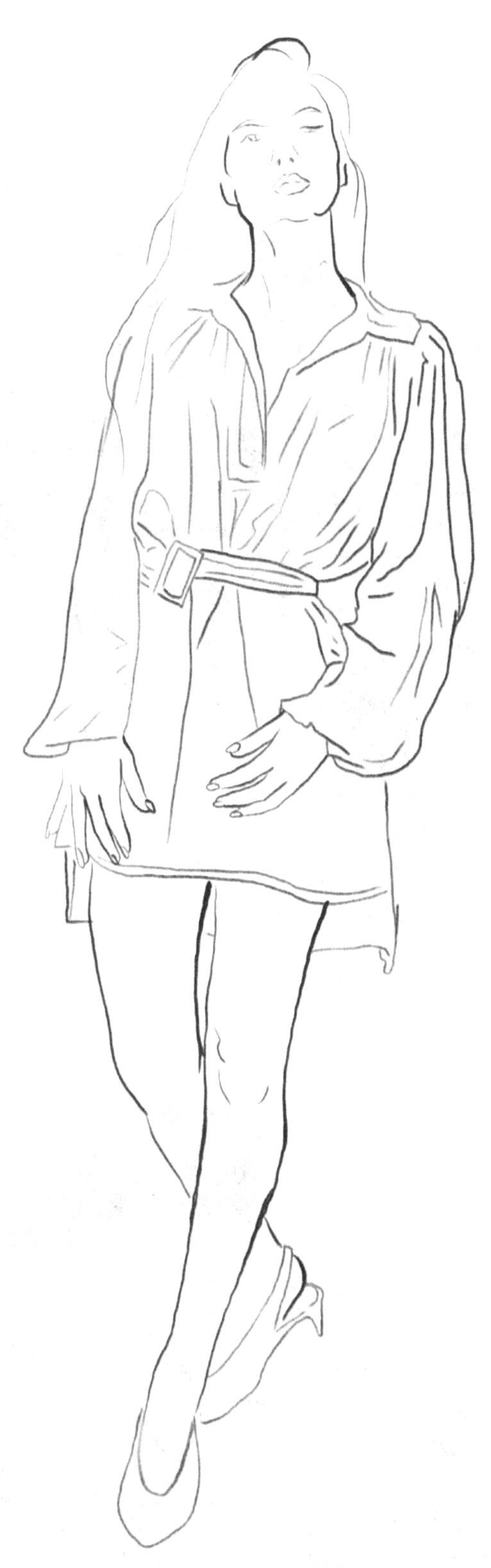

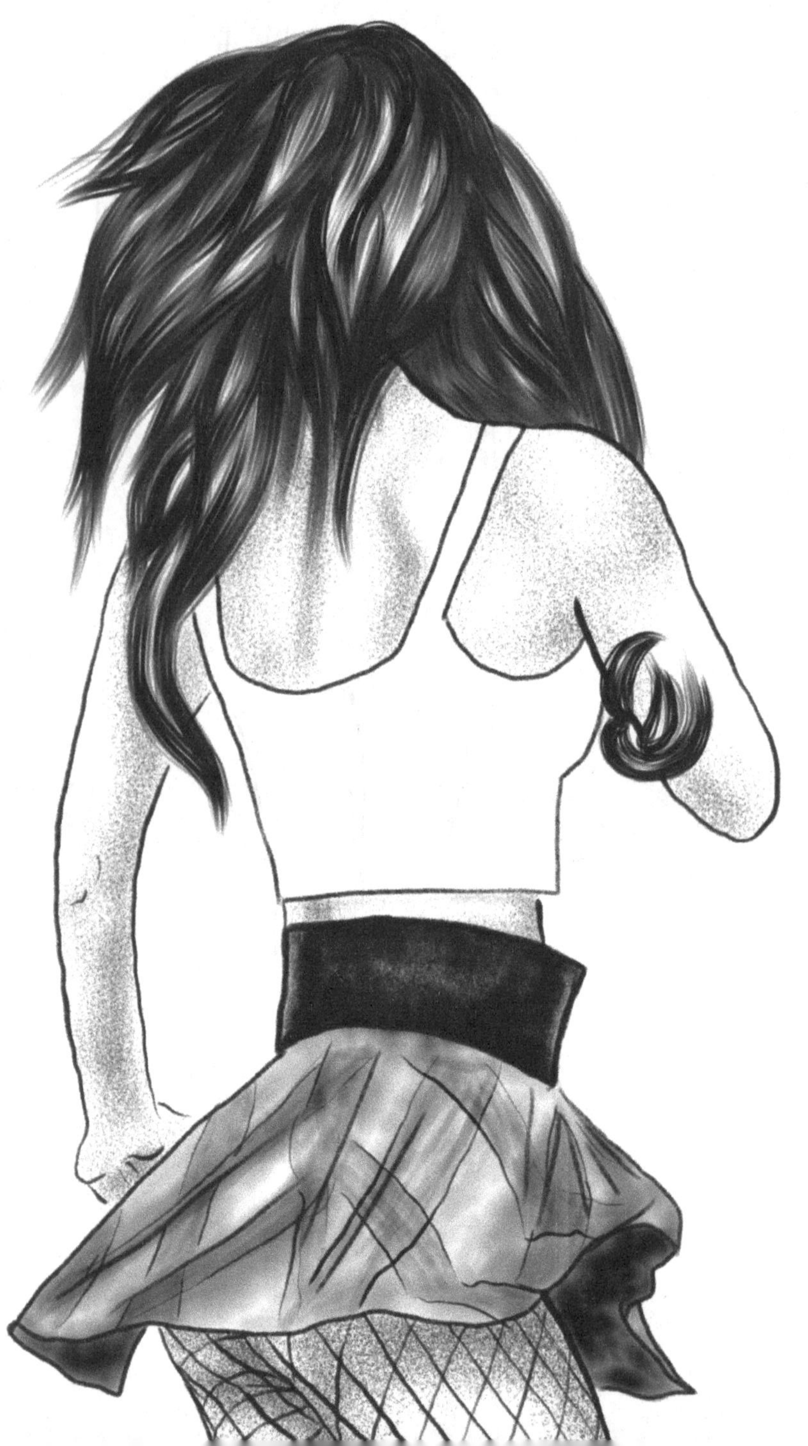

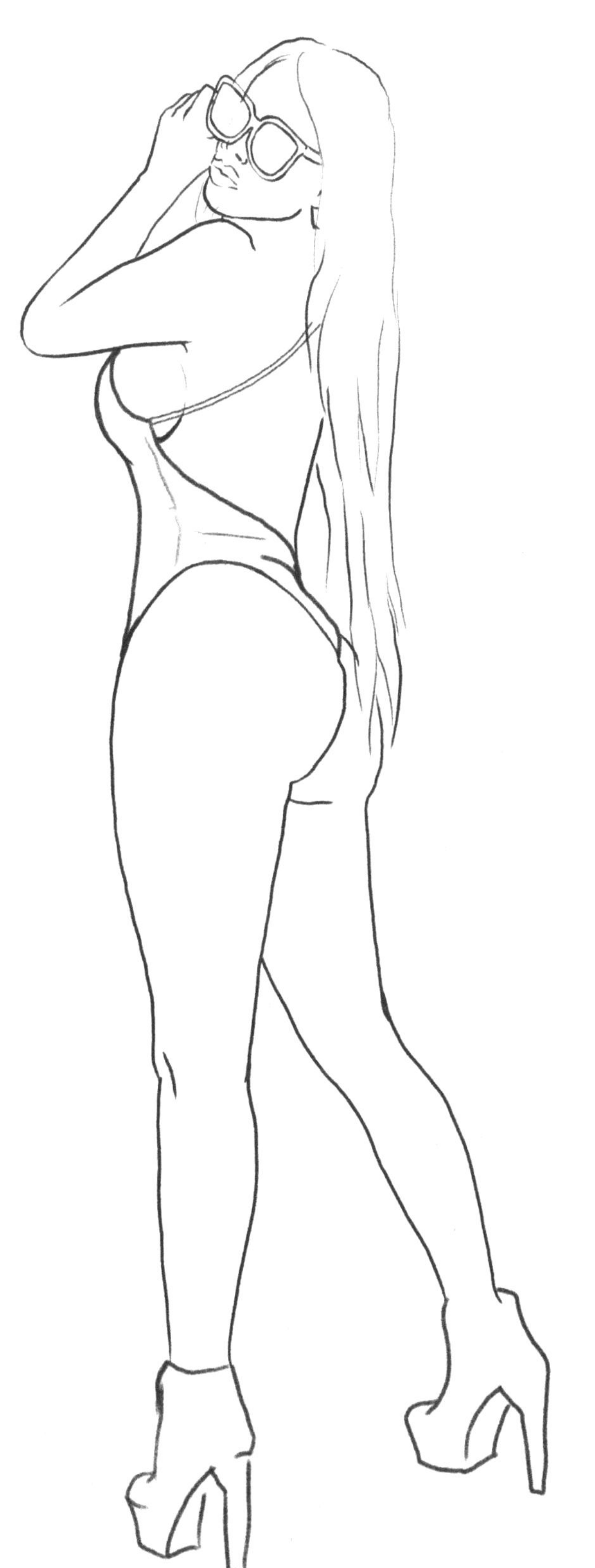

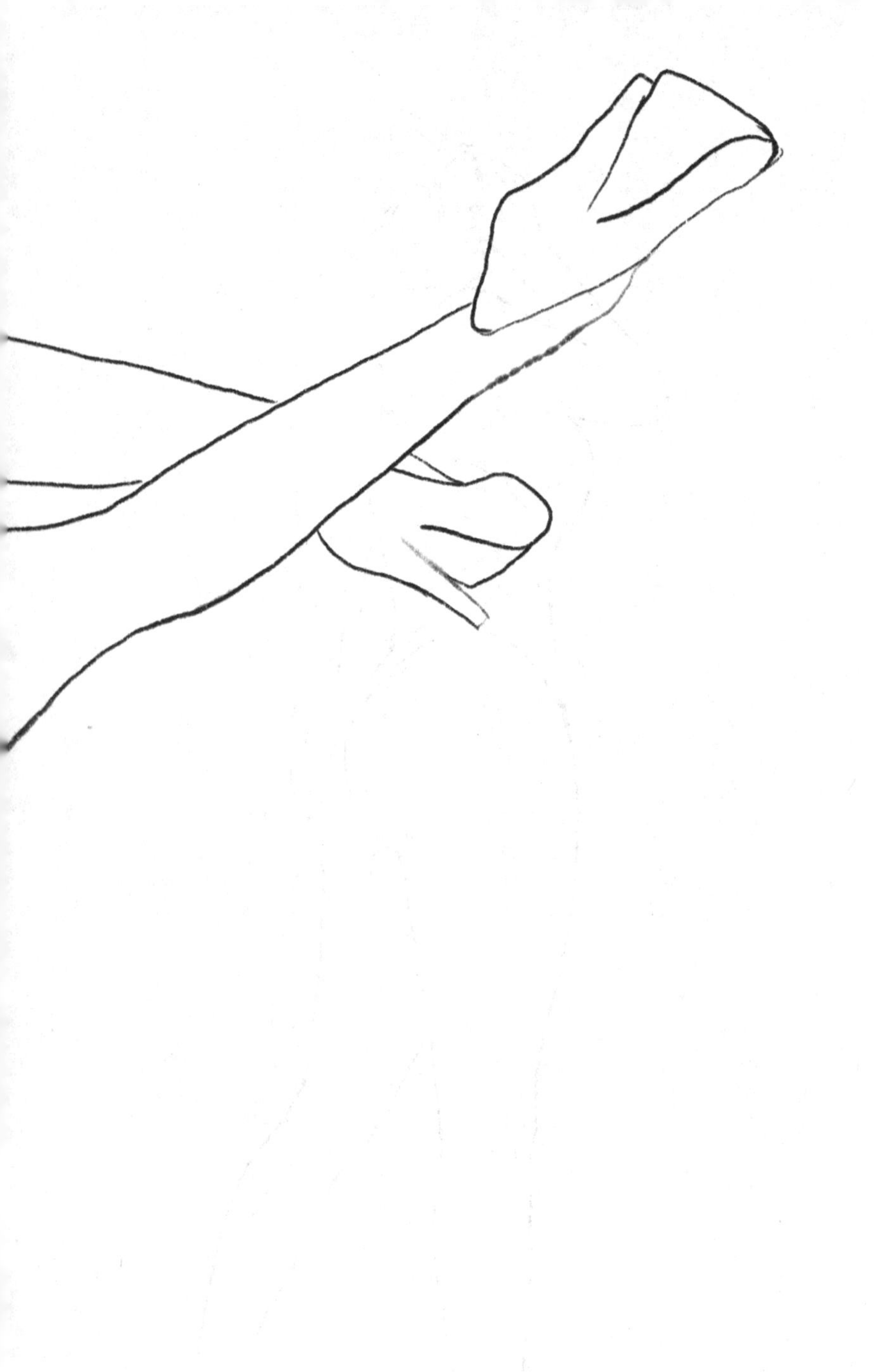

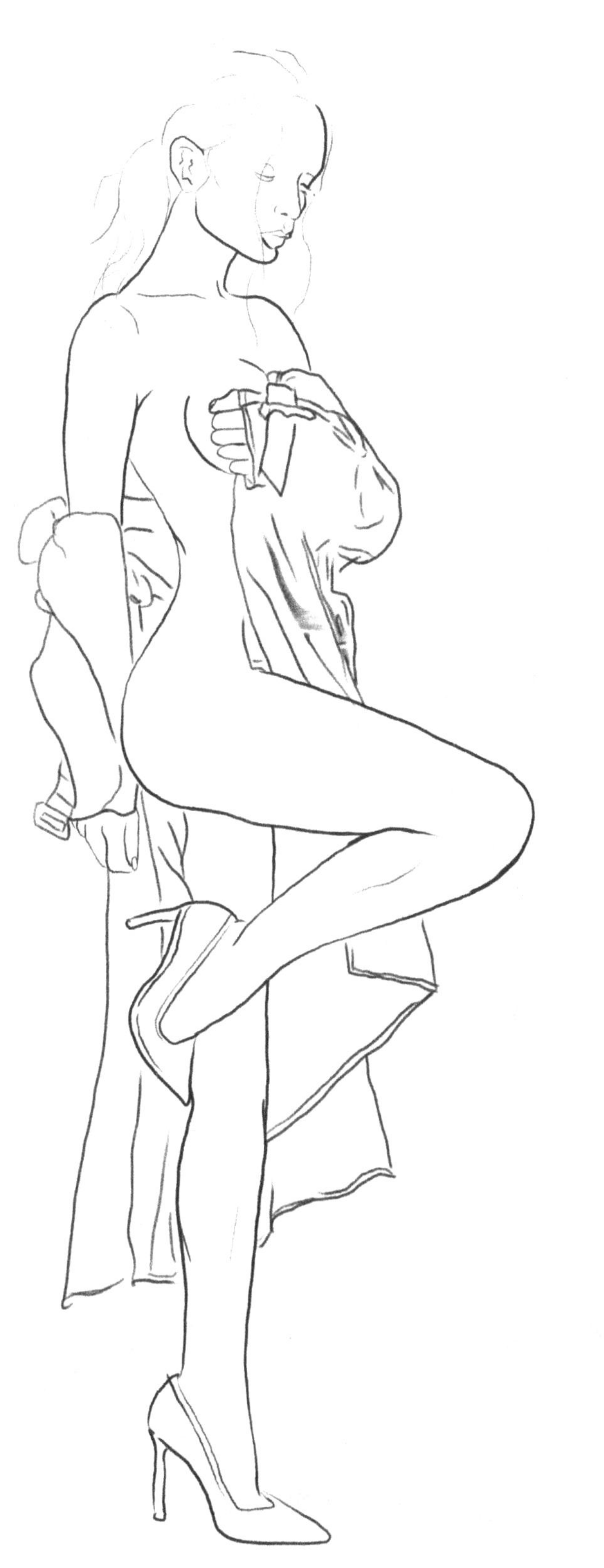

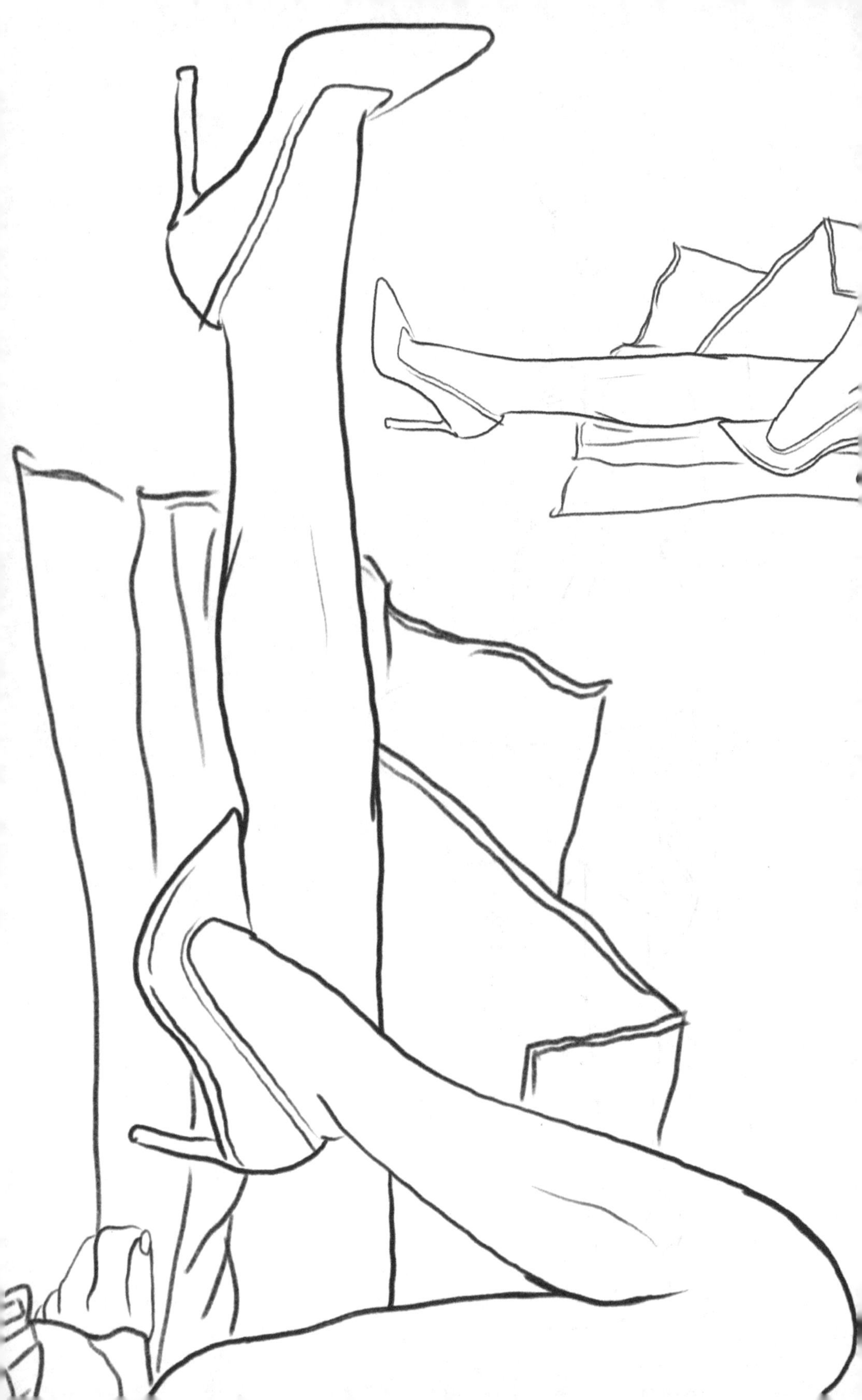

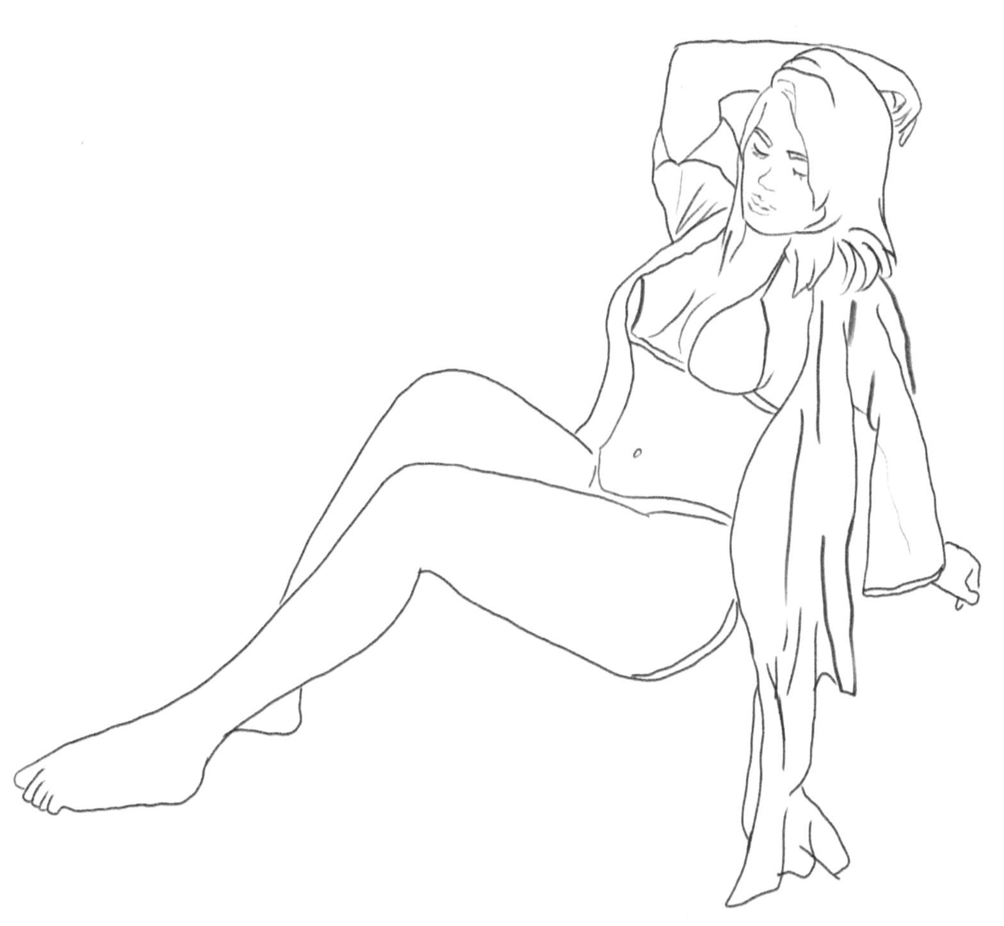

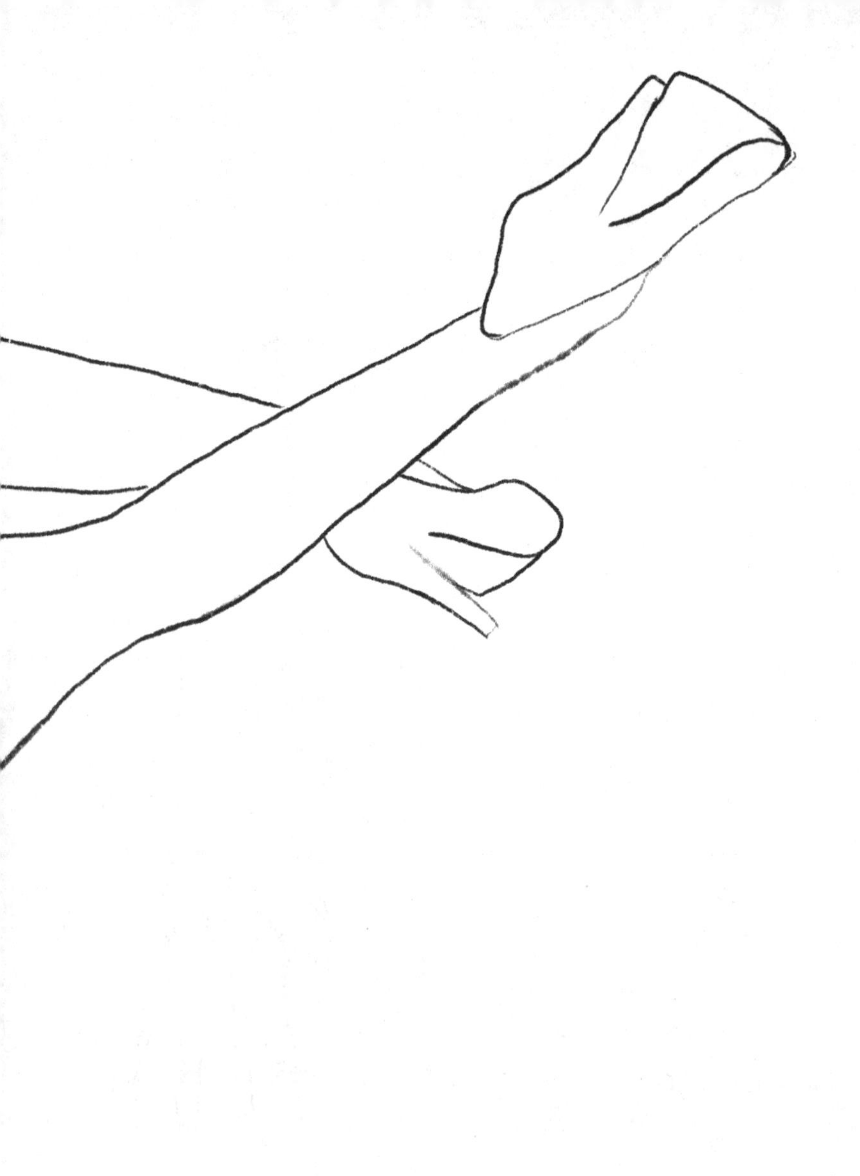

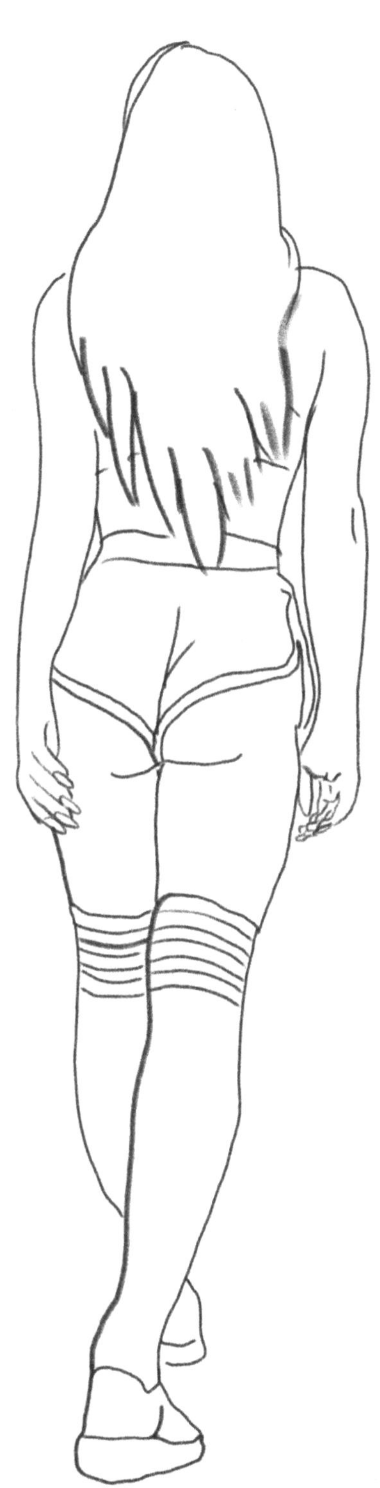

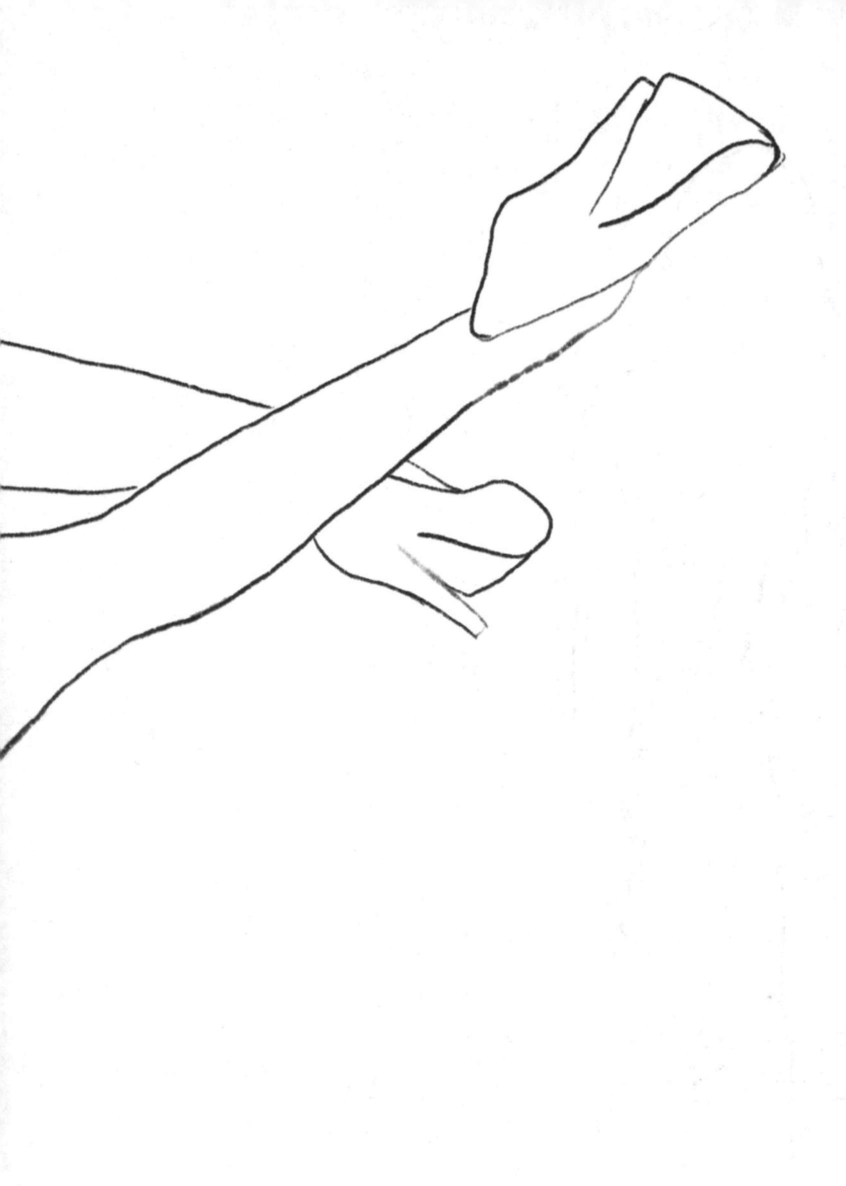

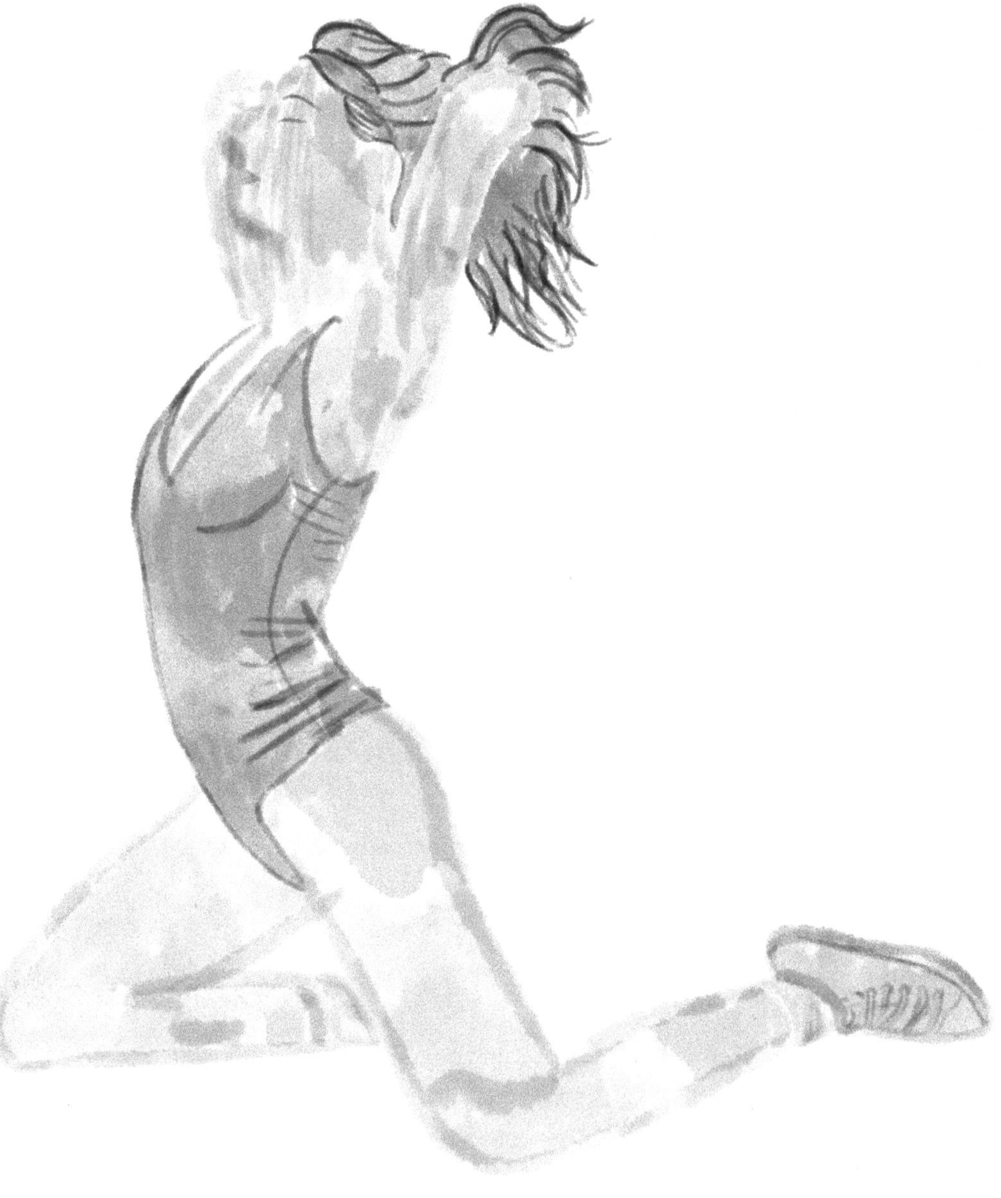

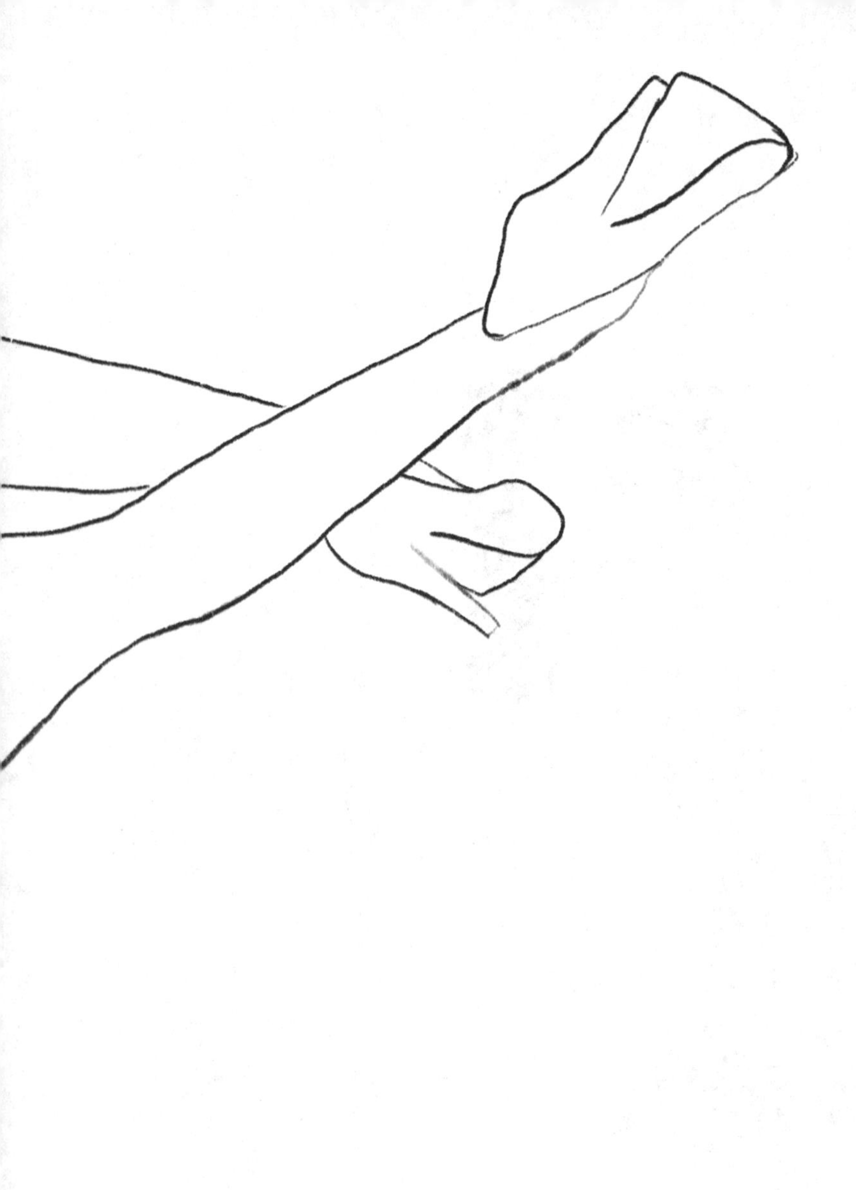

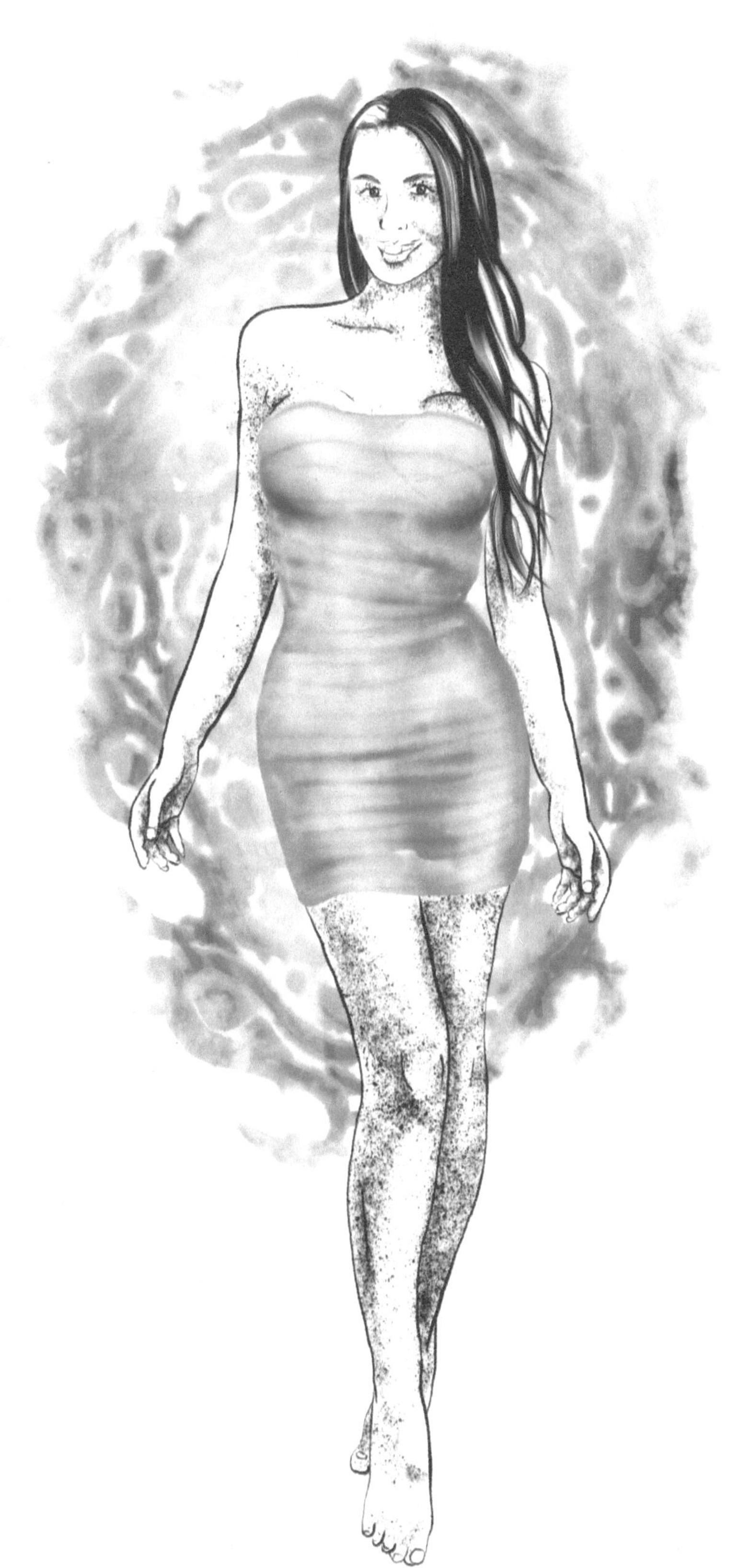

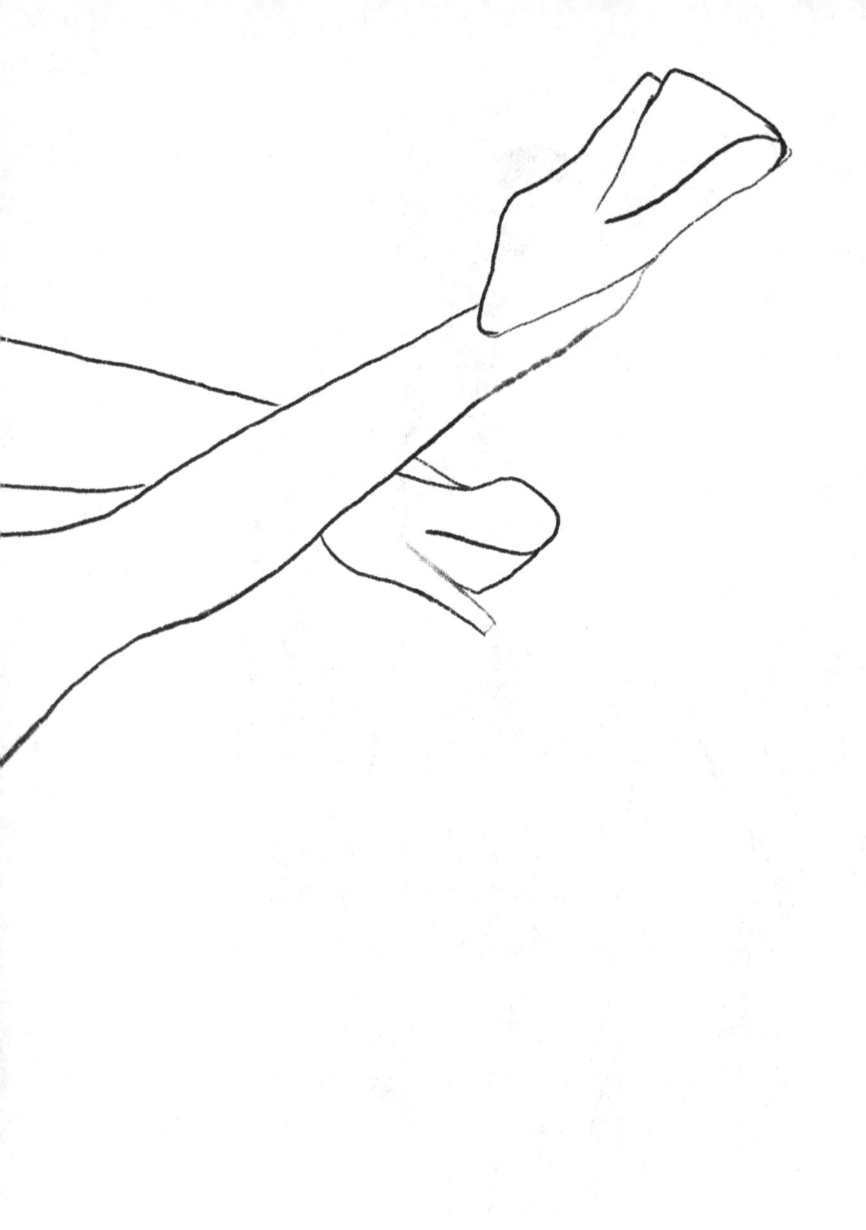

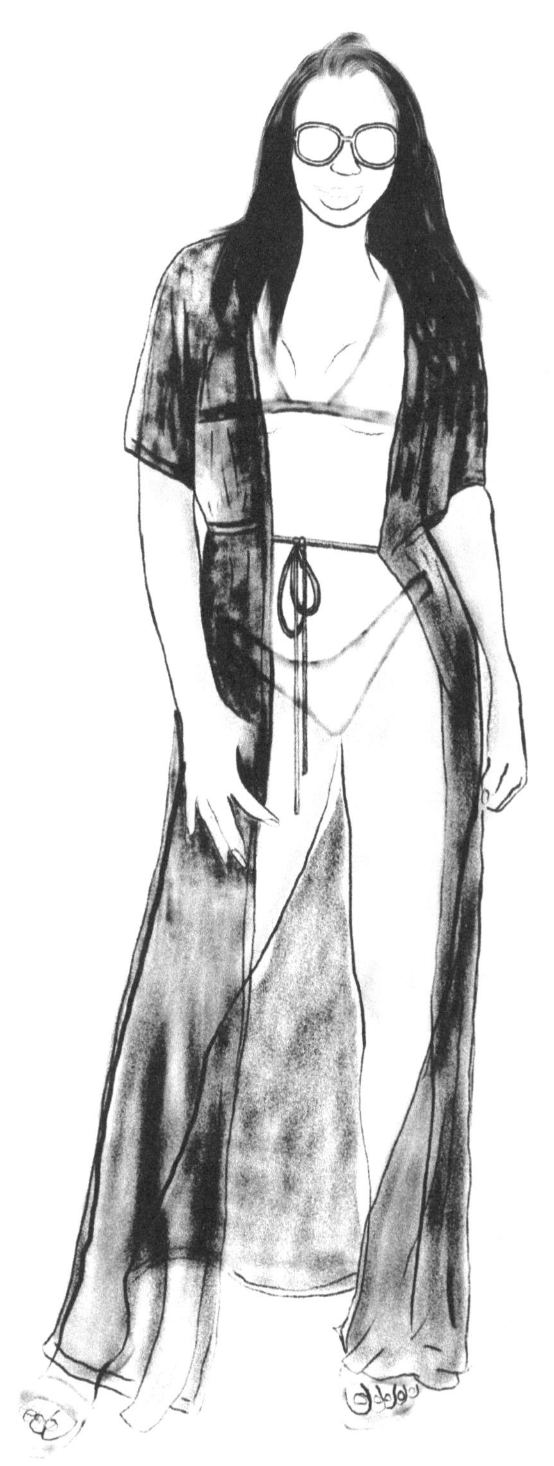

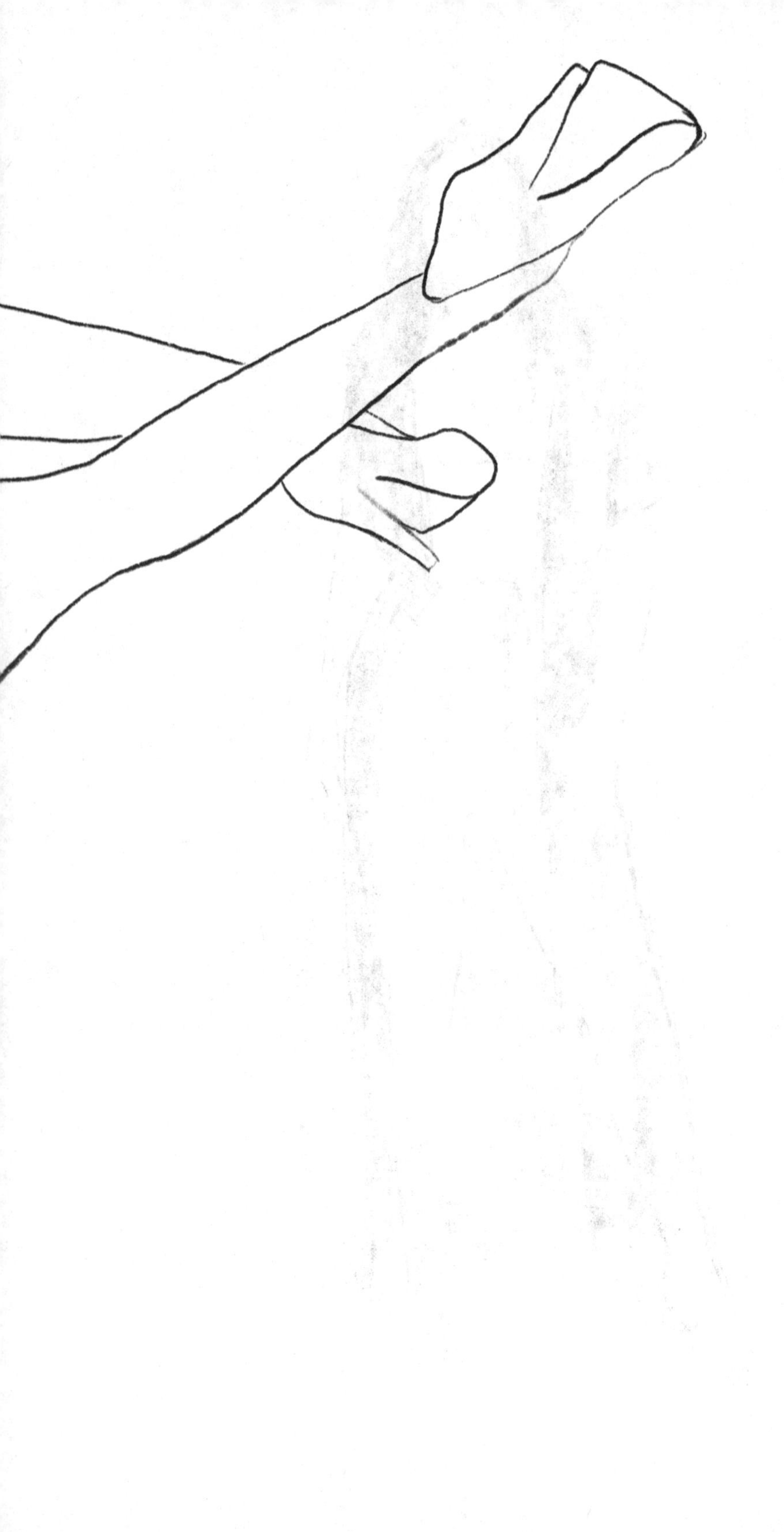

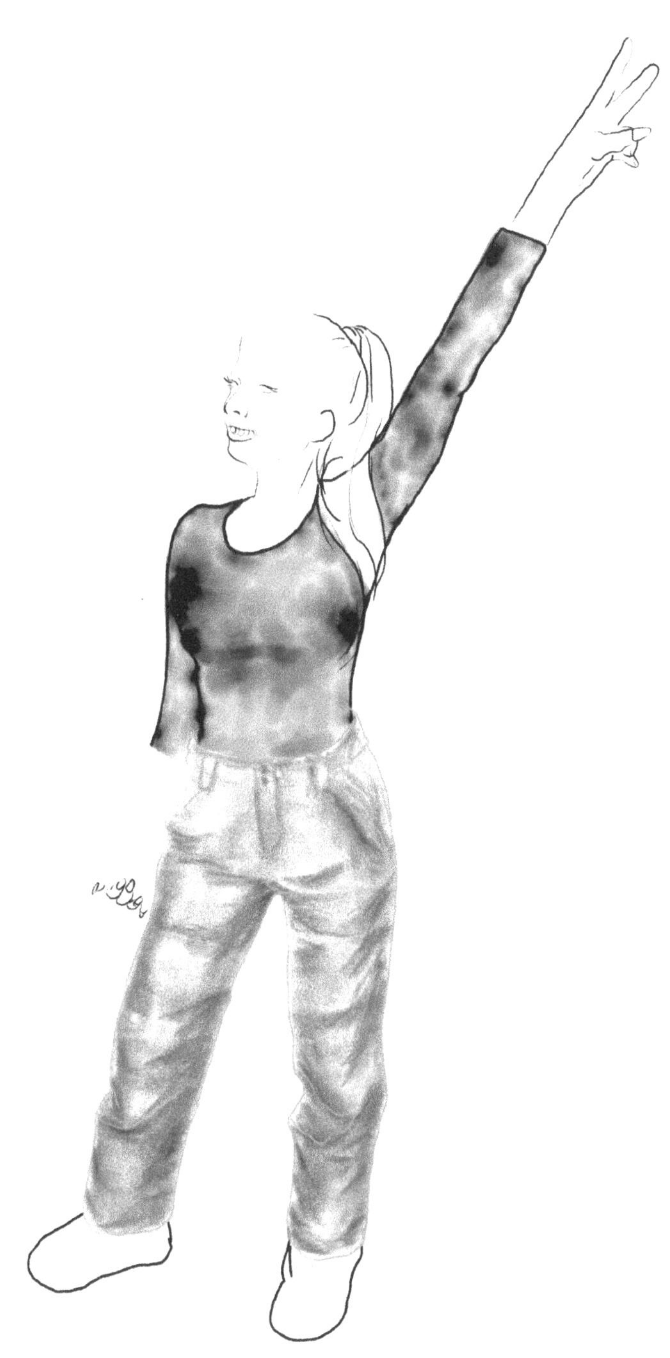

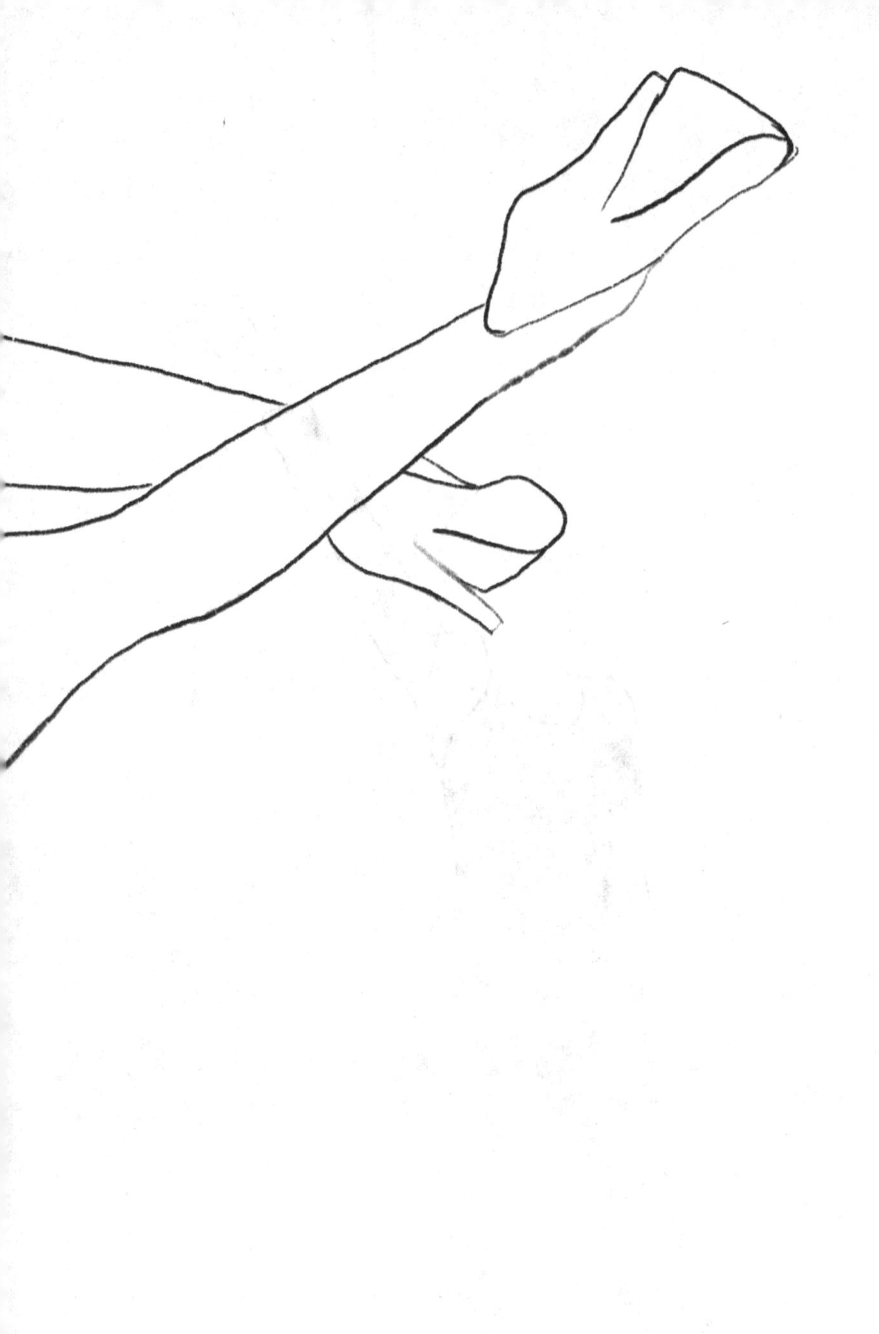

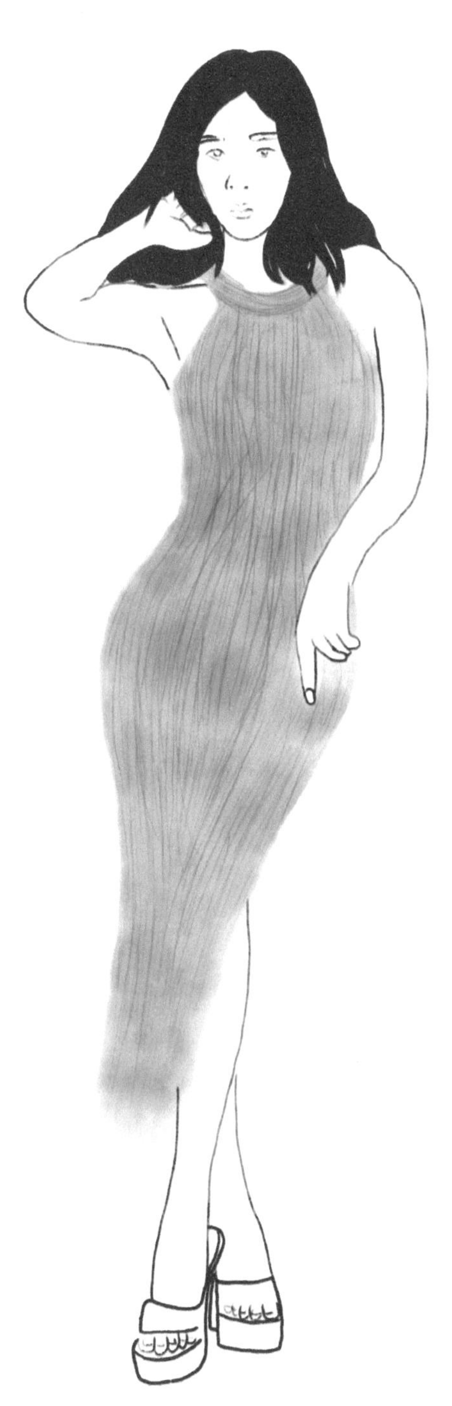

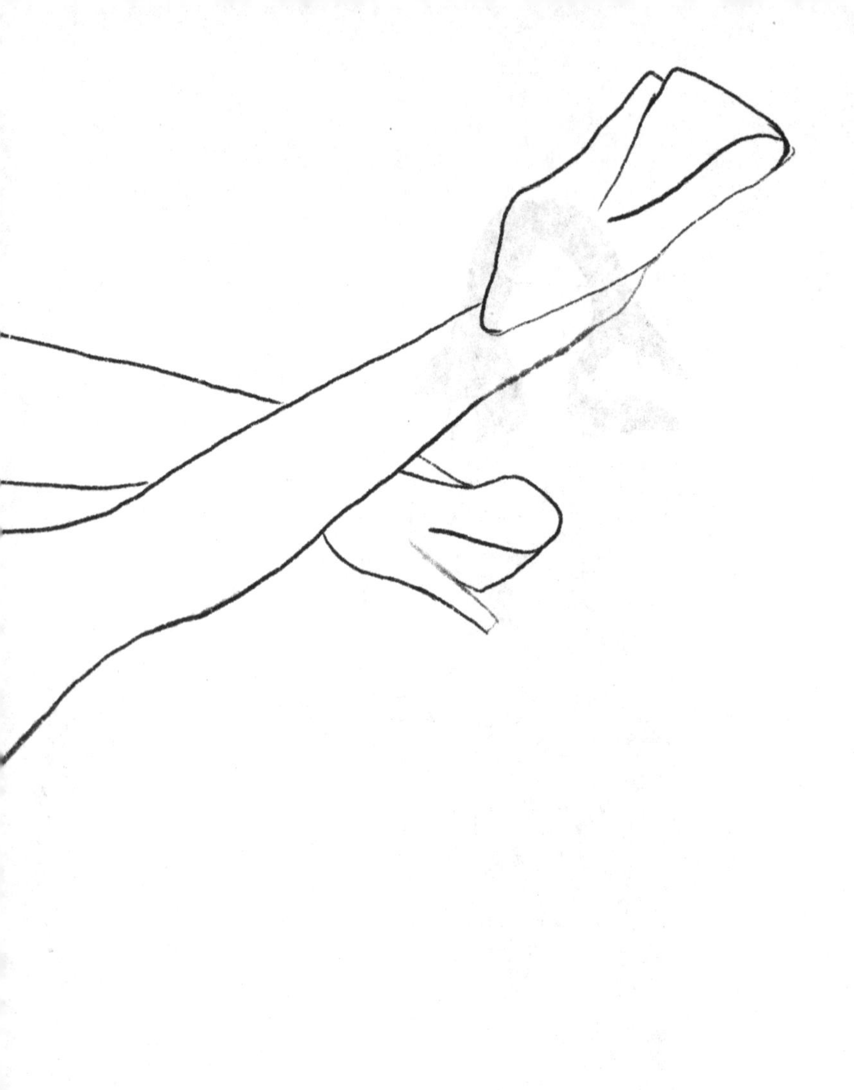

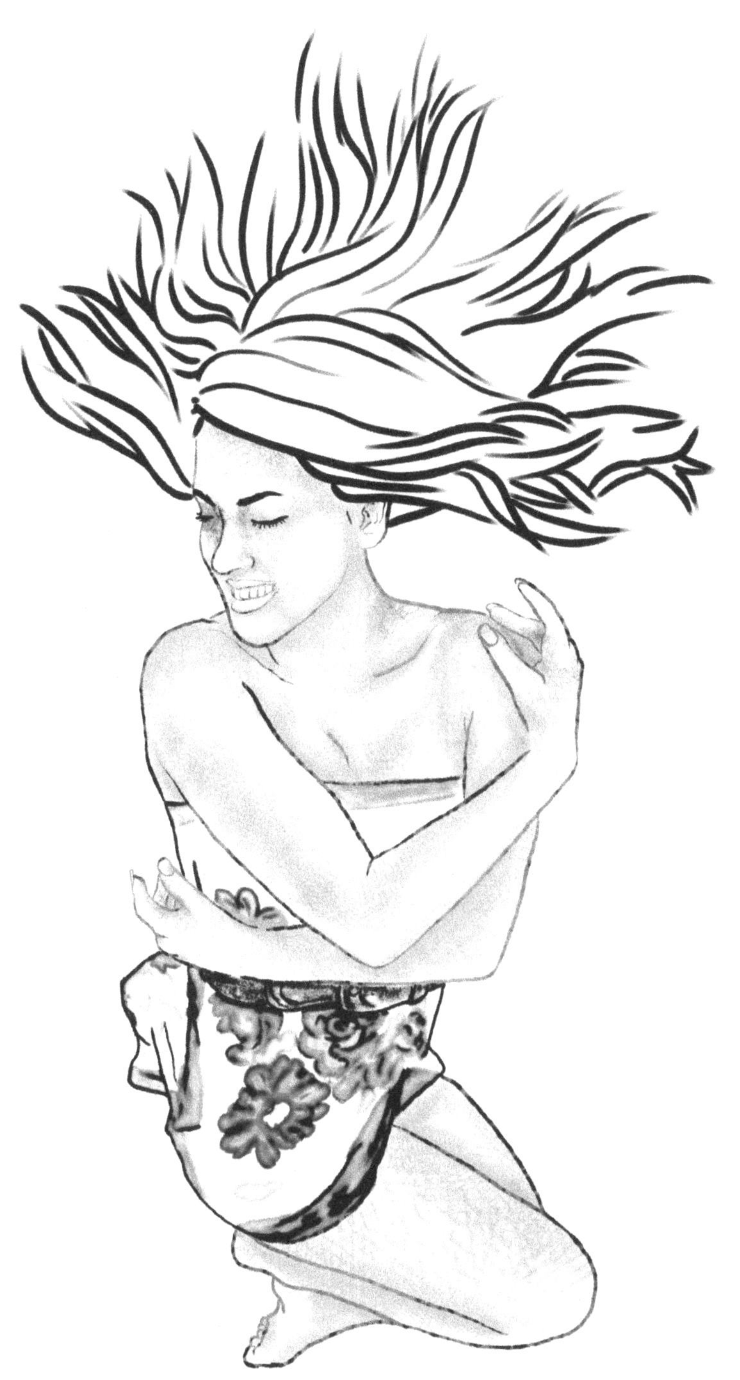

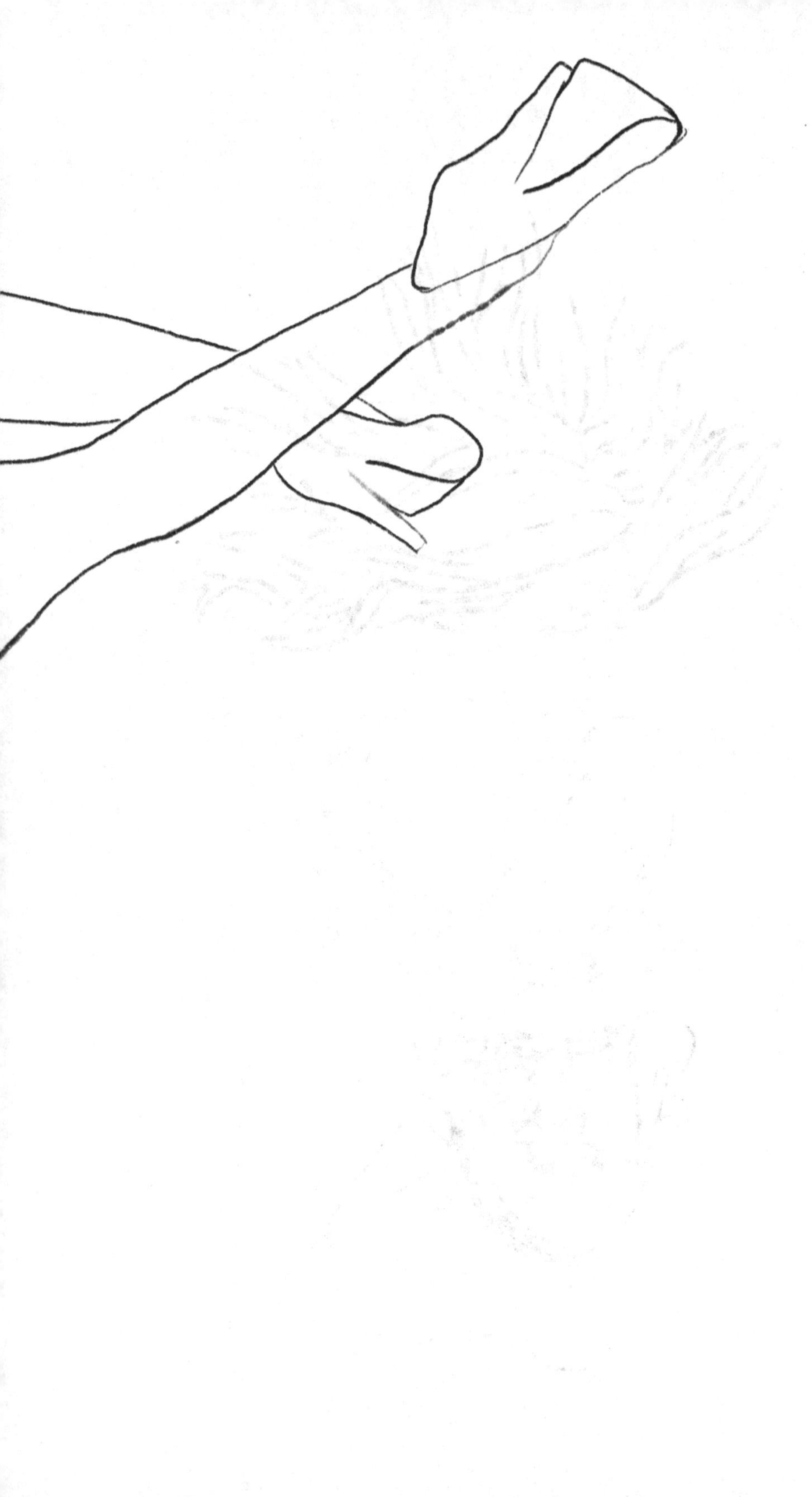

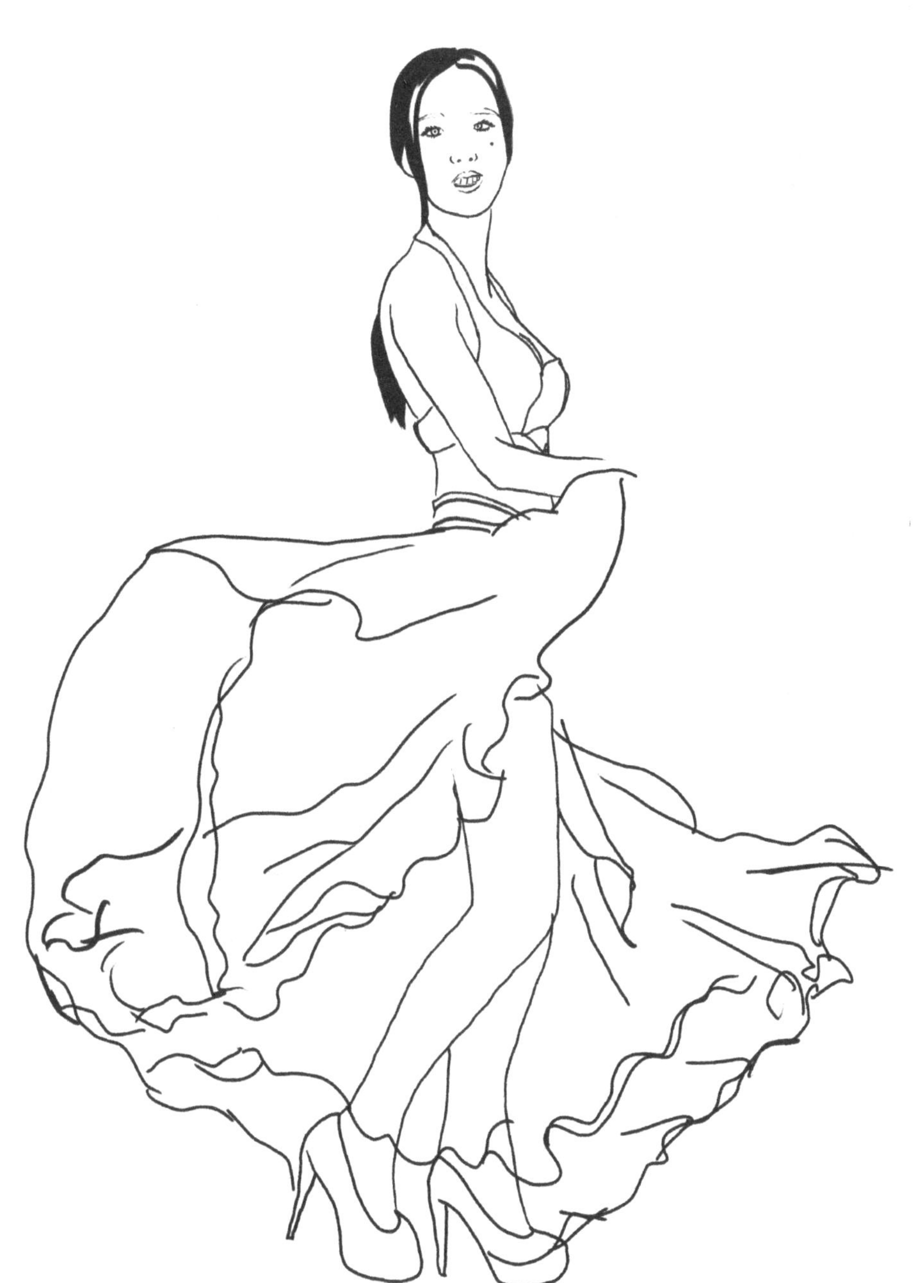

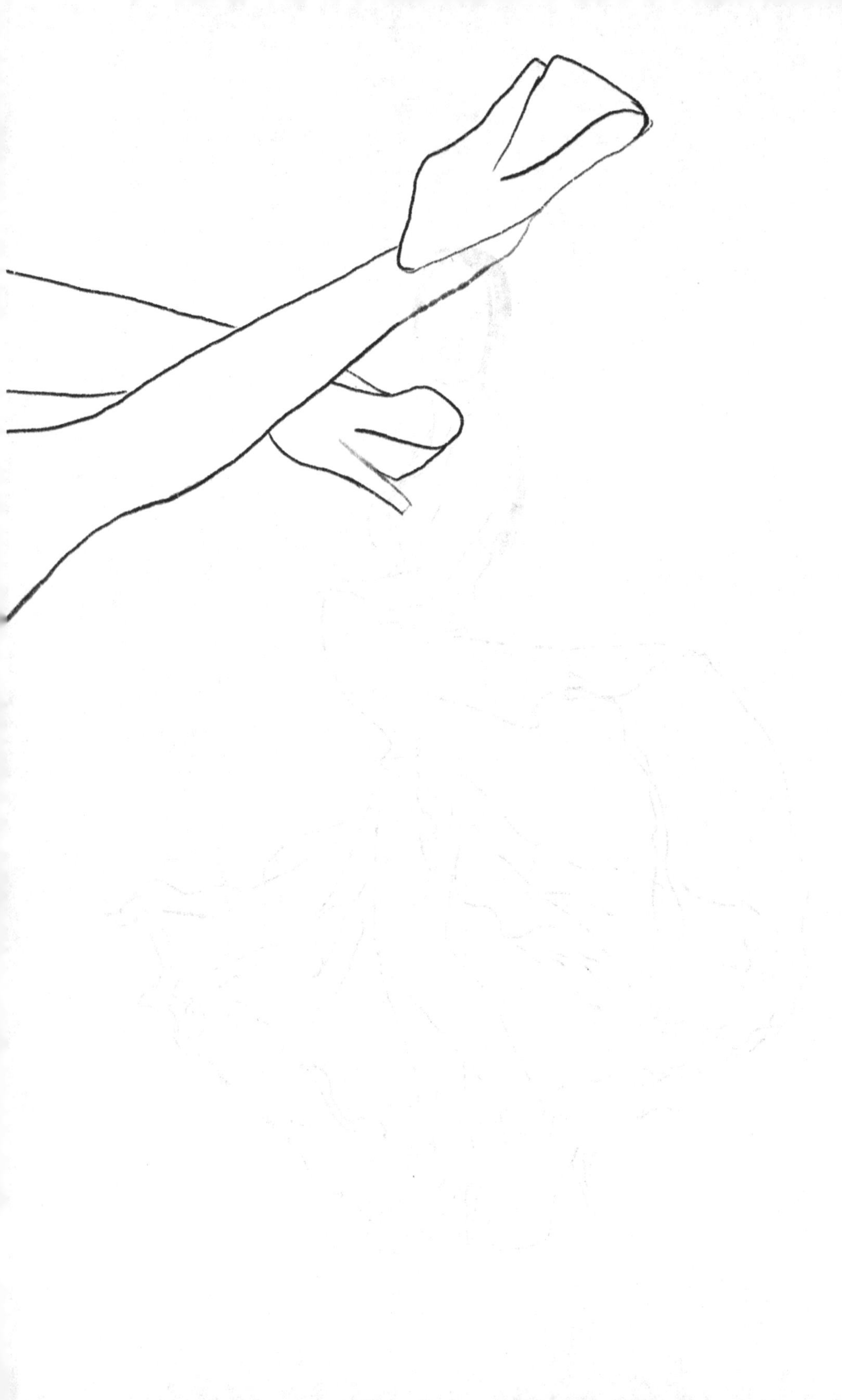

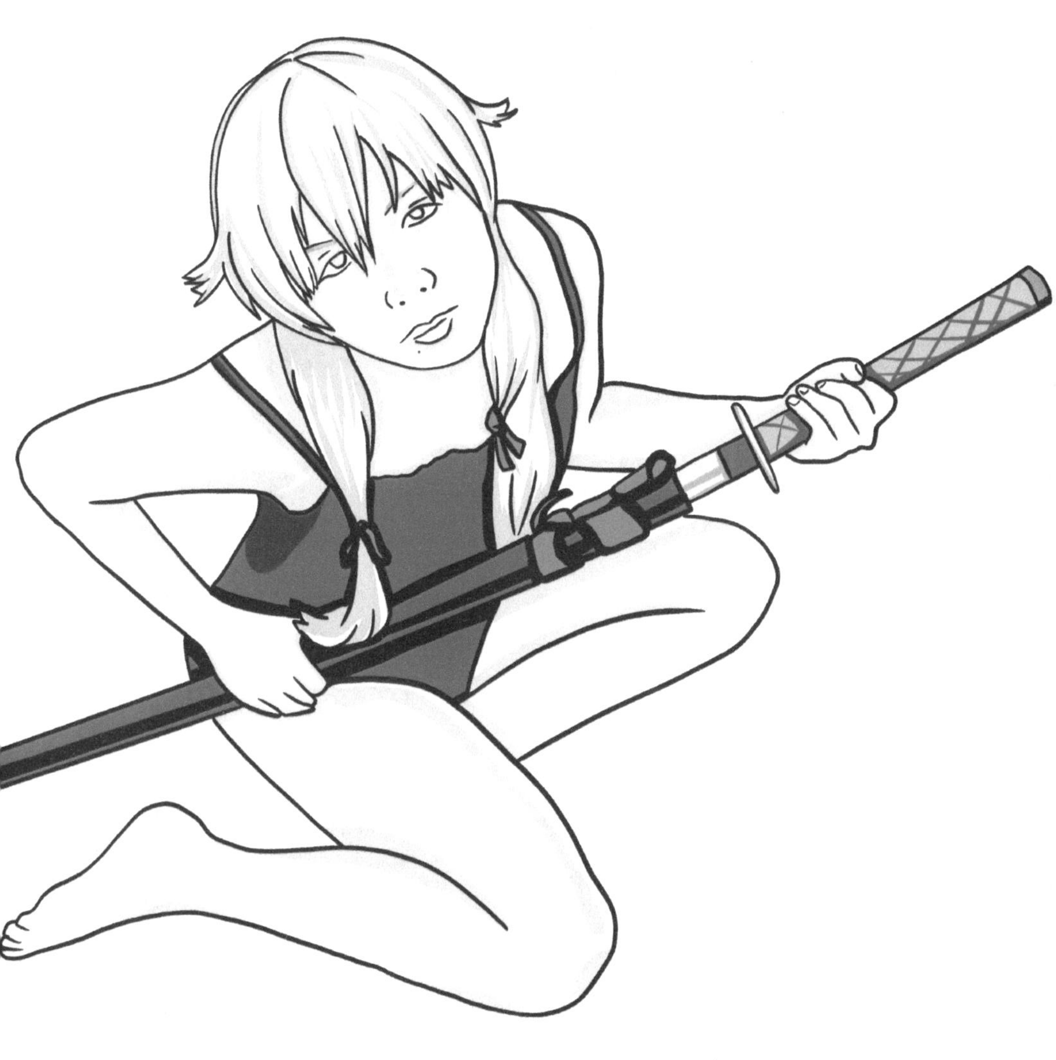

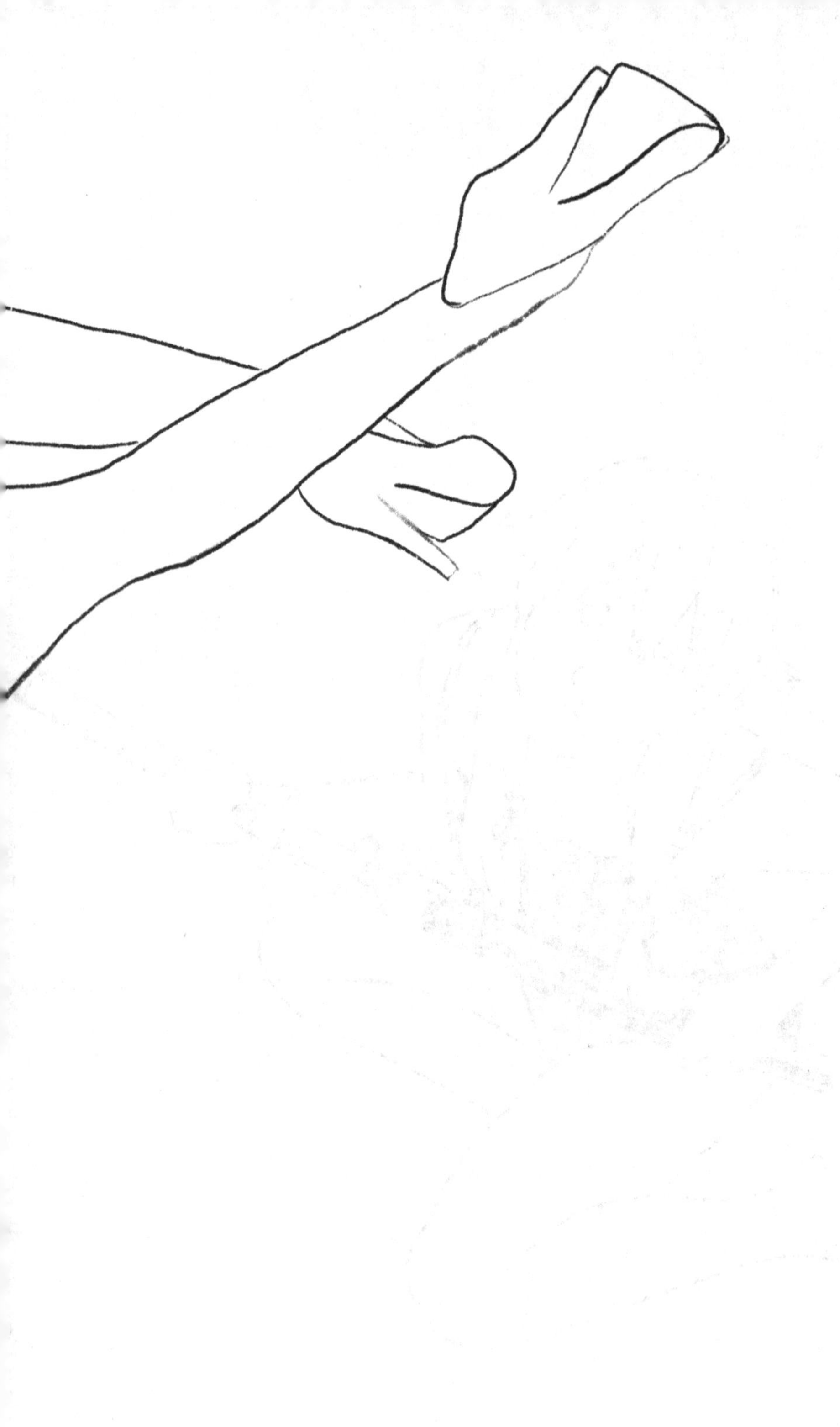

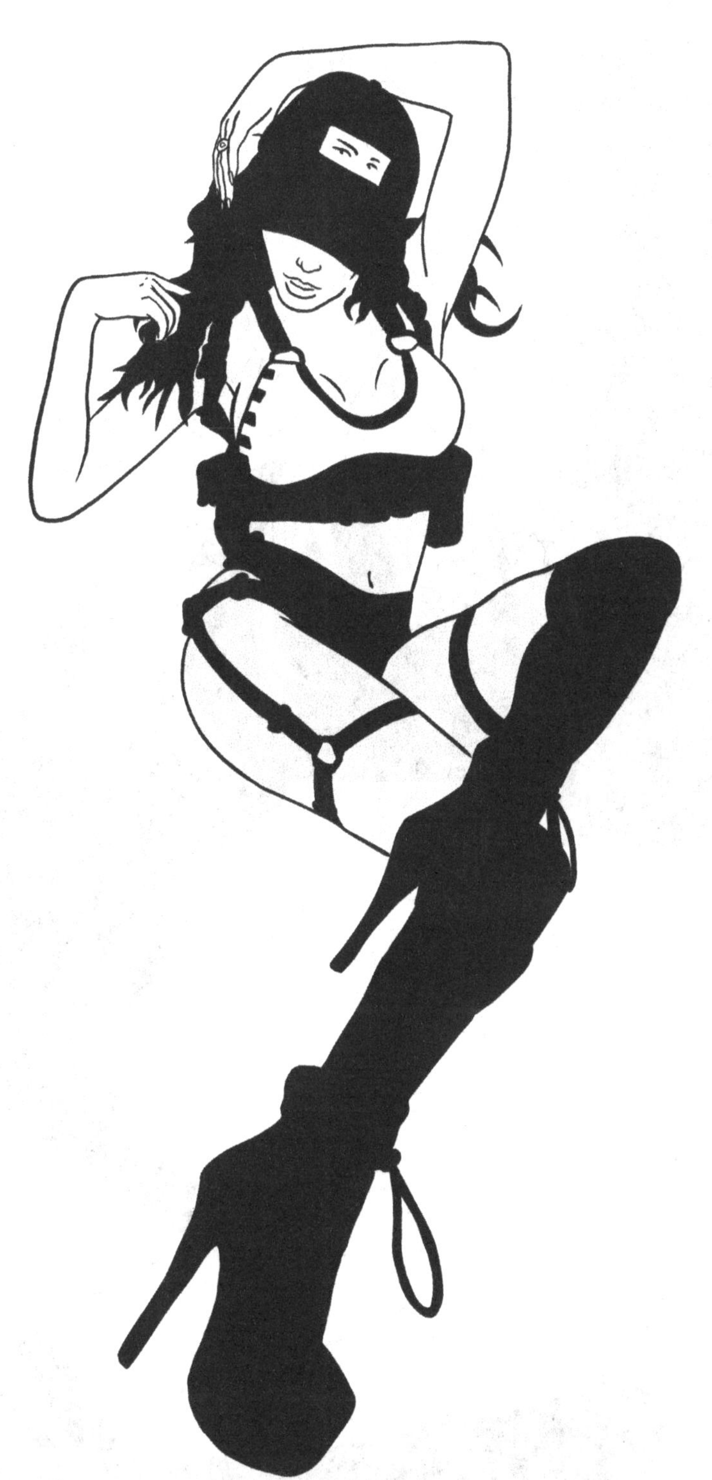

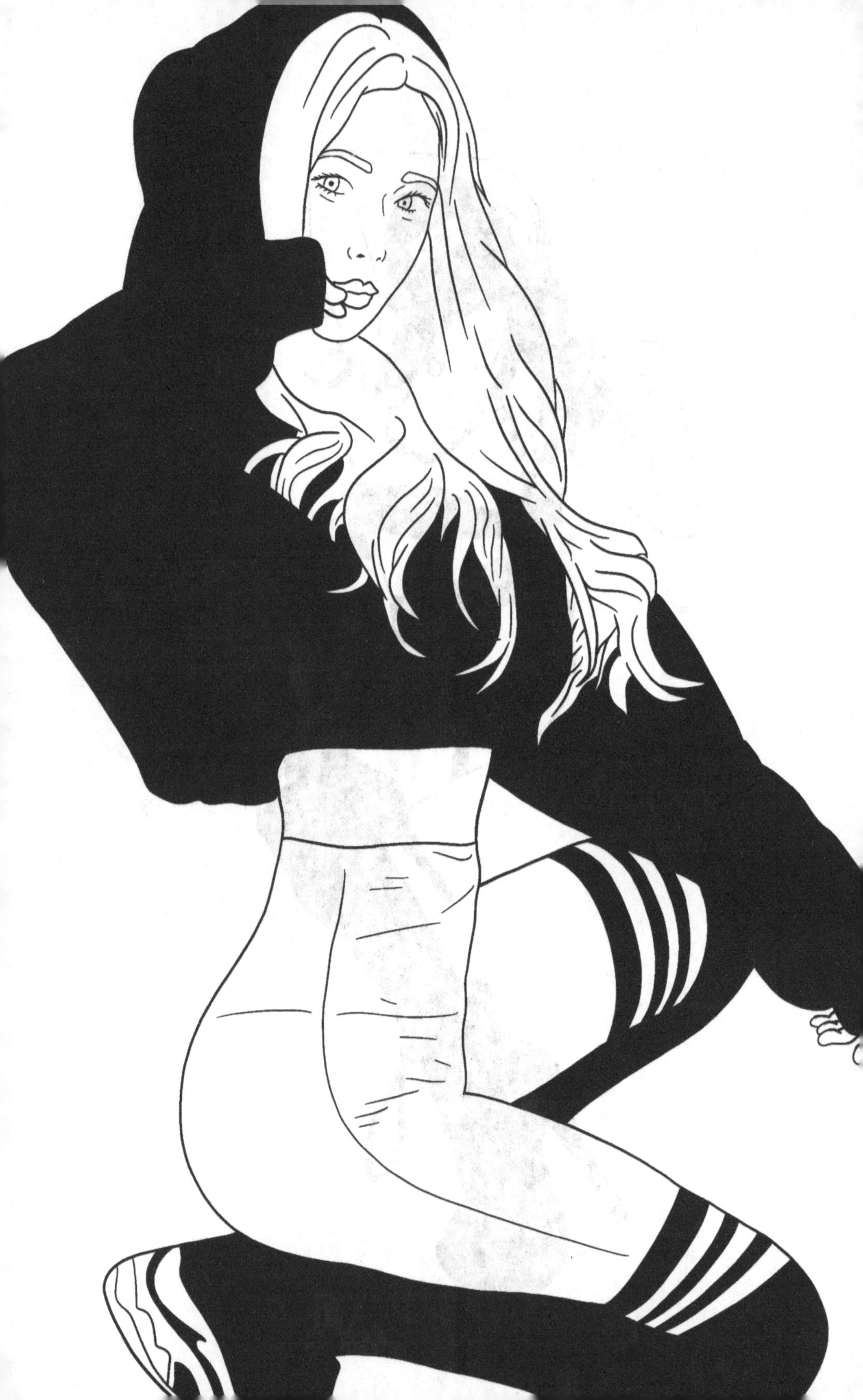

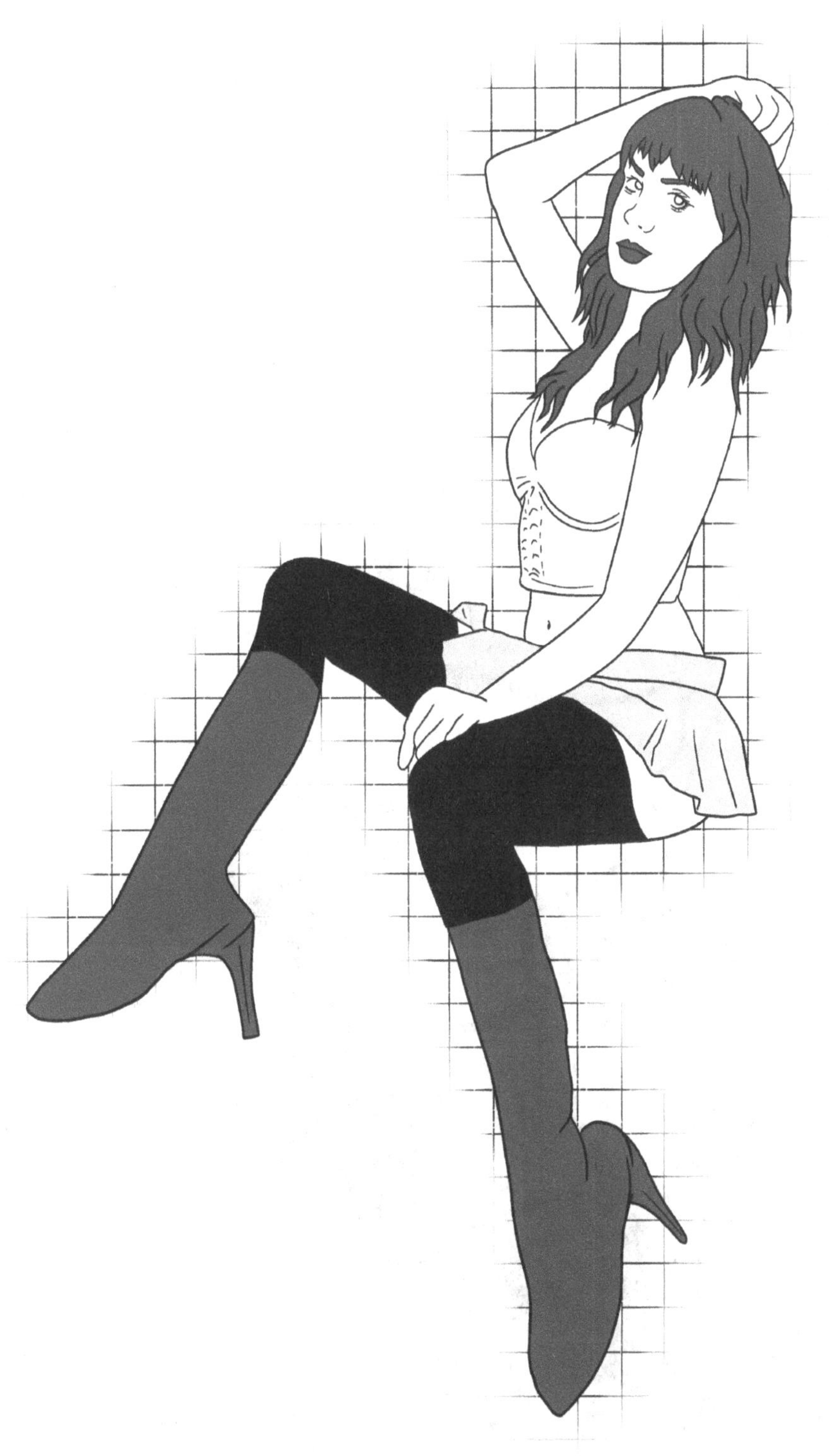

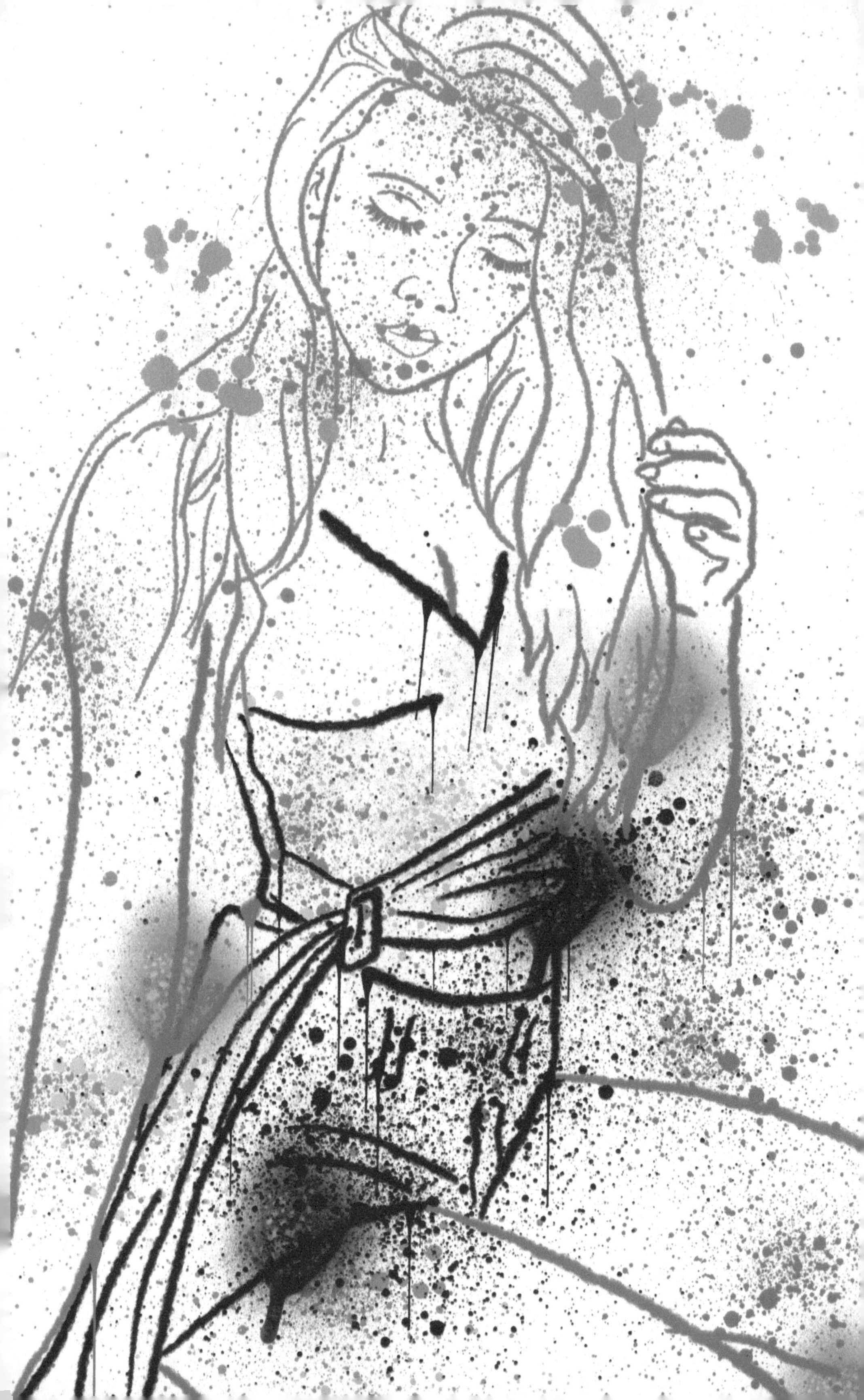

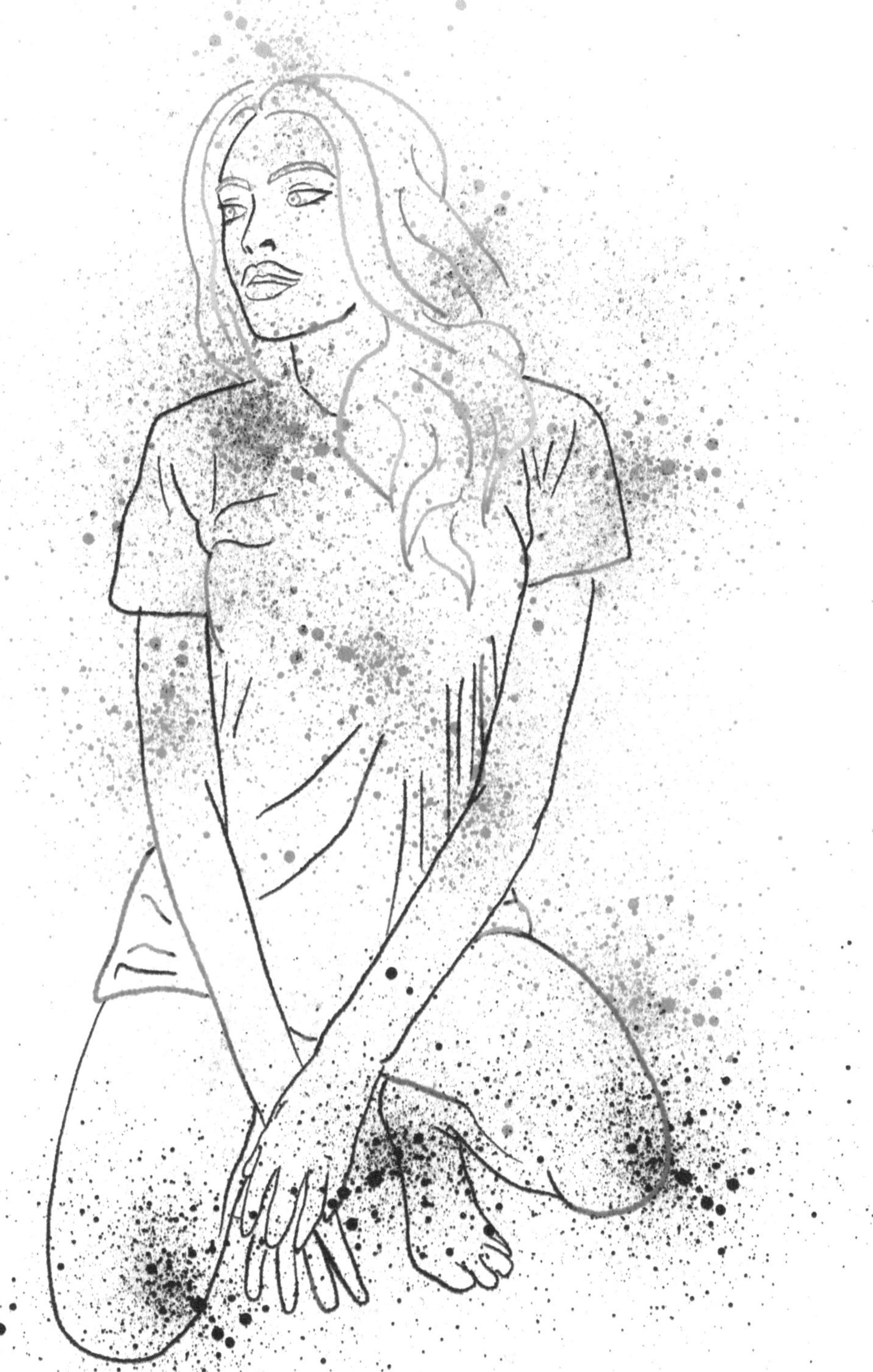

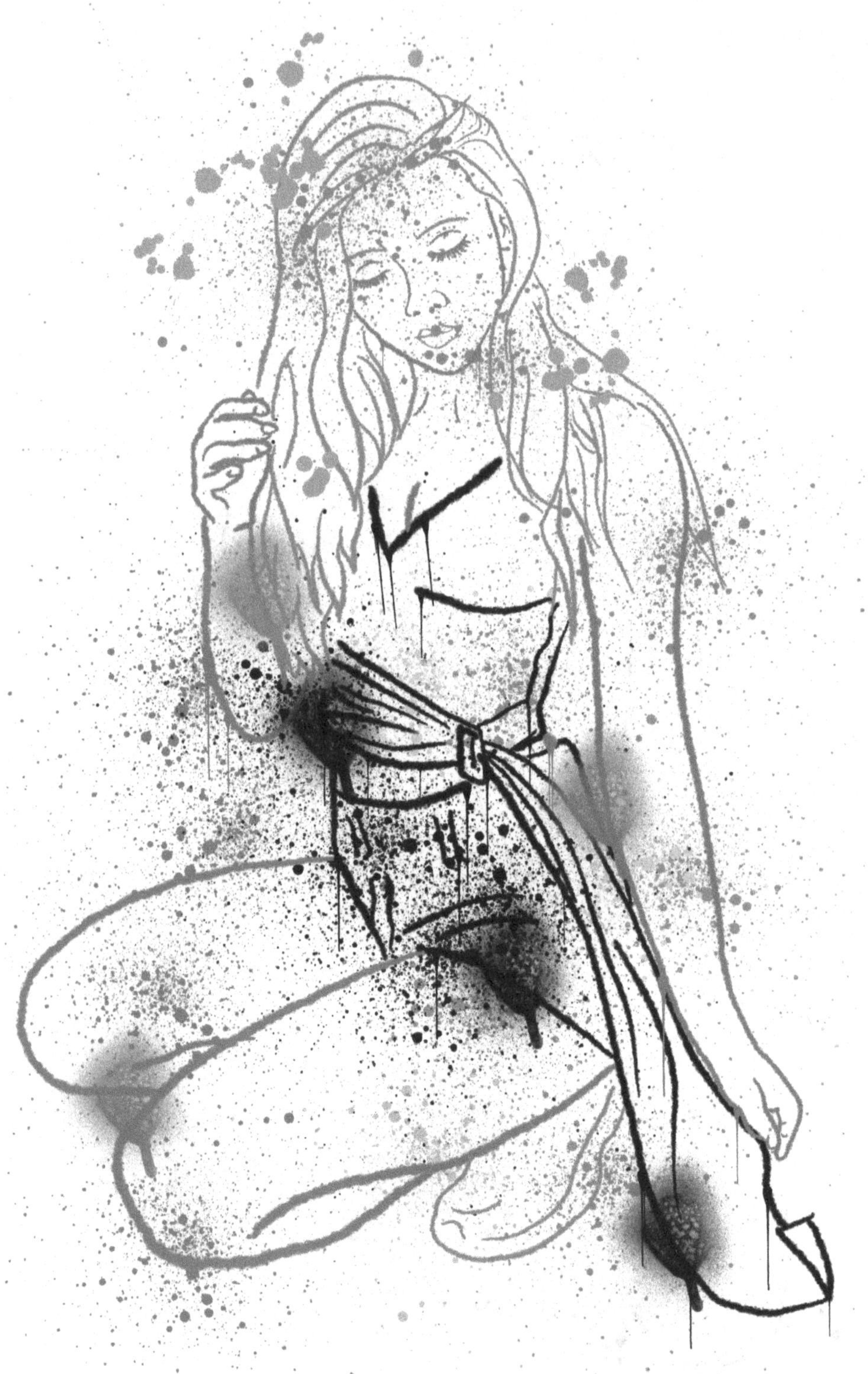

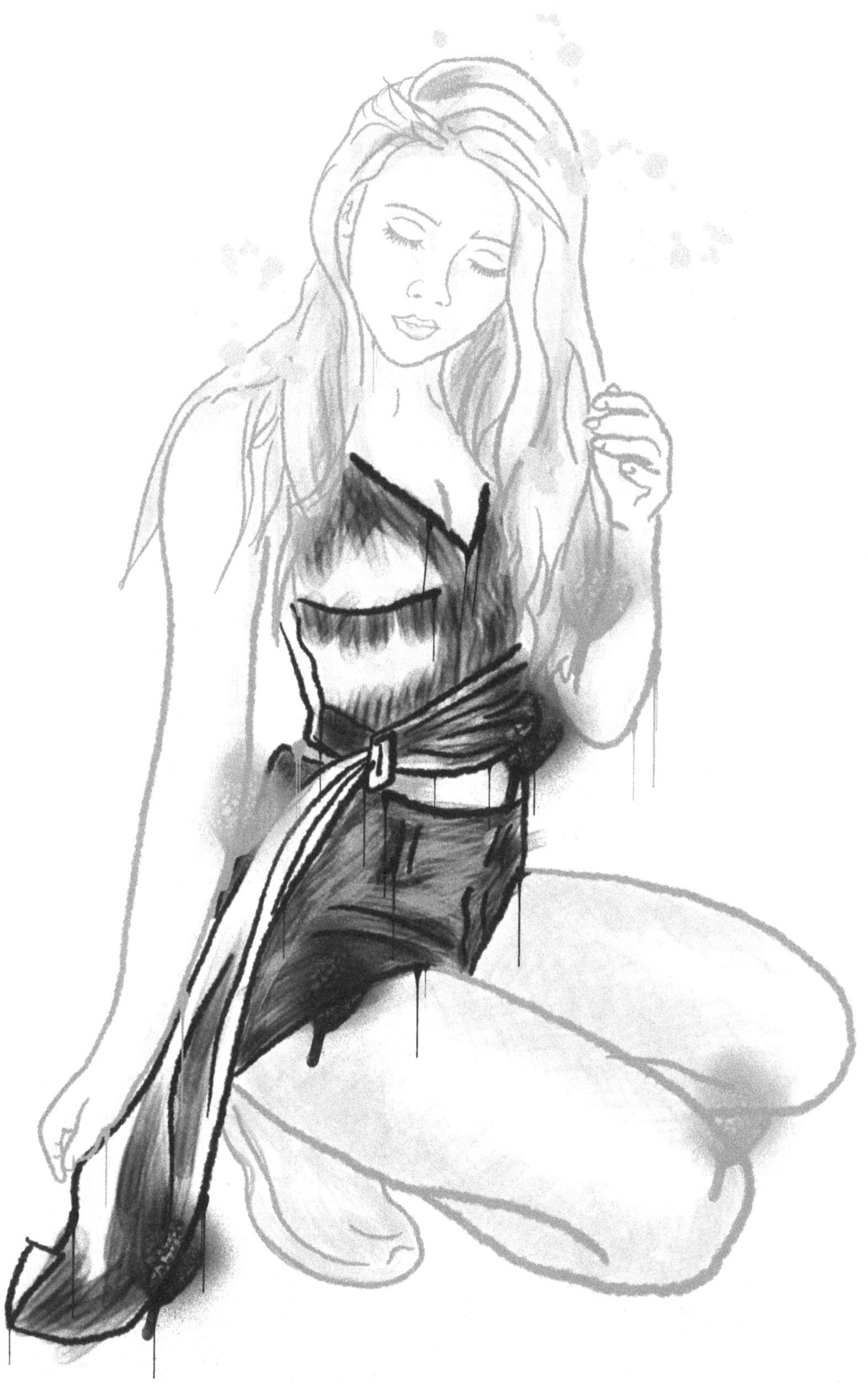

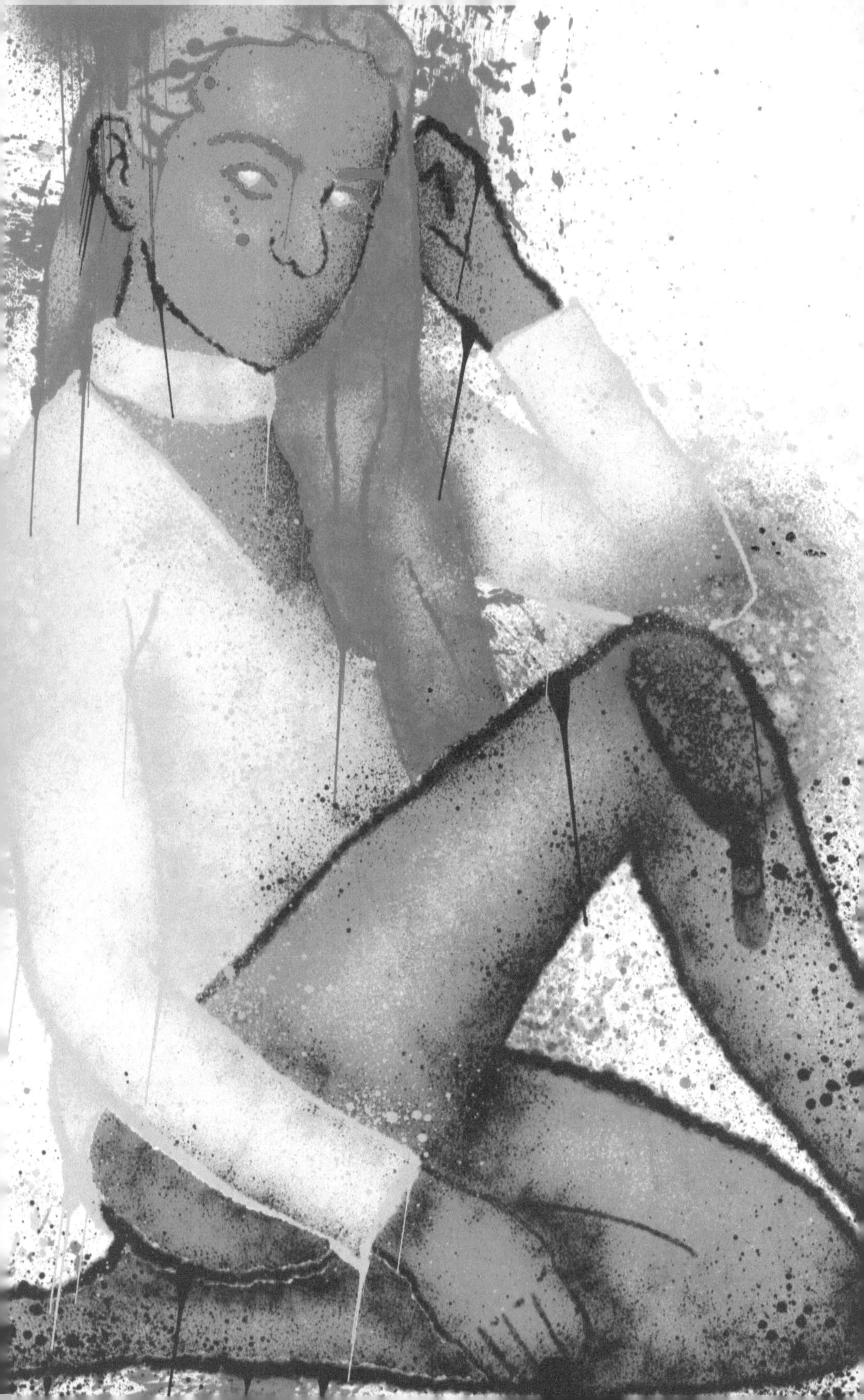

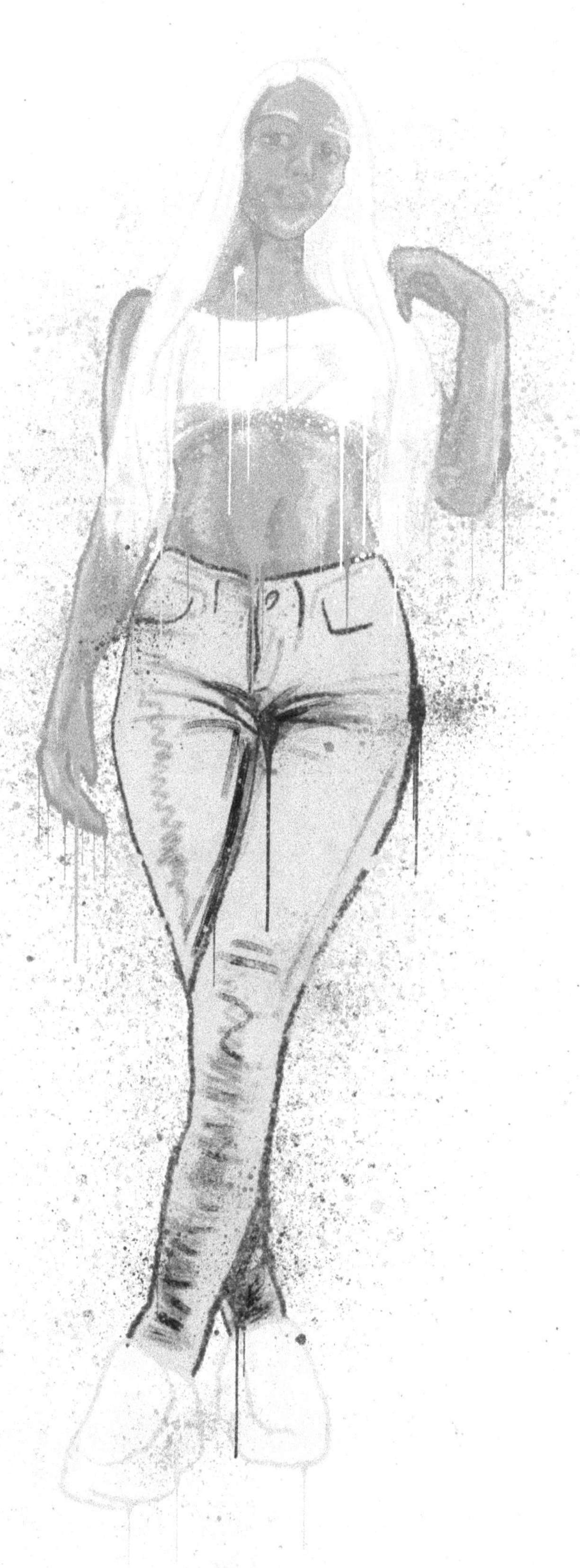

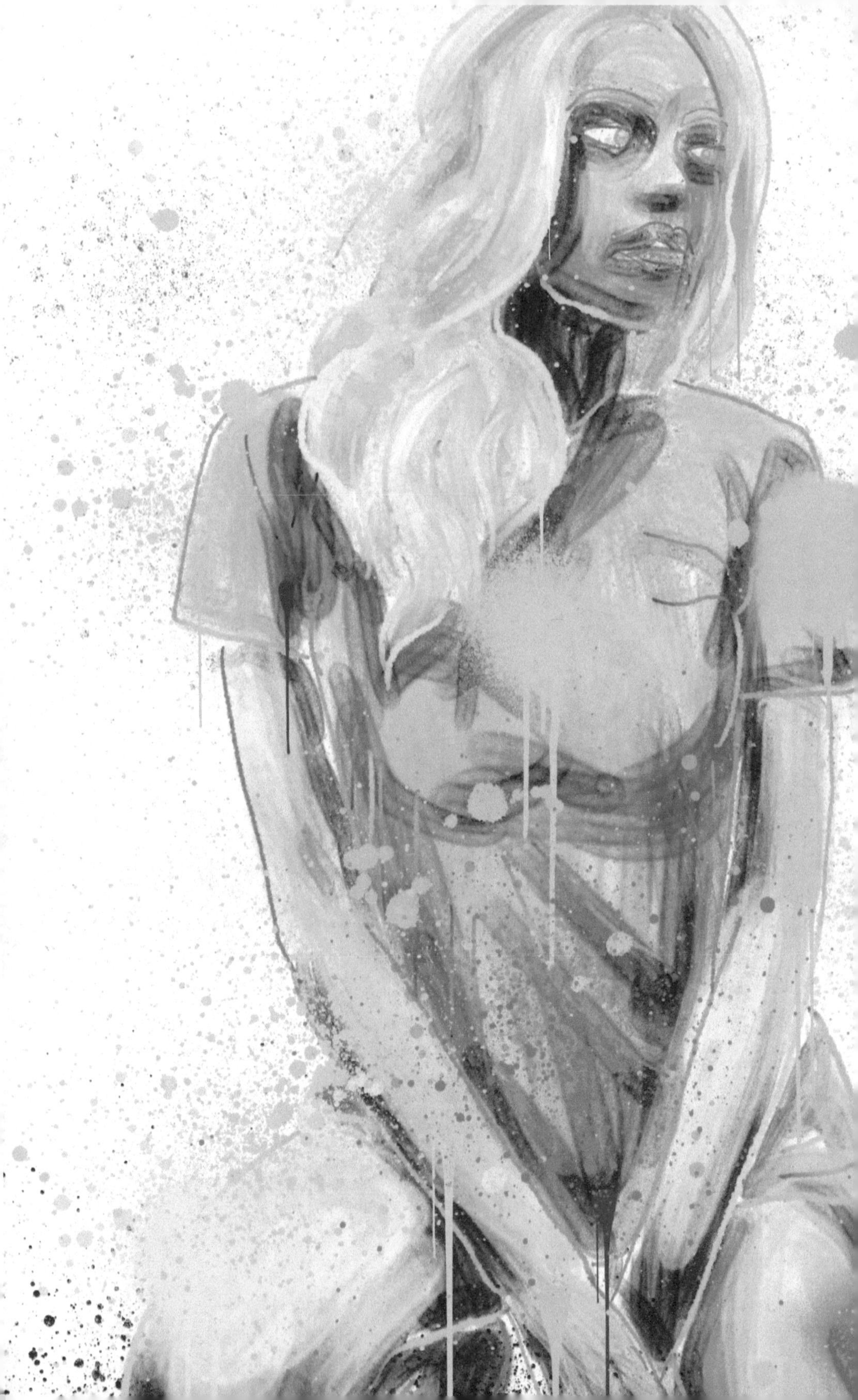

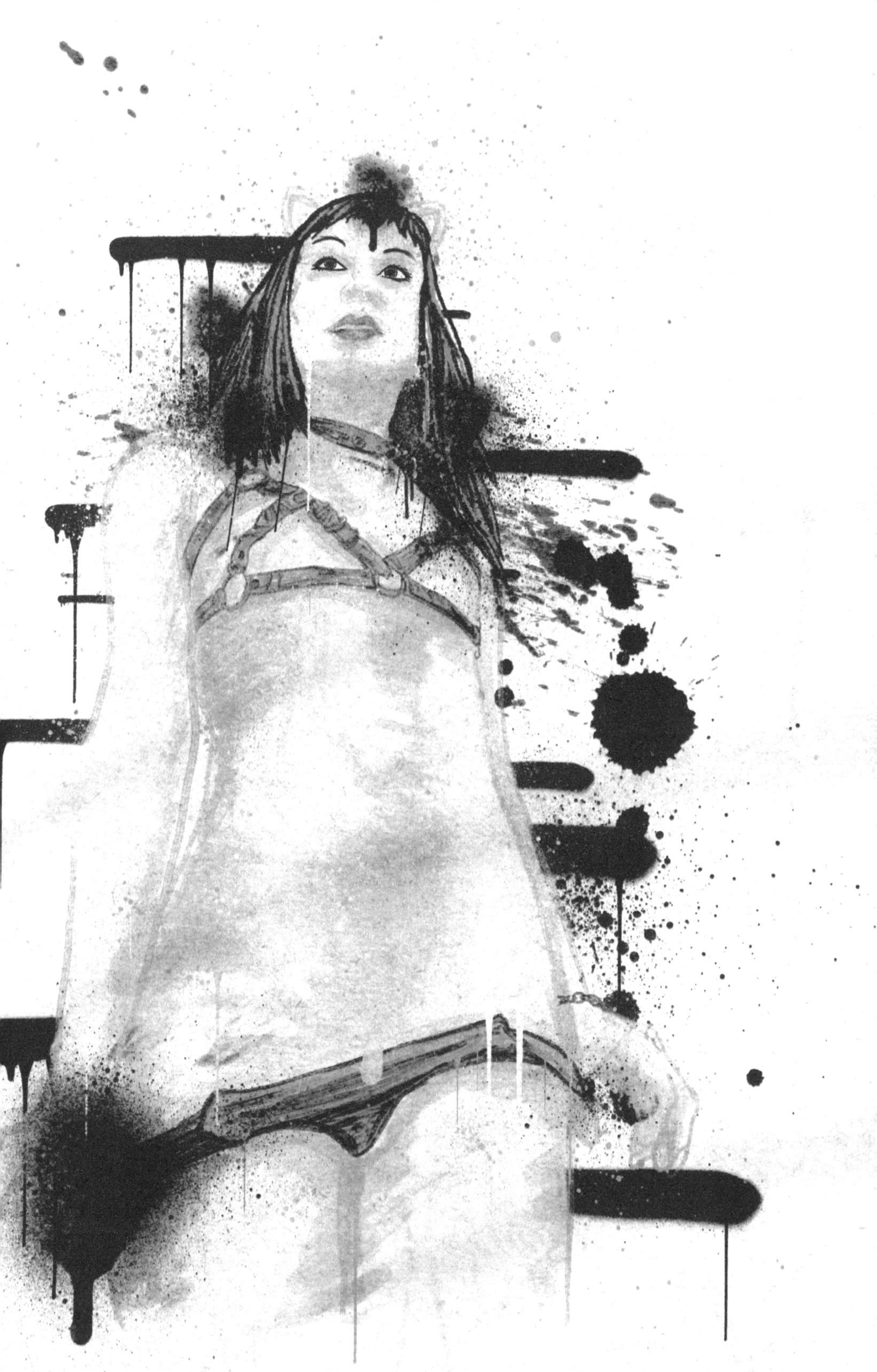

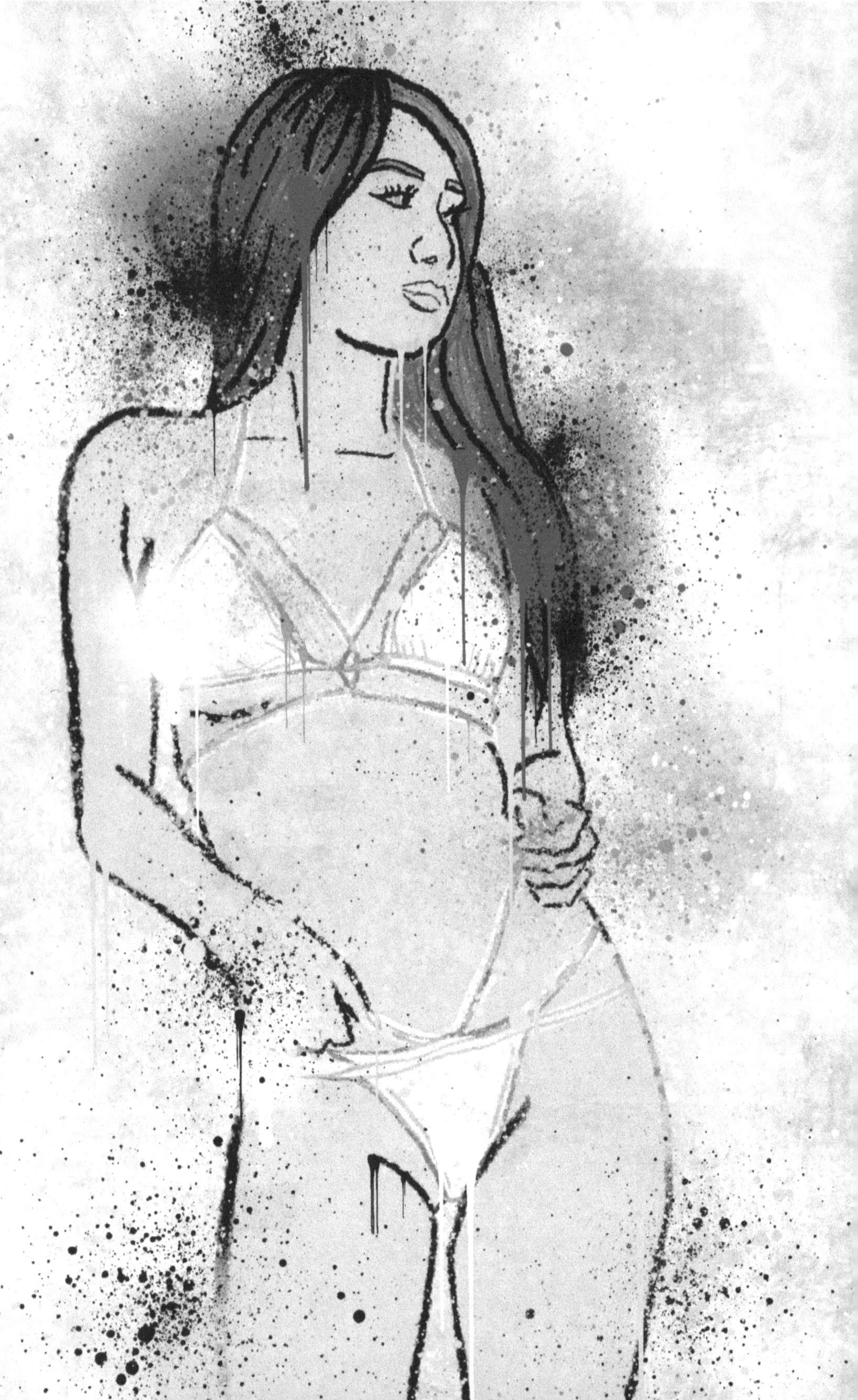

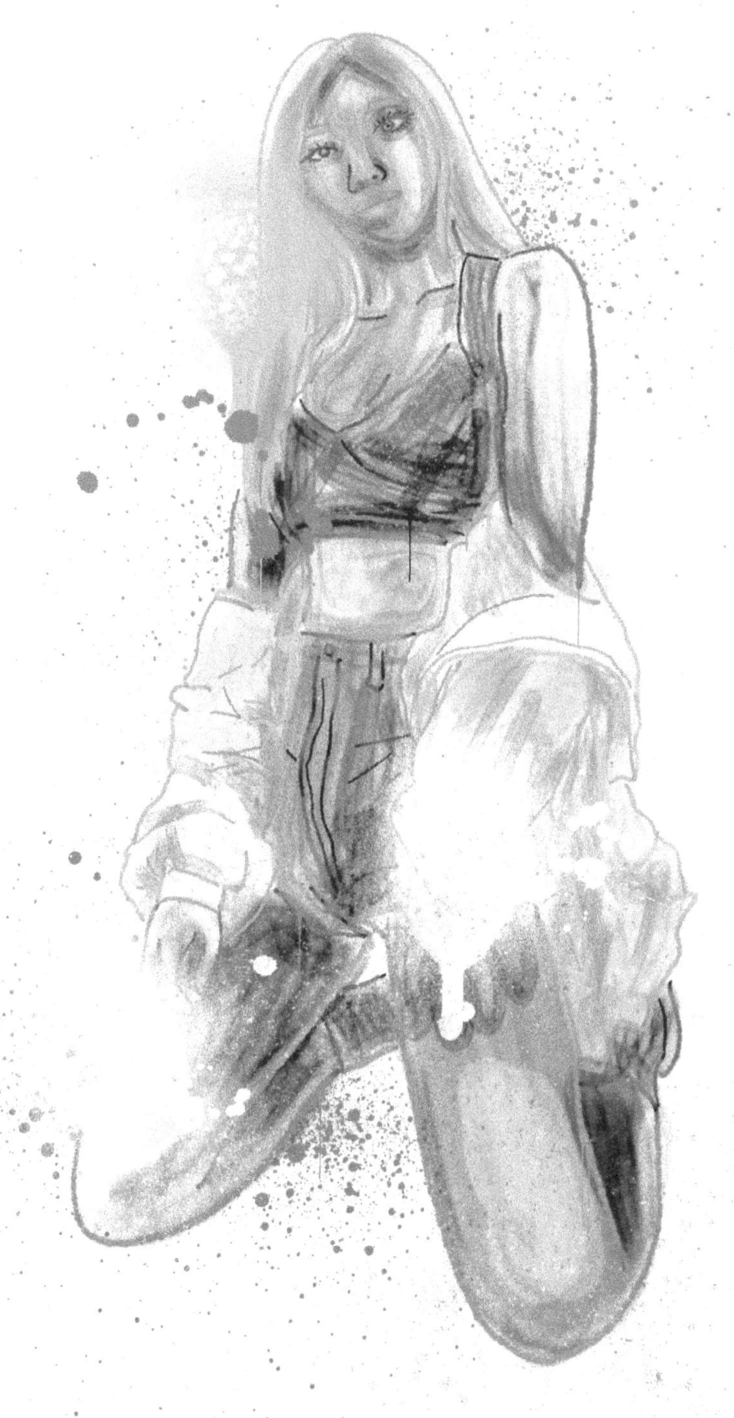

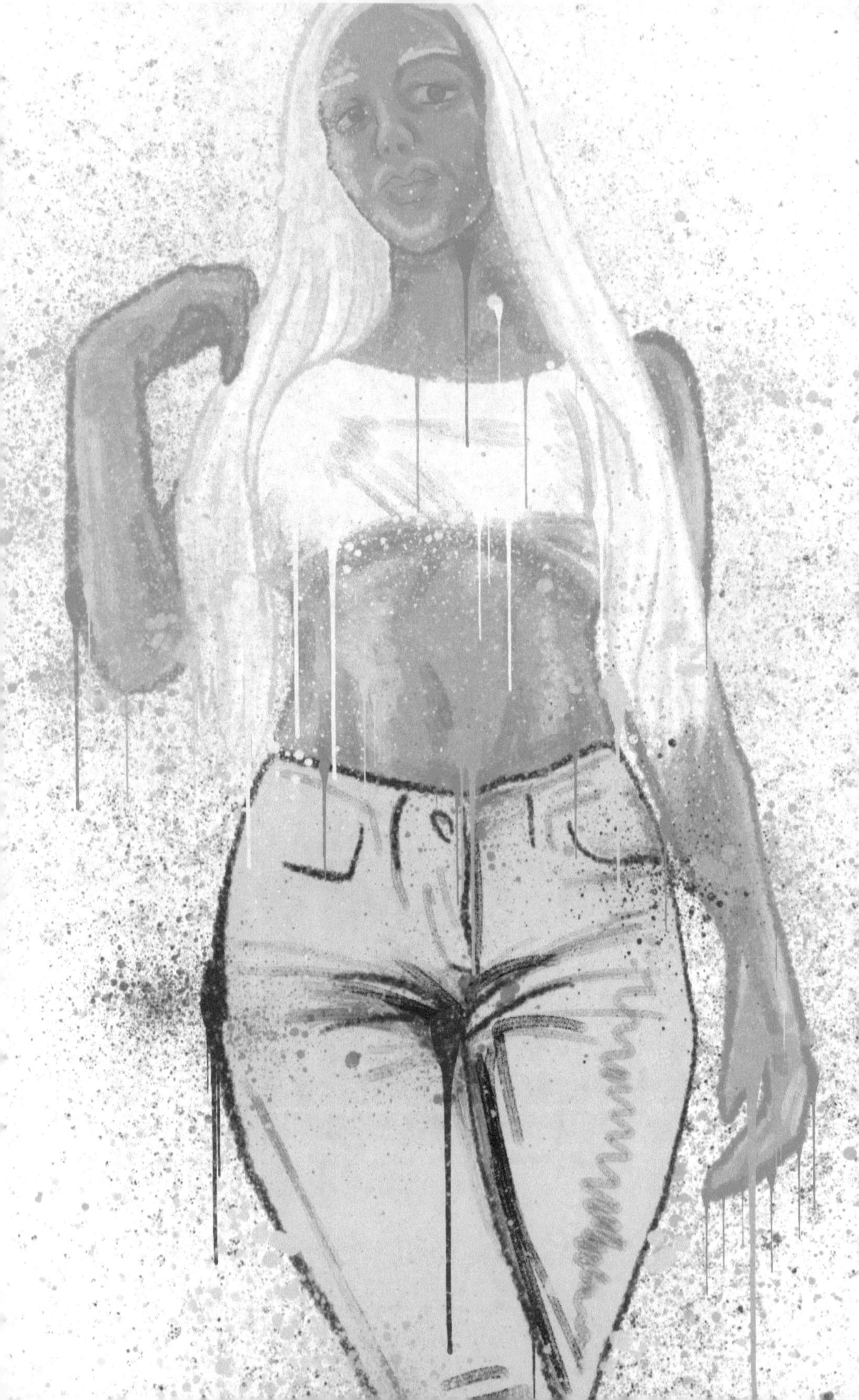

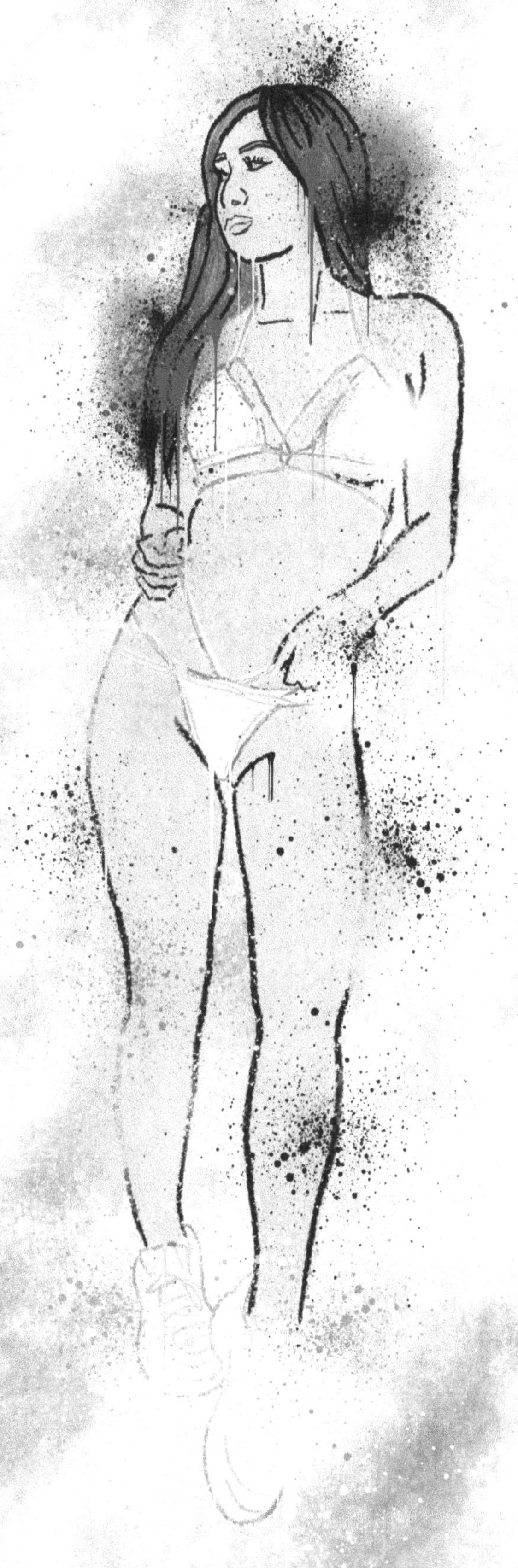

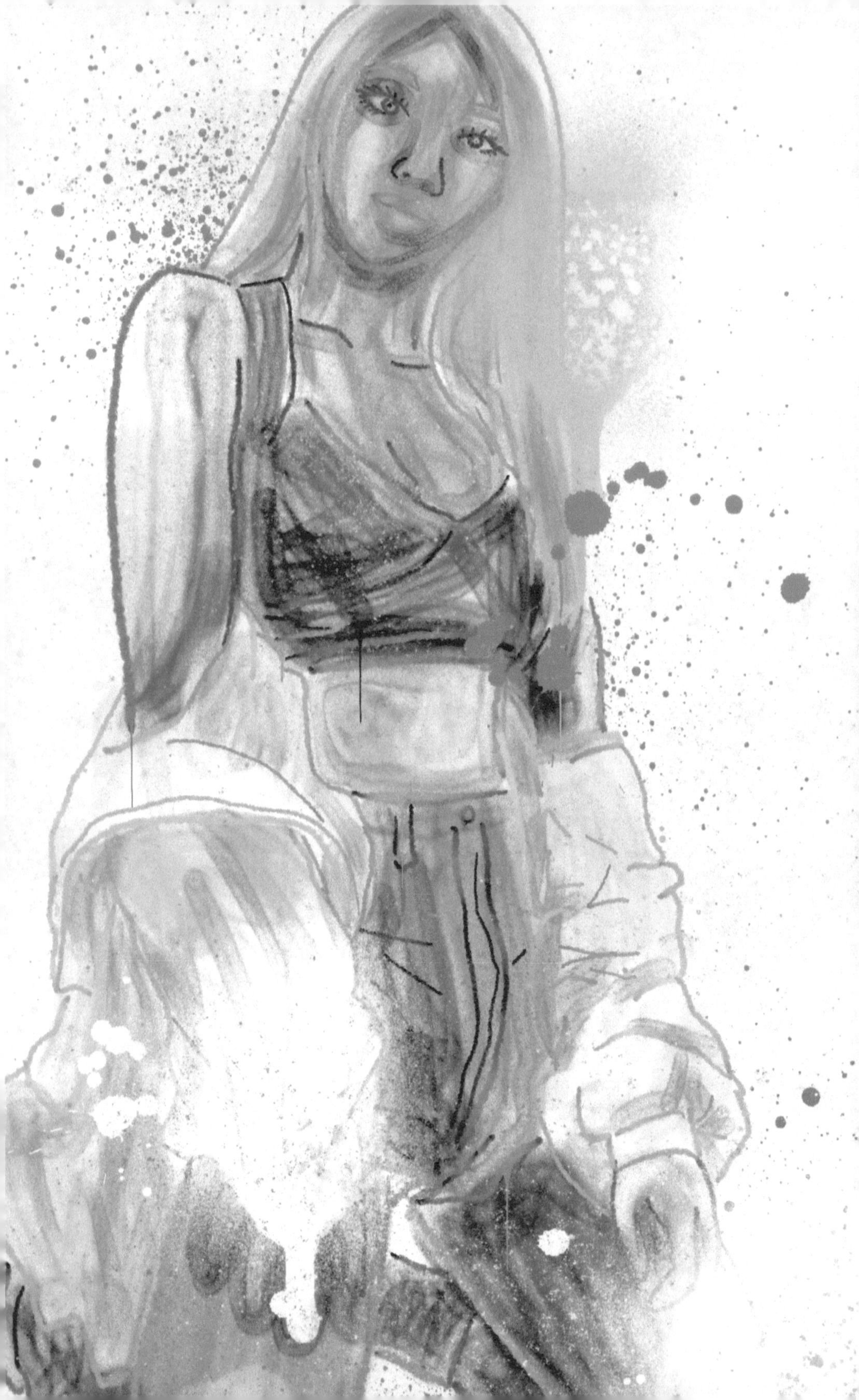

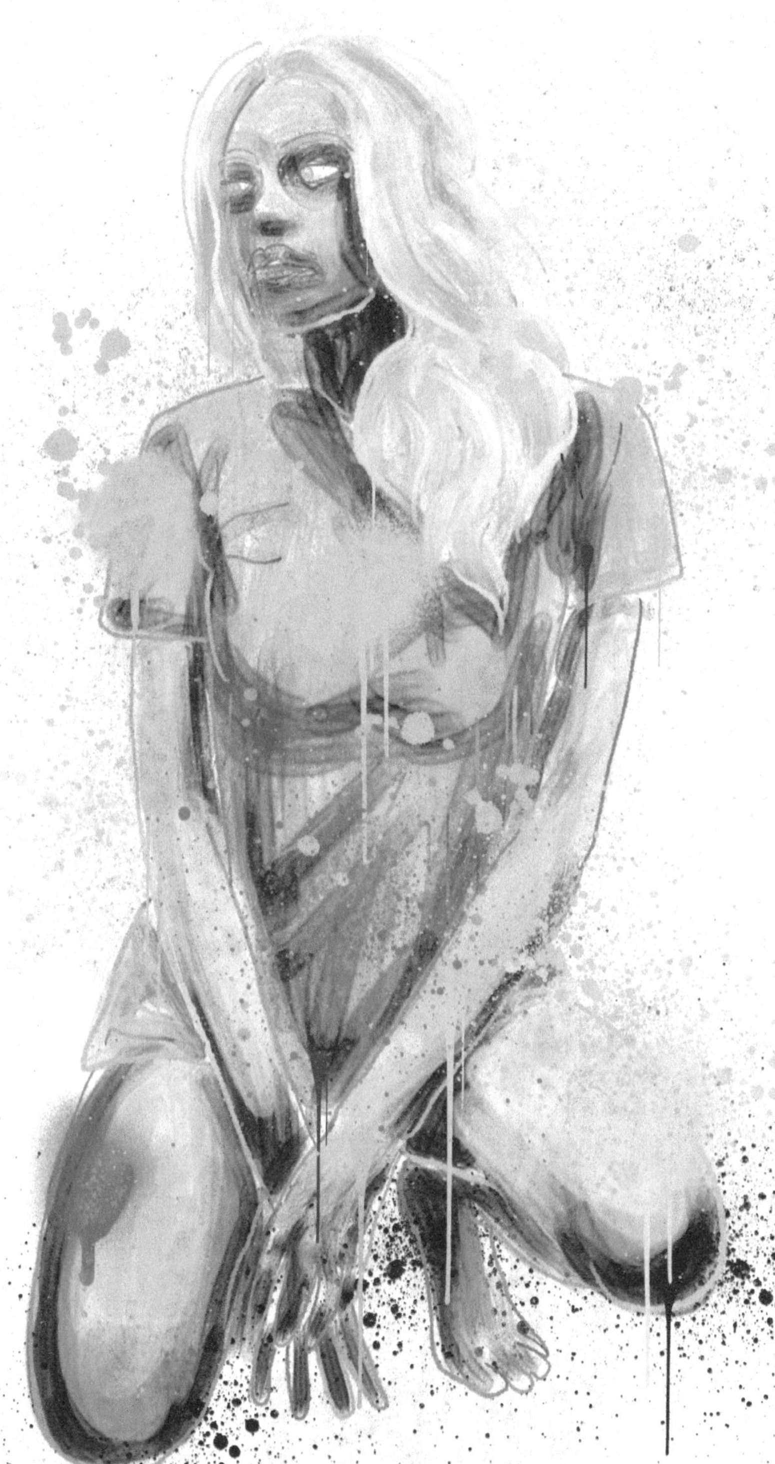

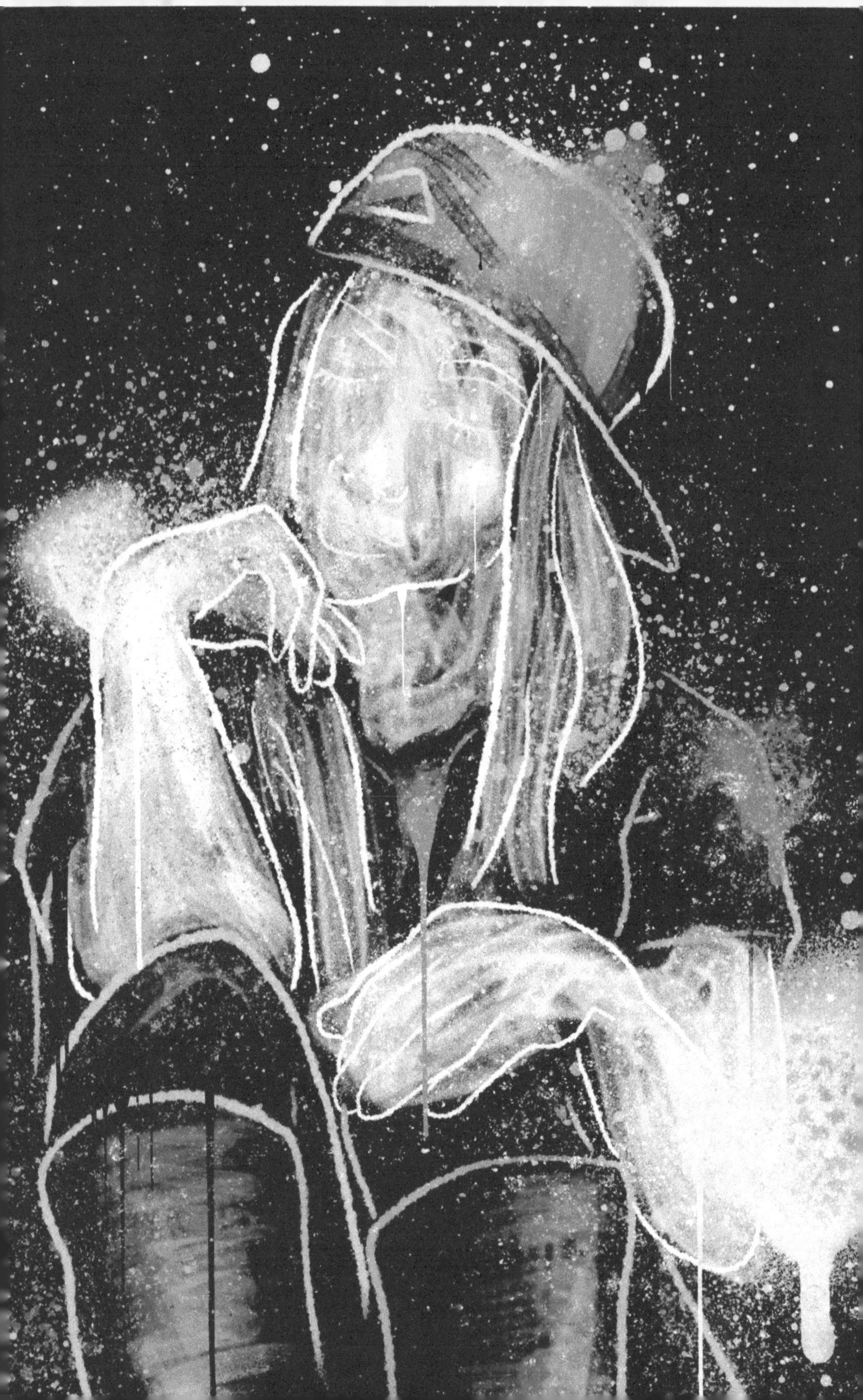

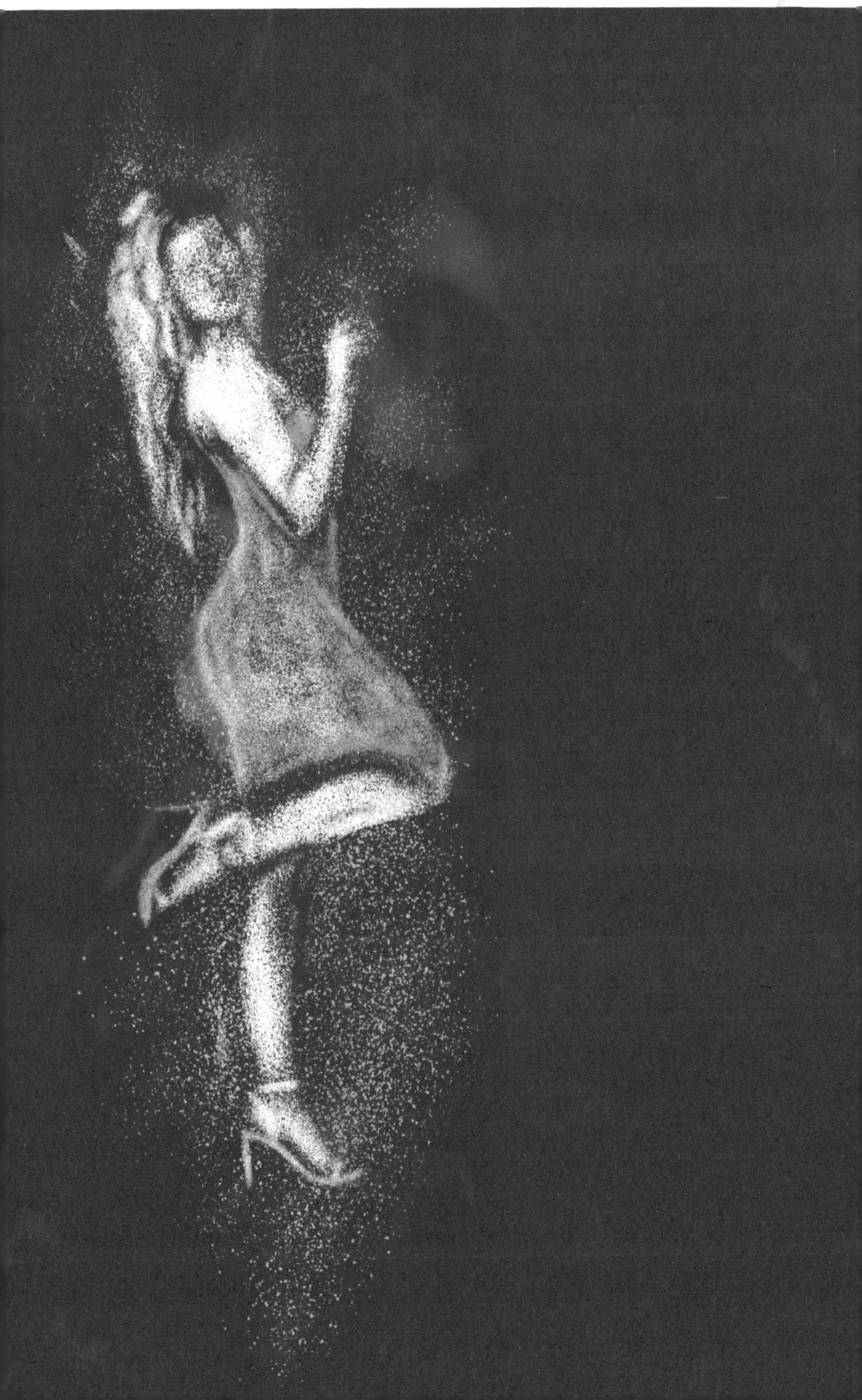

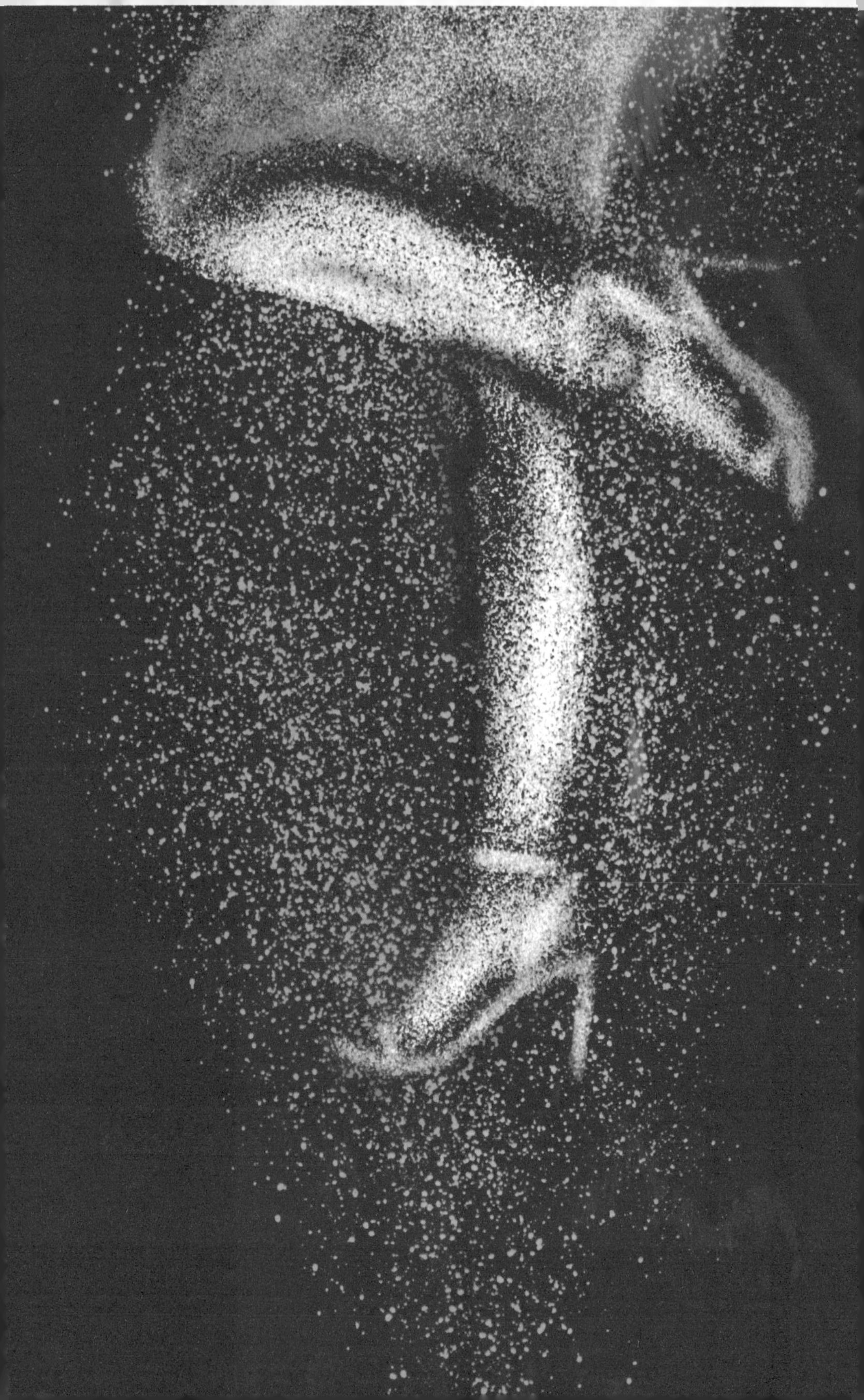

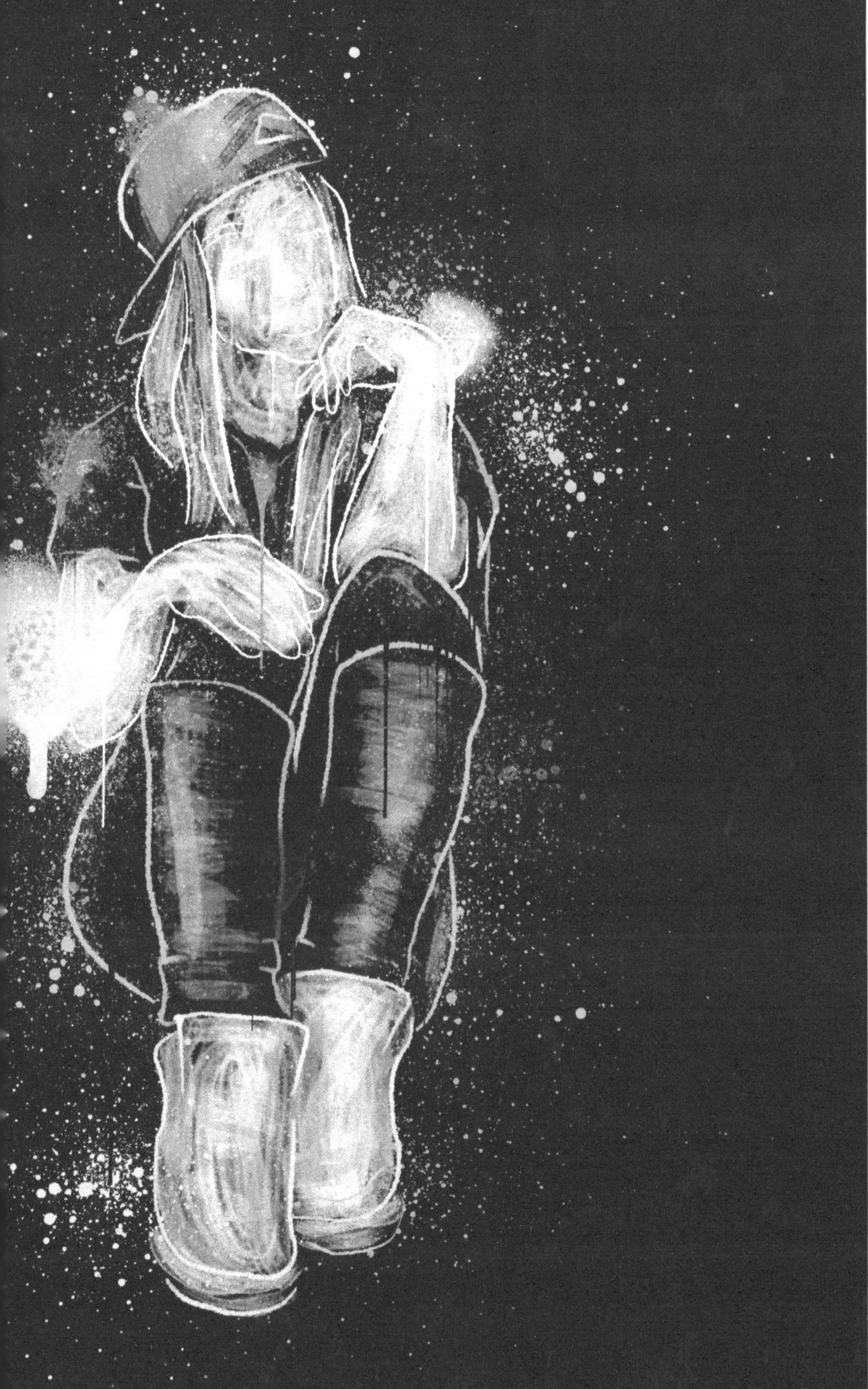

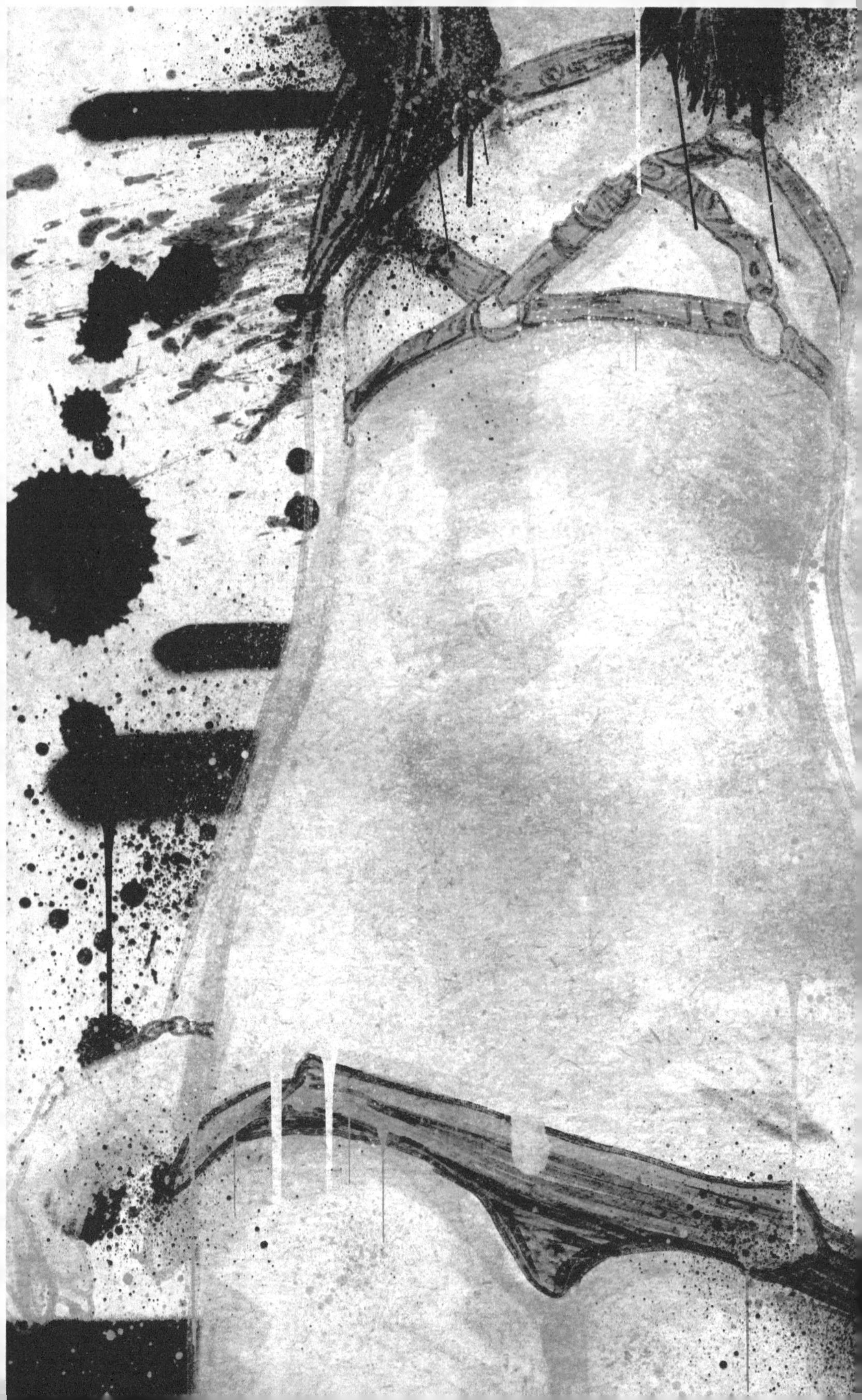

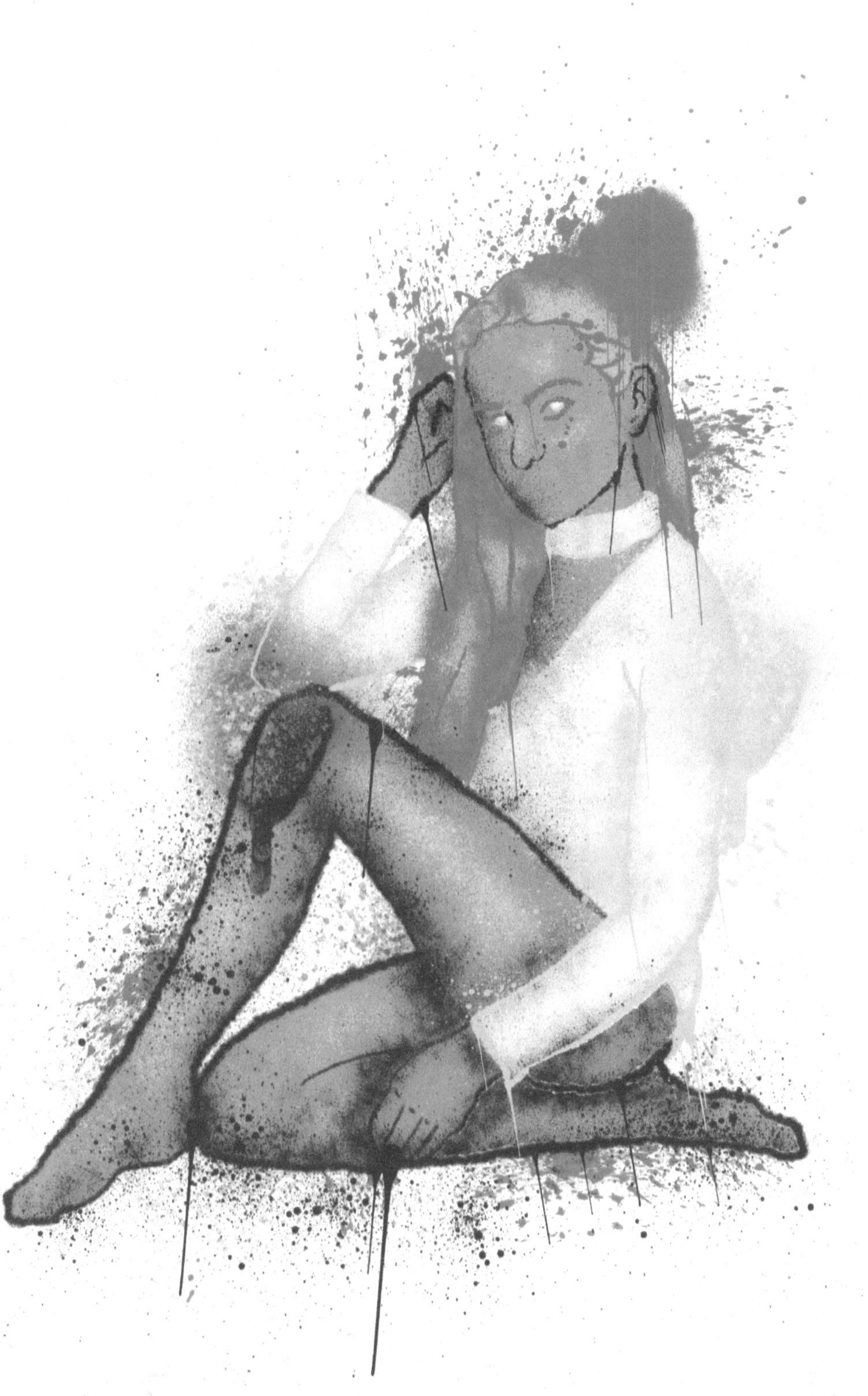

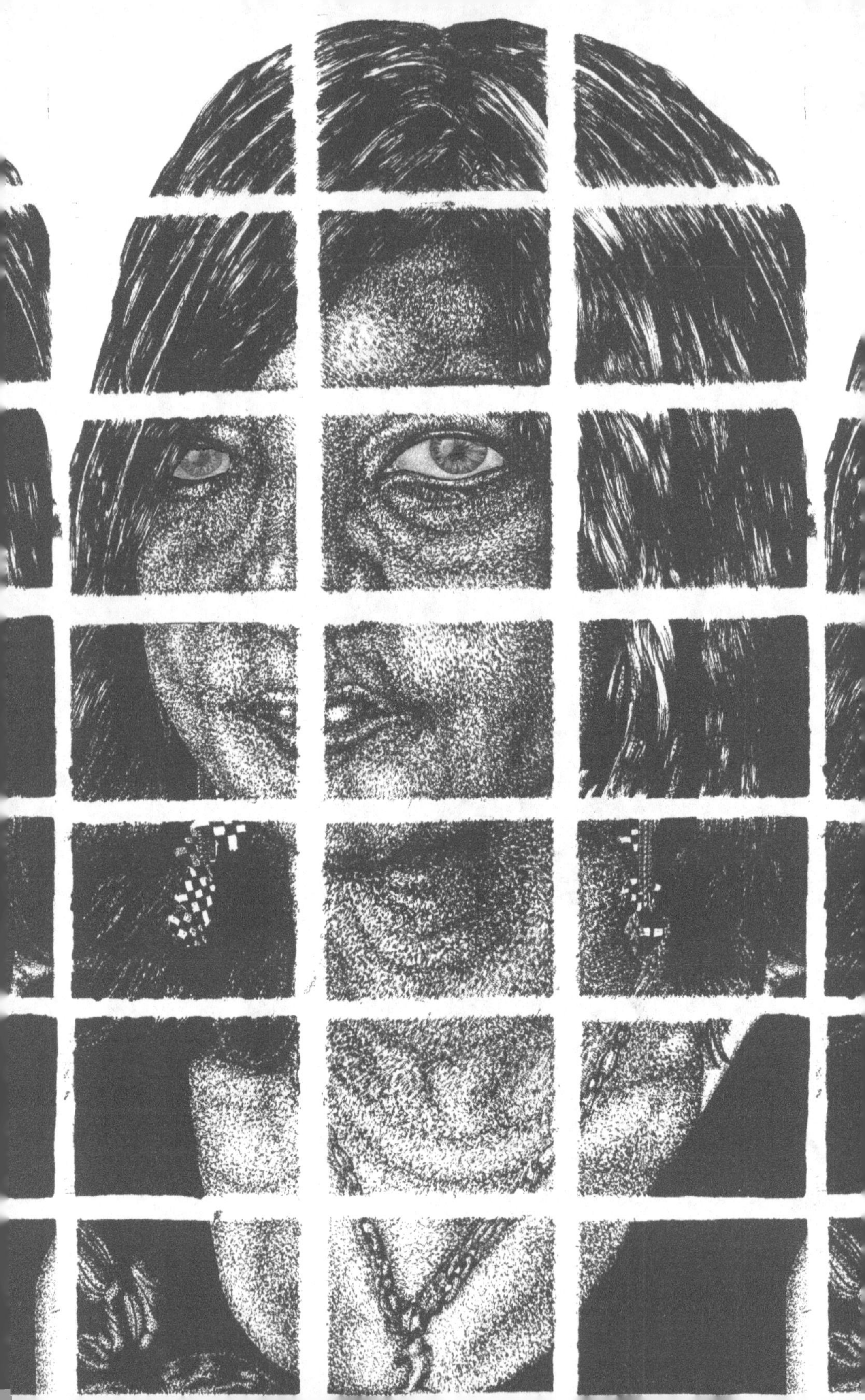

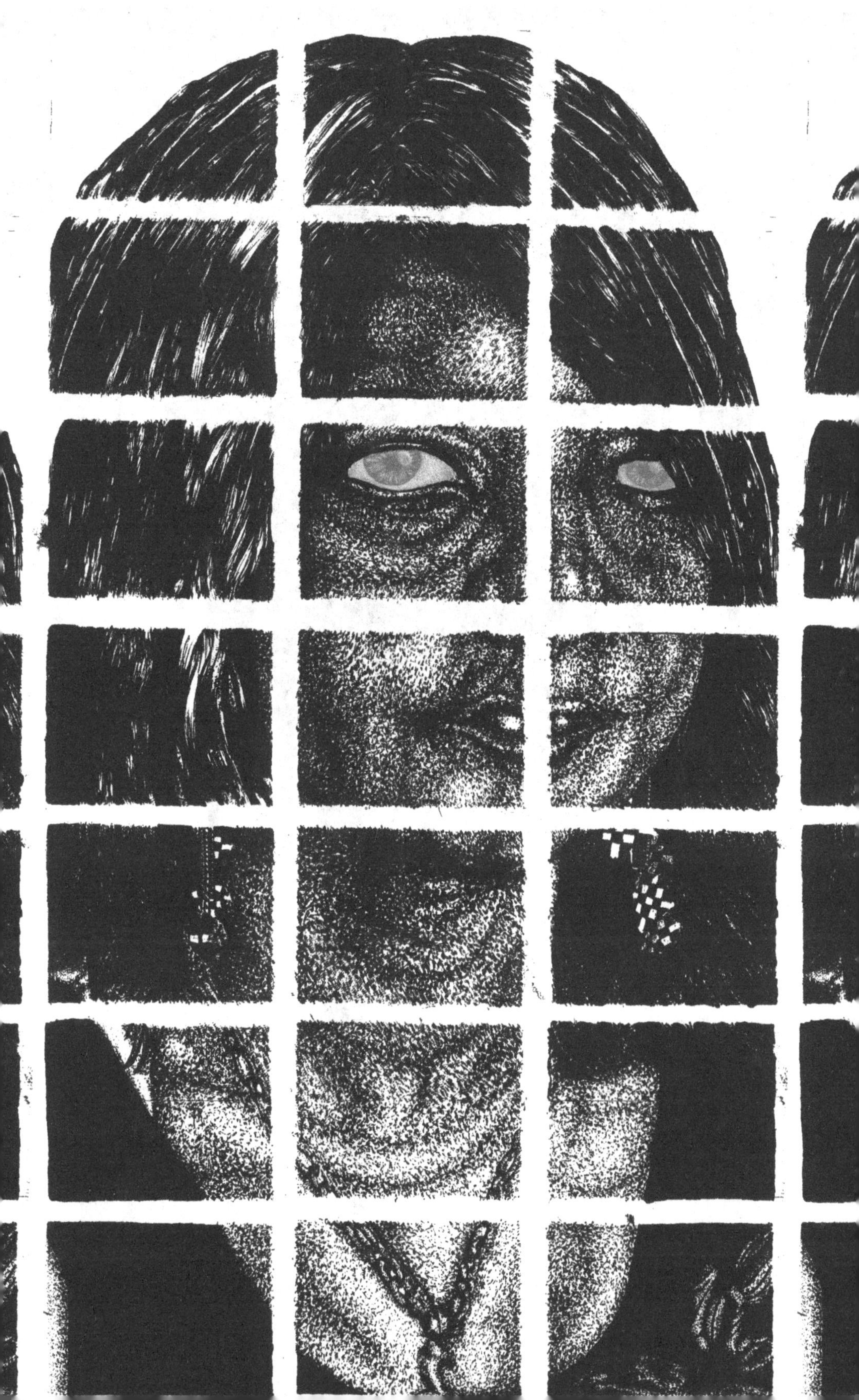

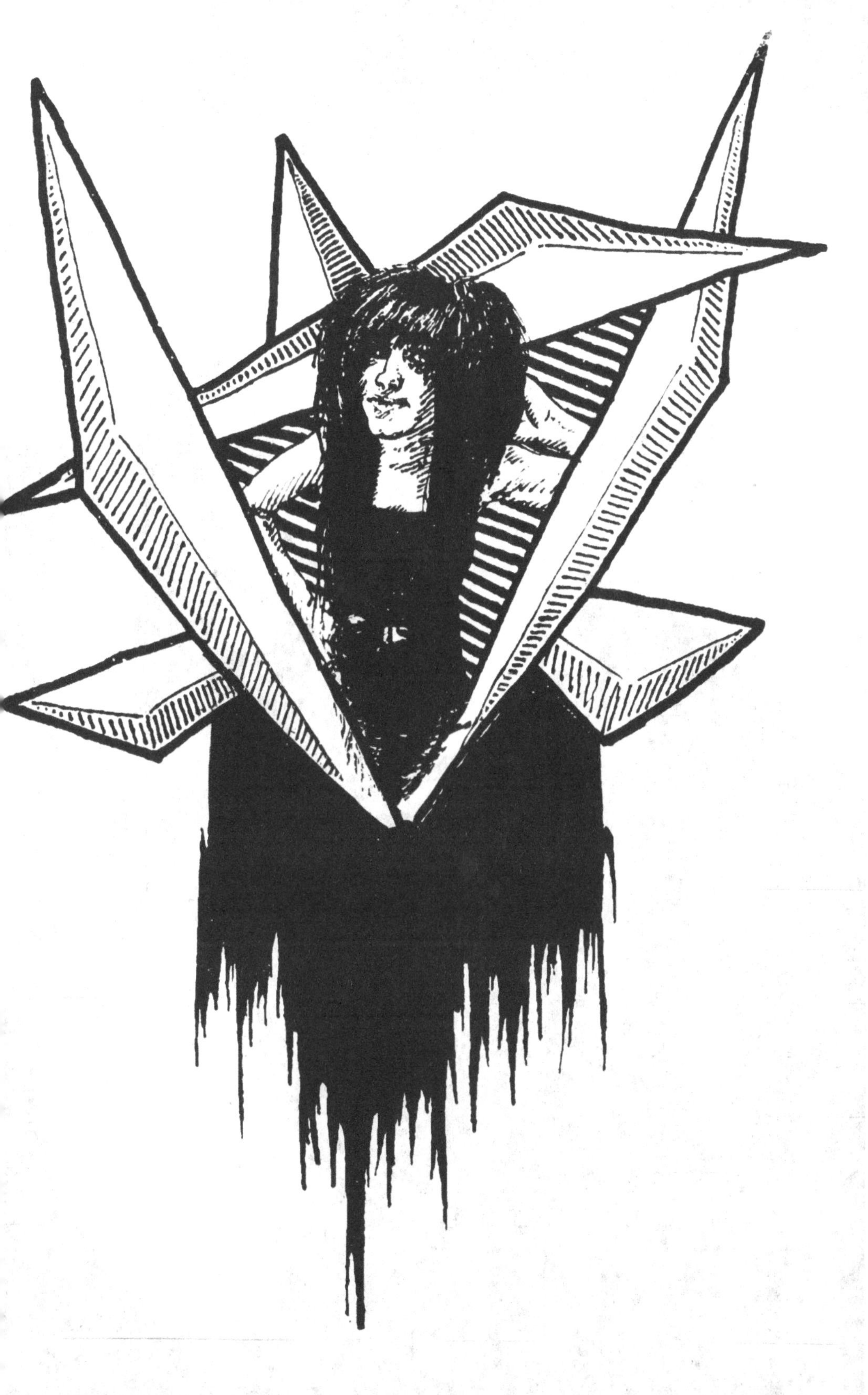

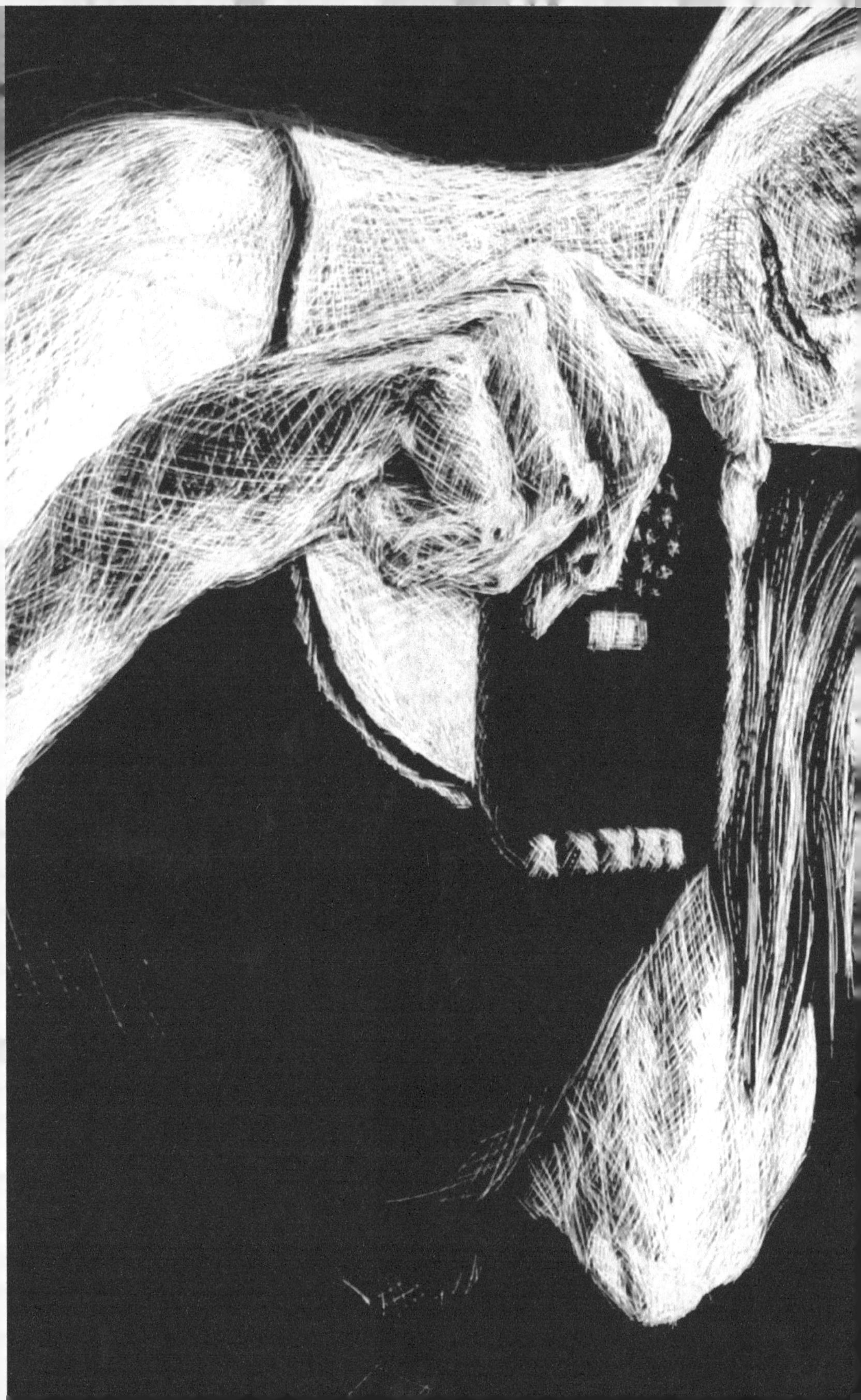

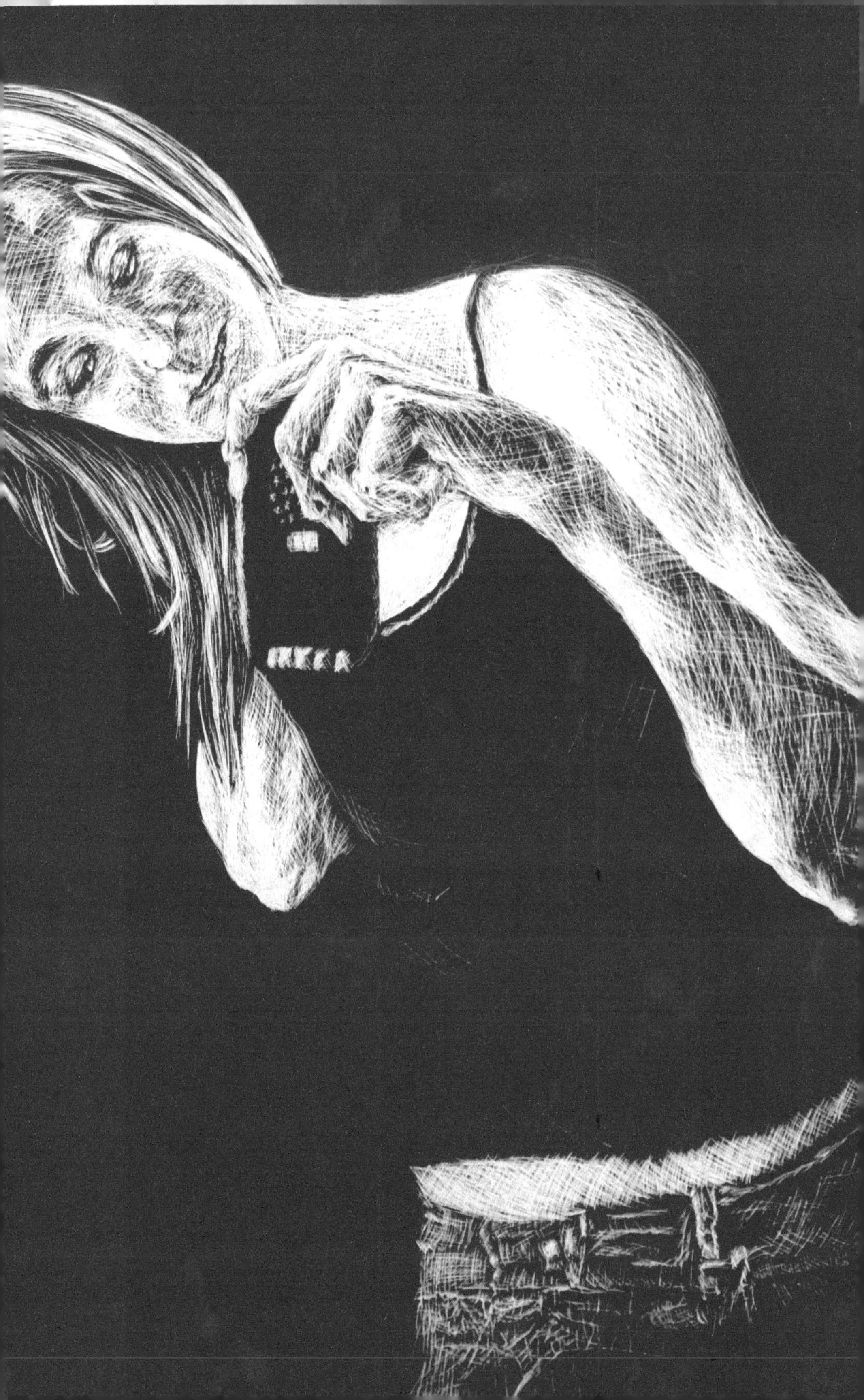

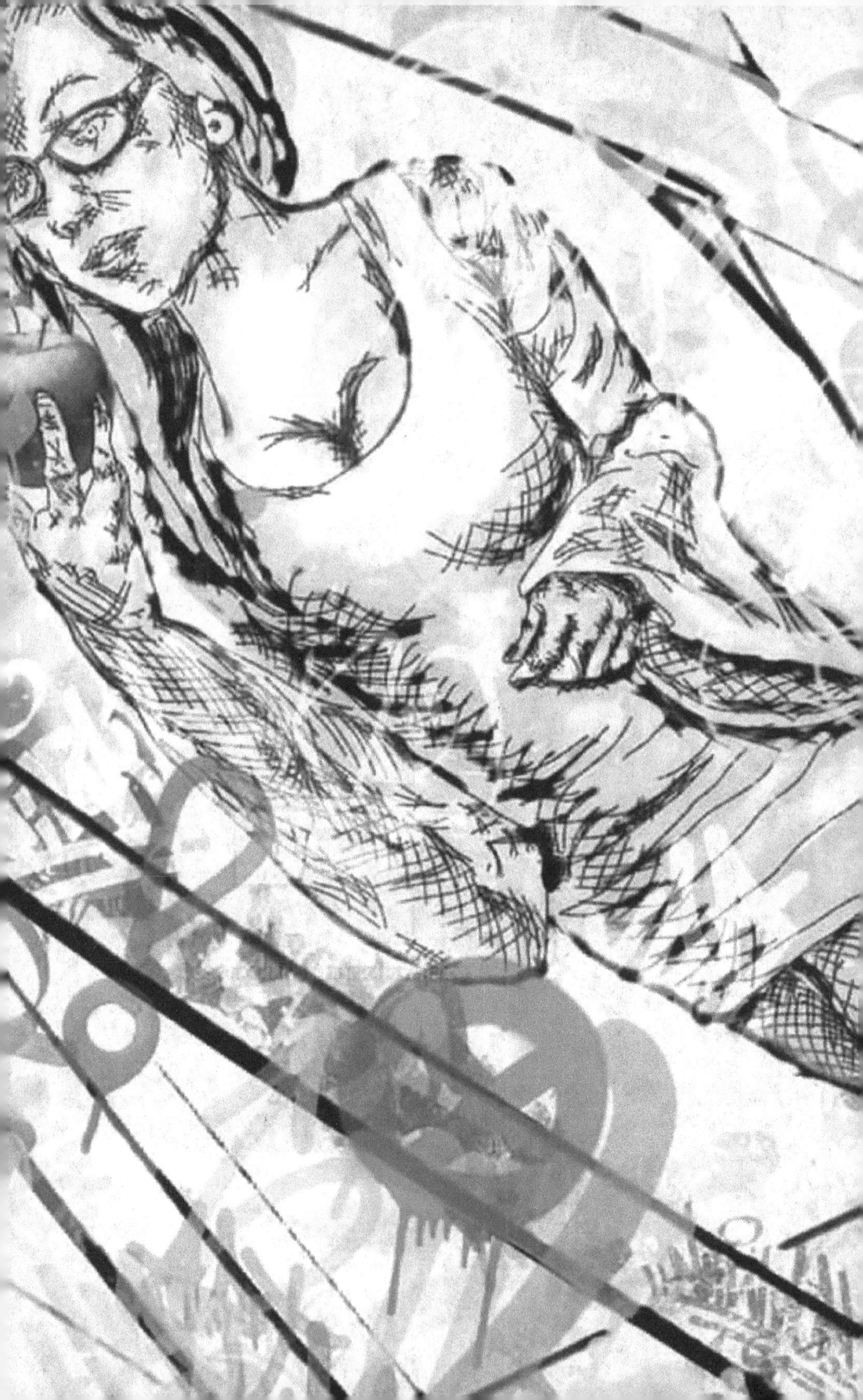

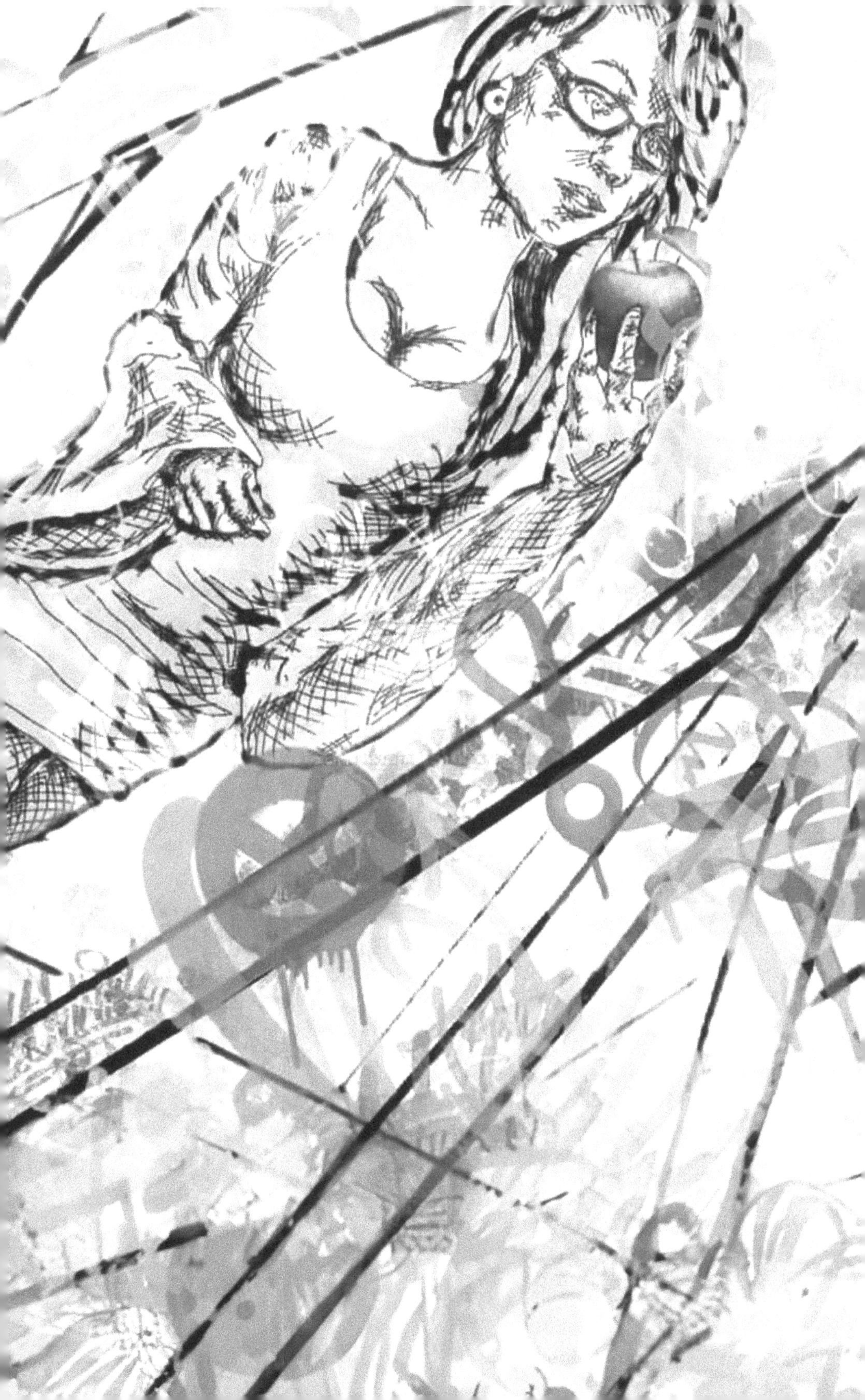

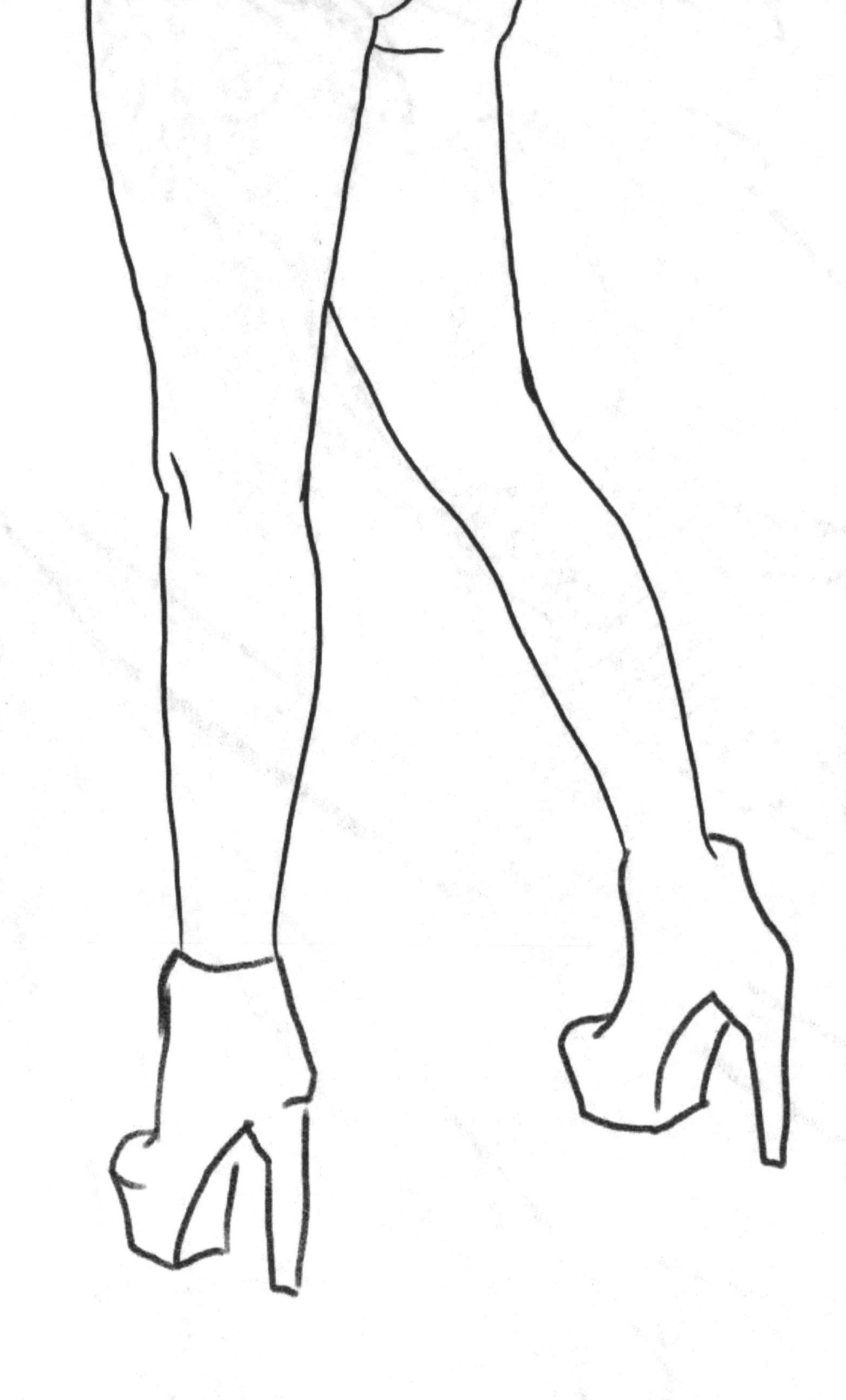

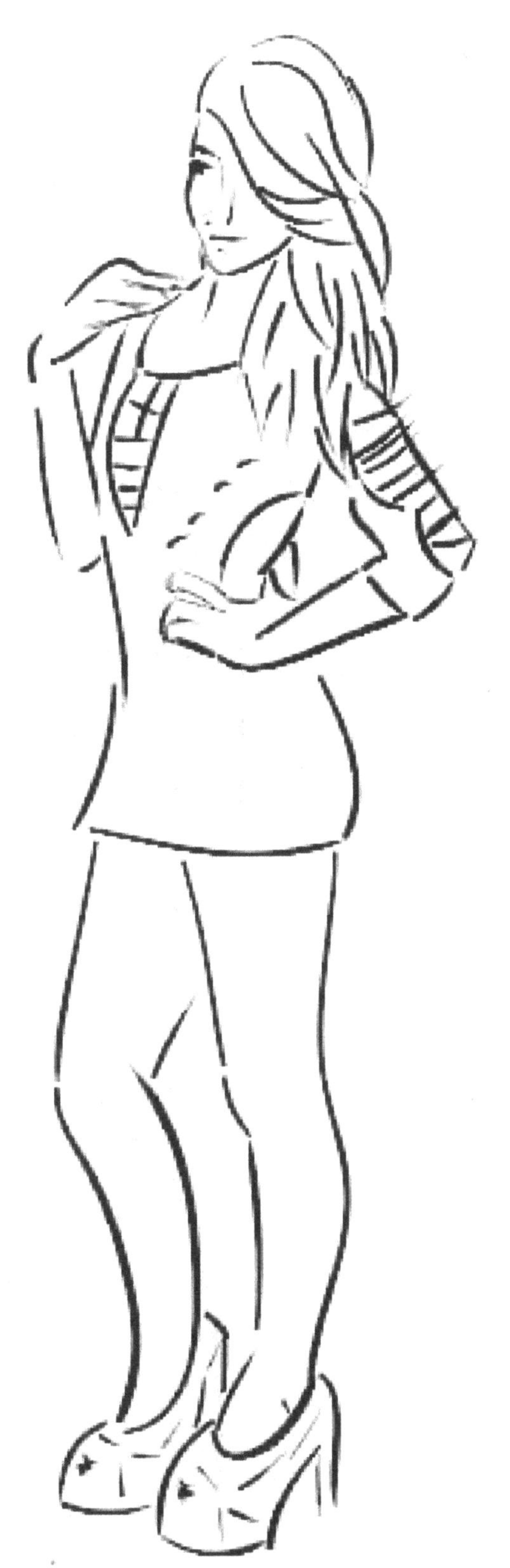

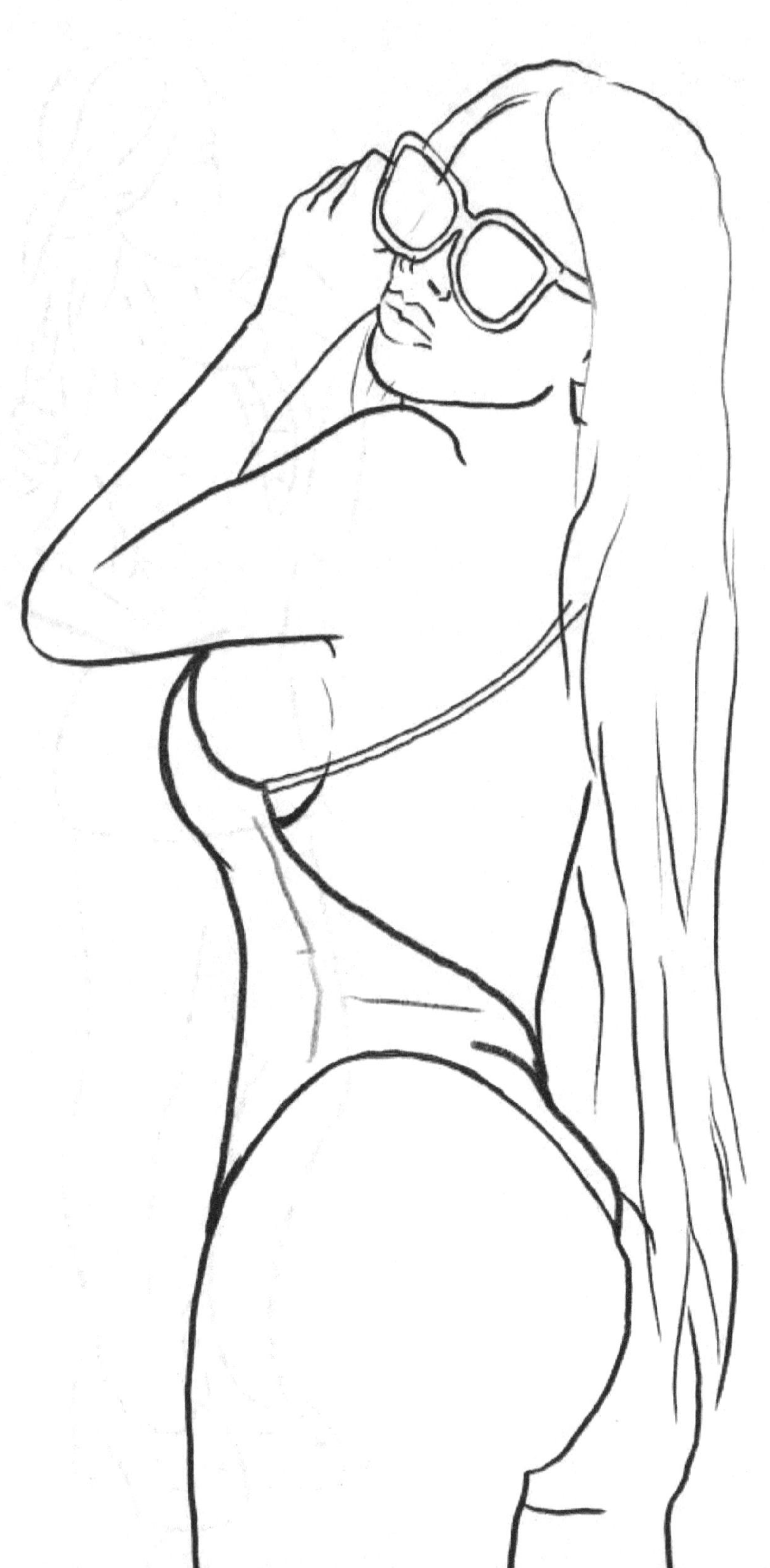

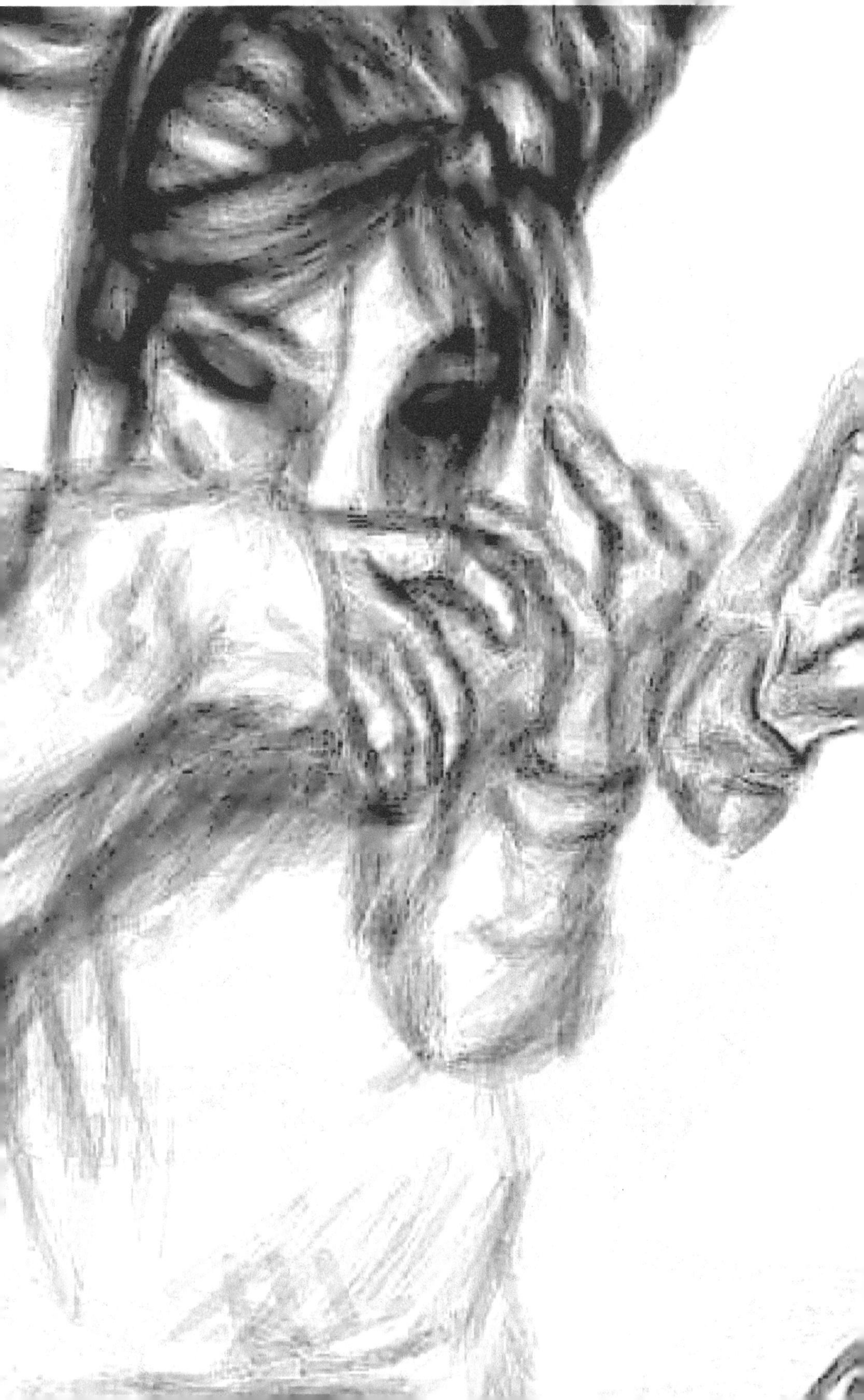

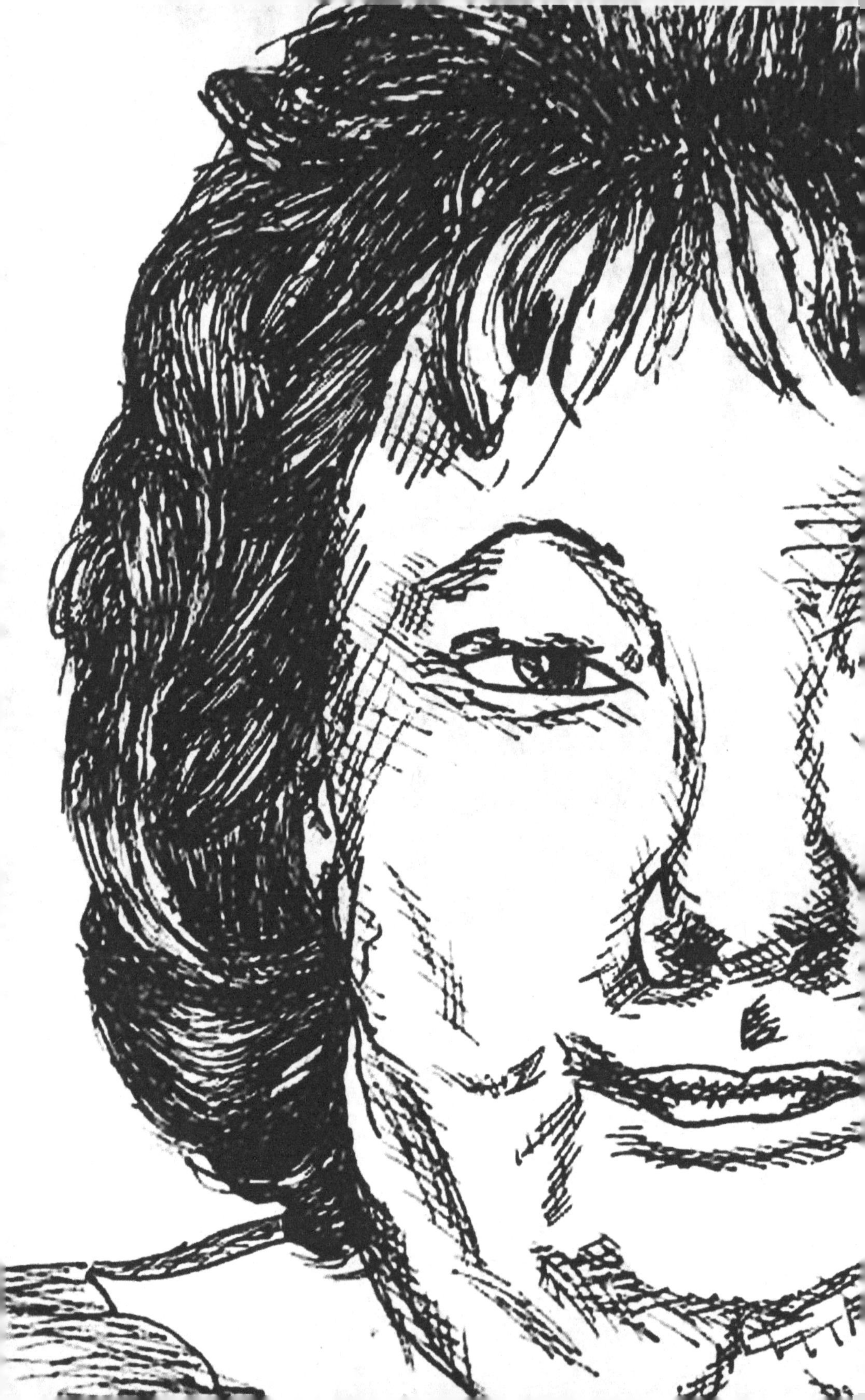

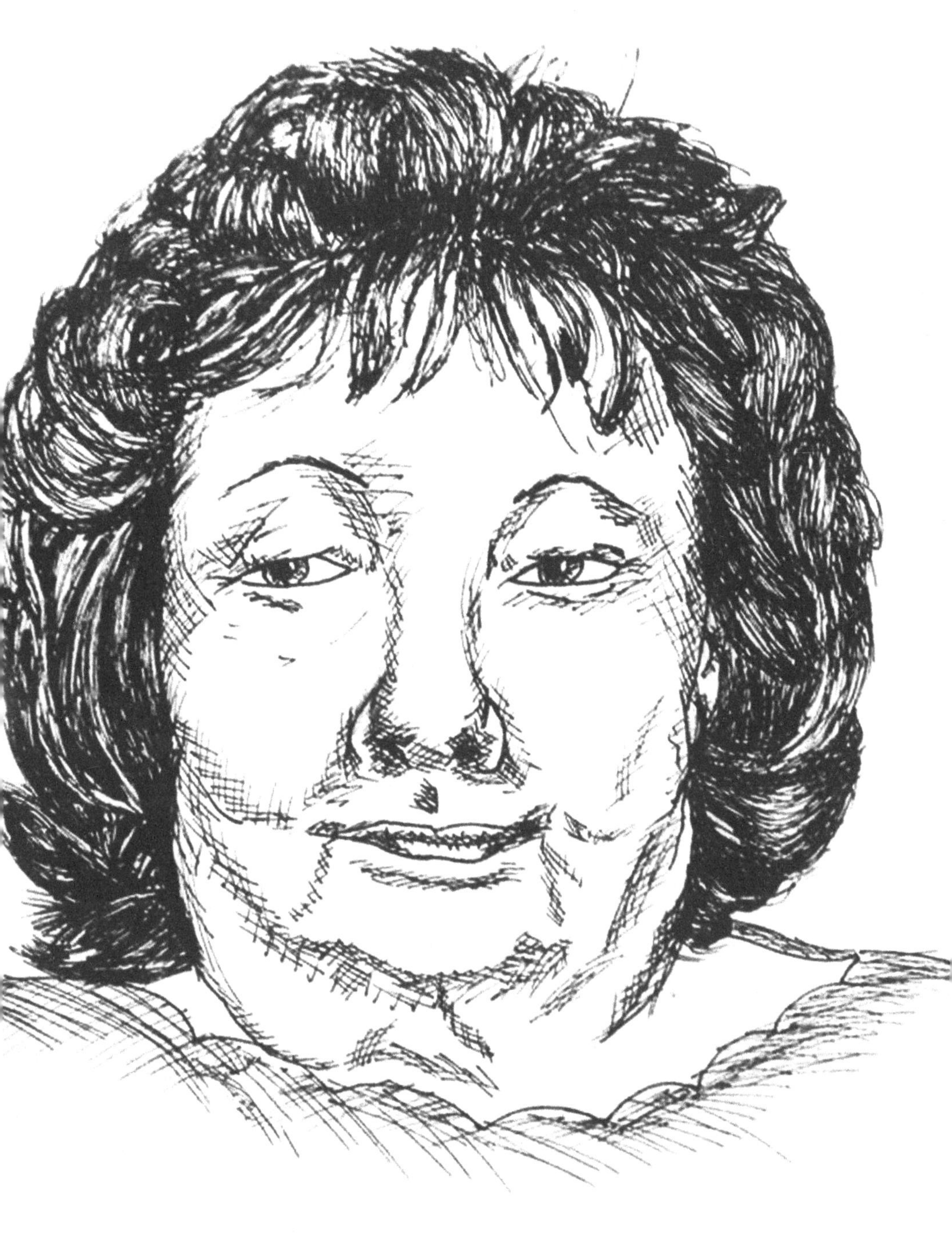

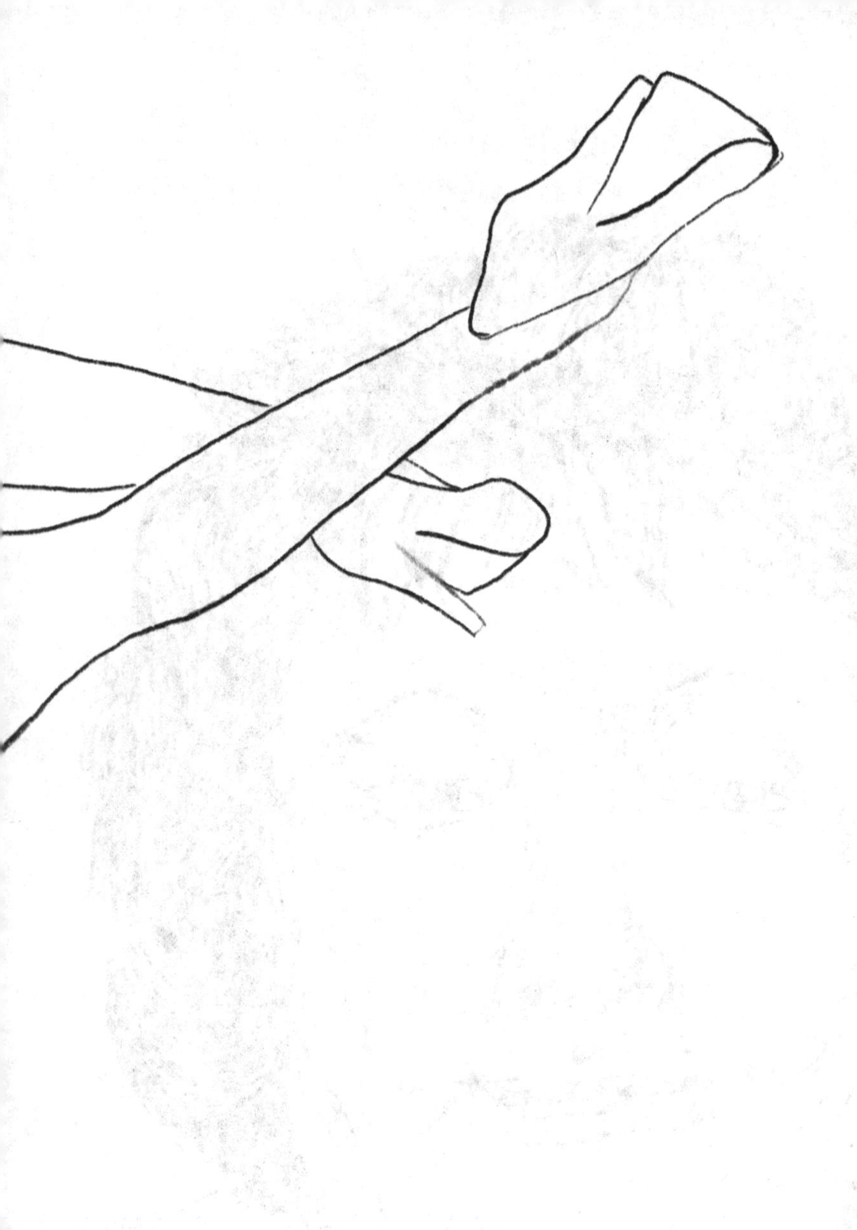

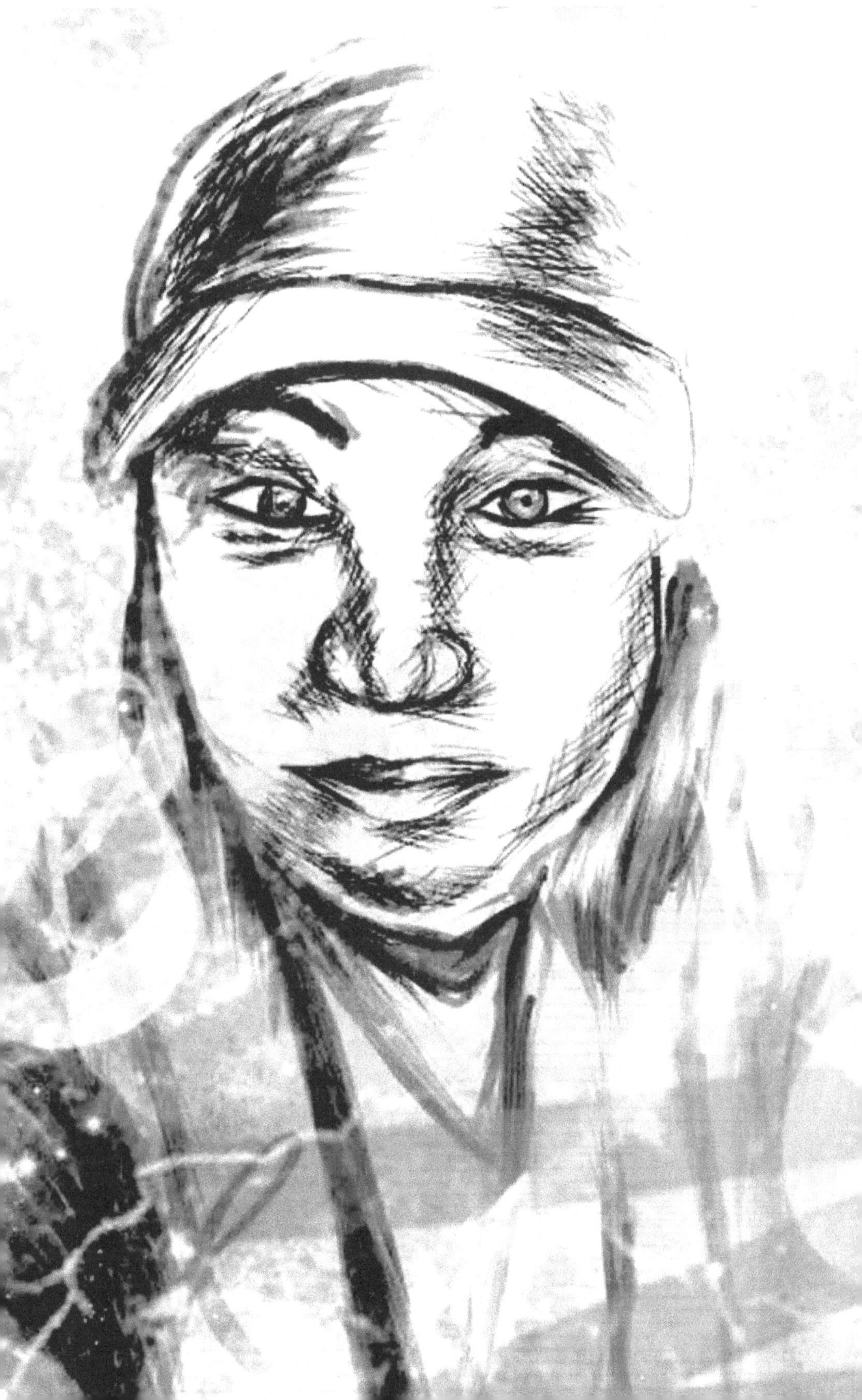

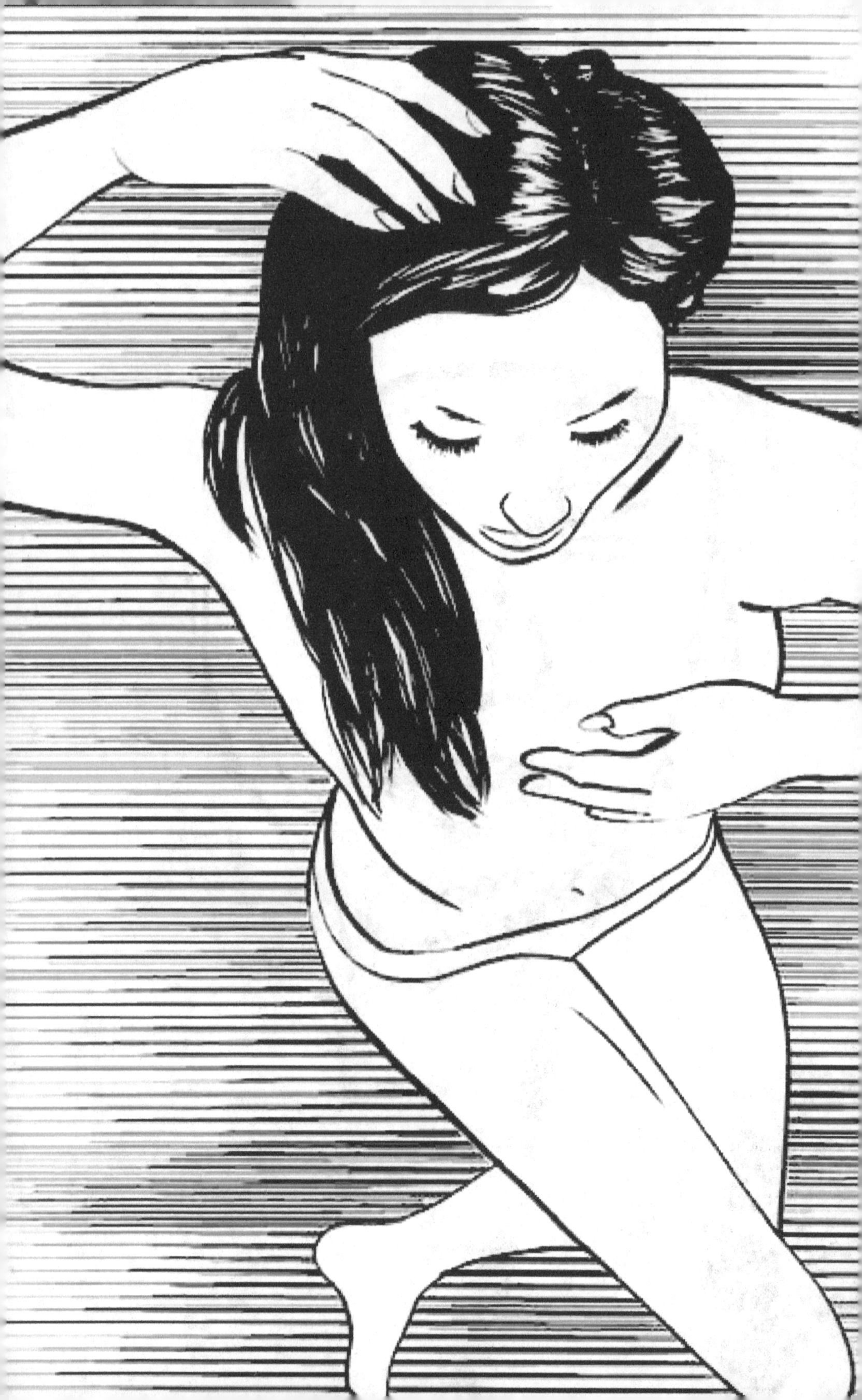

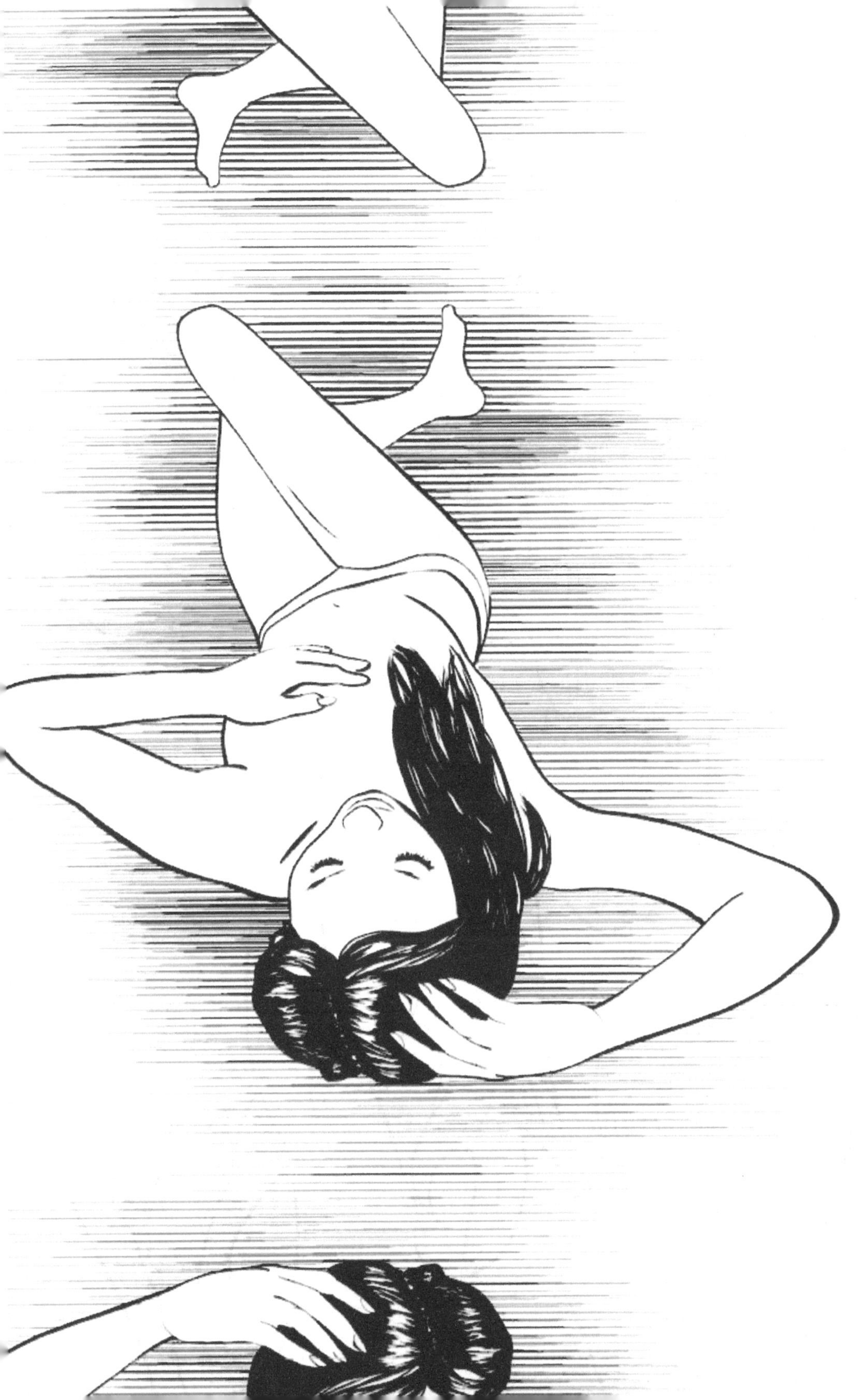

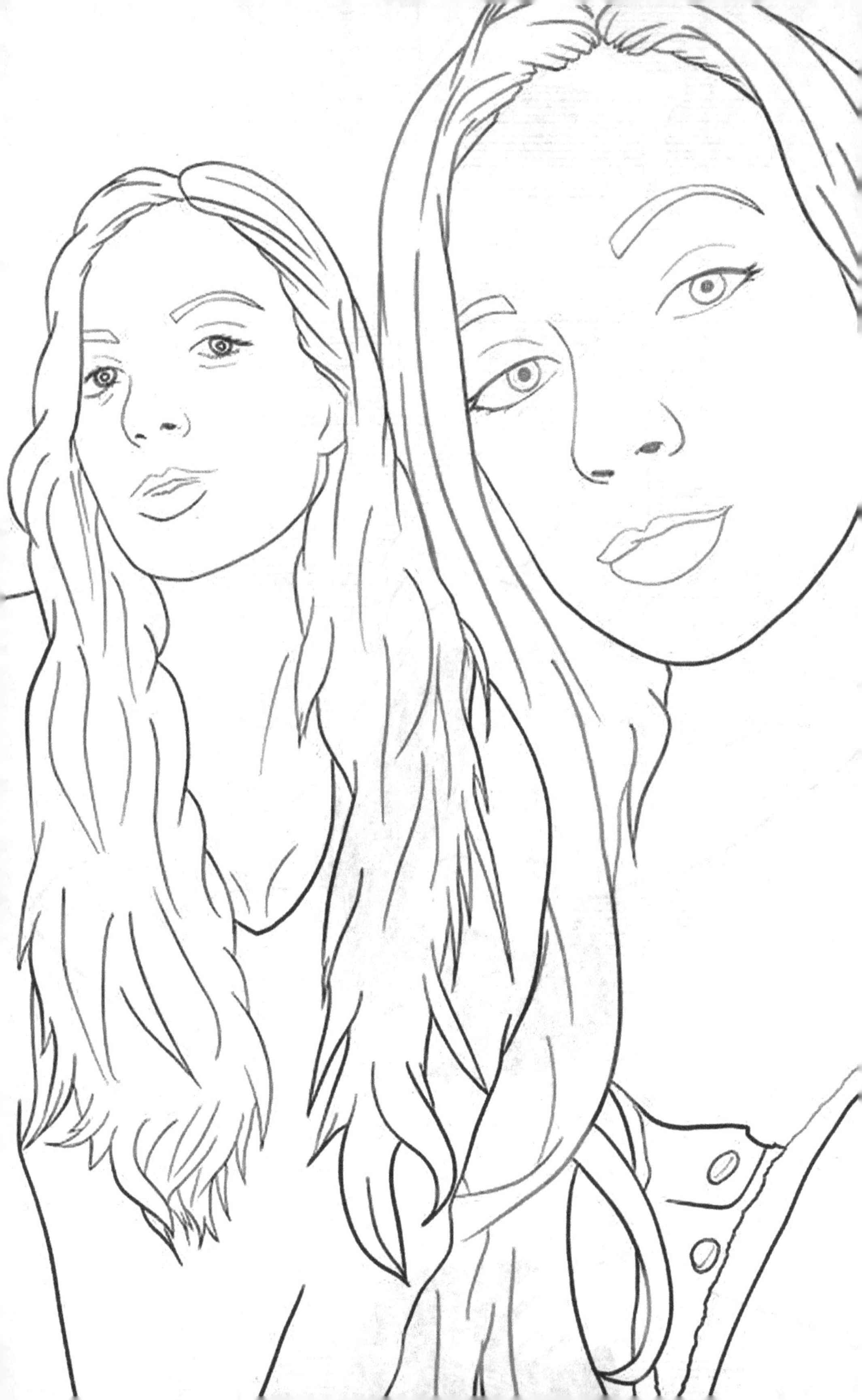

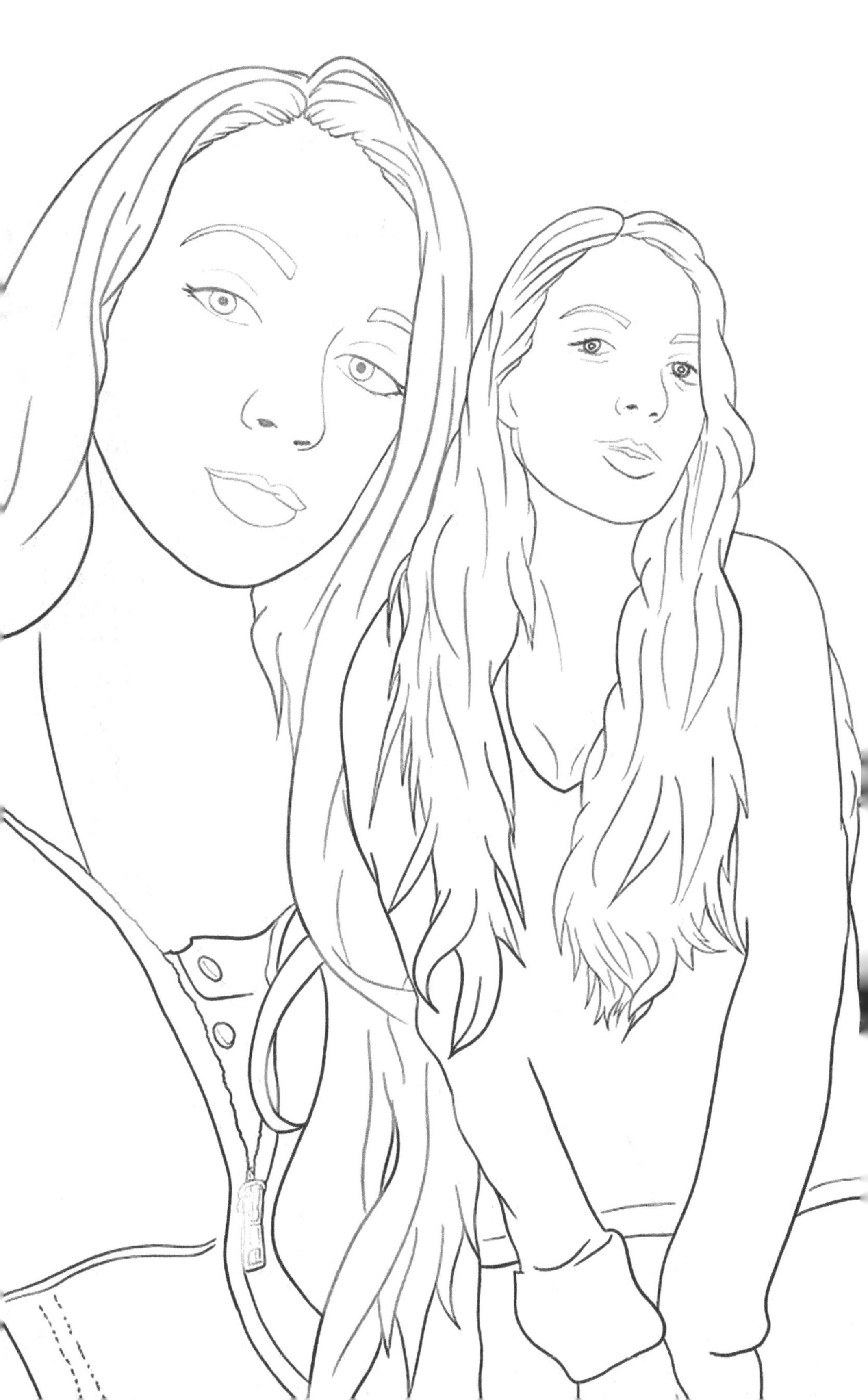

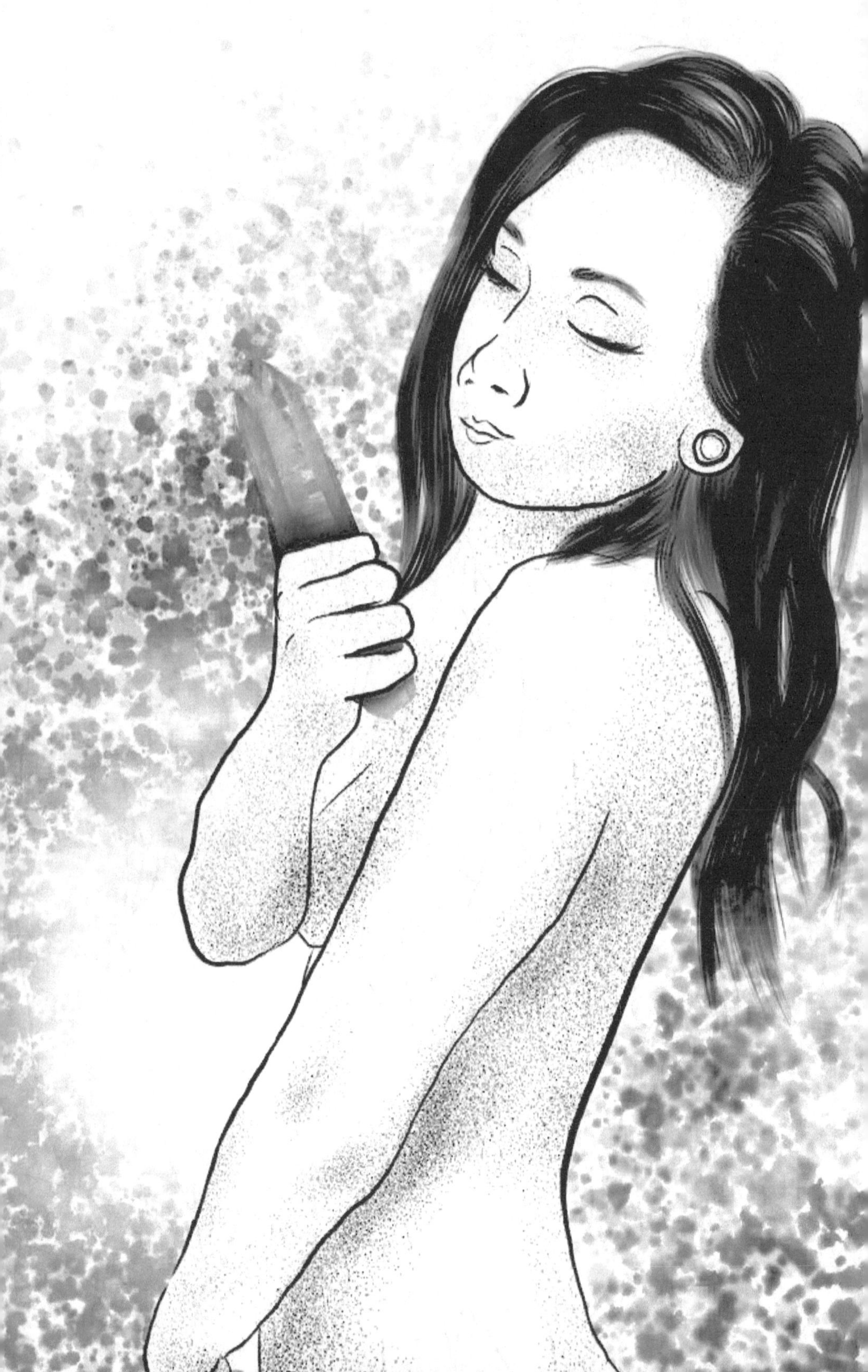

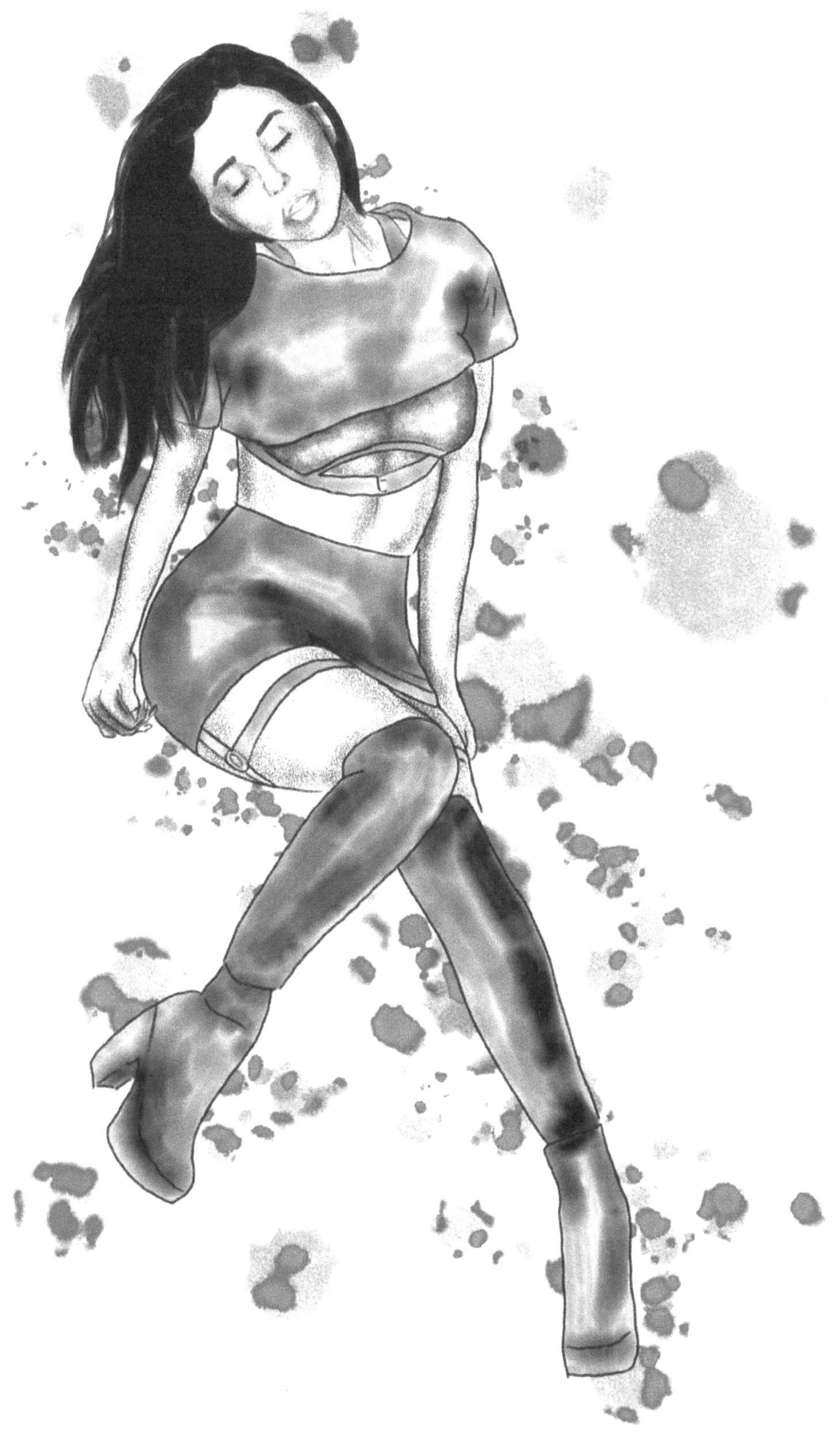

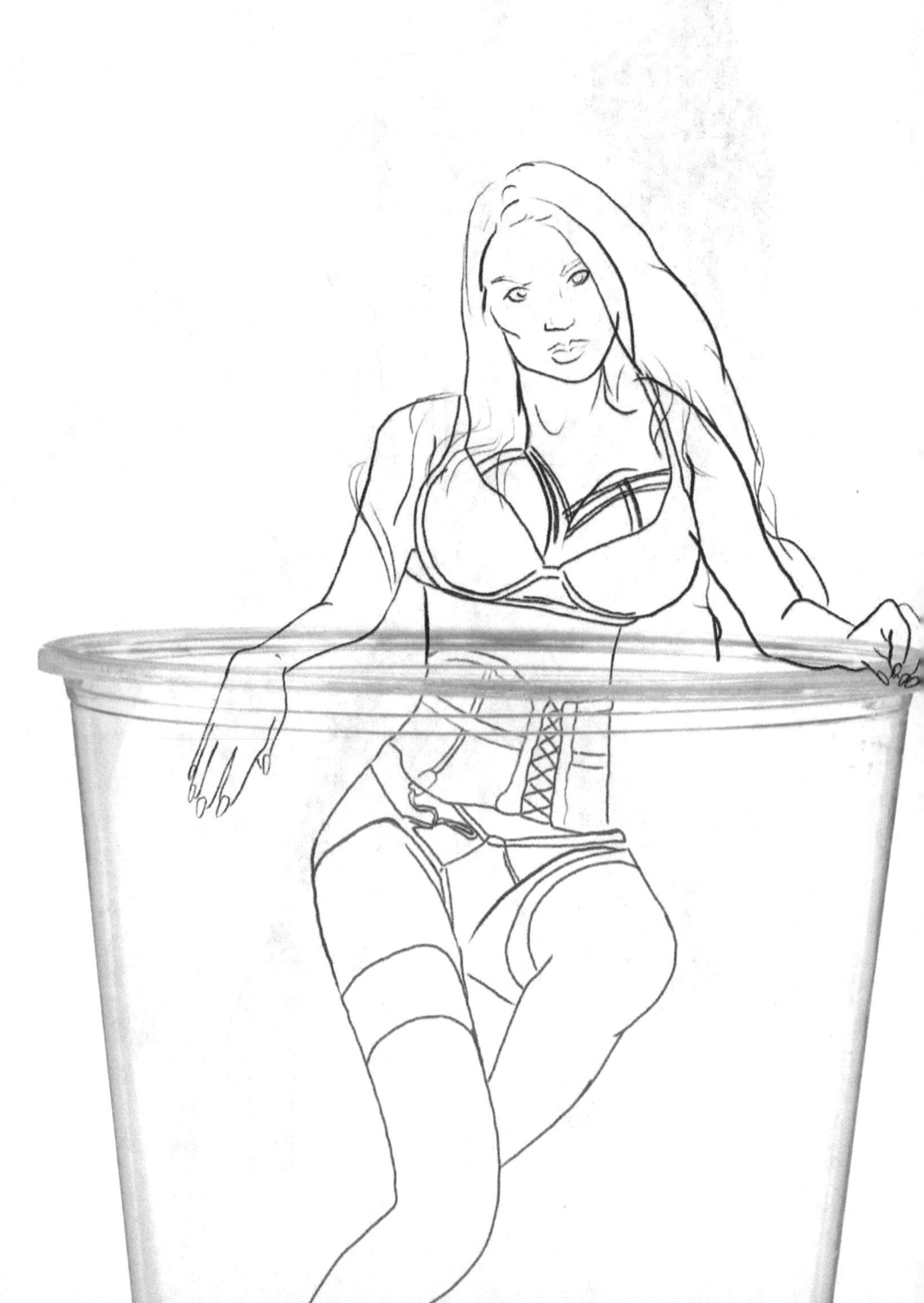

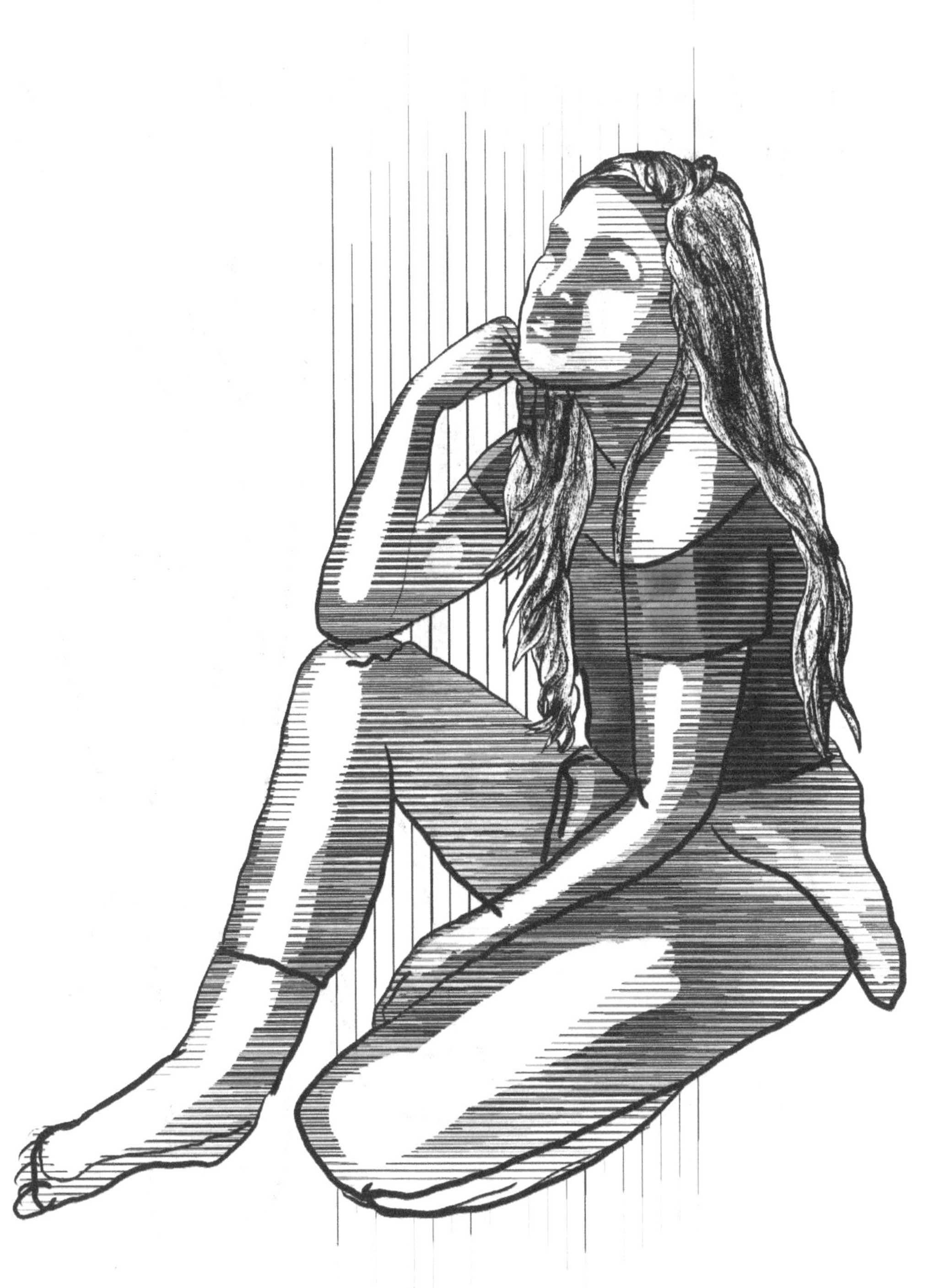

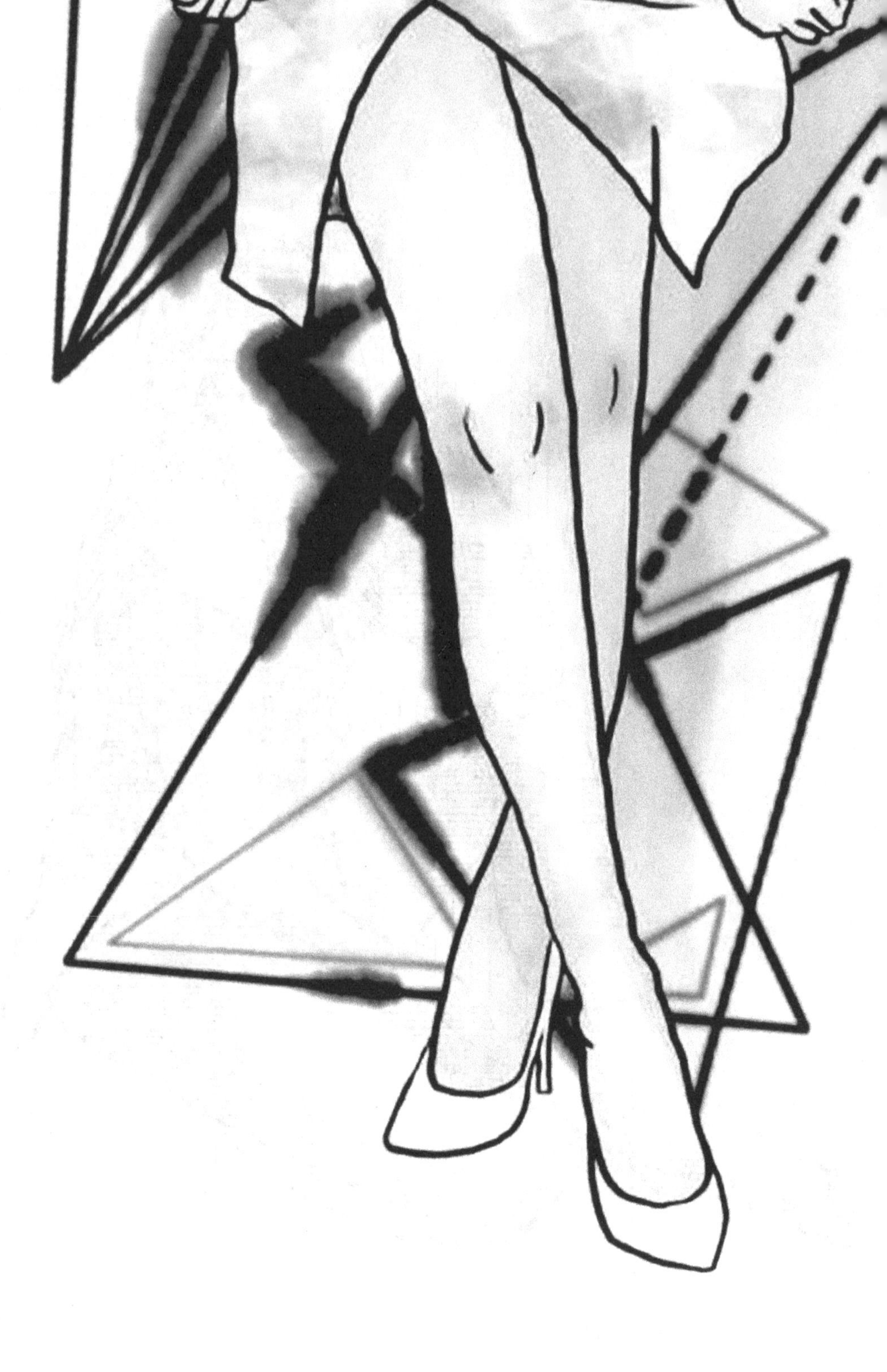

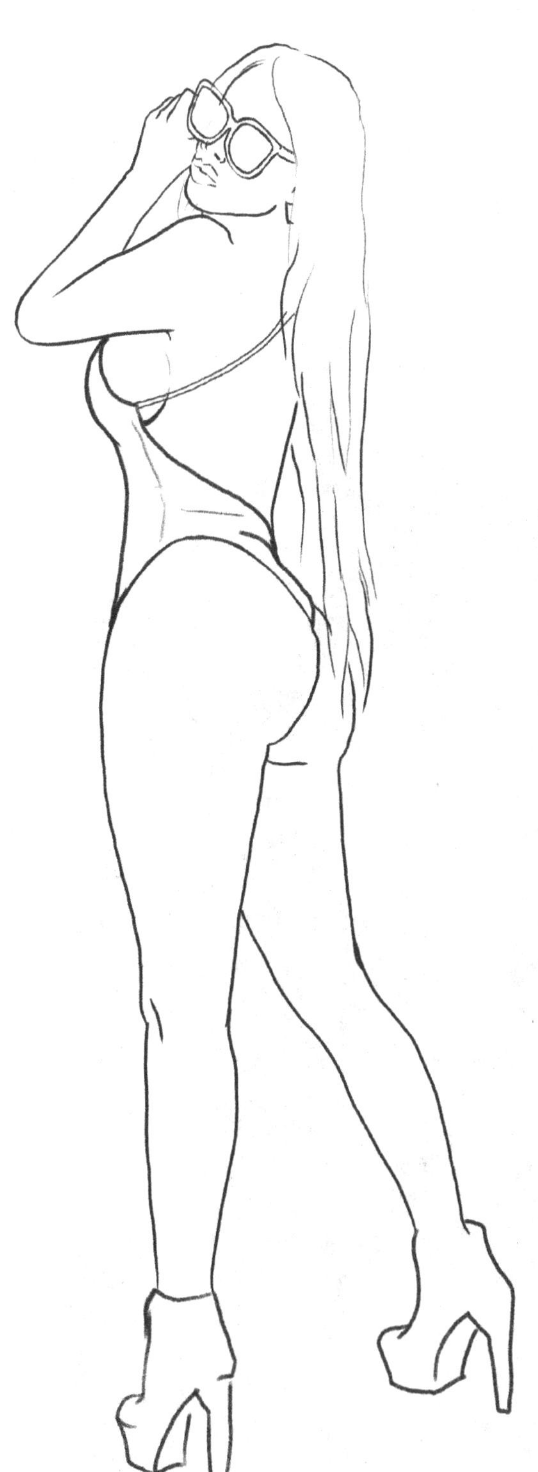

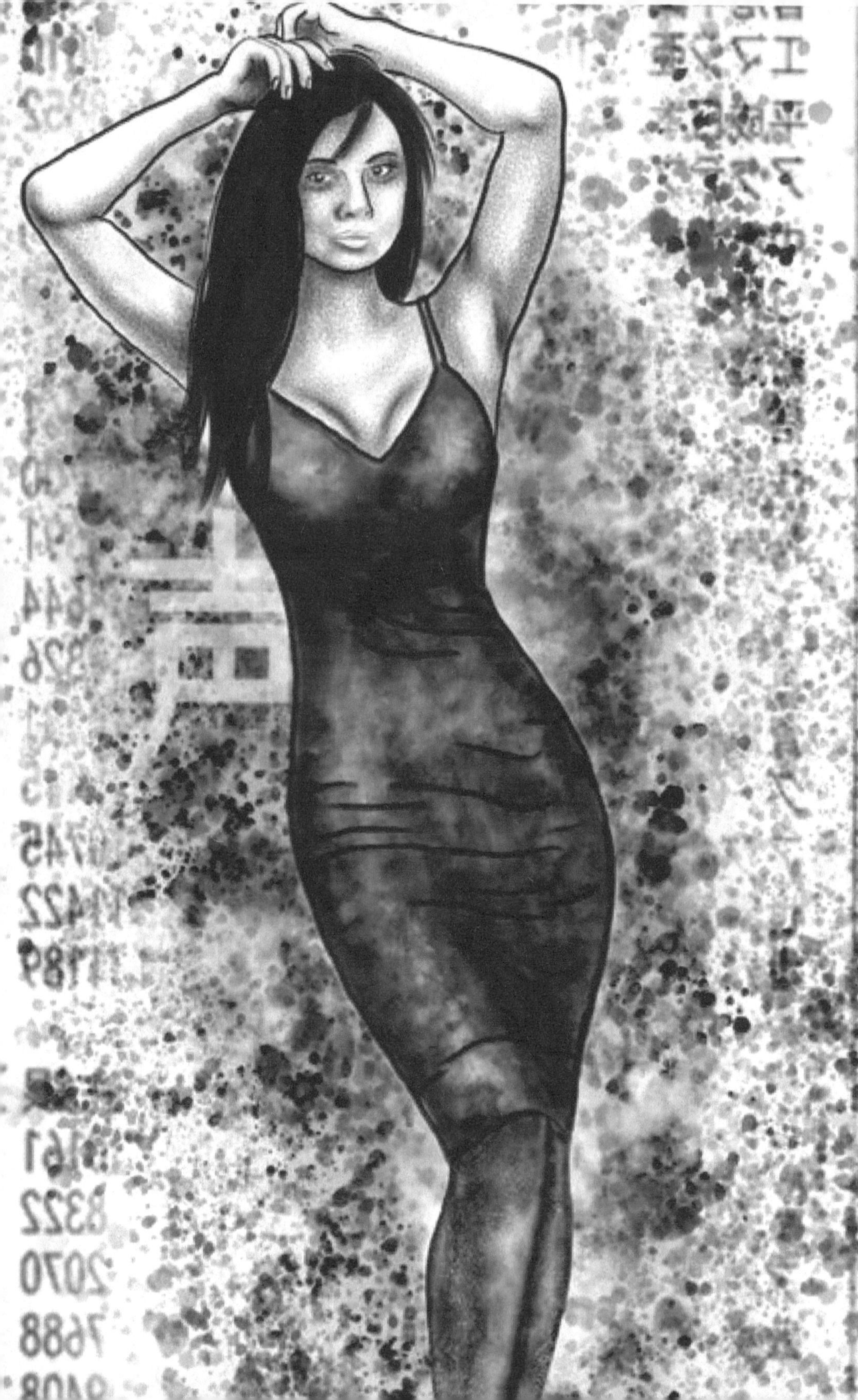

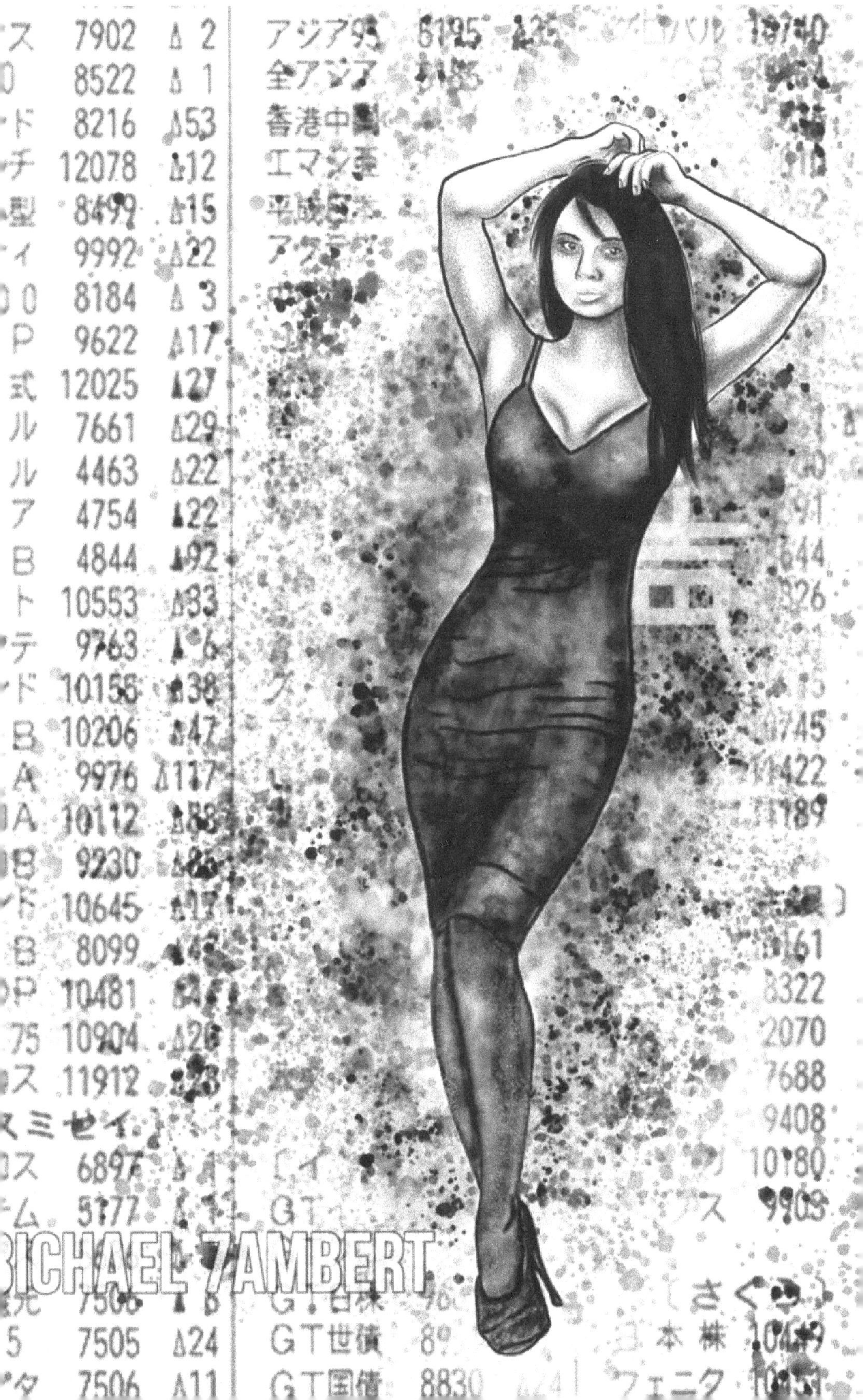

ス	7902	△ 2	アジア95	6195	
○	8522	△ 1	全アジア		
ド	8216	△53	香港中国		
チ	12078	△12	エマン東		
型	8499	△15	平成		
イ	9992	△22	アフ		
○○	8184	△ 3			
Ｐ	9622	△17			
式	12025	△27			
ル	7661	△29			
ル	4463	△22			
ア	4754	△22			
Ｂ	4844	△92			
ト	10553	△33			
テ	9763	△ 6			
ド	10156	△38			
Ｂ	10206	△47			
Ａ	9976	△117			
Ａ	10112	△88			
Ｂ	9230	△22			
ド	10645	△17			
Ｂ	8099				
Ｐ	10481				
75	10904	△20			
ス	11912	△23			
スミセイ					
コス	6897		イ		10180
ム	5177		ＧＴ		ス 9909
元	7506	△ 6	ＧＴ日株		さく
5	7505	△24	ＧＴ世横	8	本 株
タ	7506	△11	ＧＴ国債	8830	フェニク

MICHAEL ZAMBERT

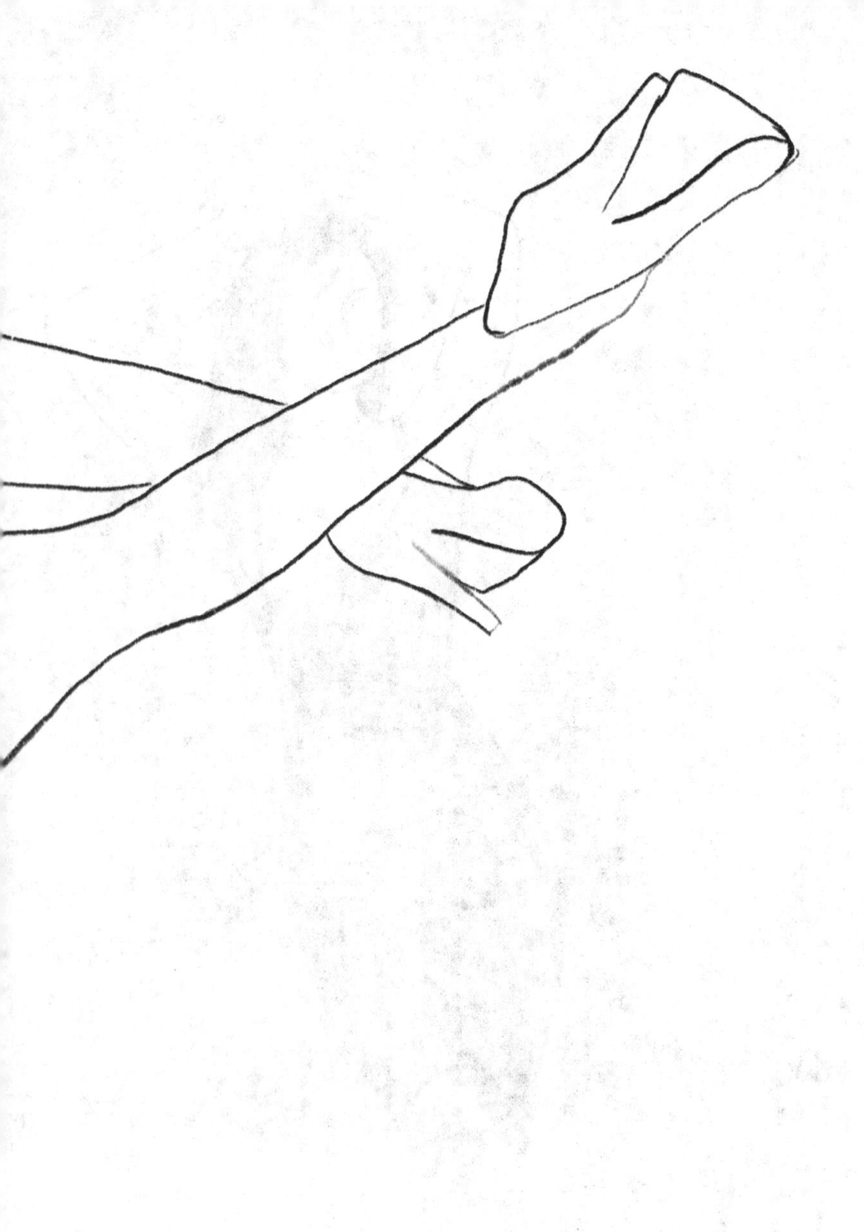

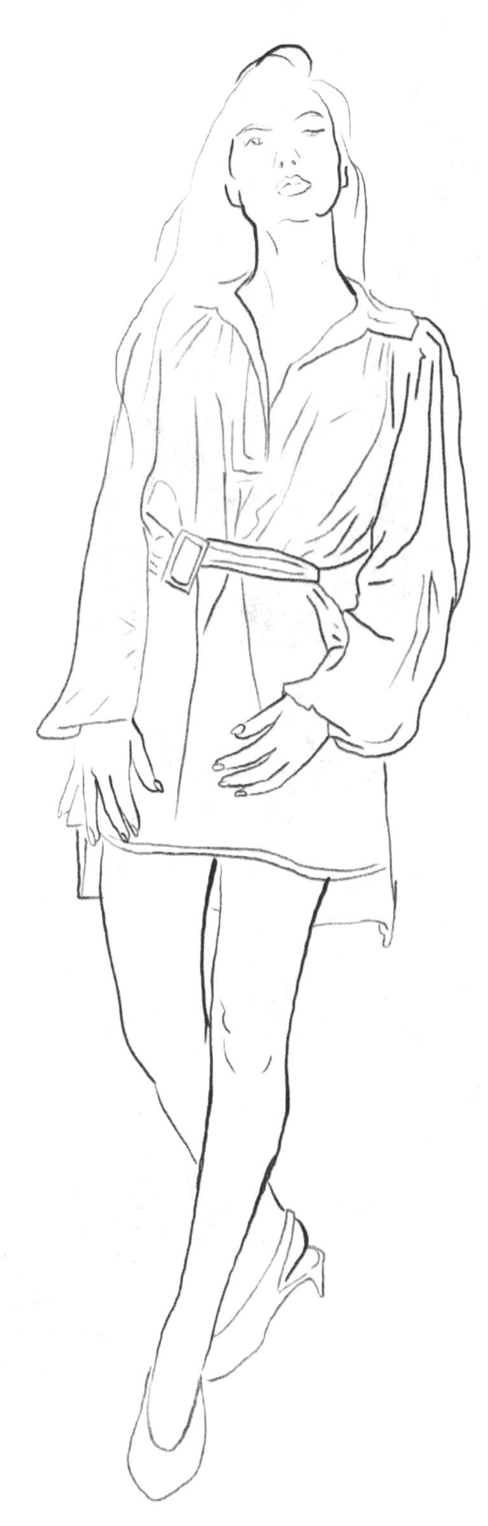

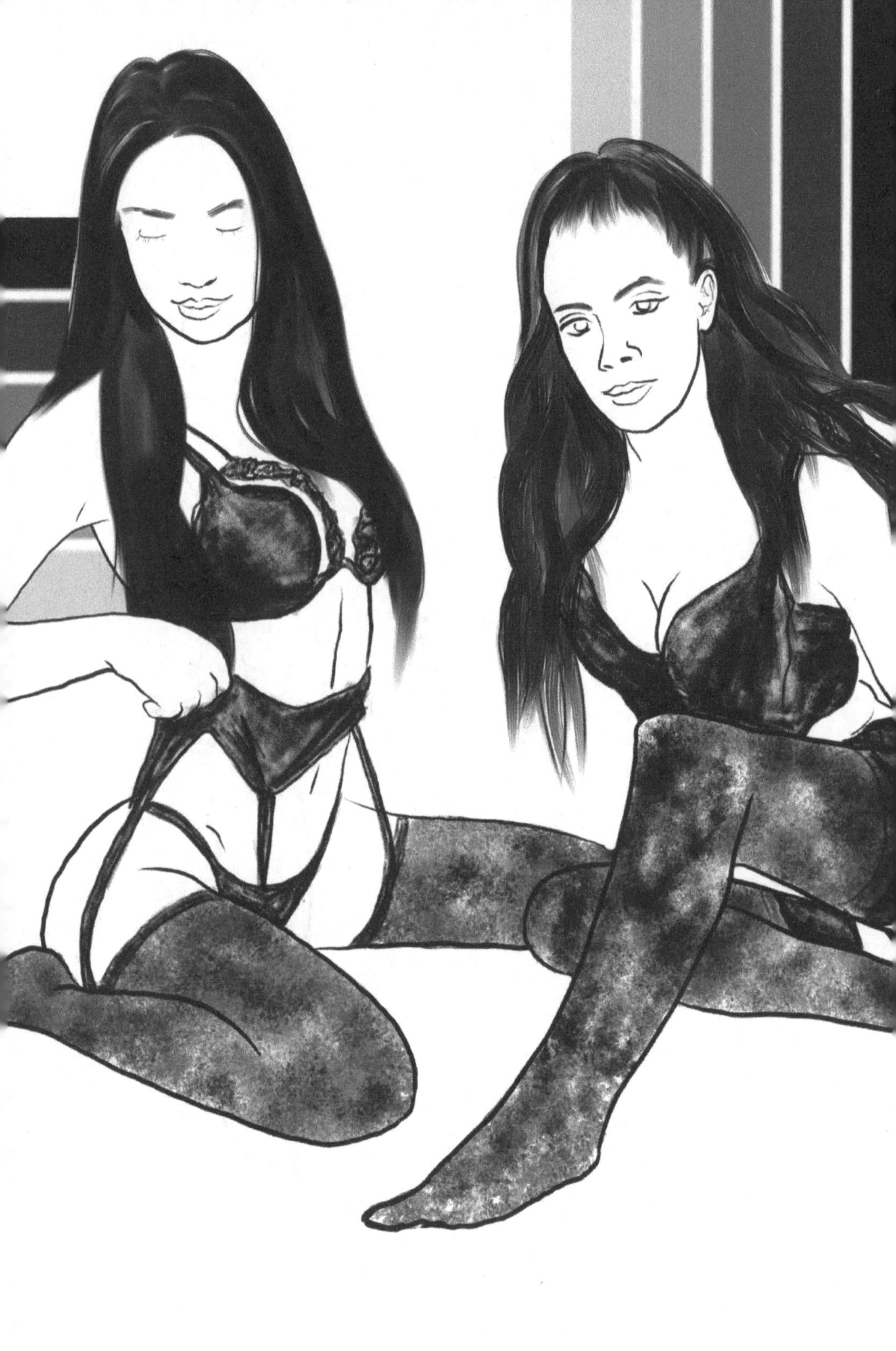

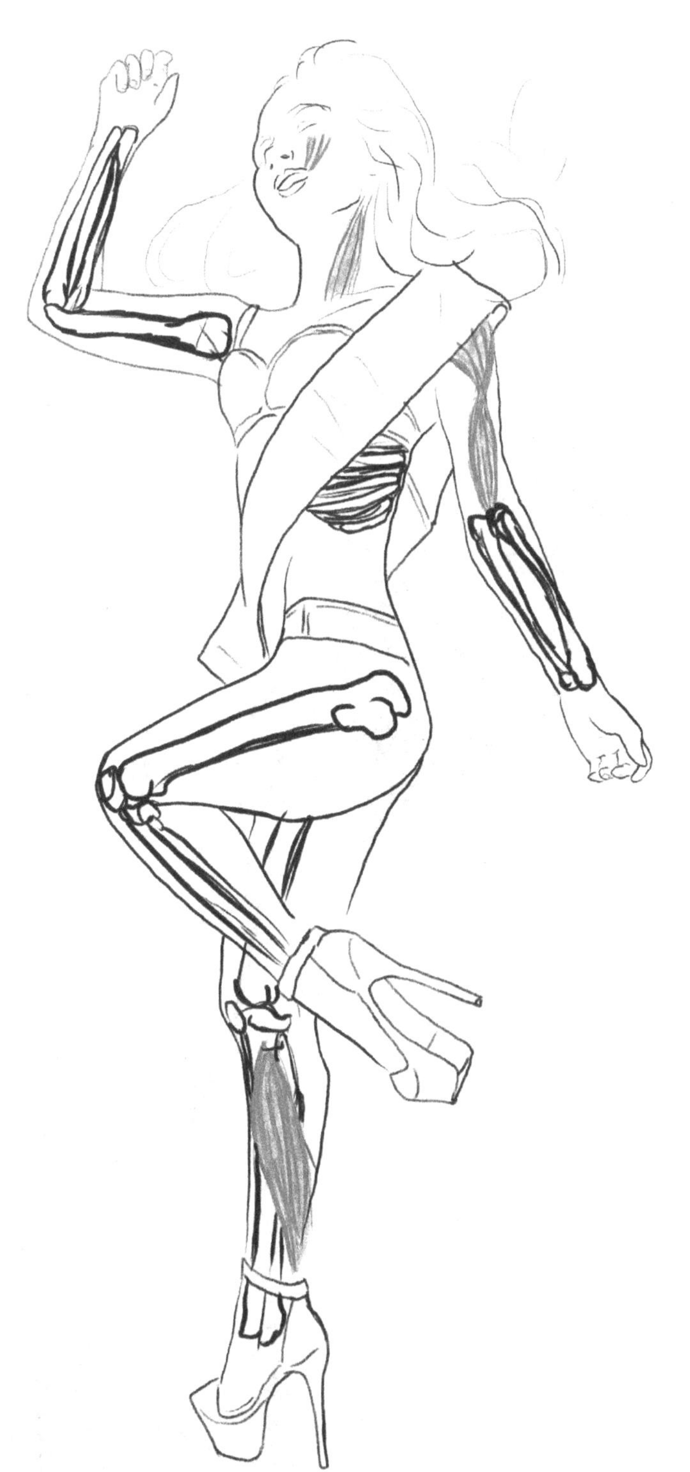

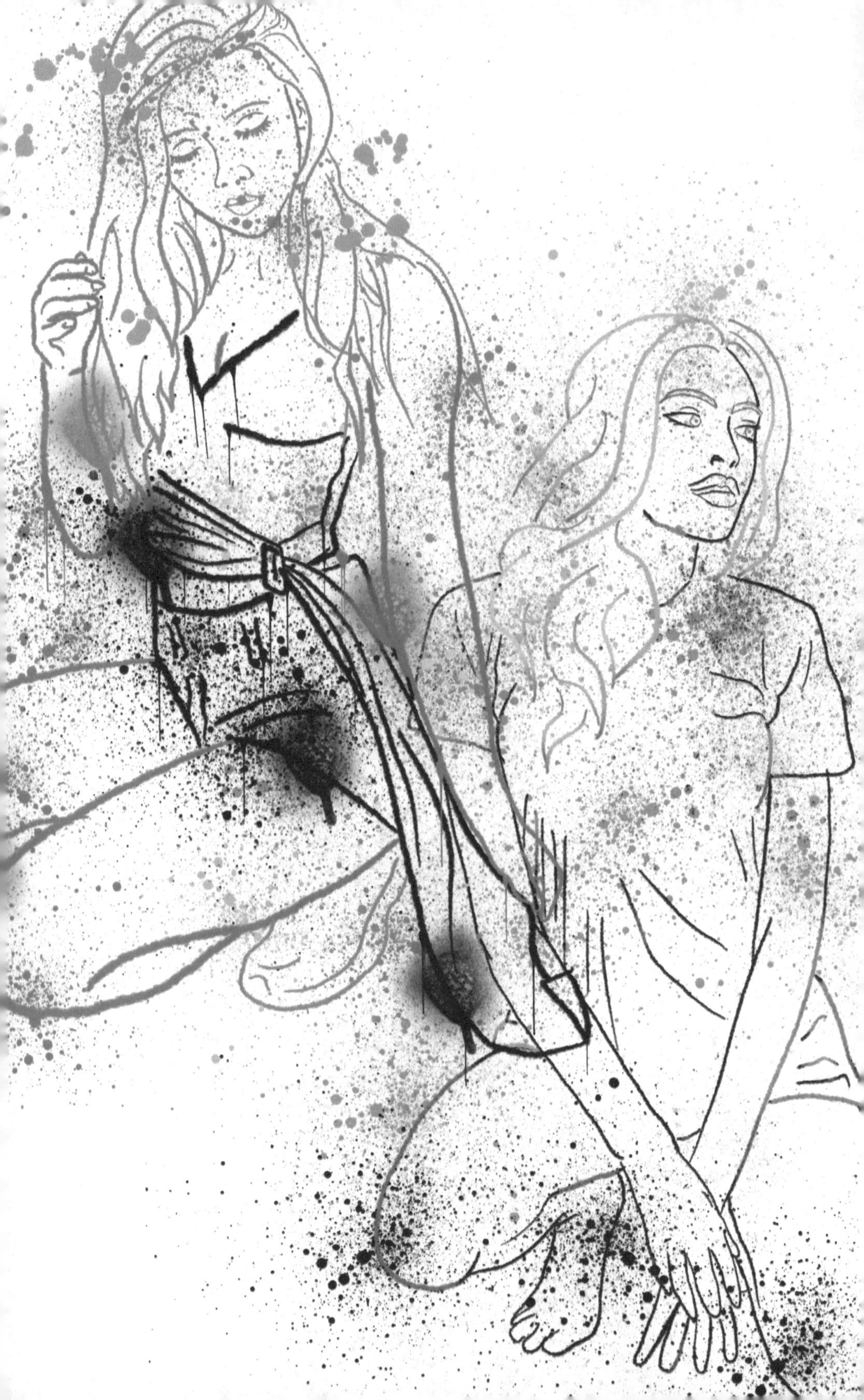

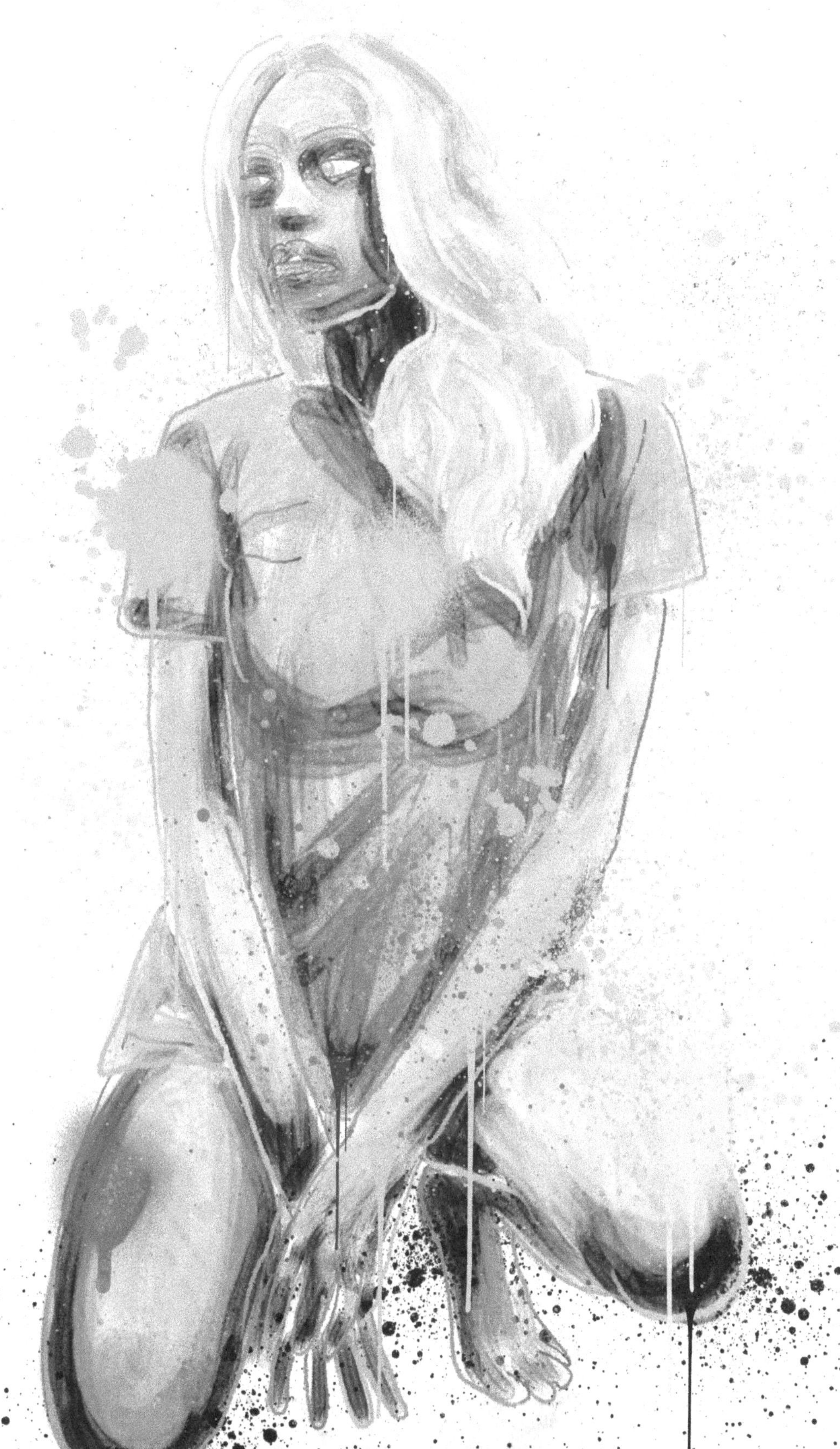

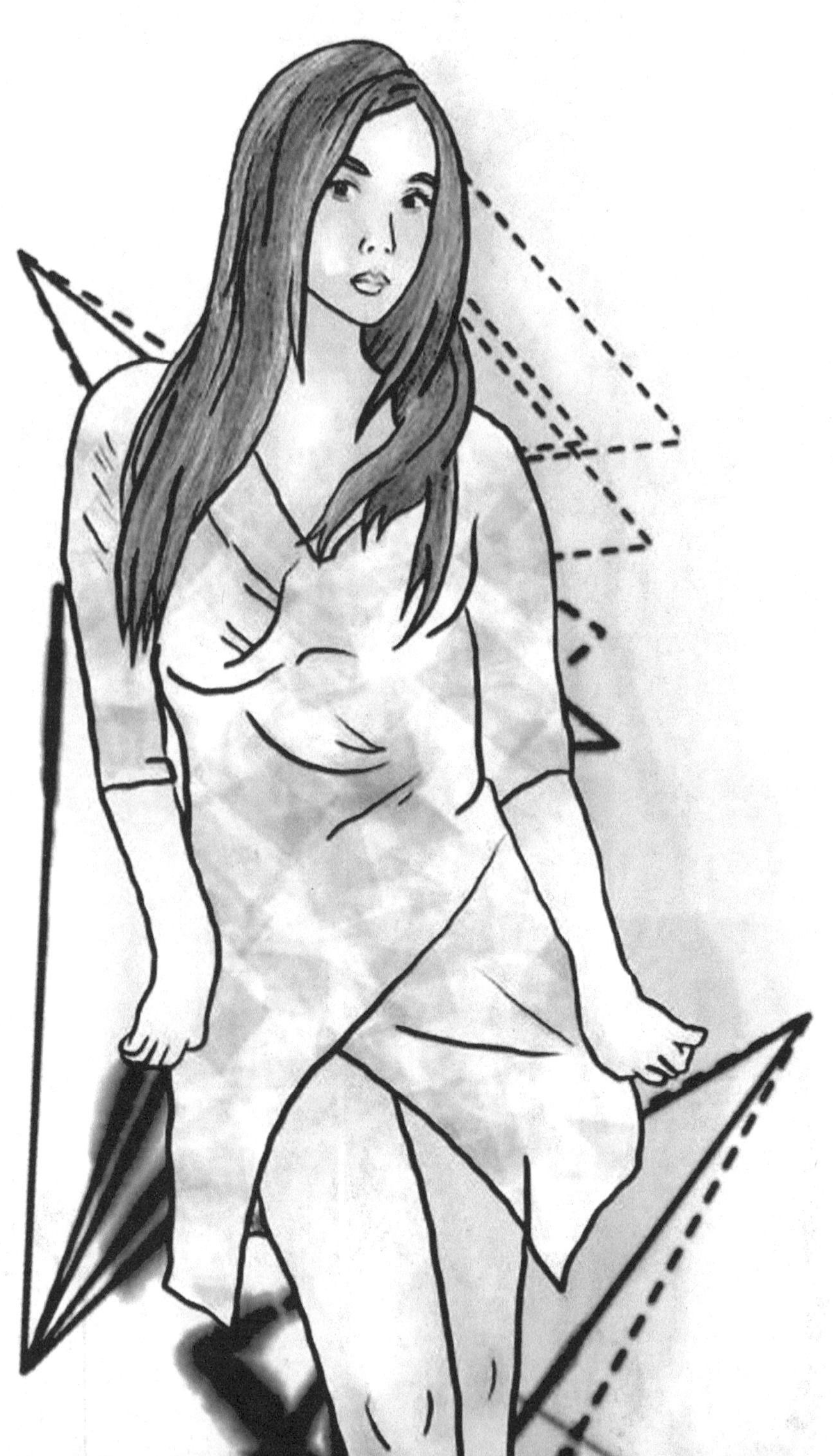

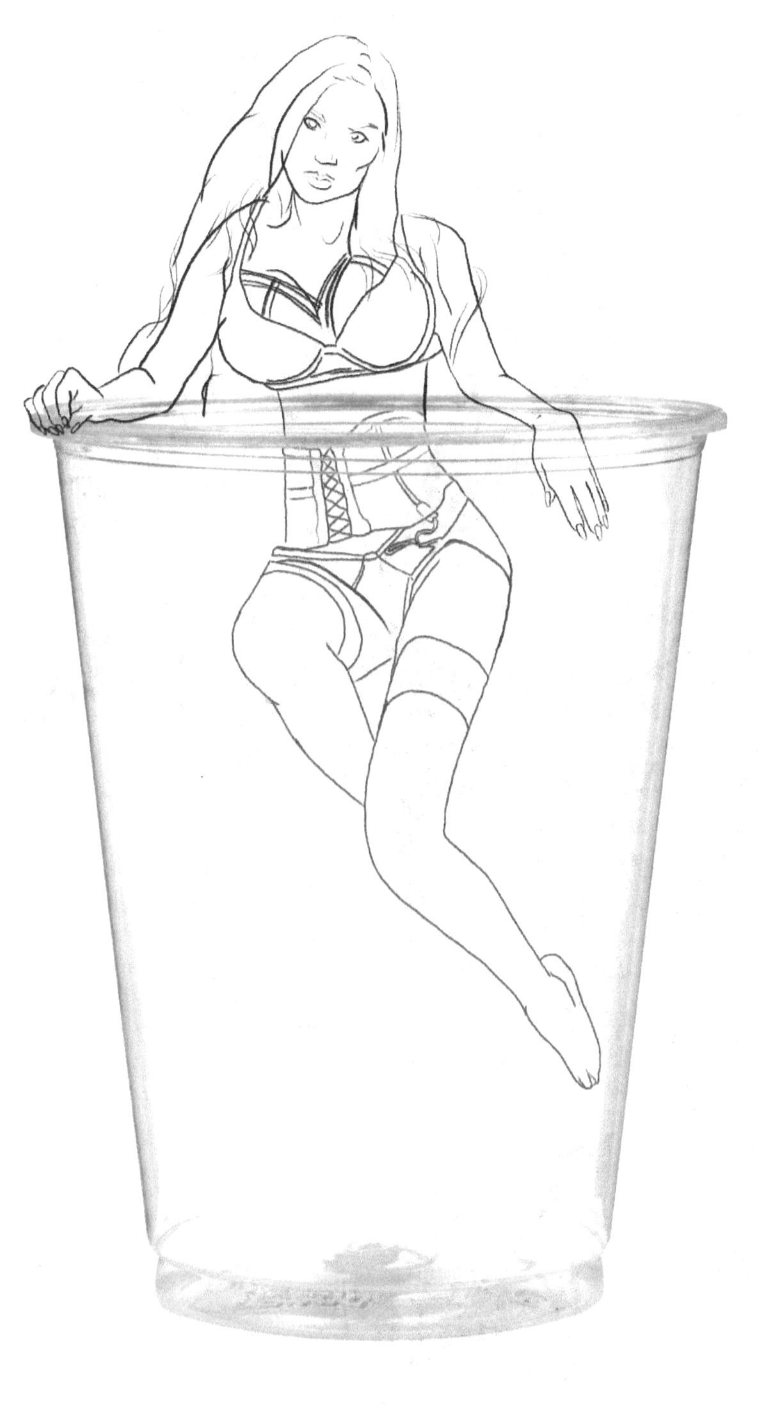

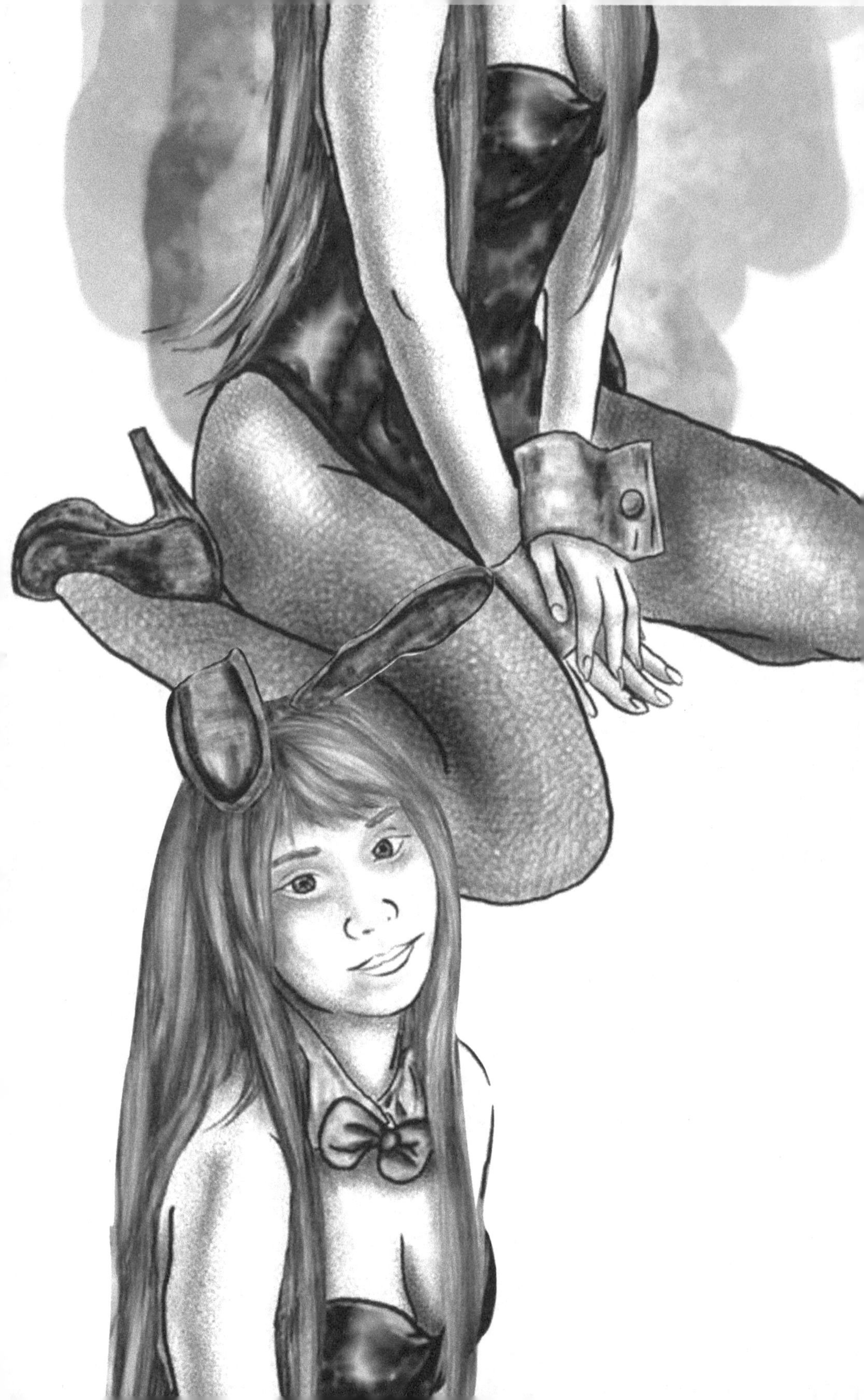

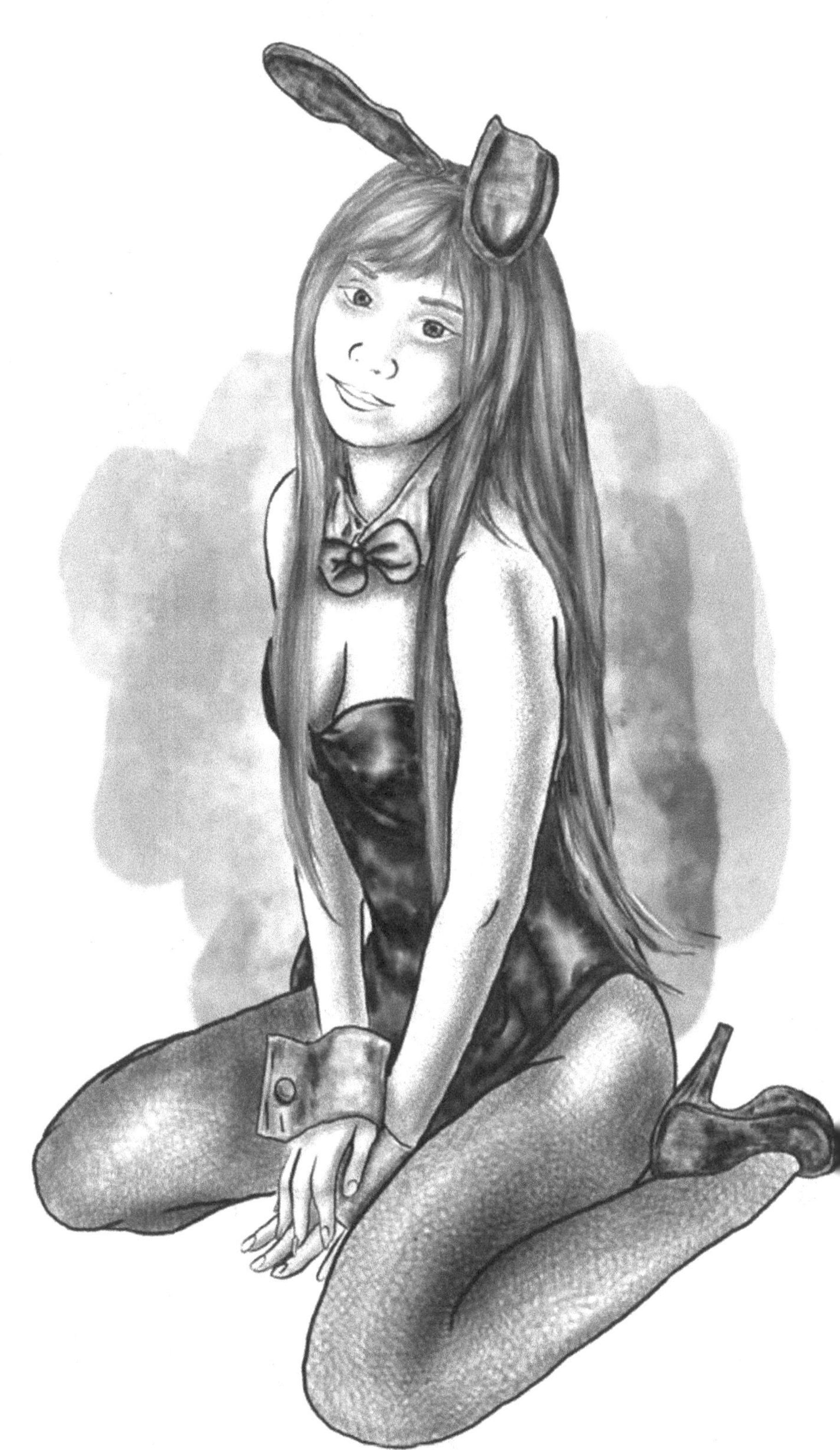

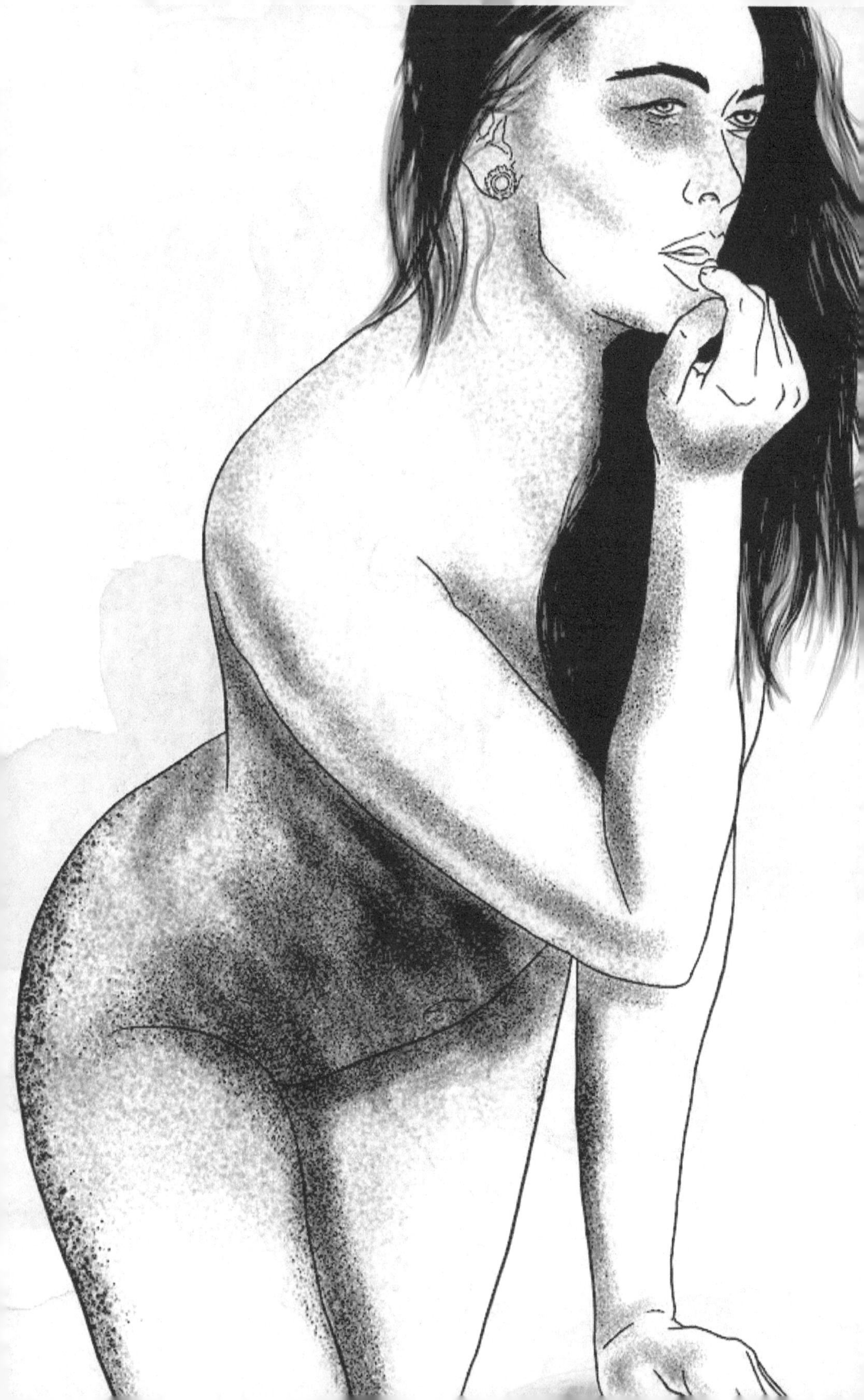

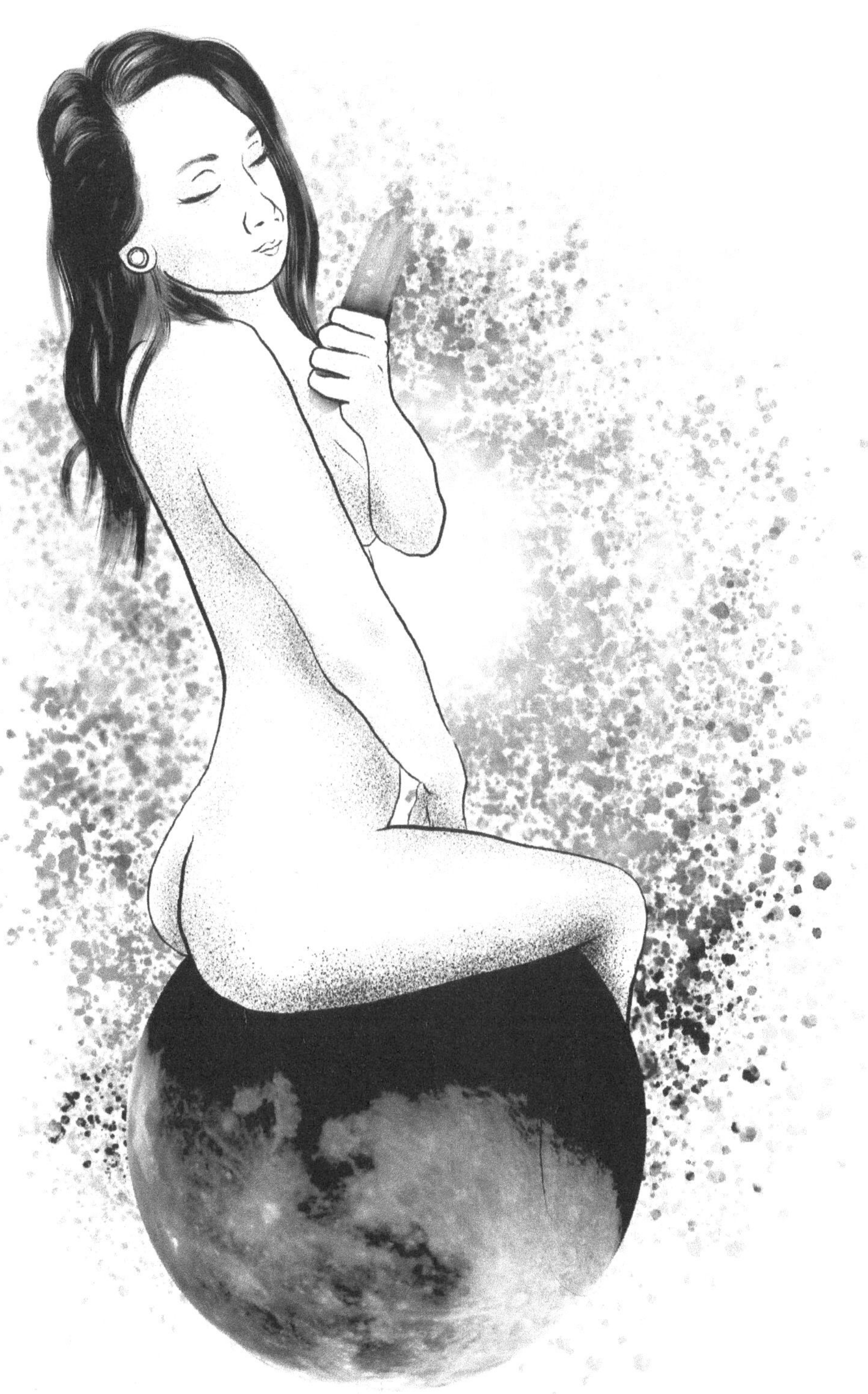

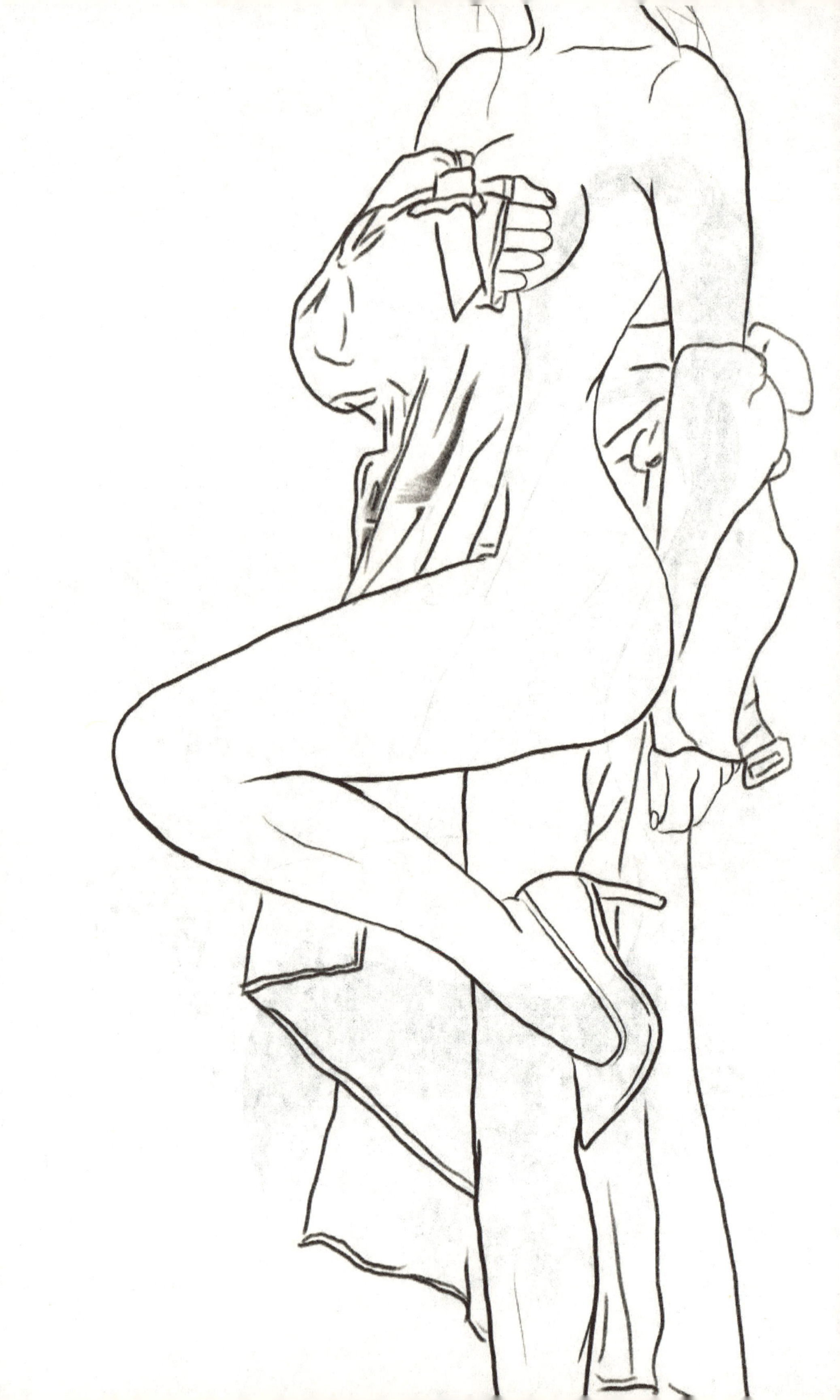

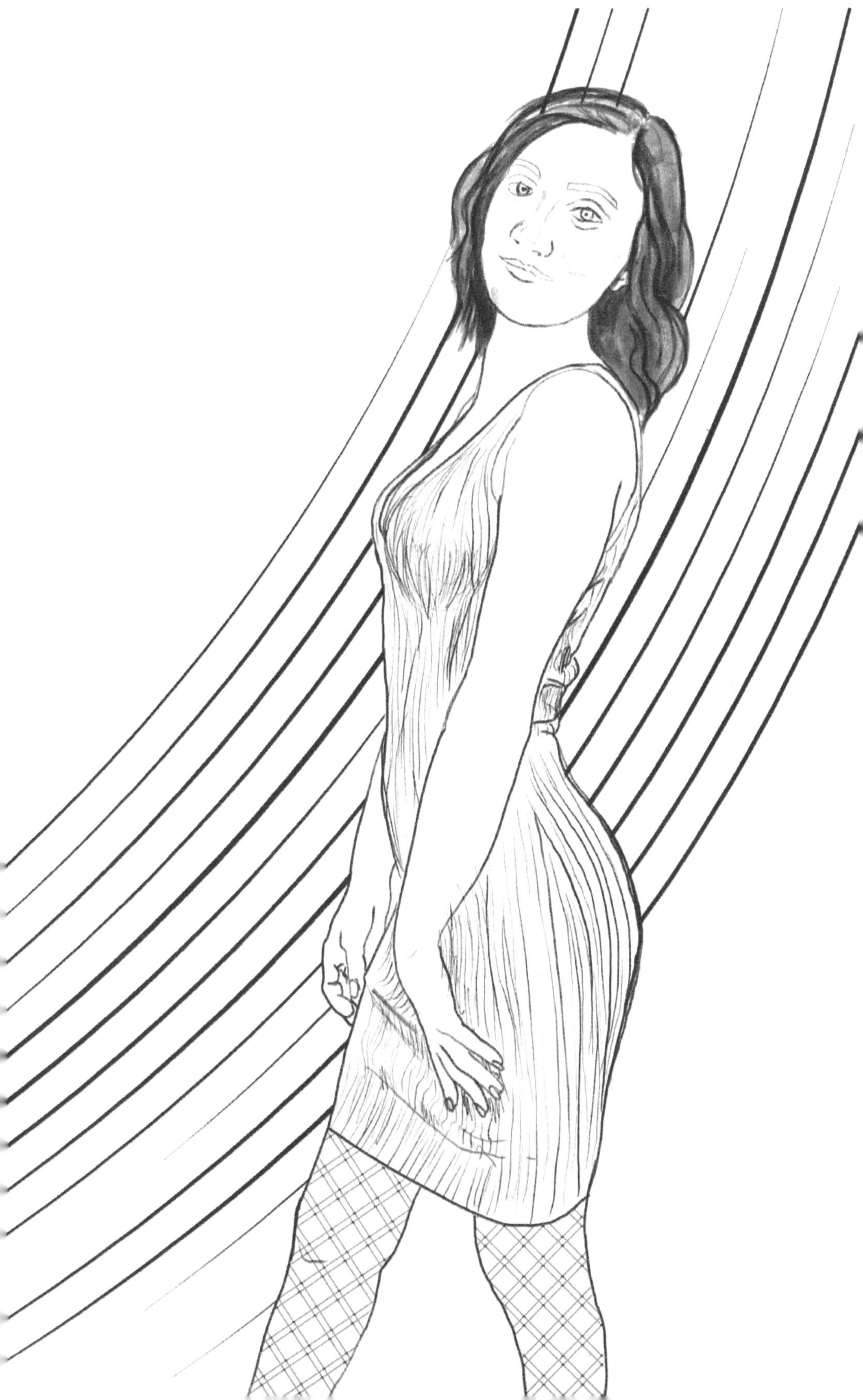

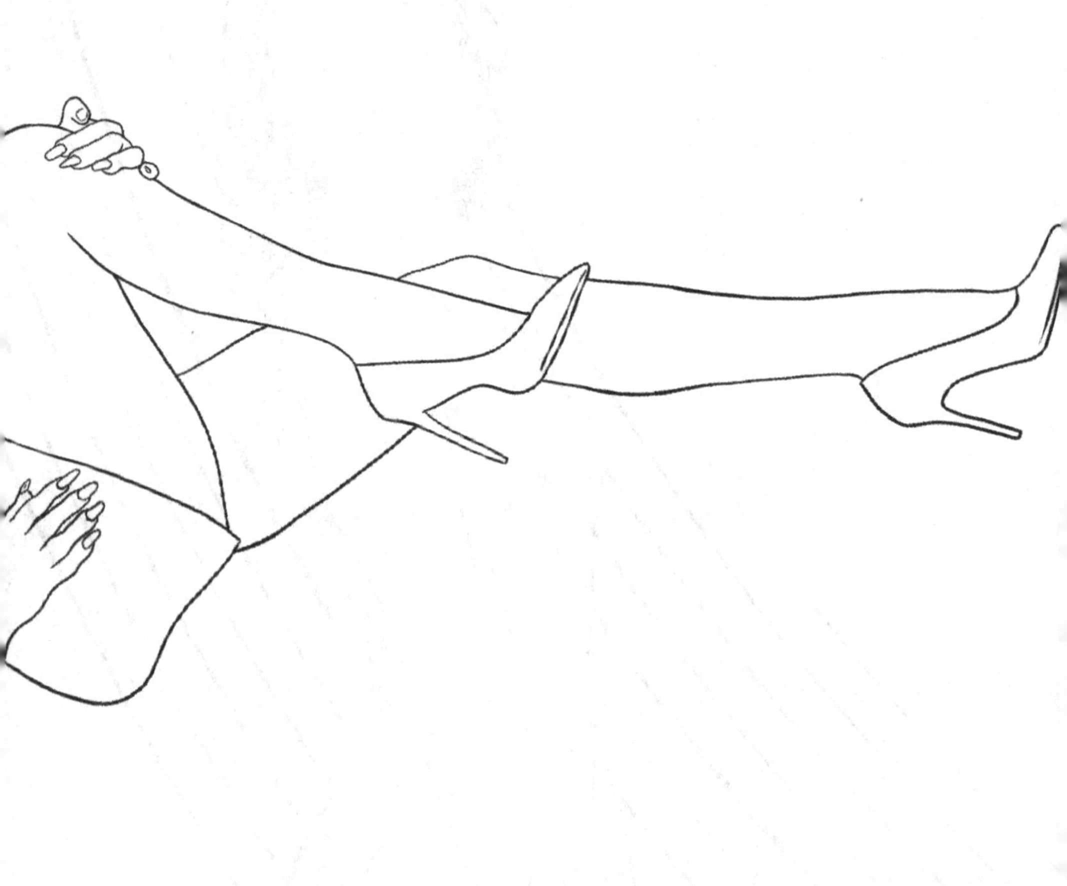

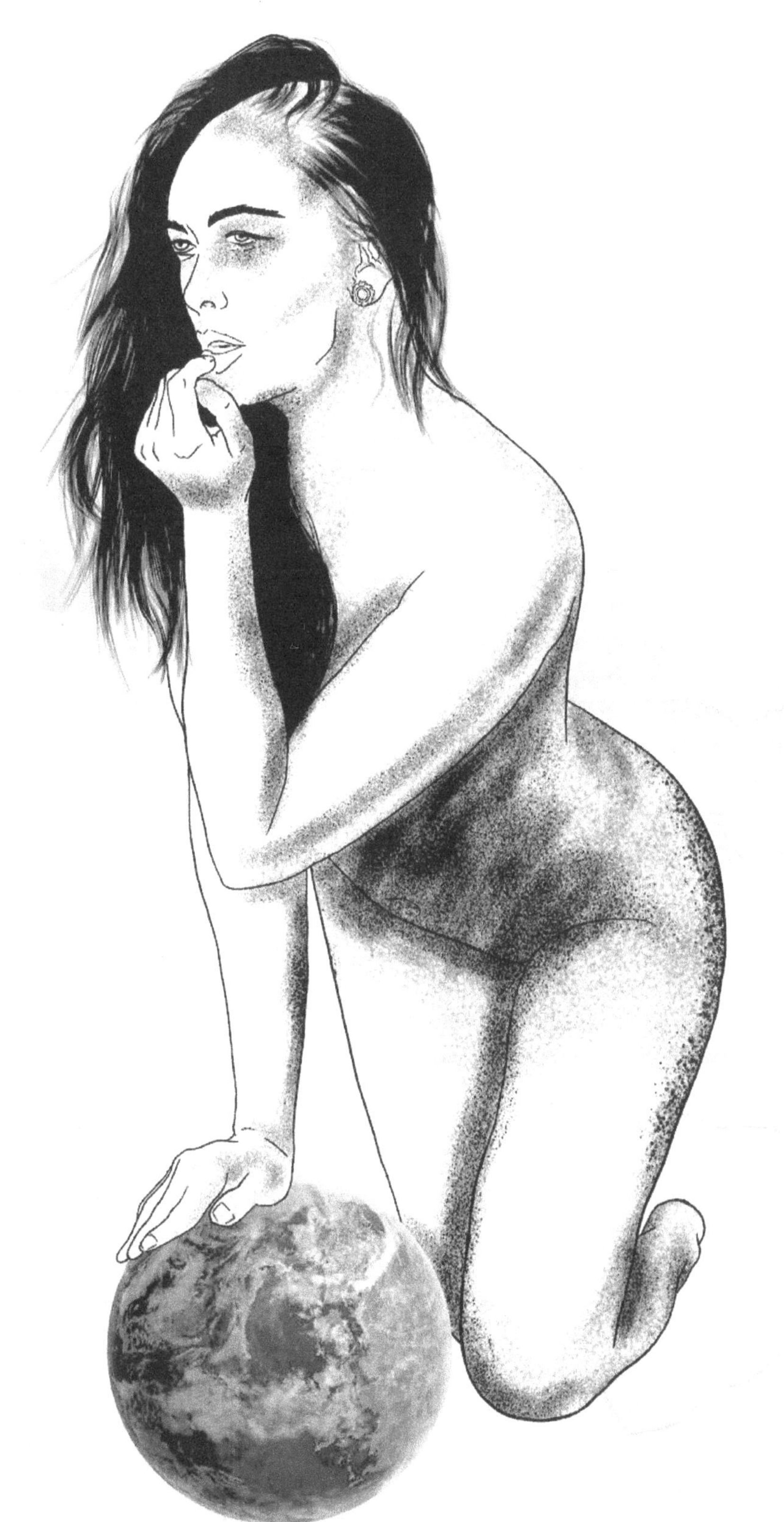

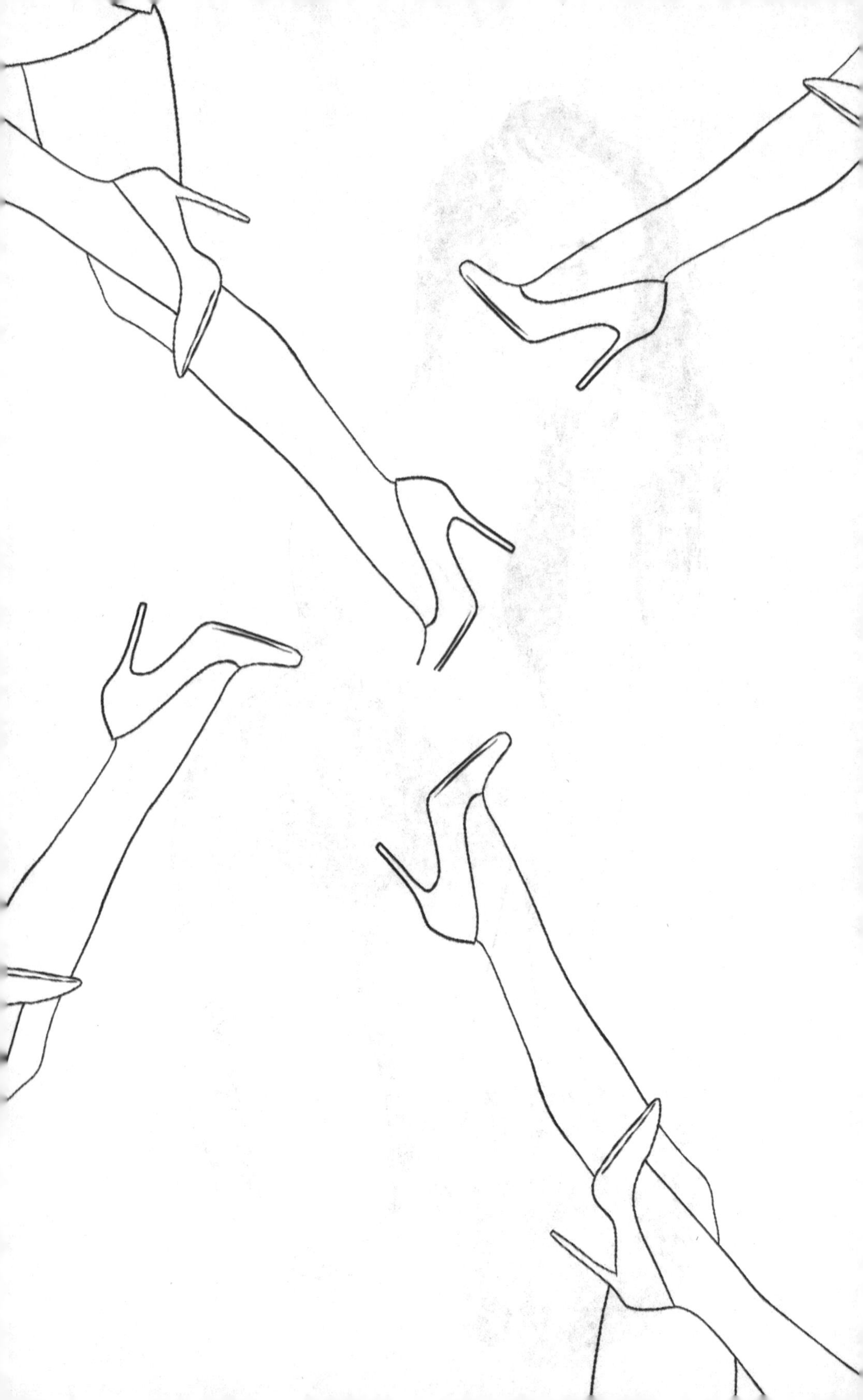

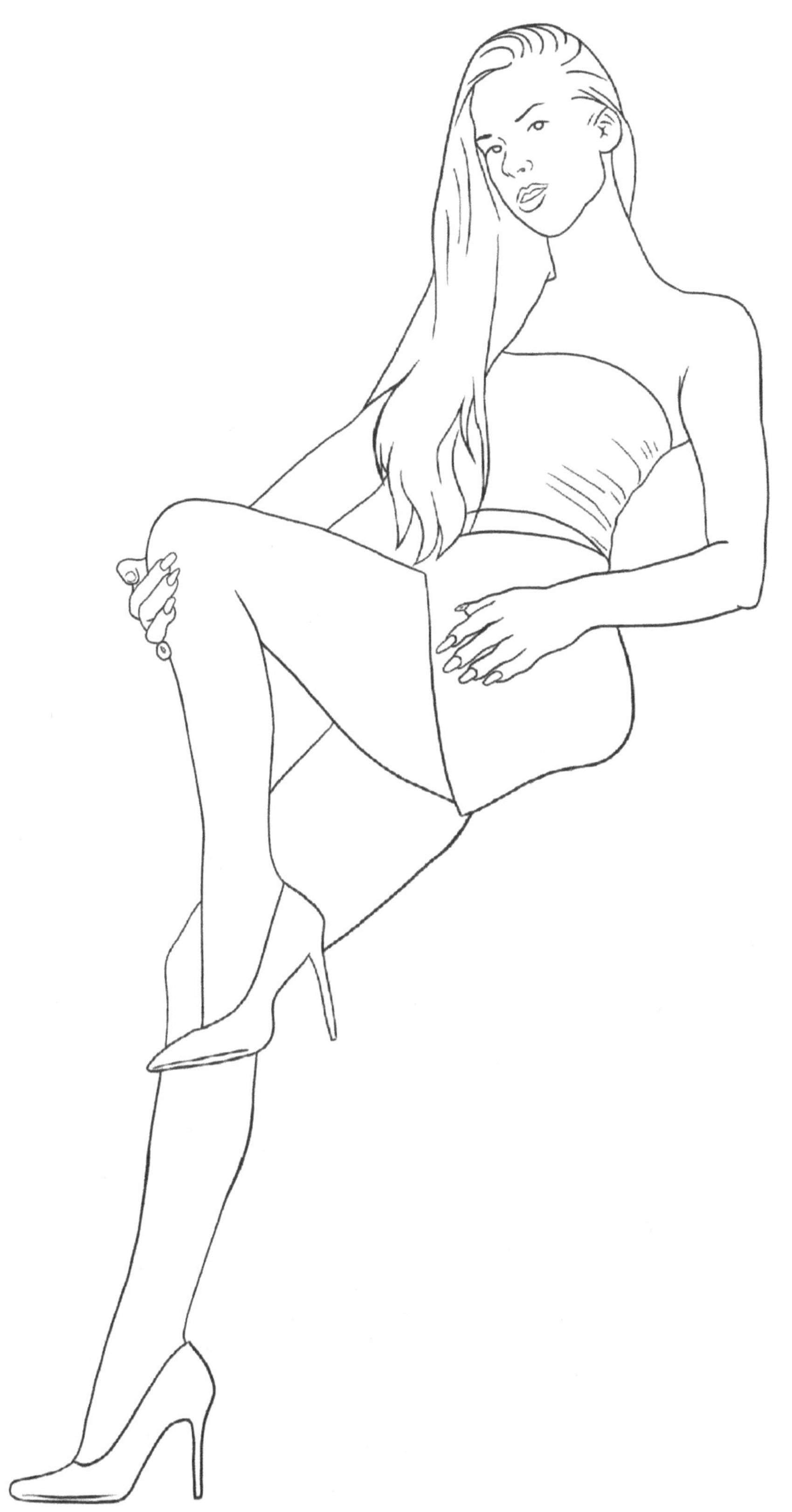

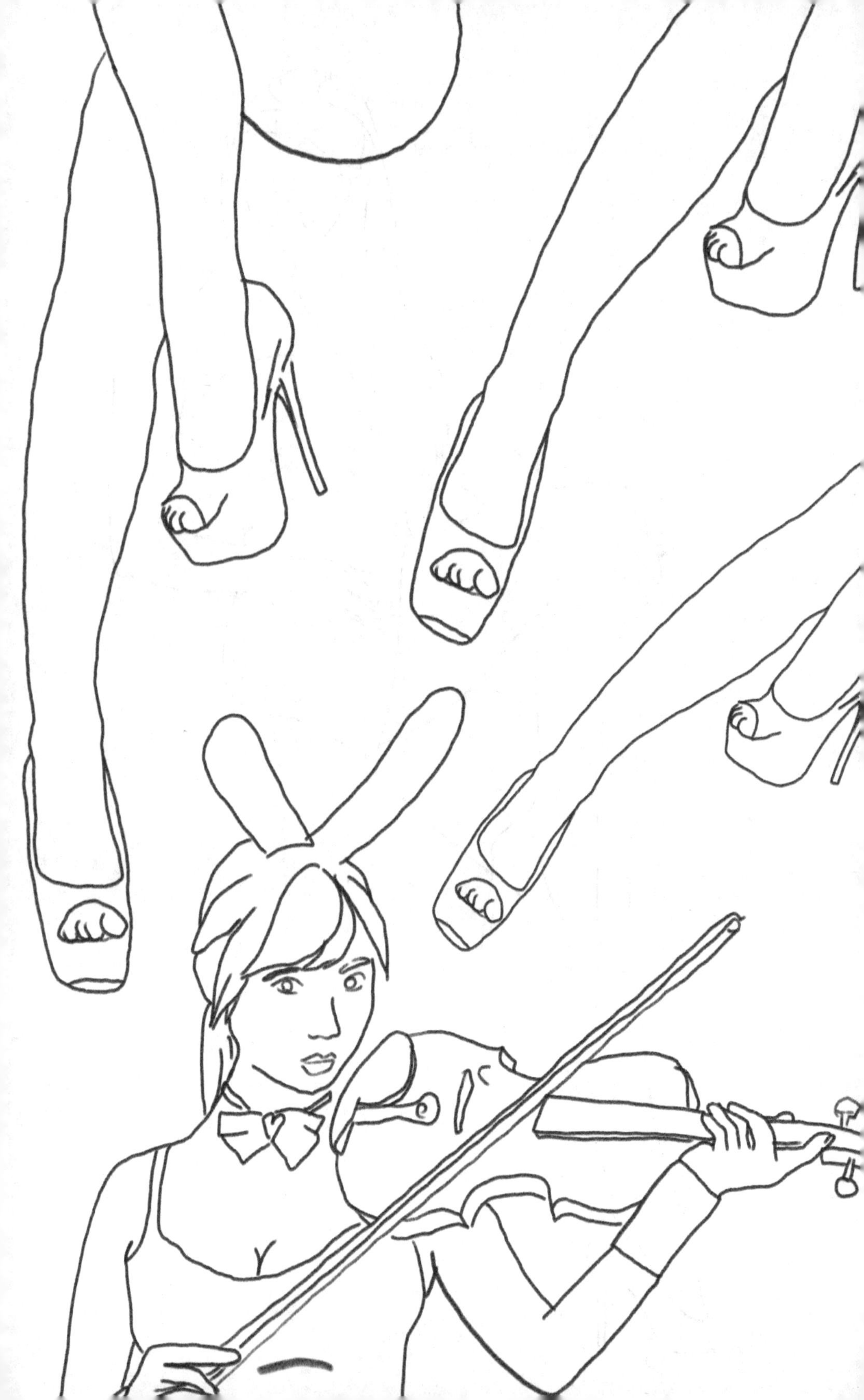

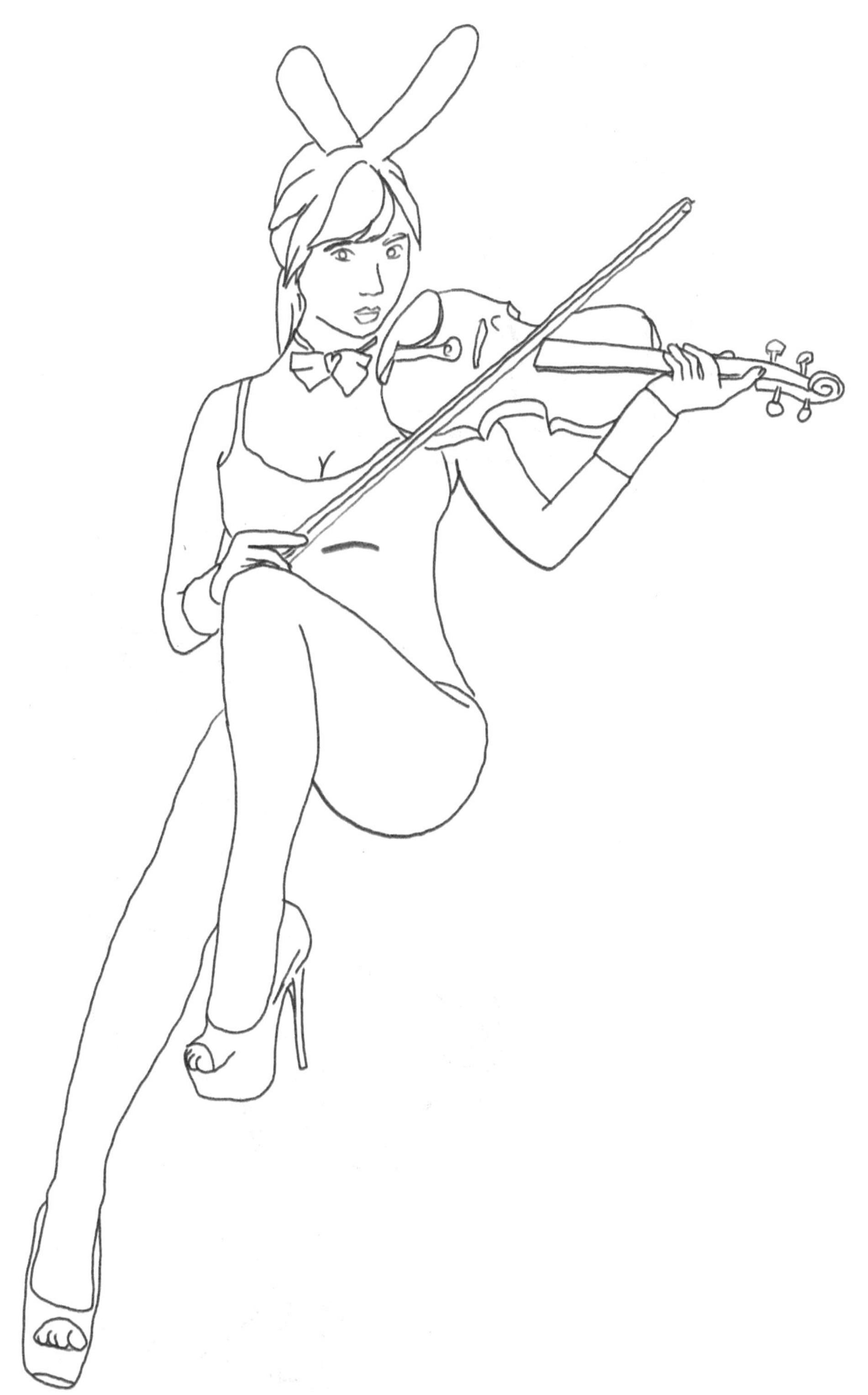

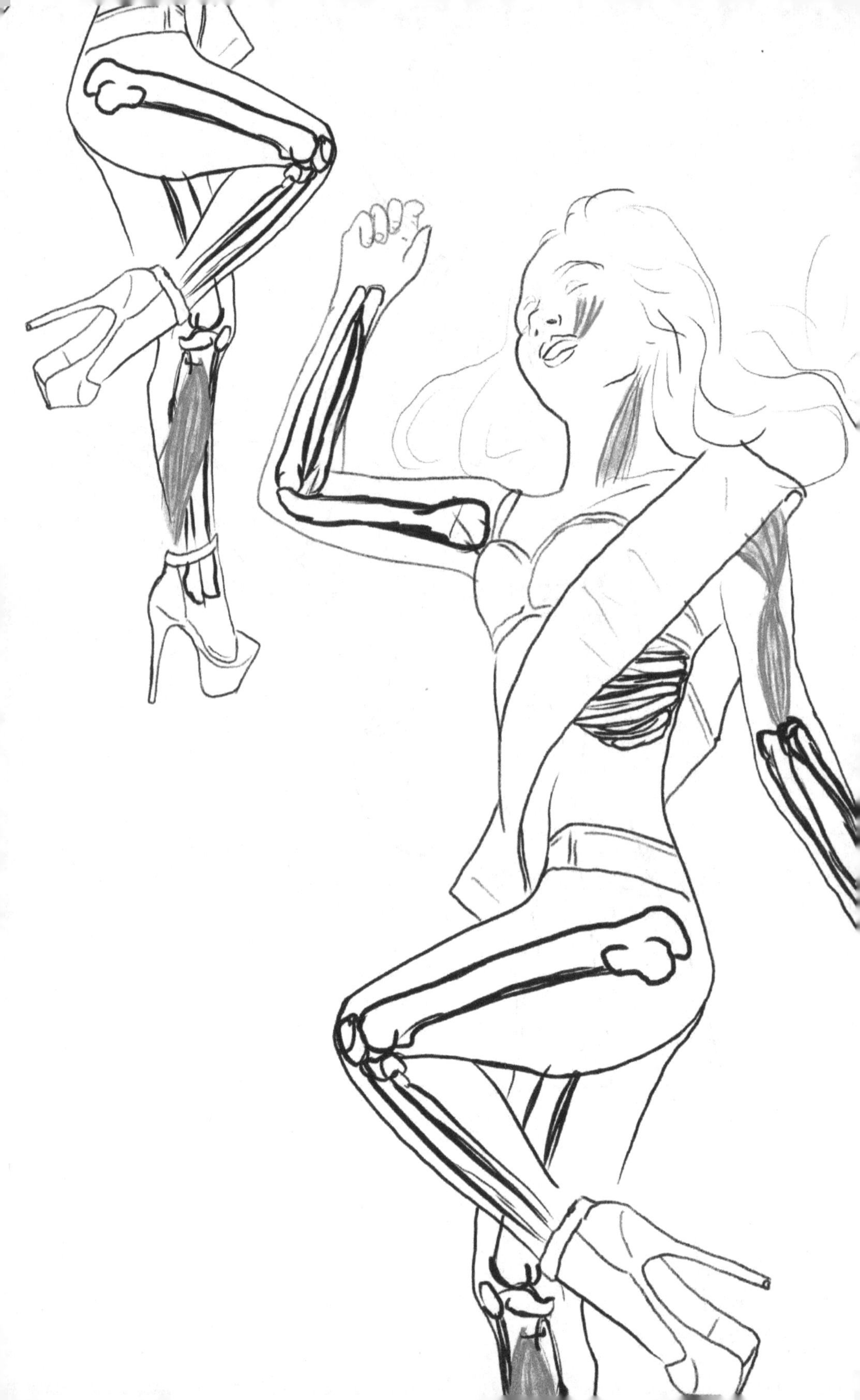

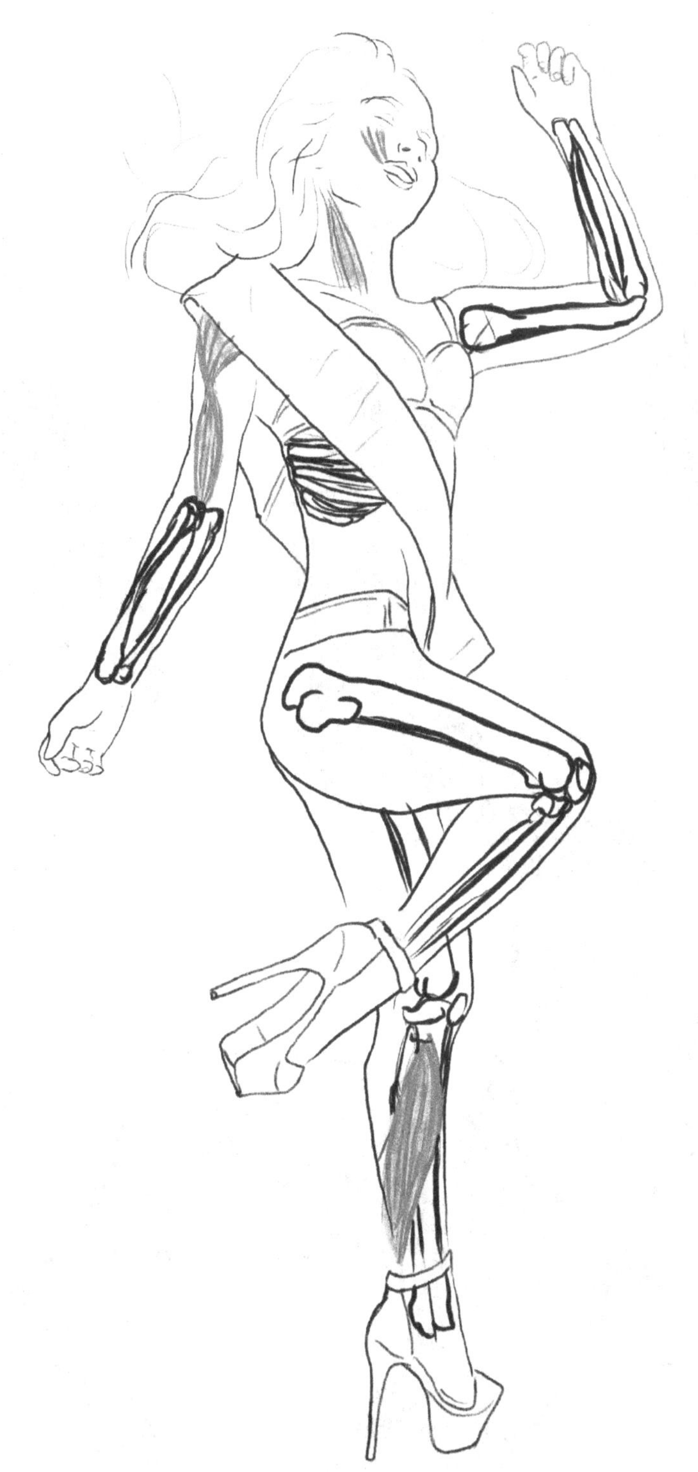

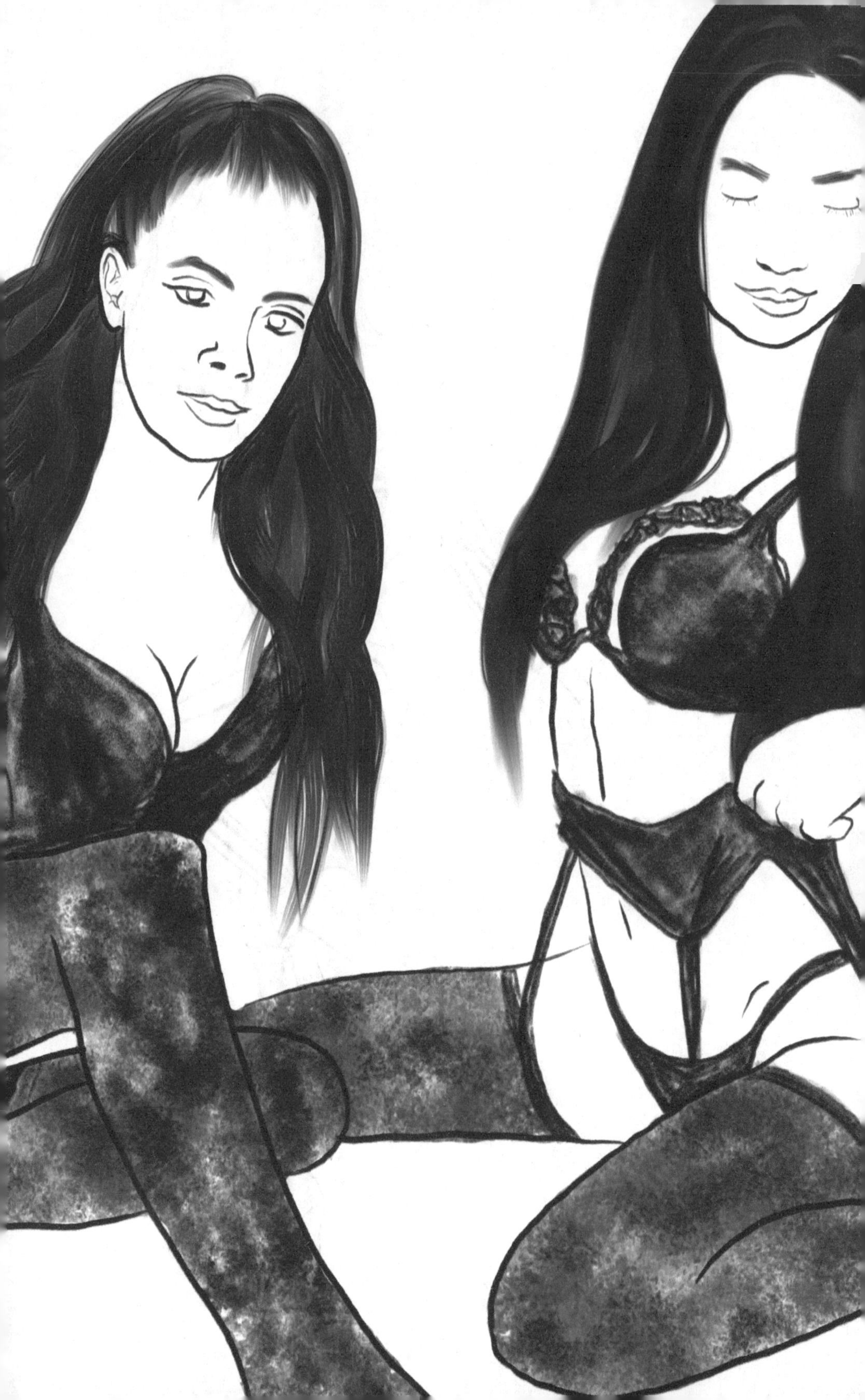

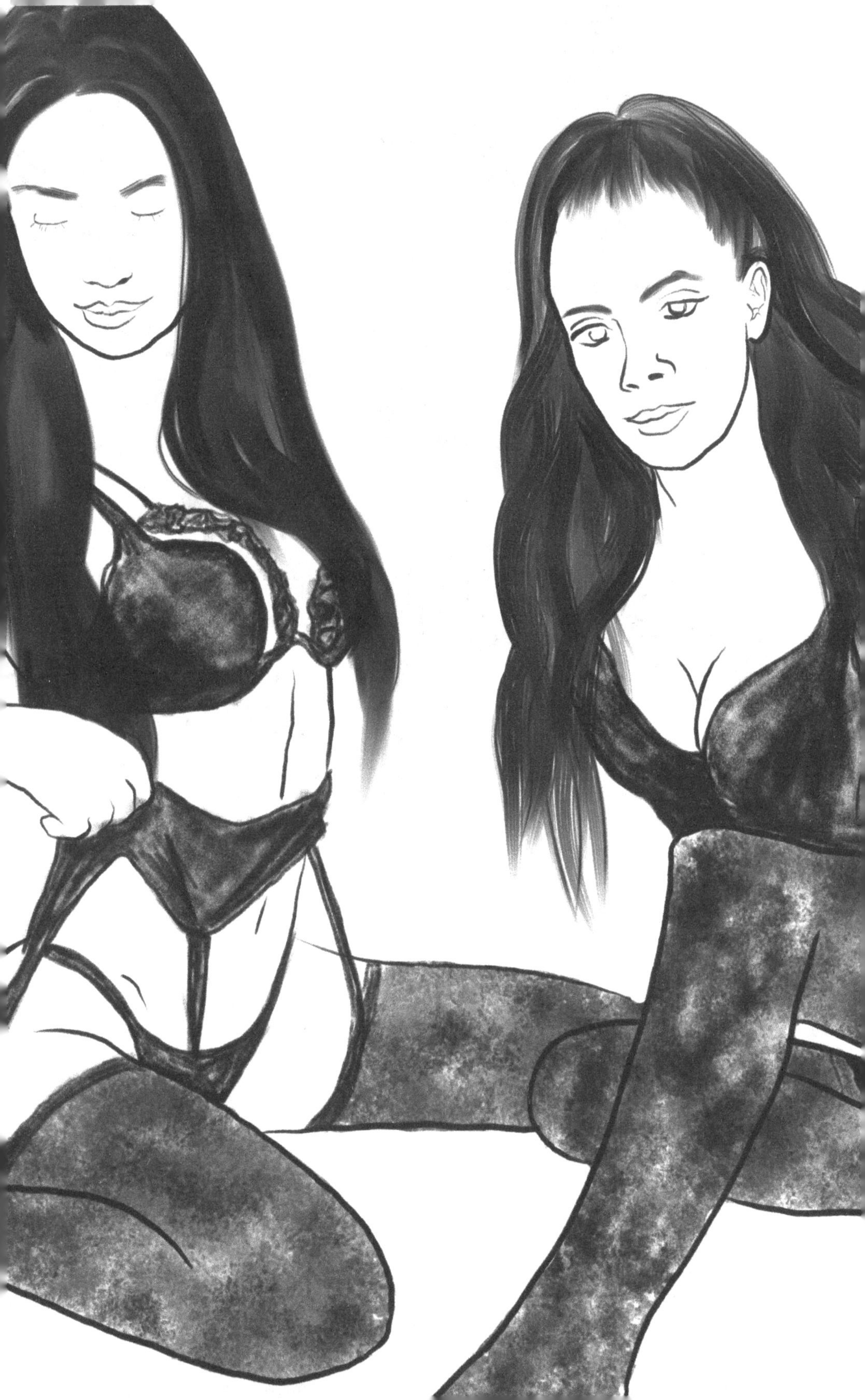

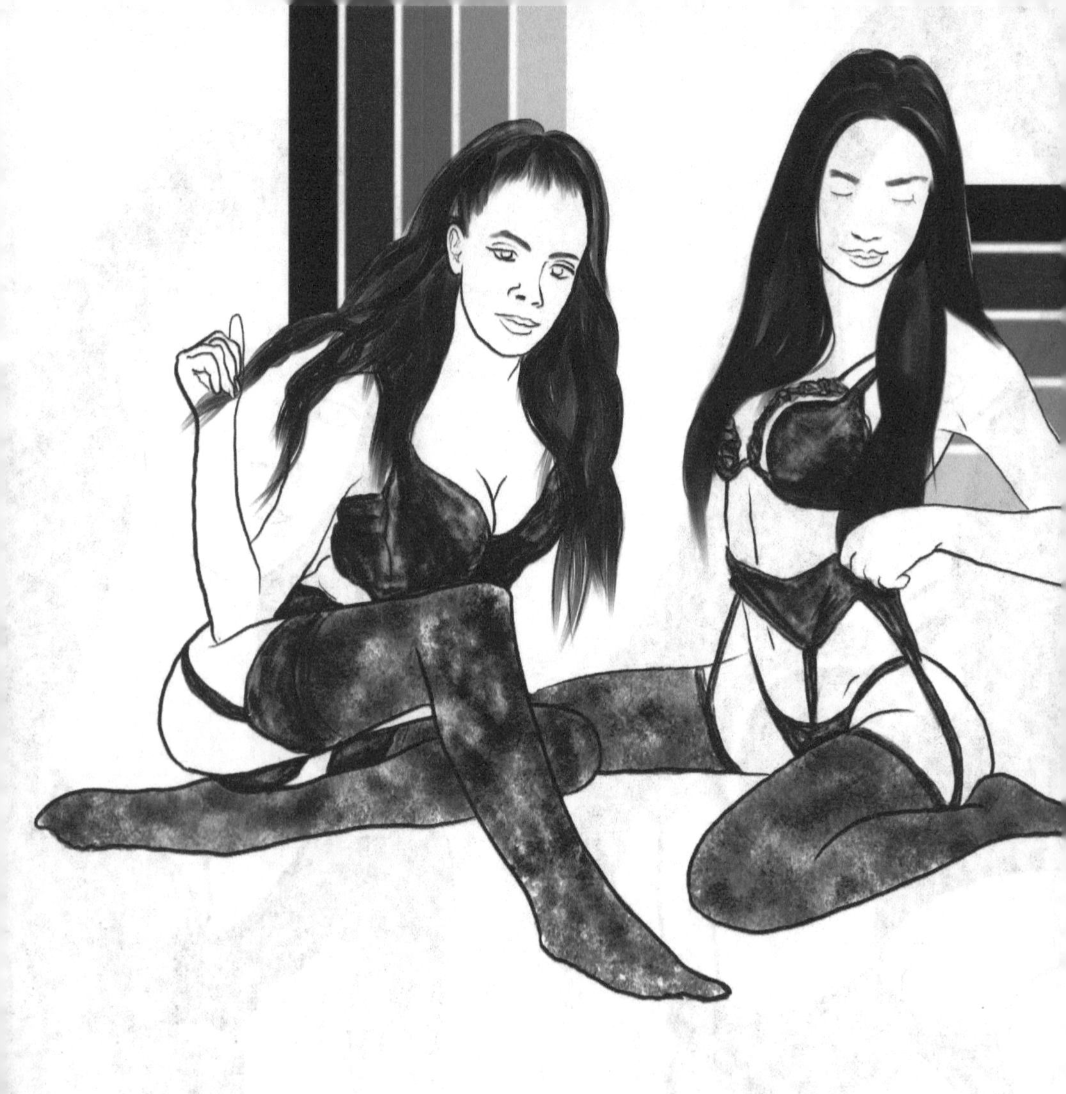

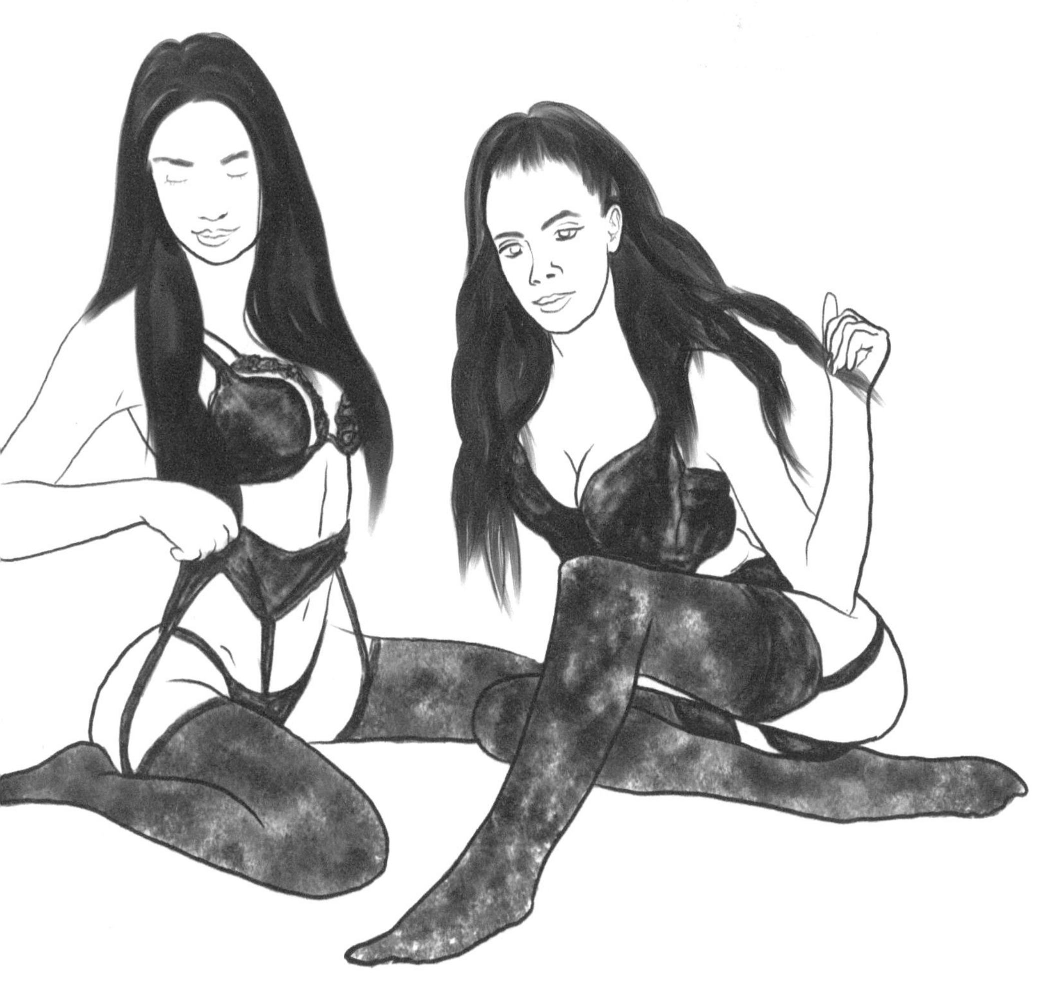

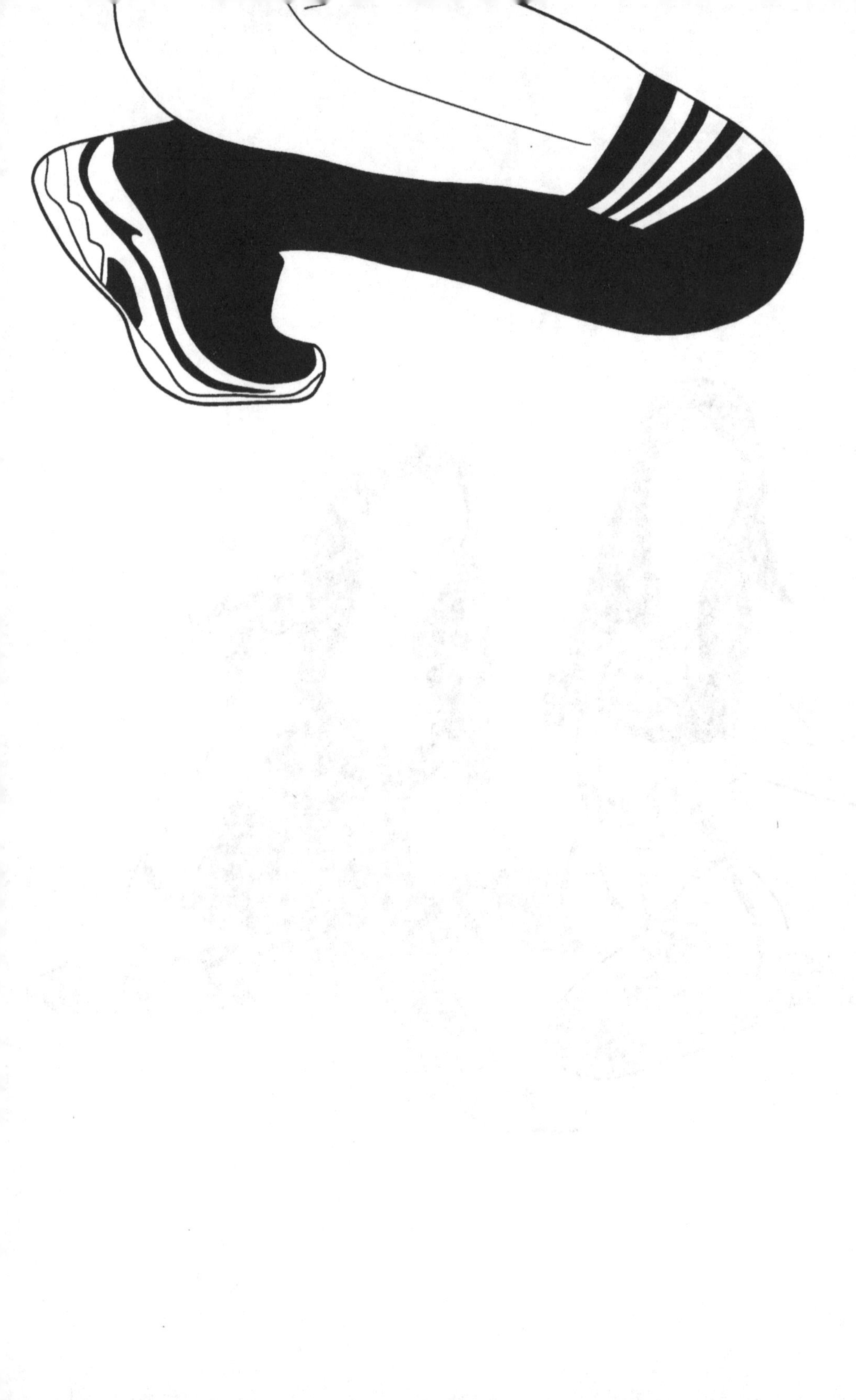

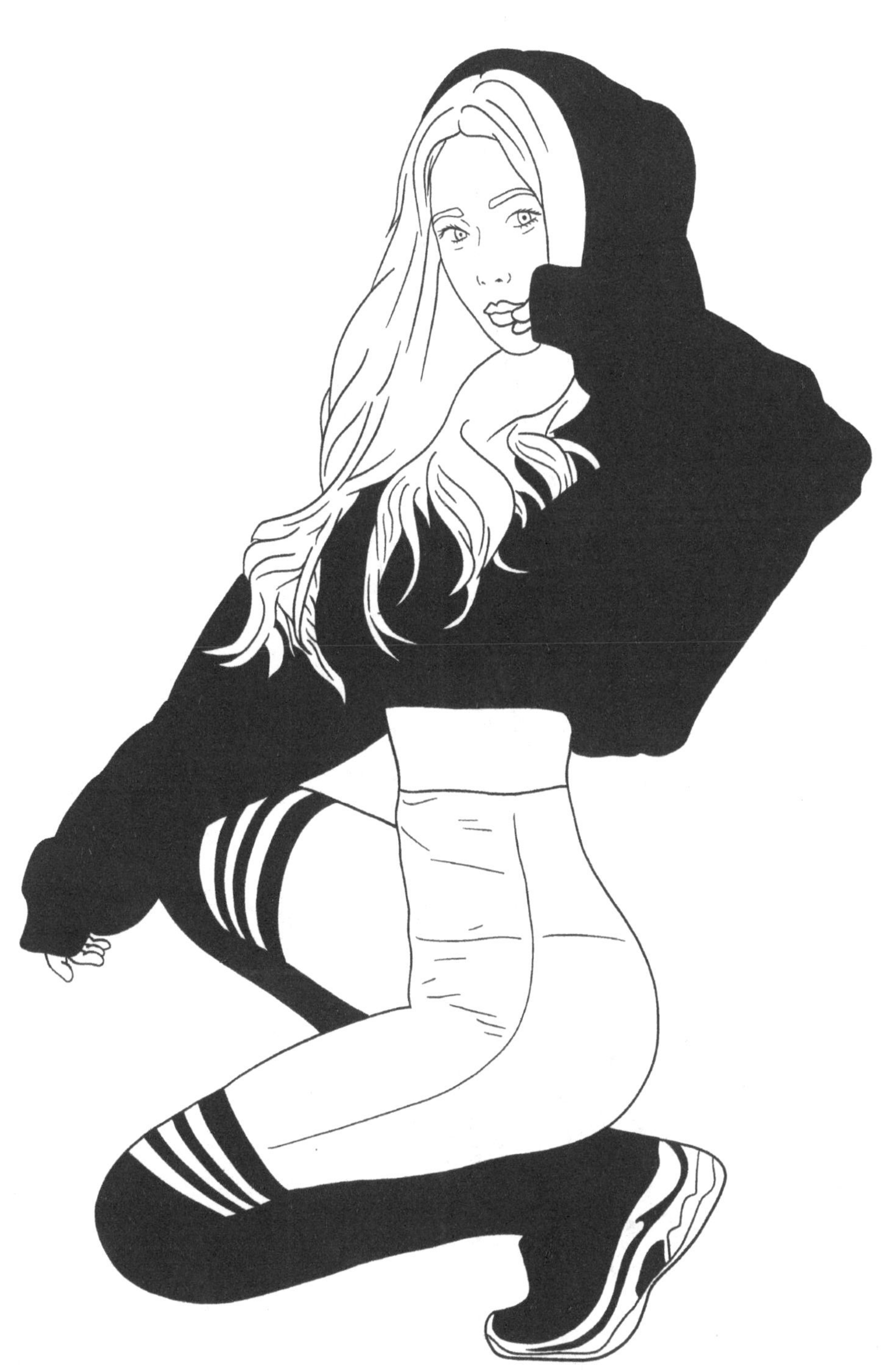

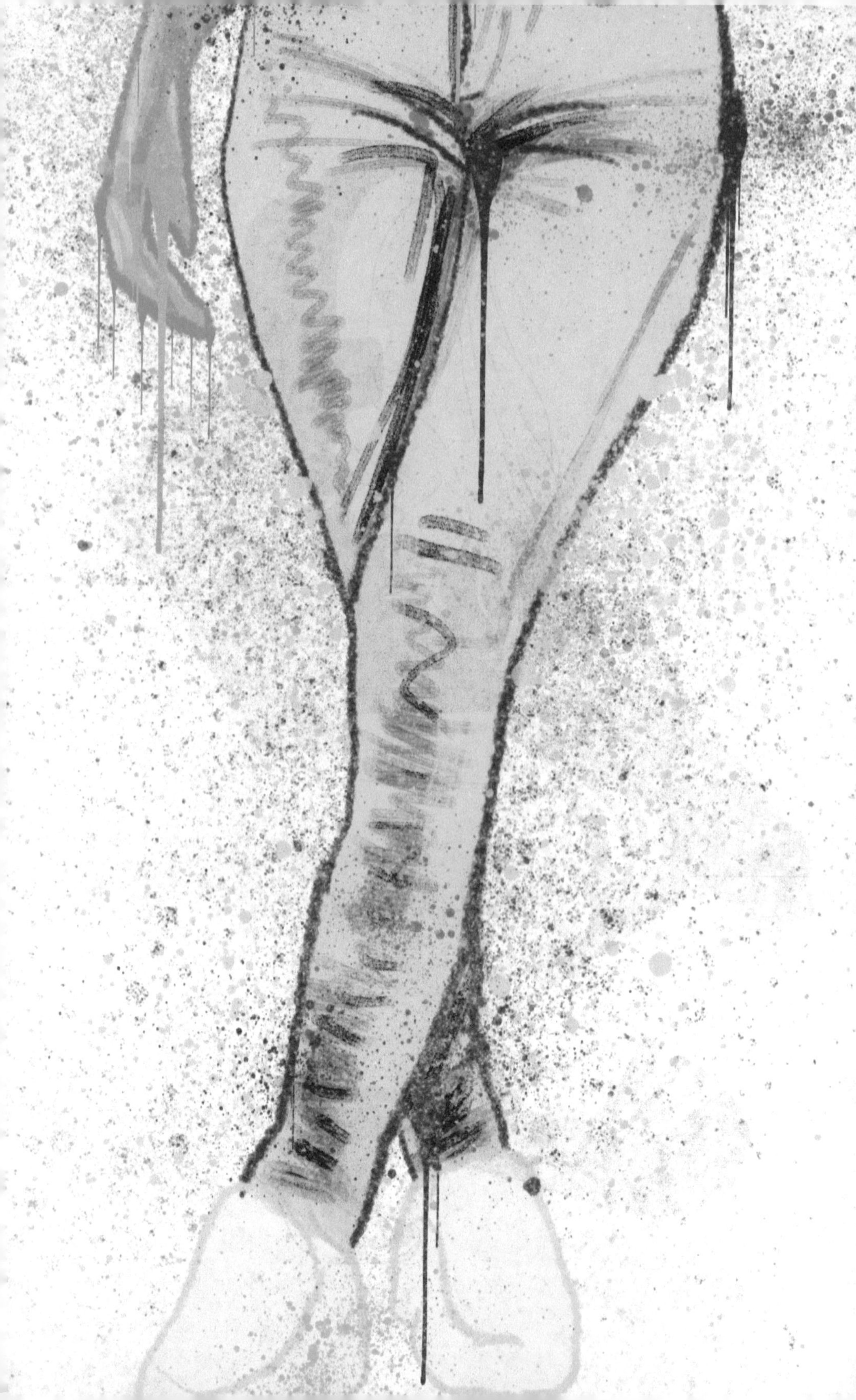

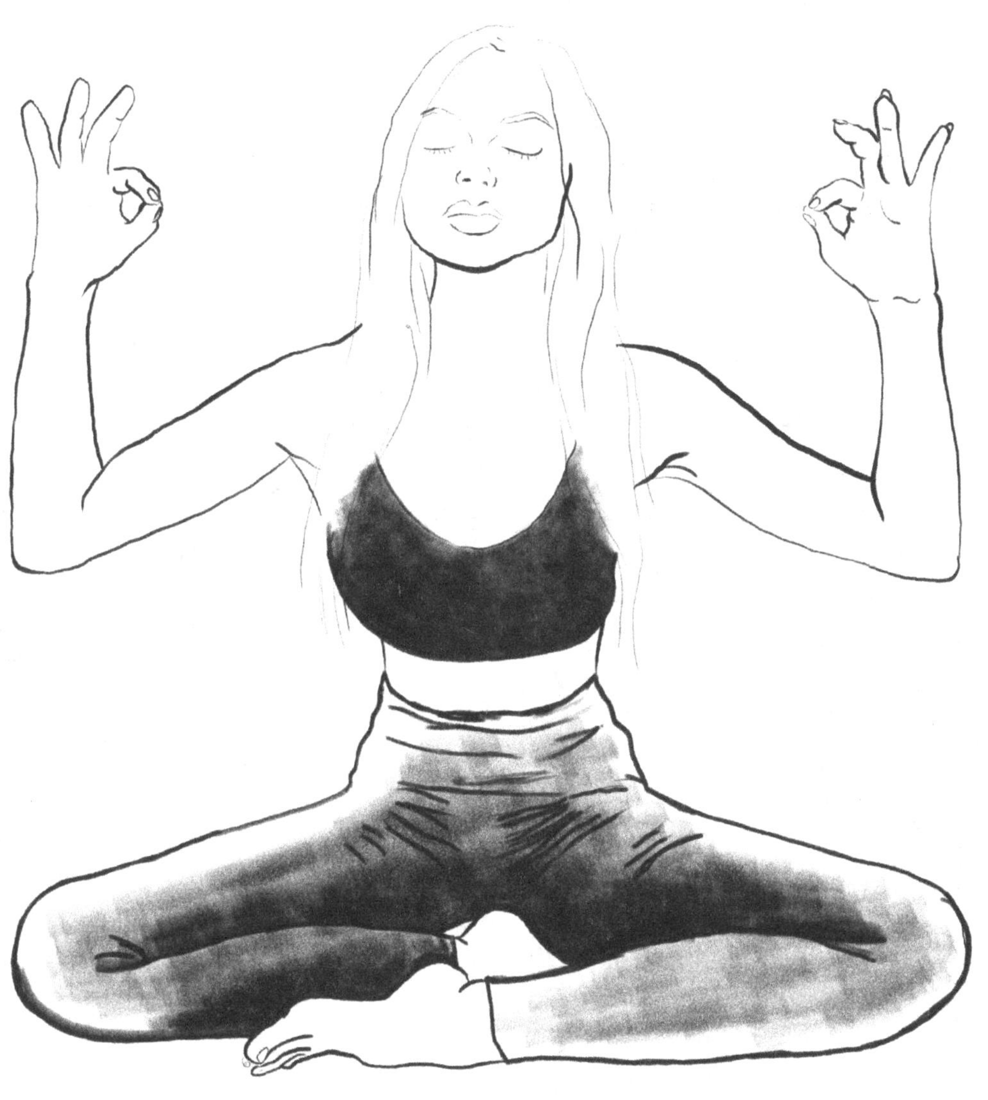

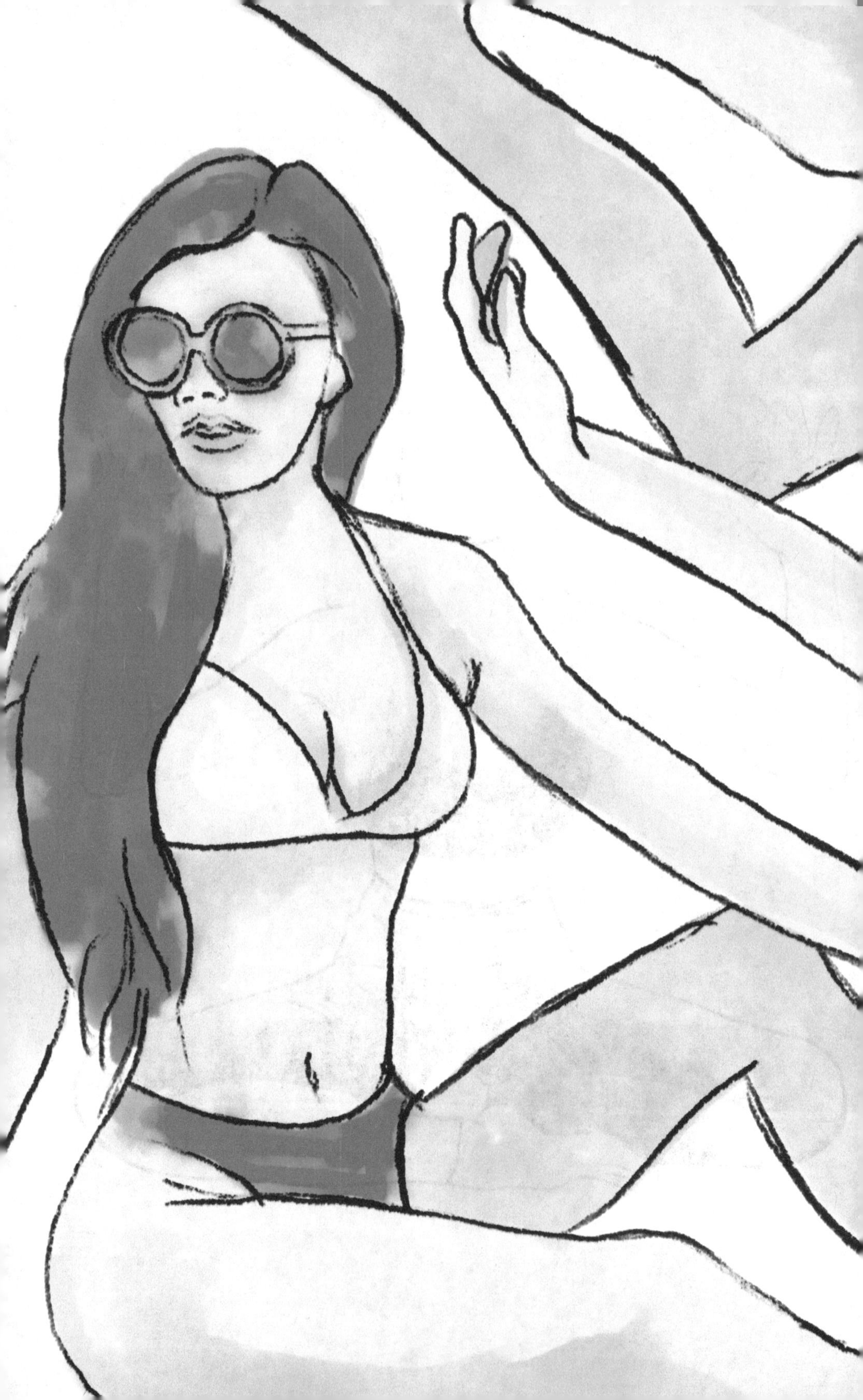

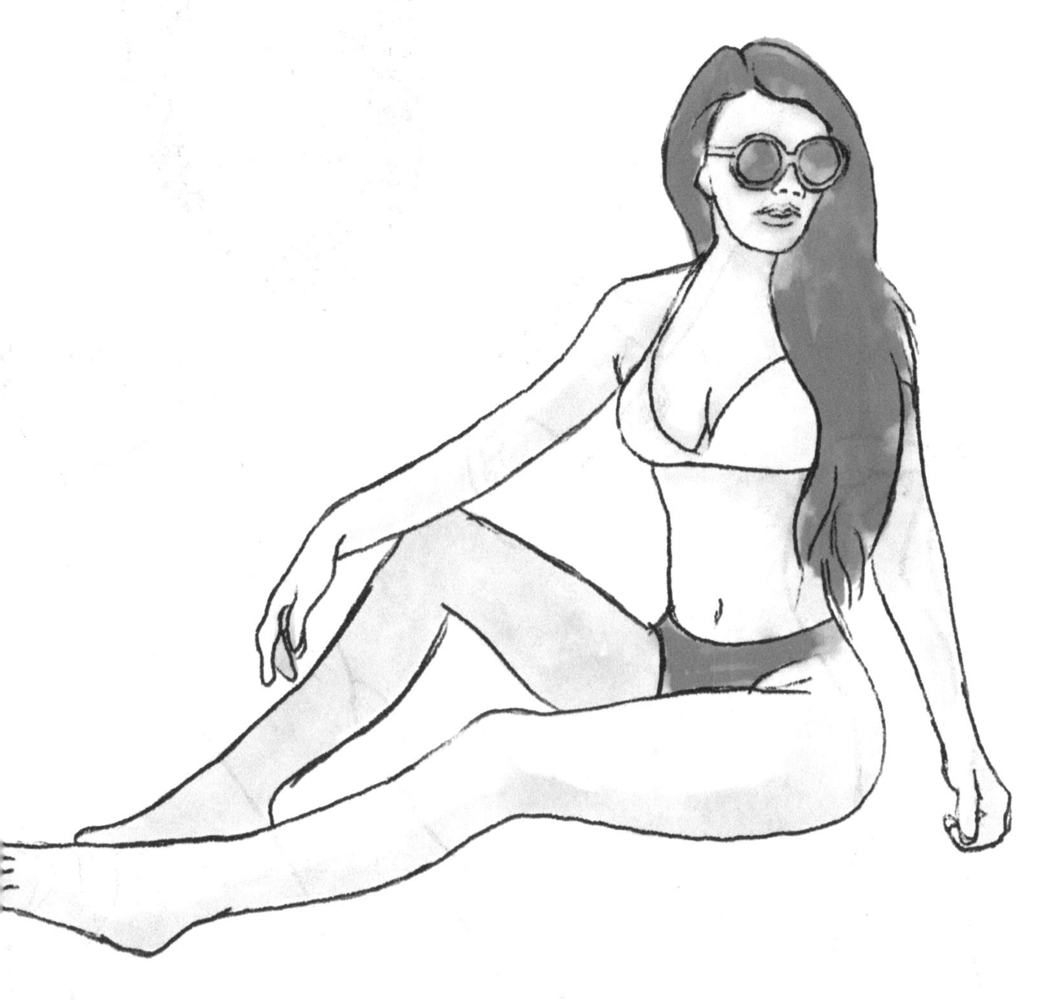

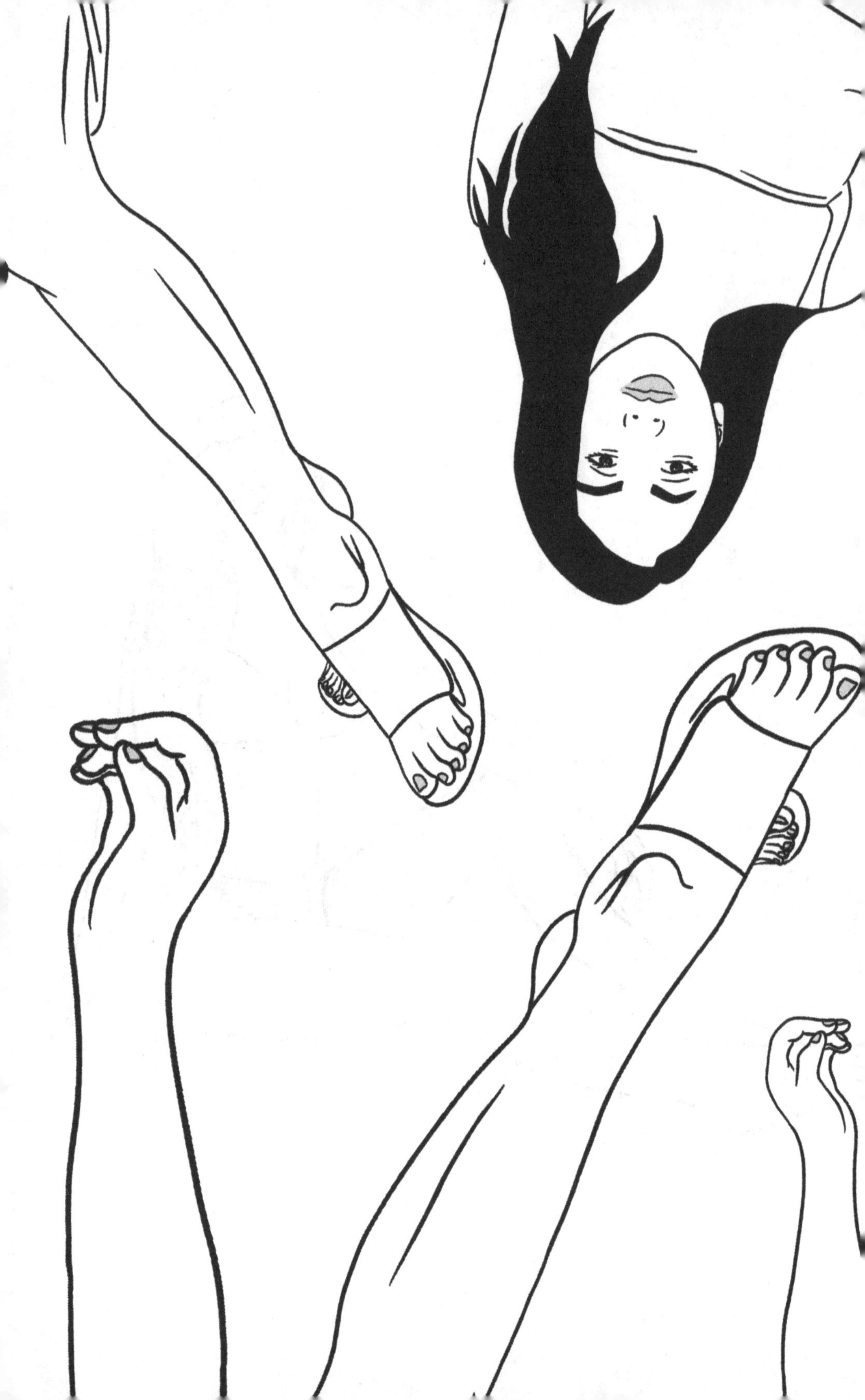

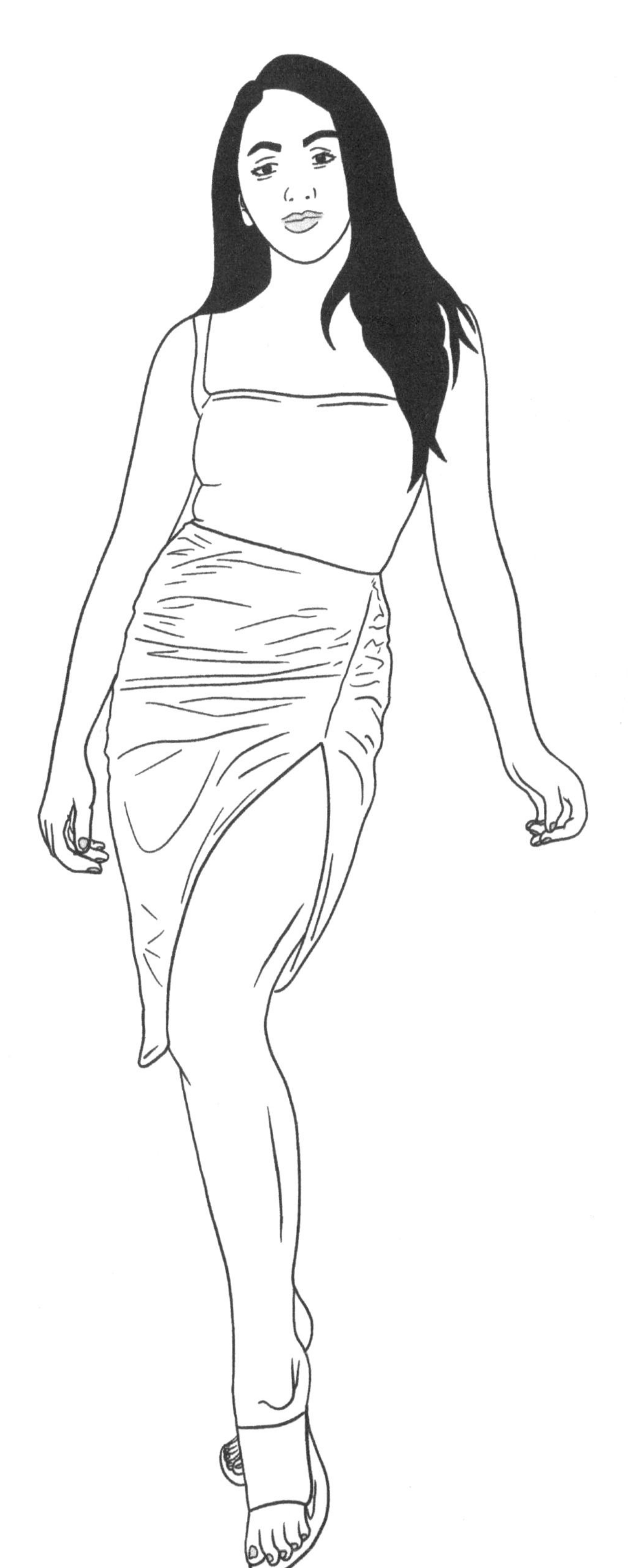

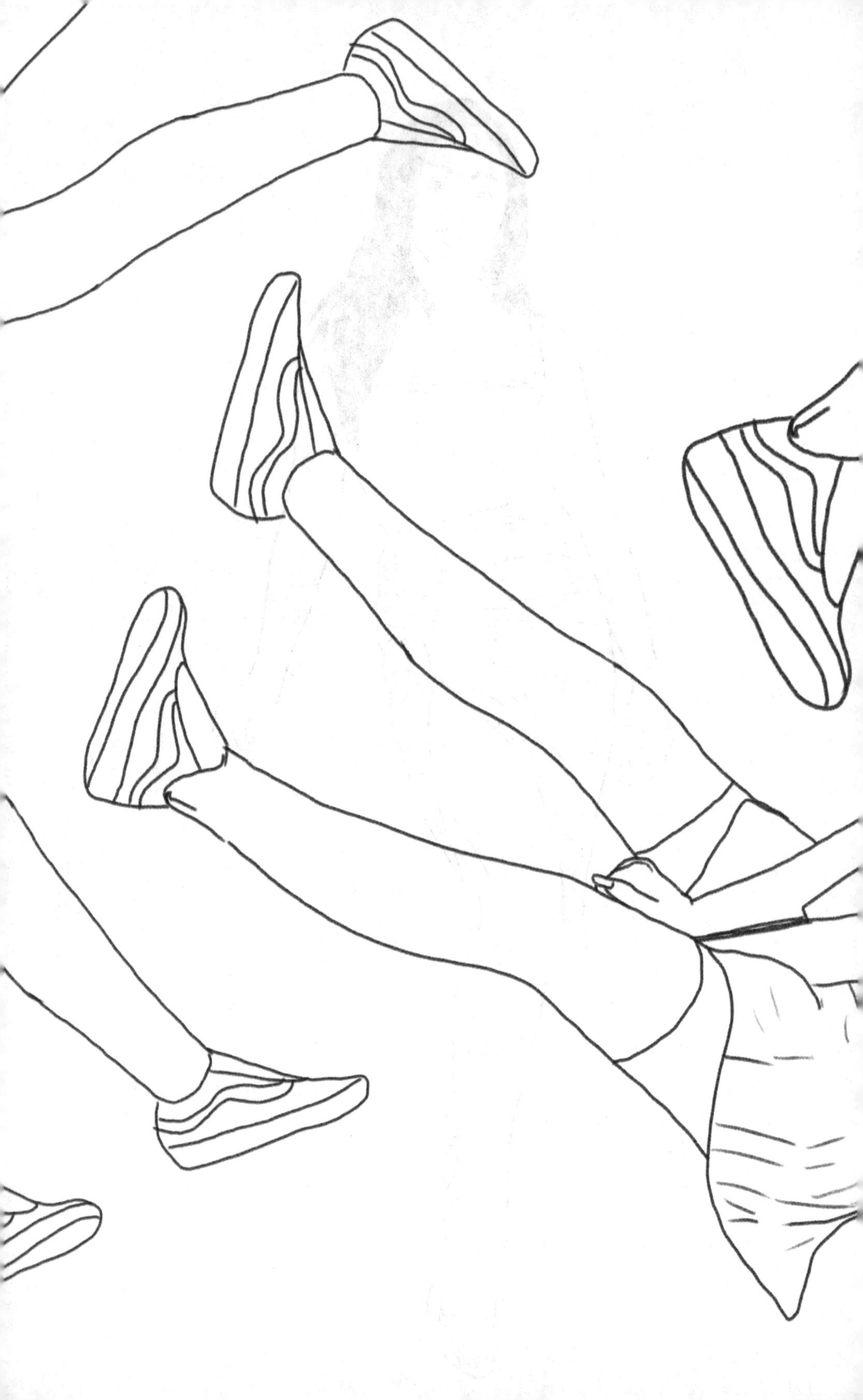

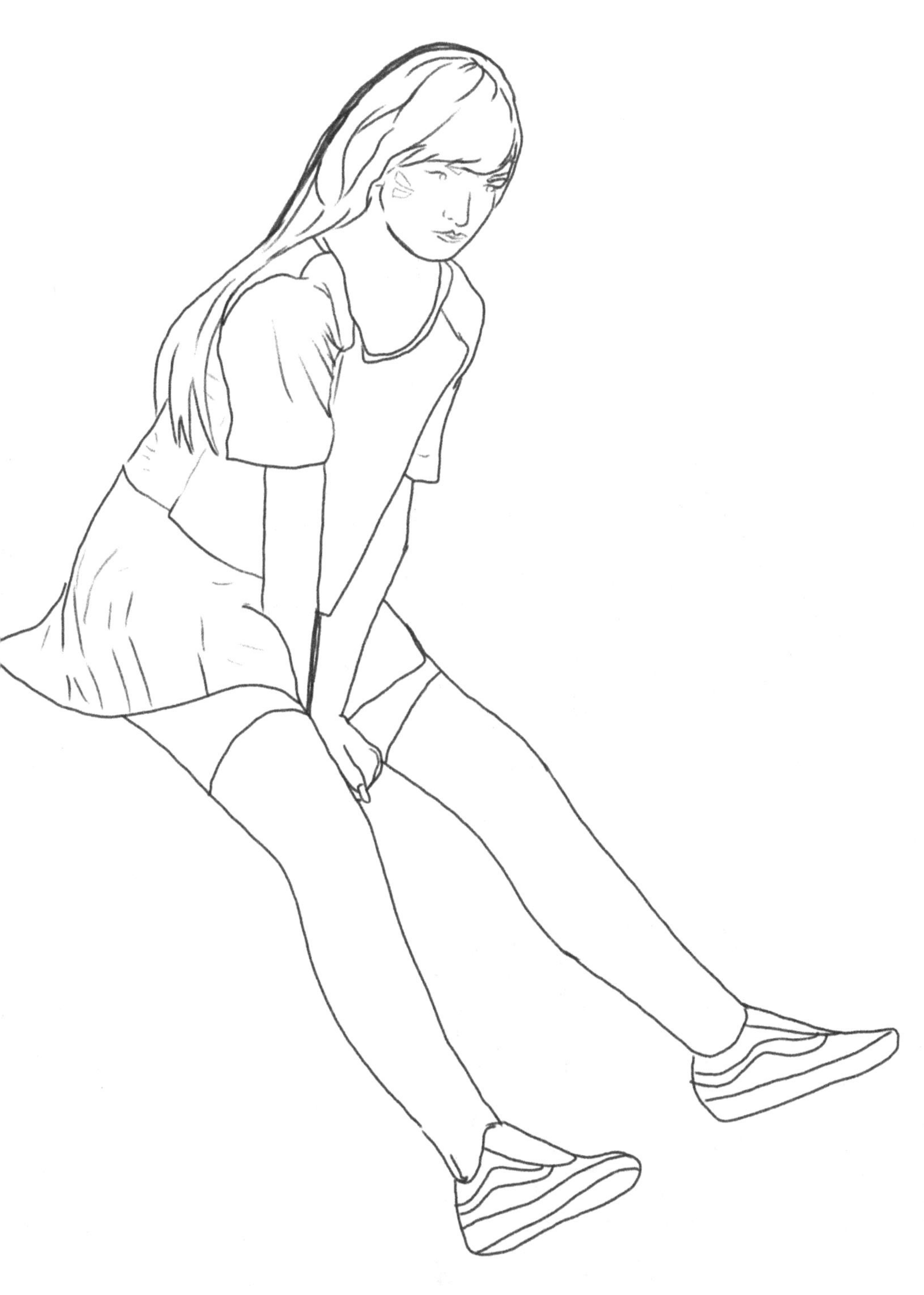

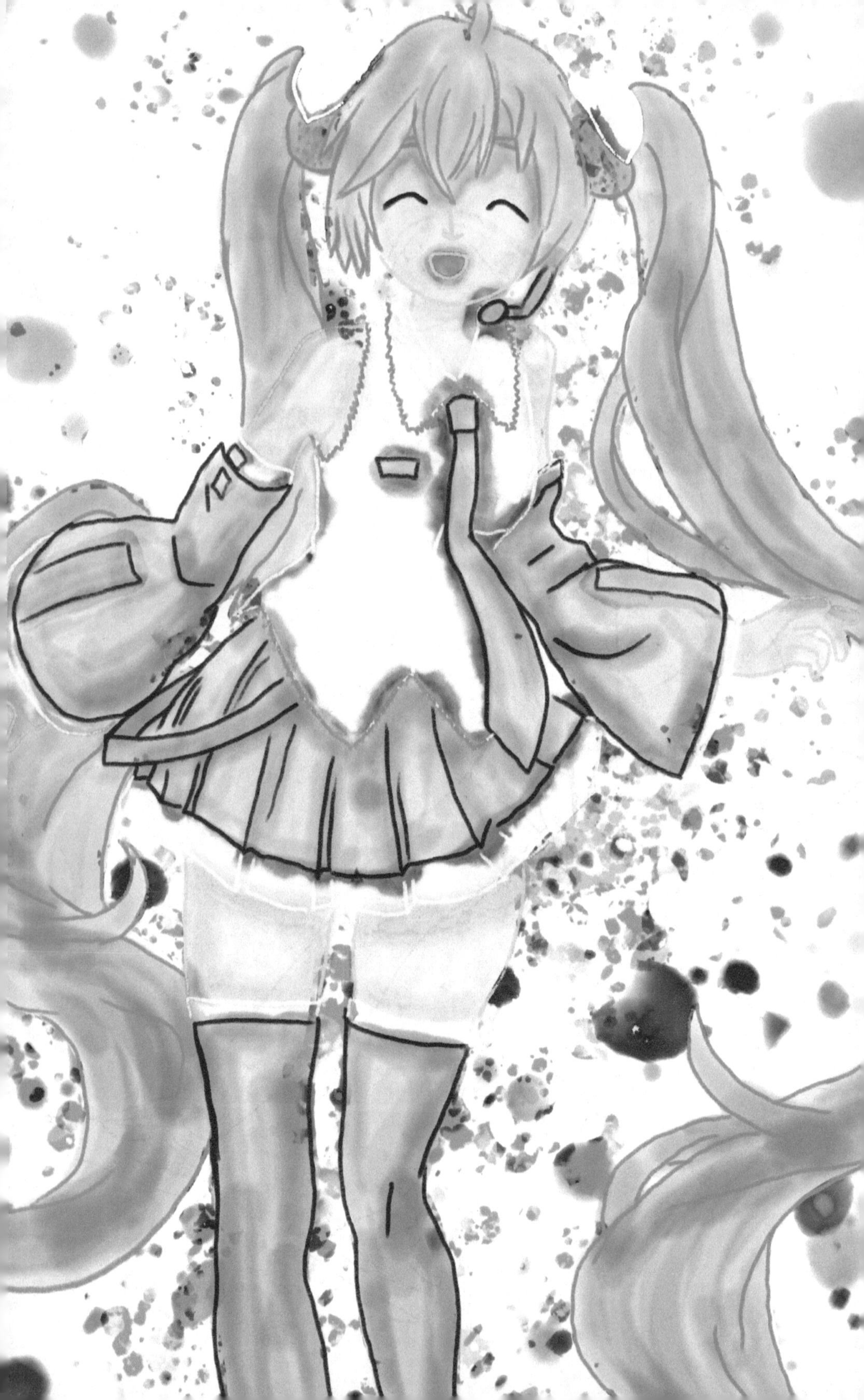

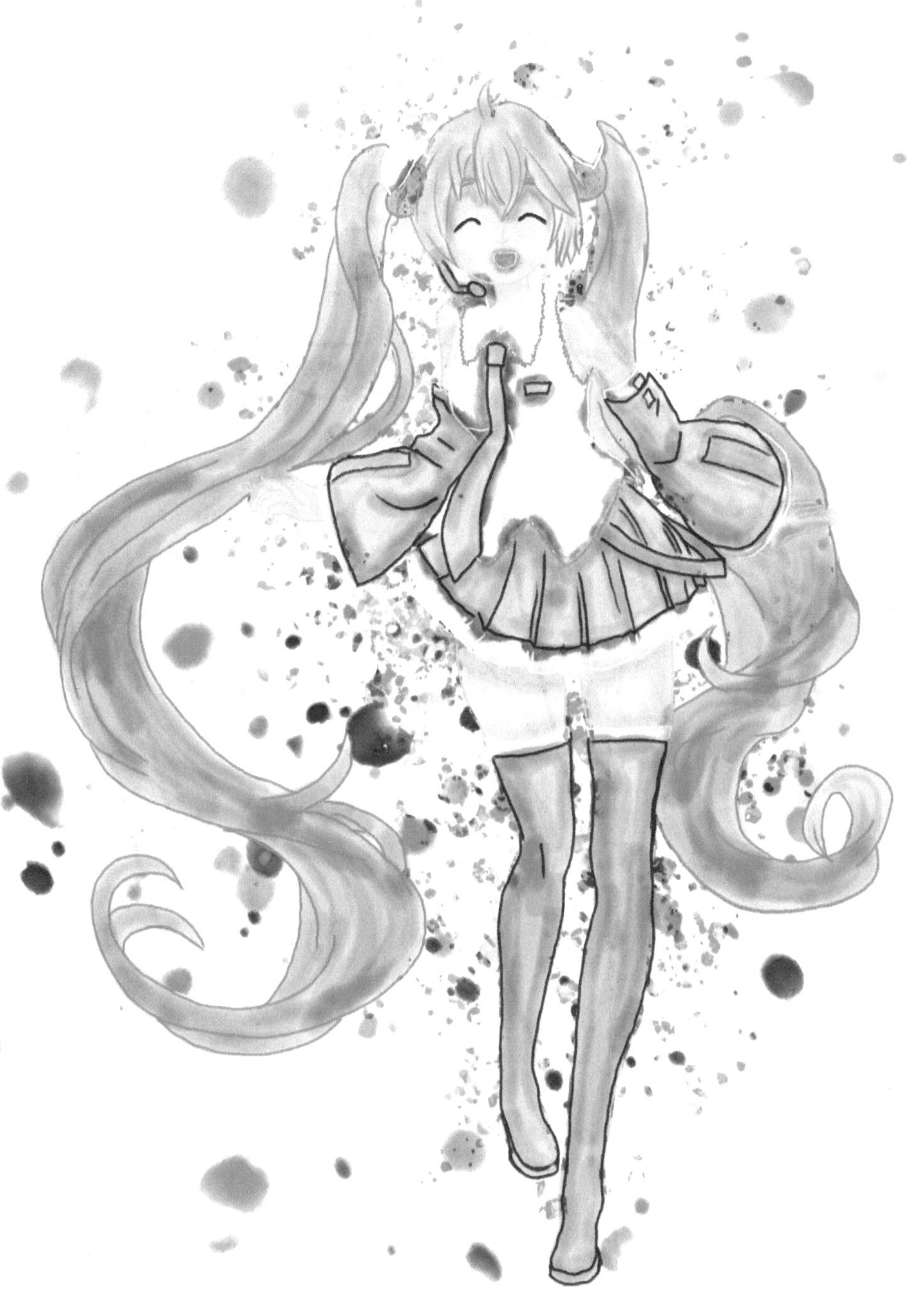

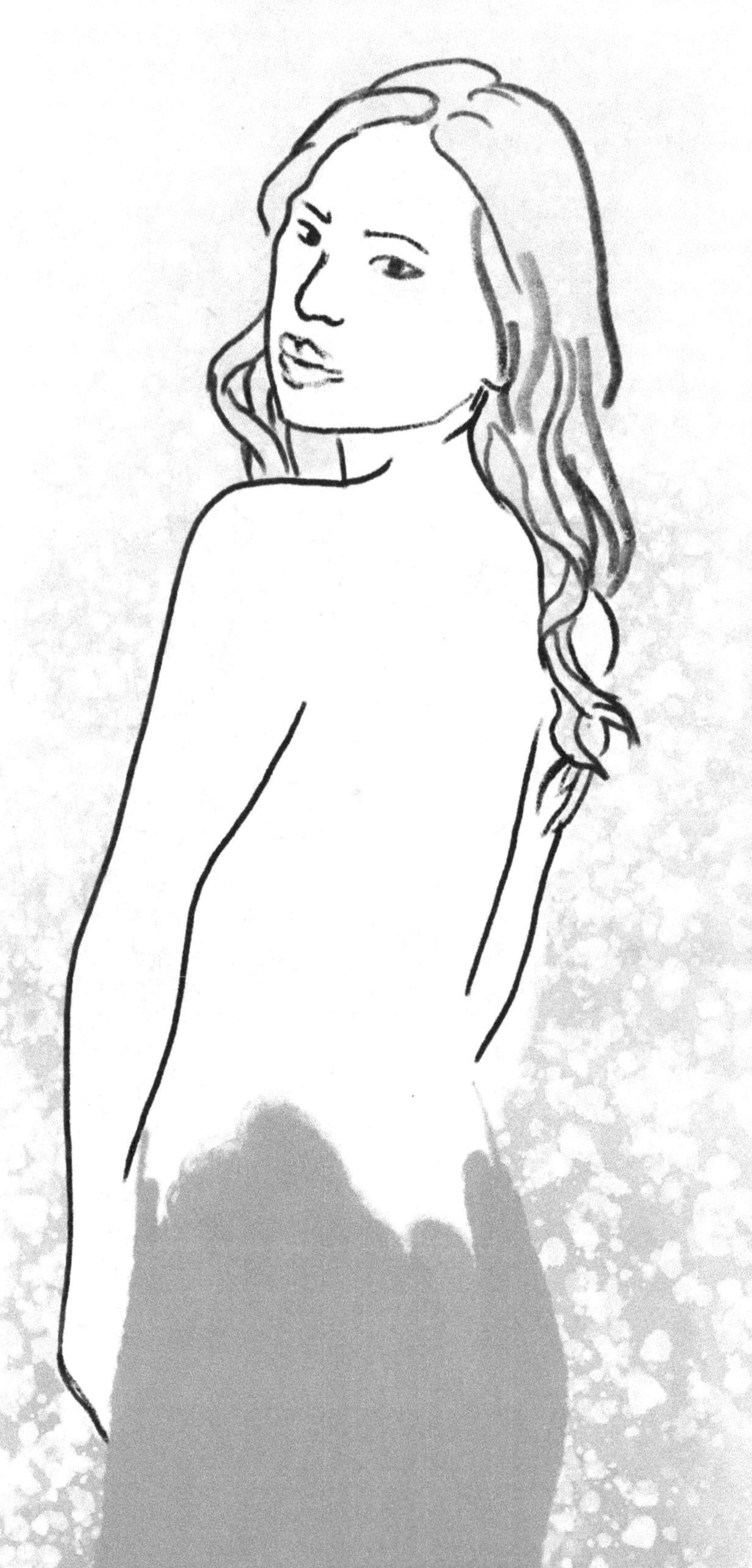

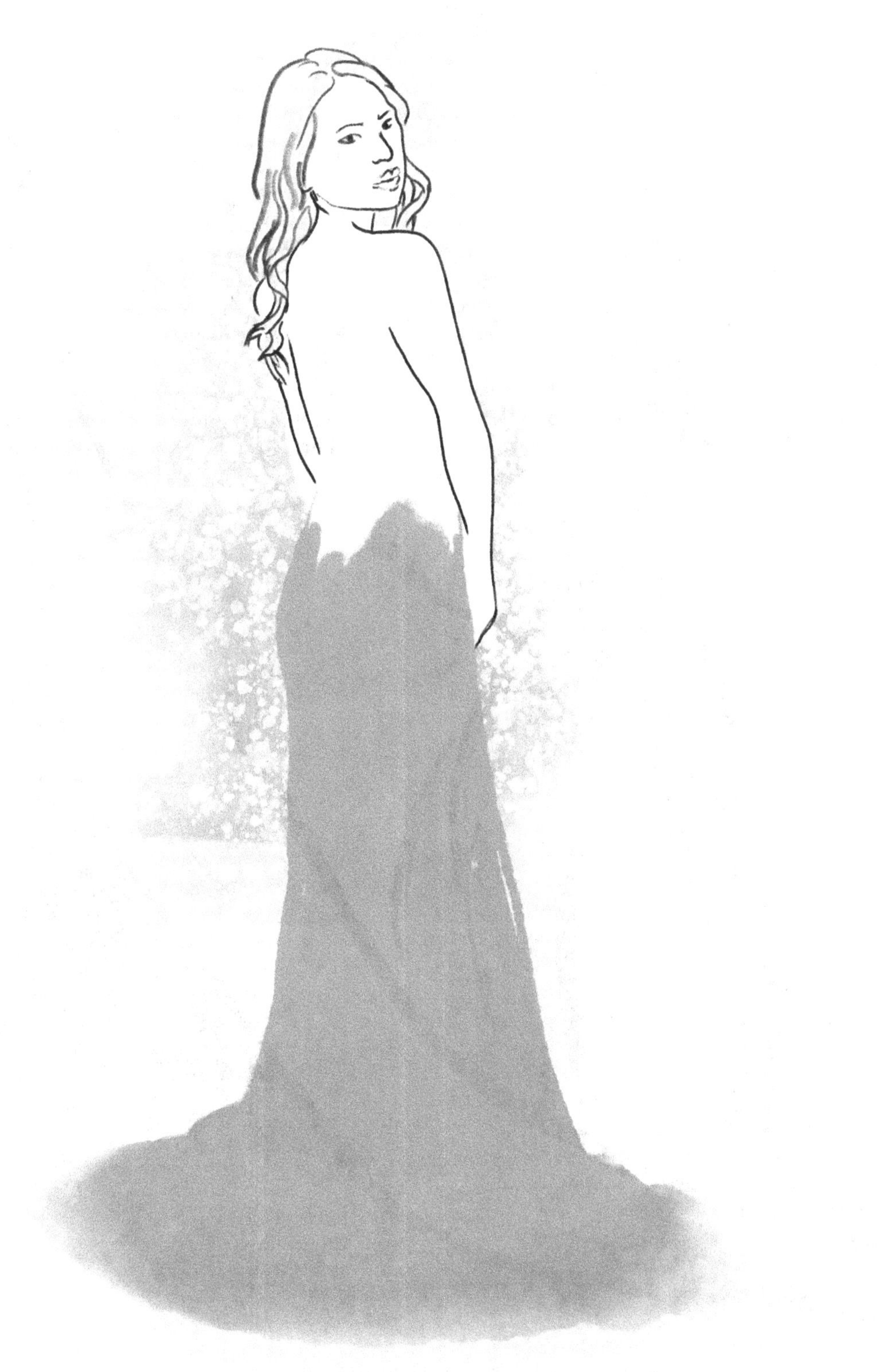

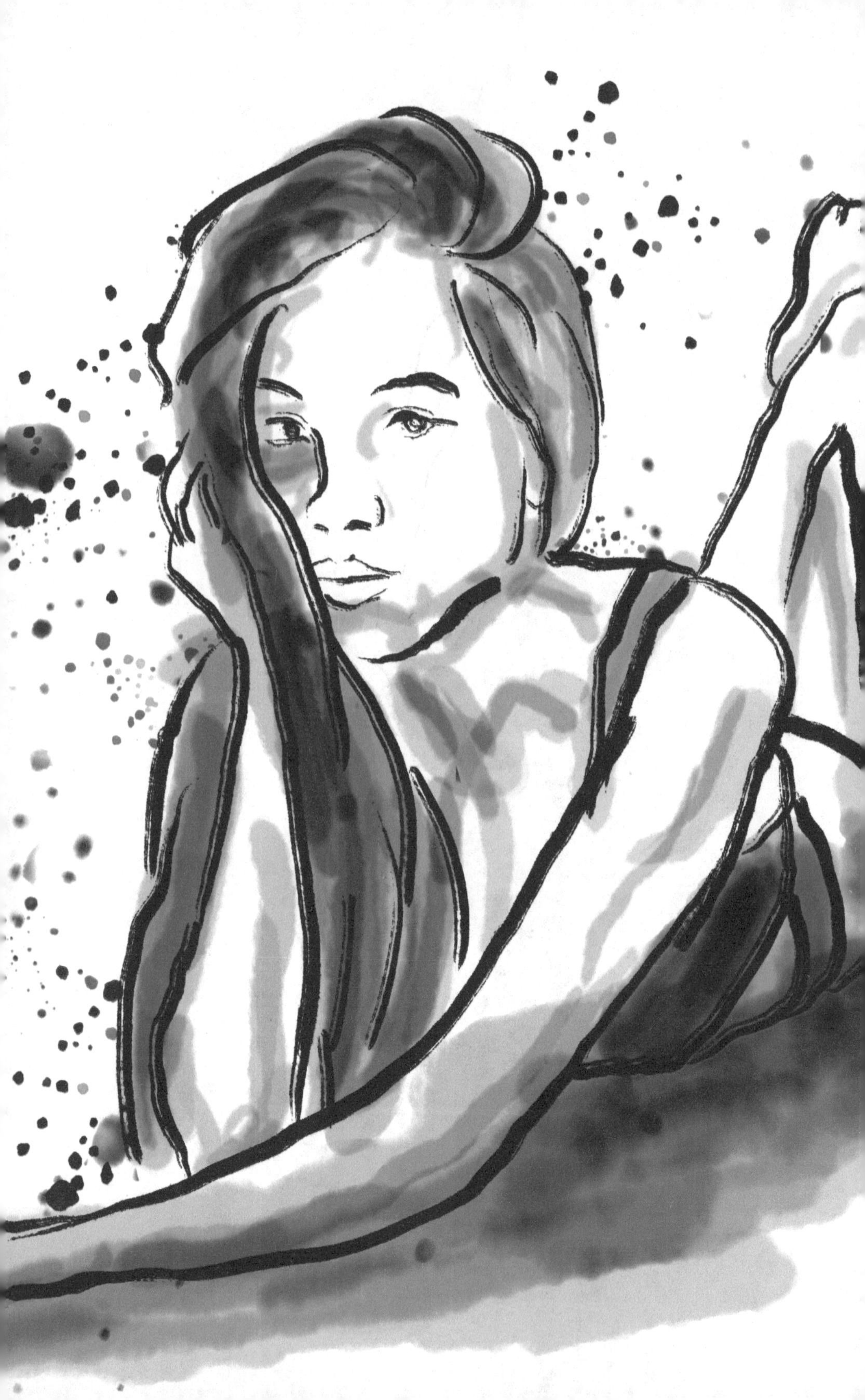

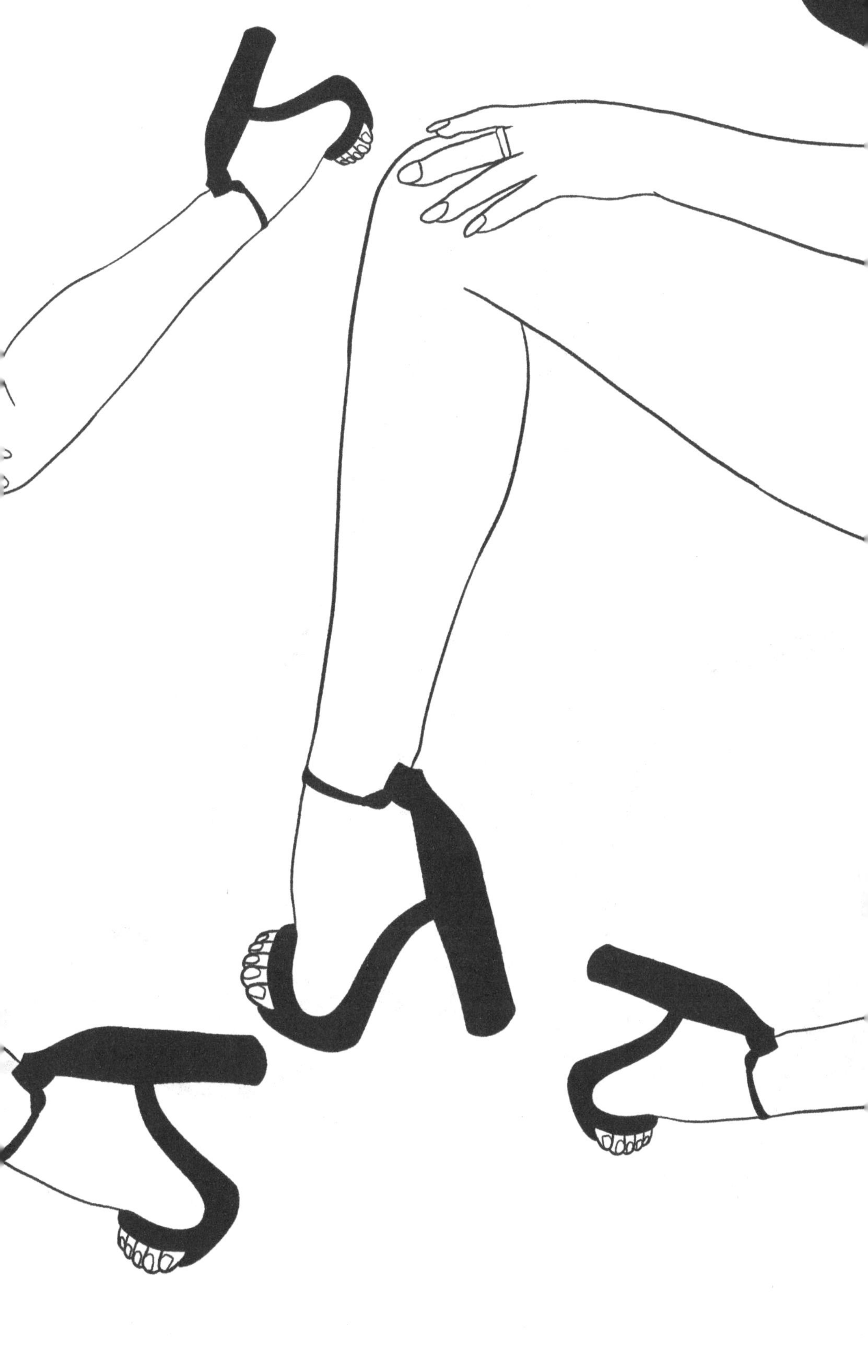

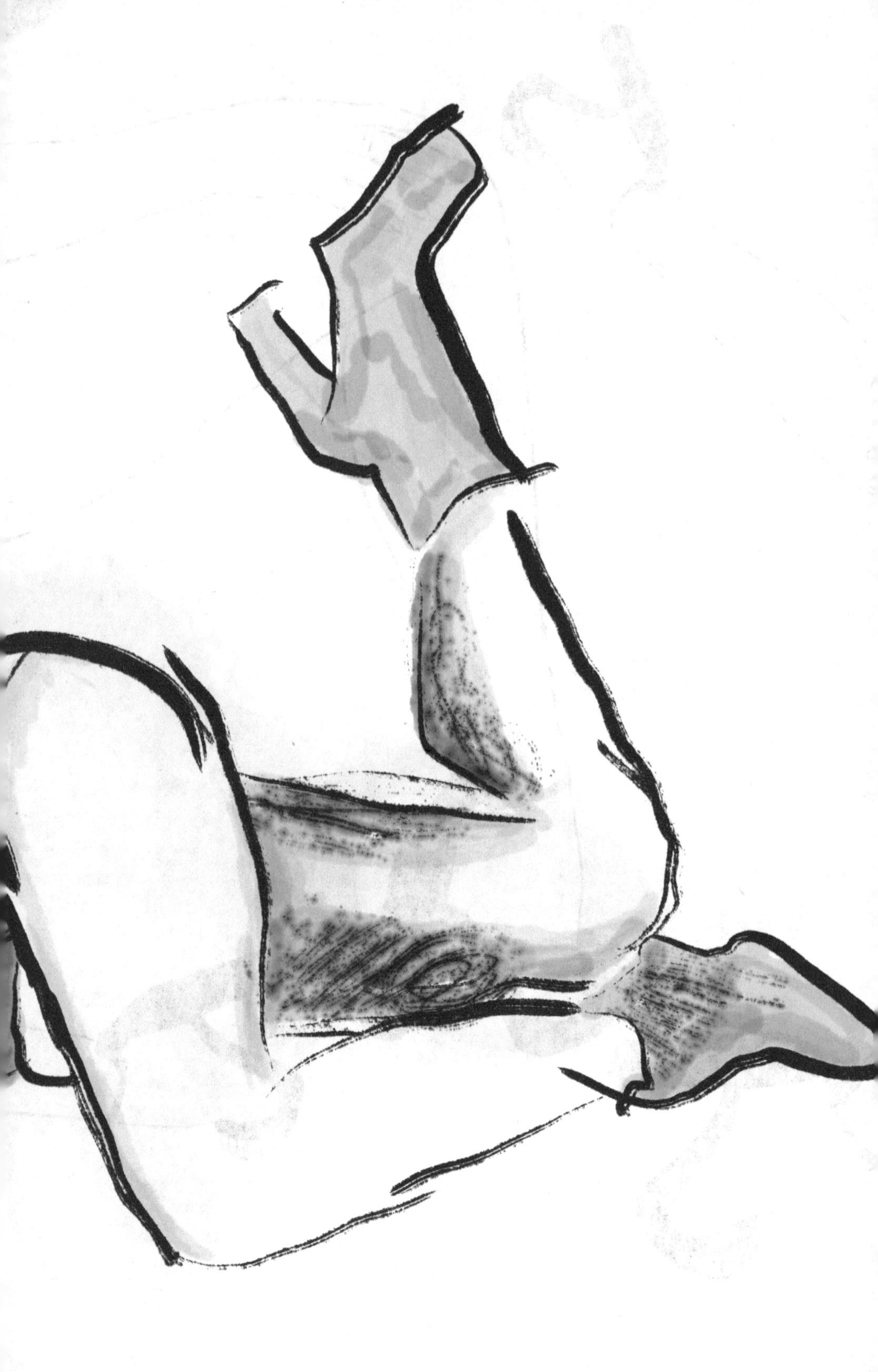

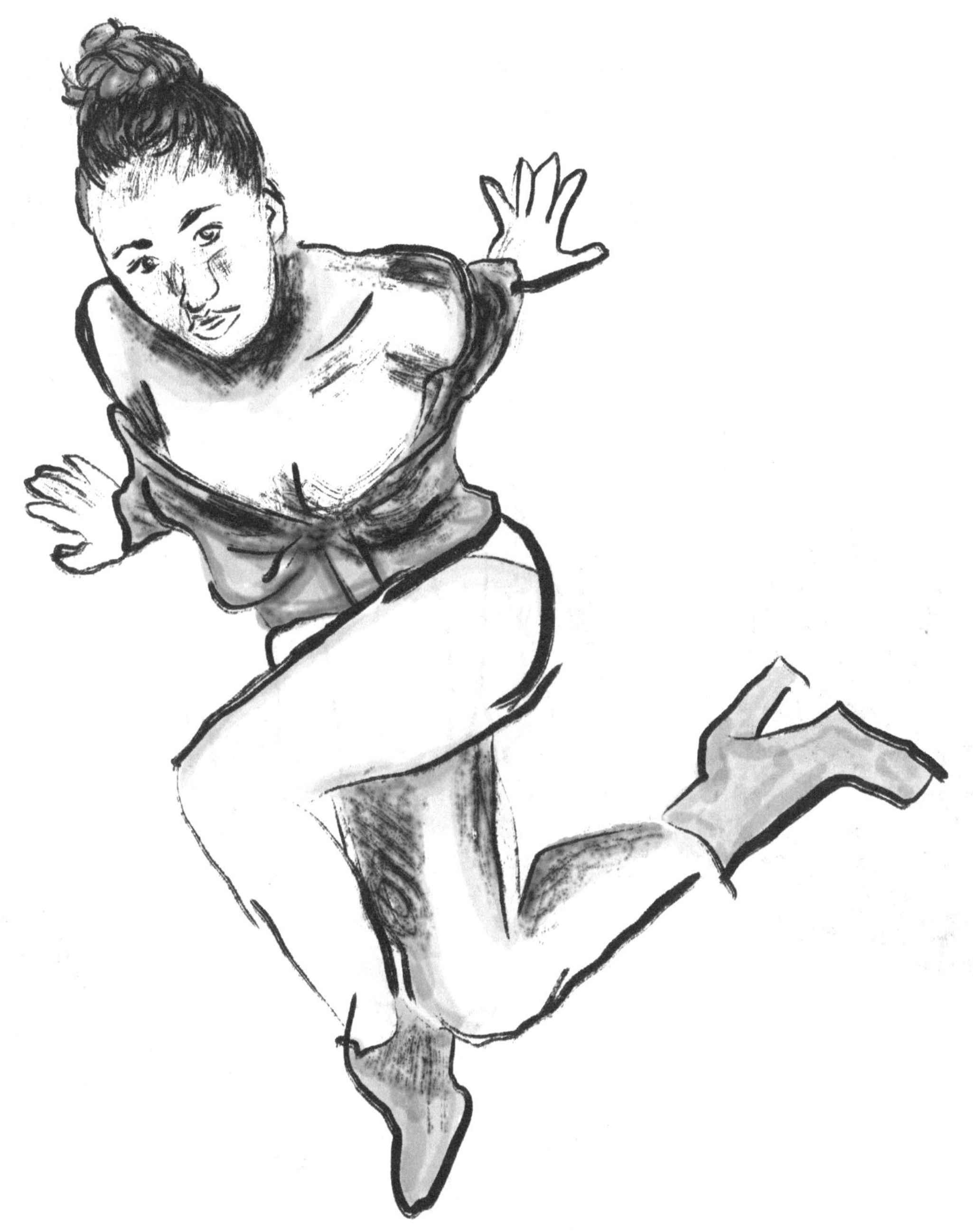

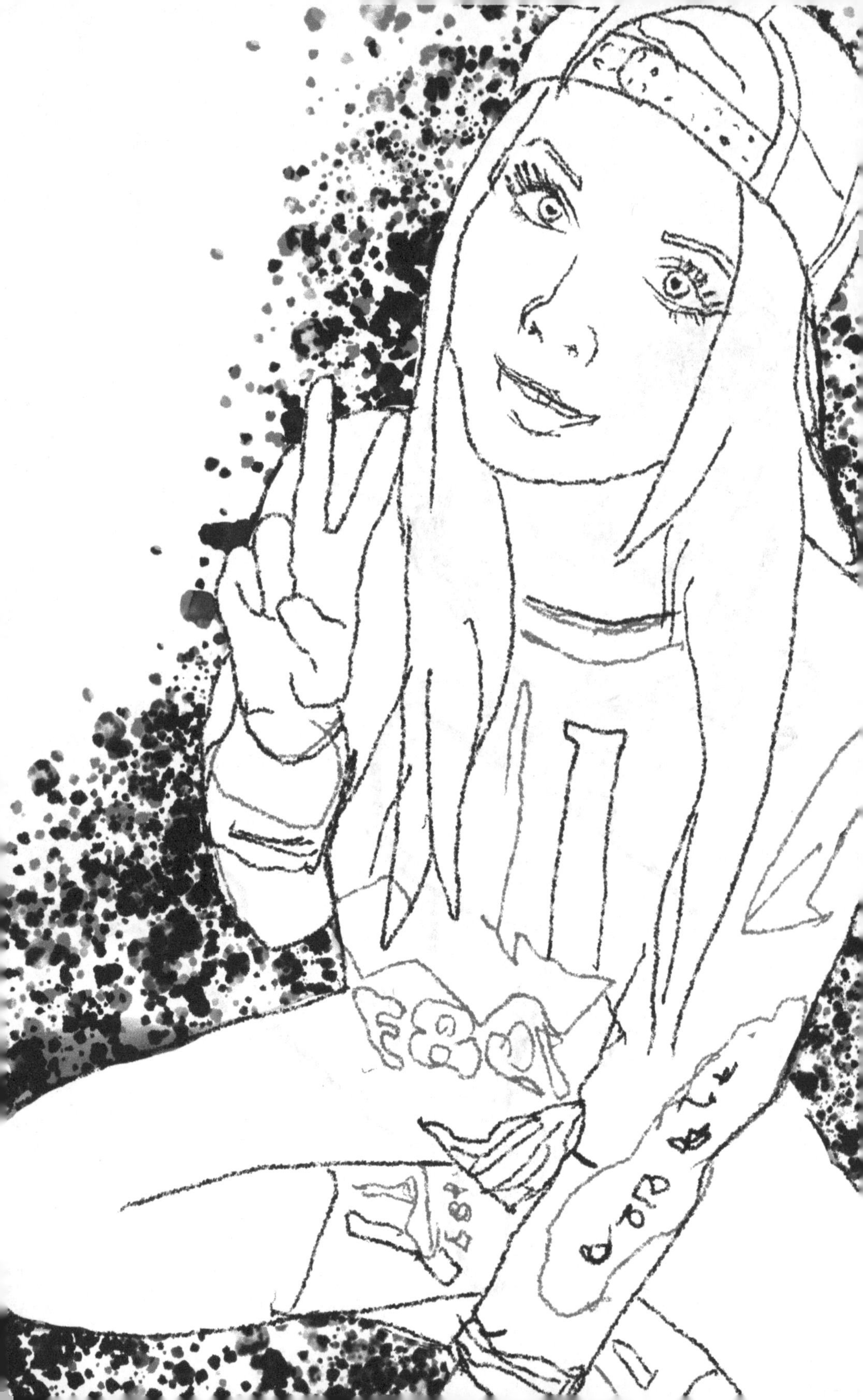

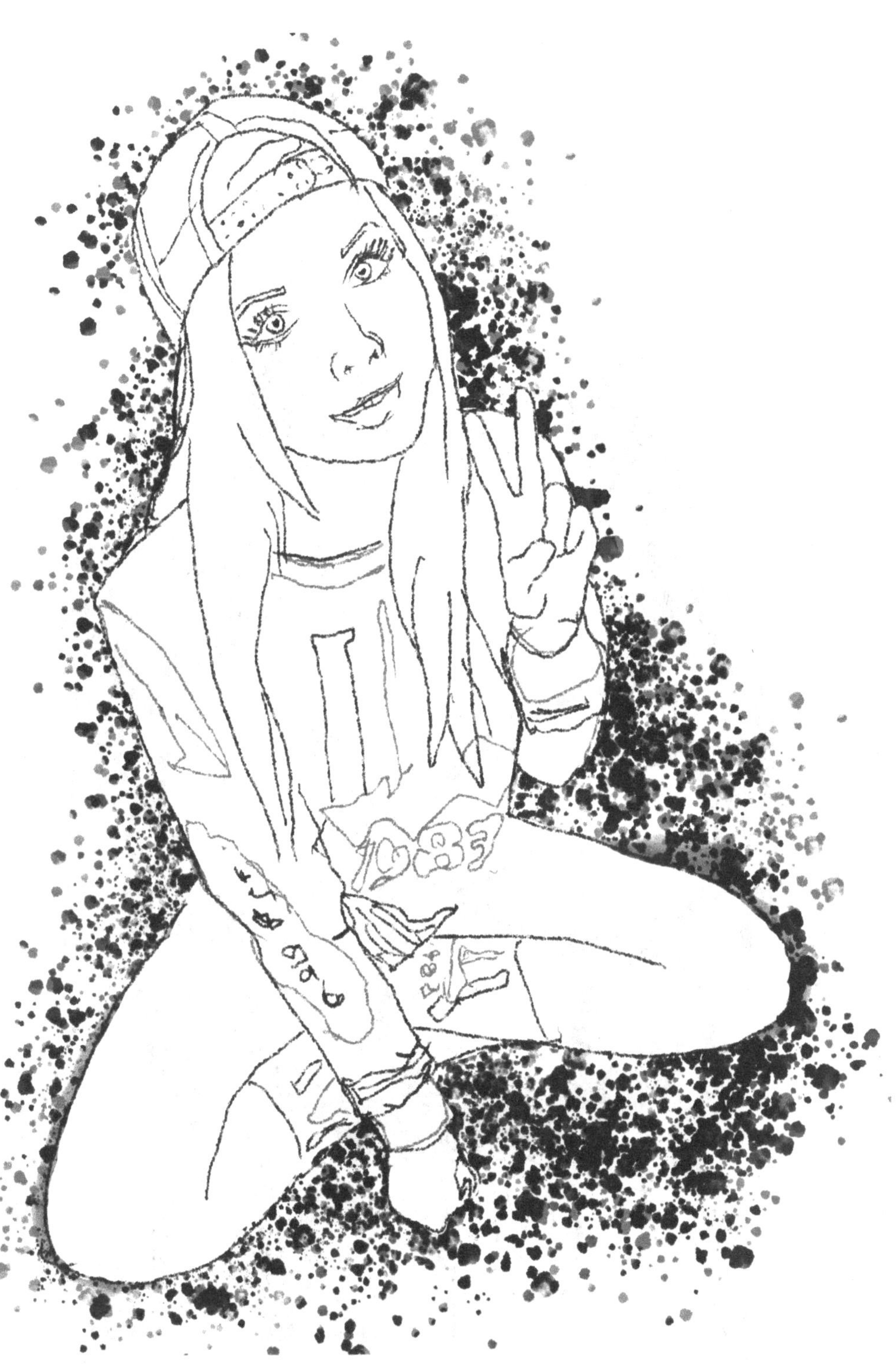

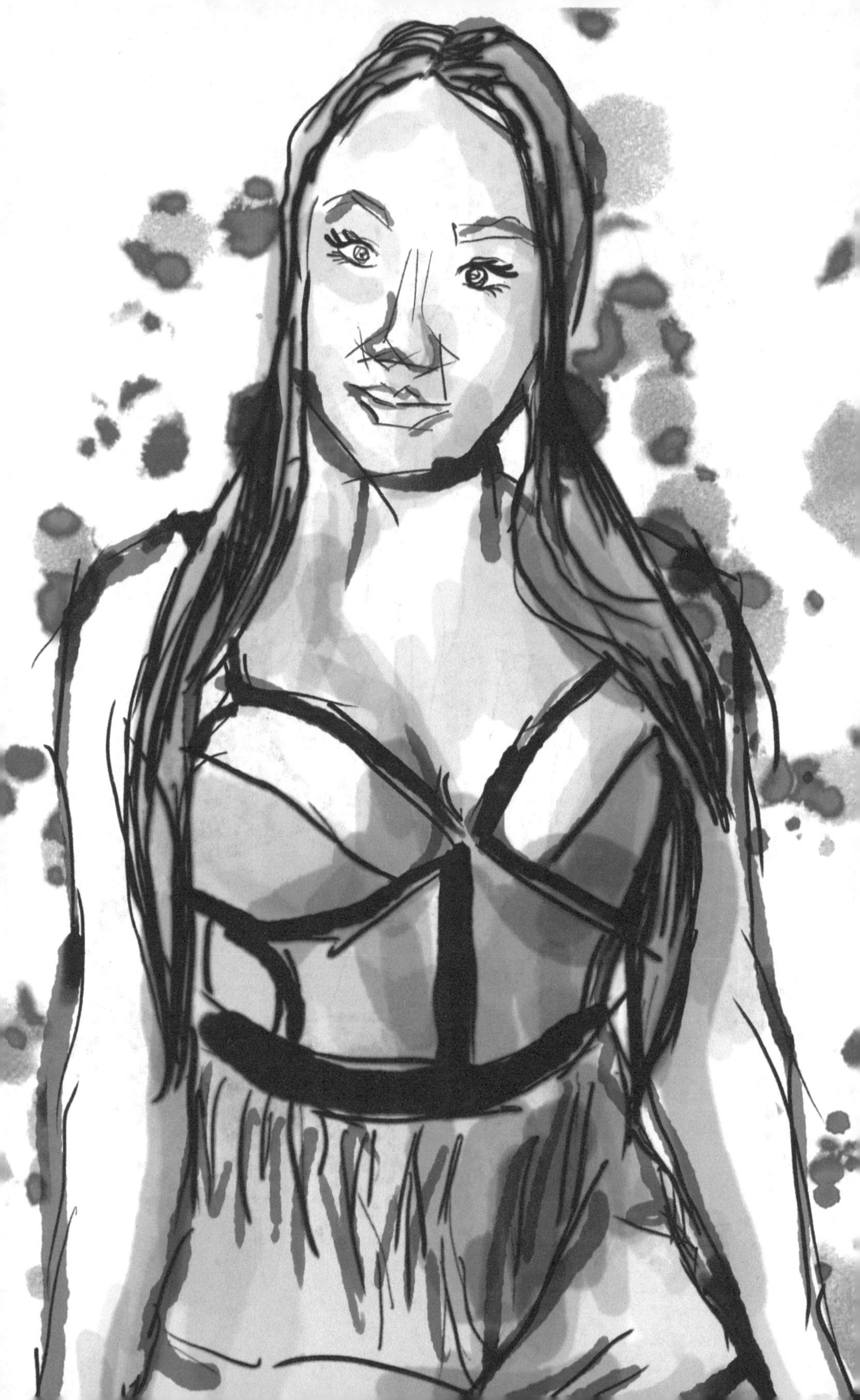

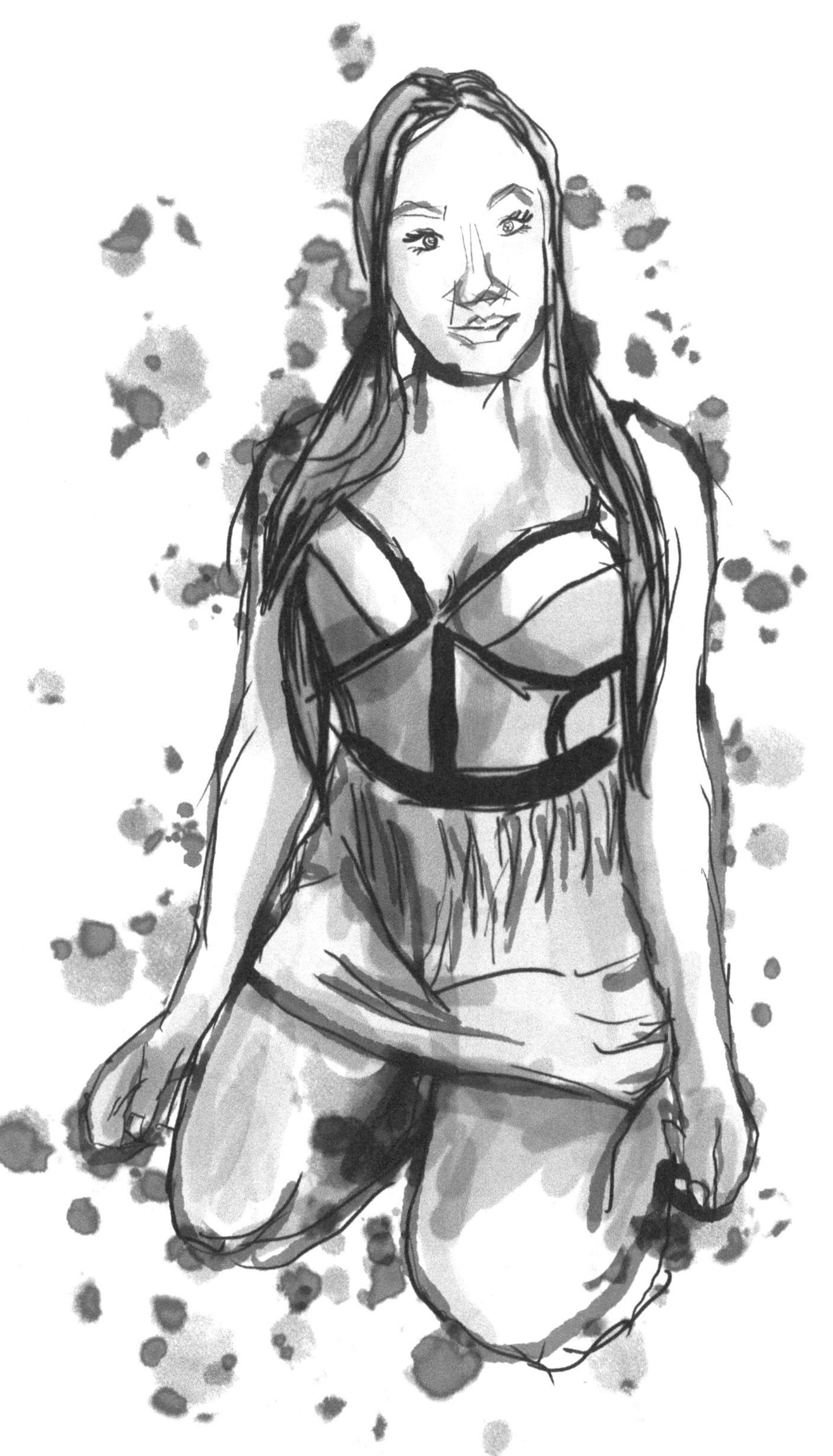

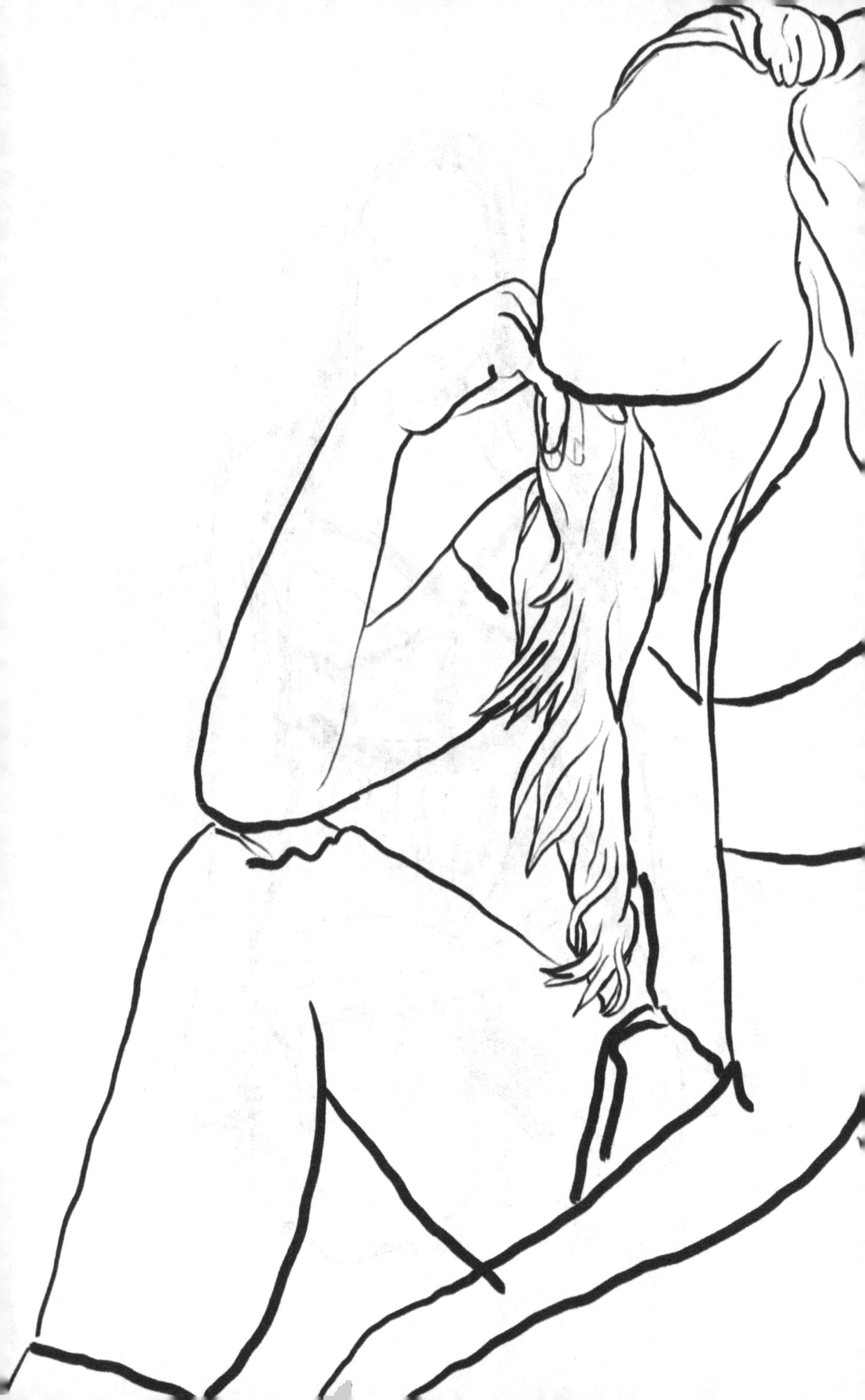

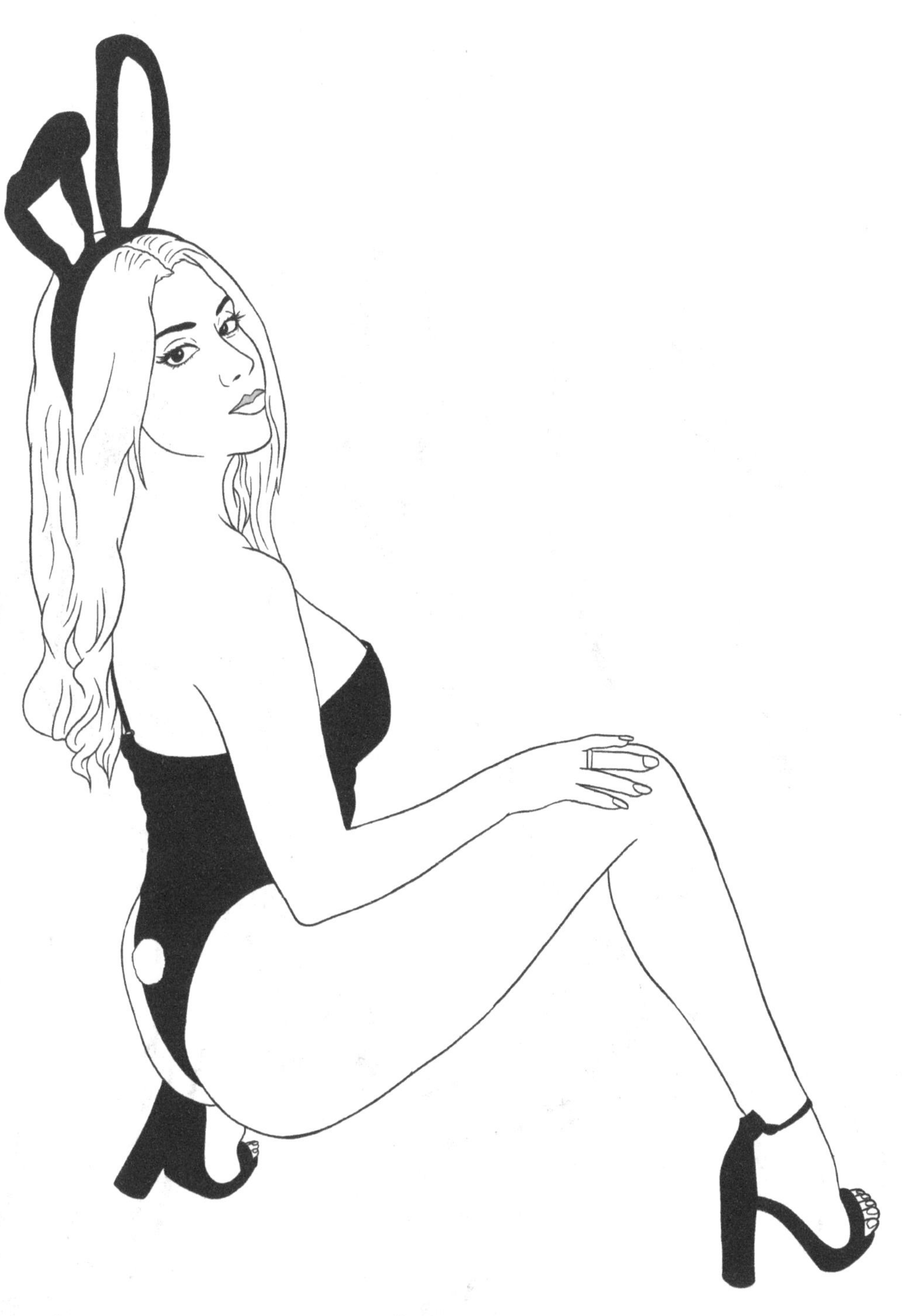

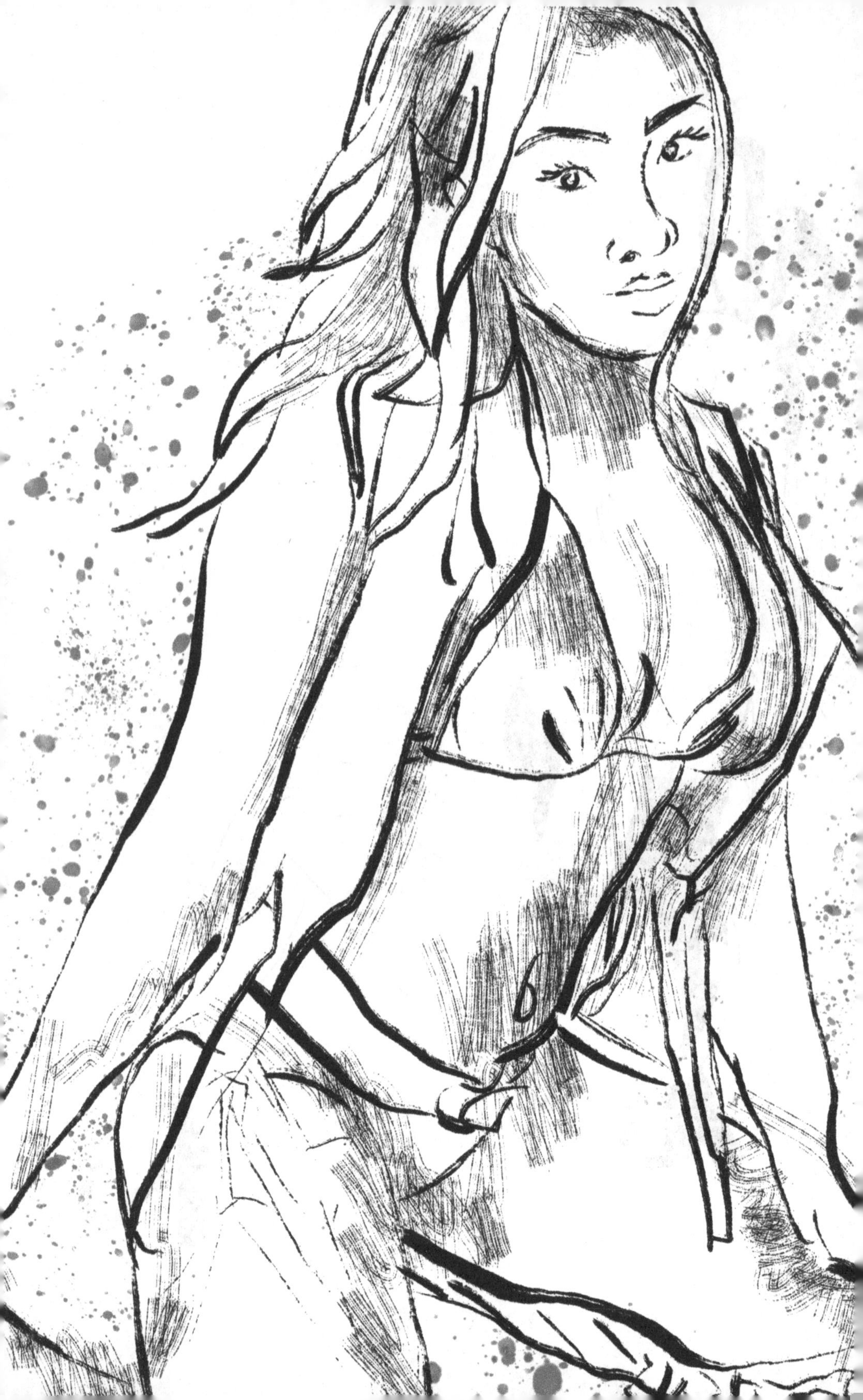

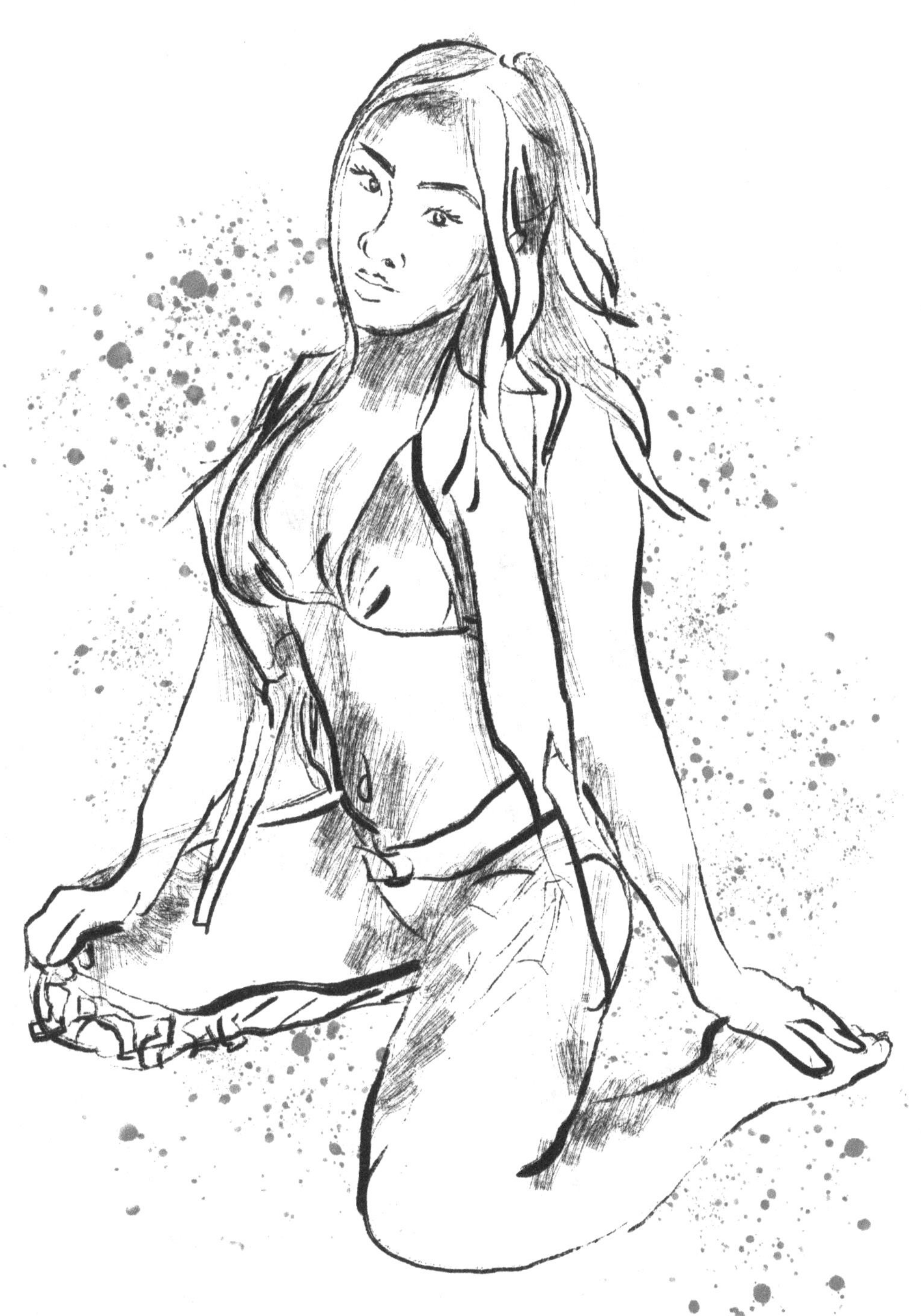

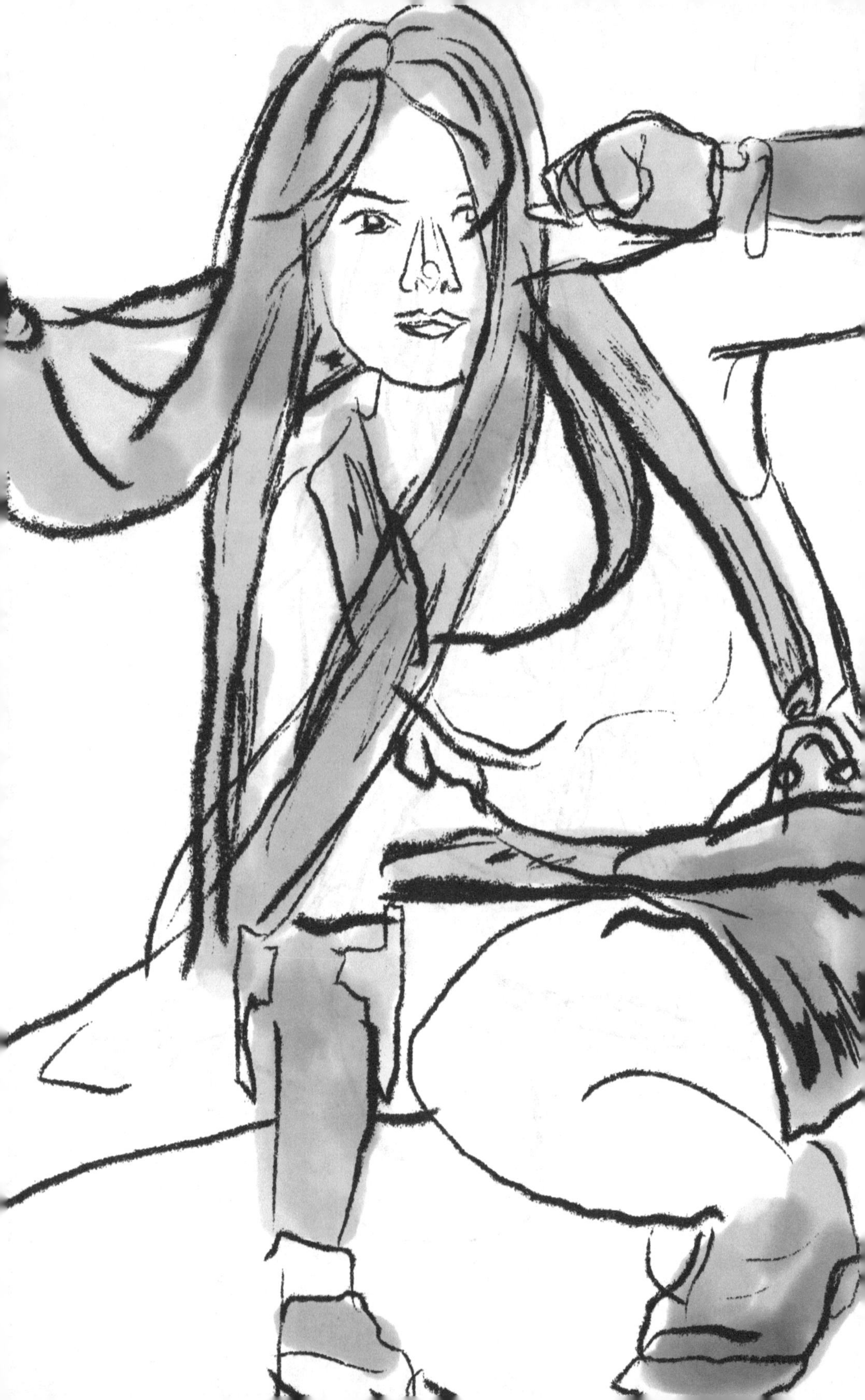

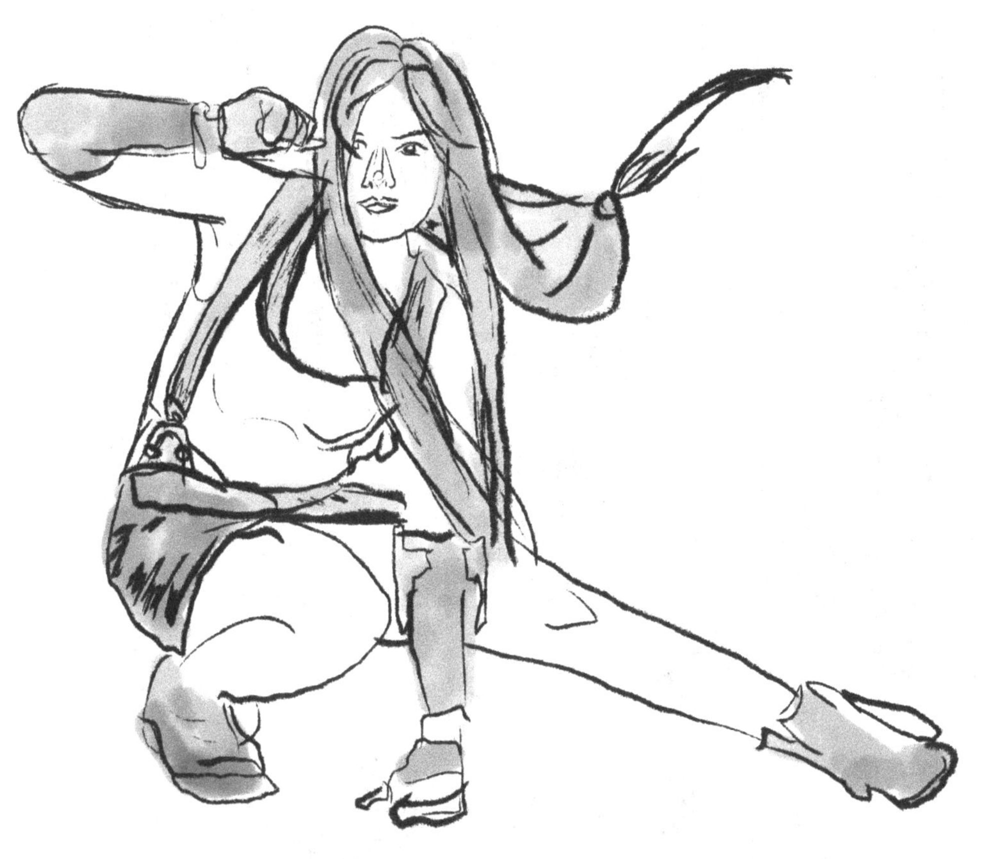

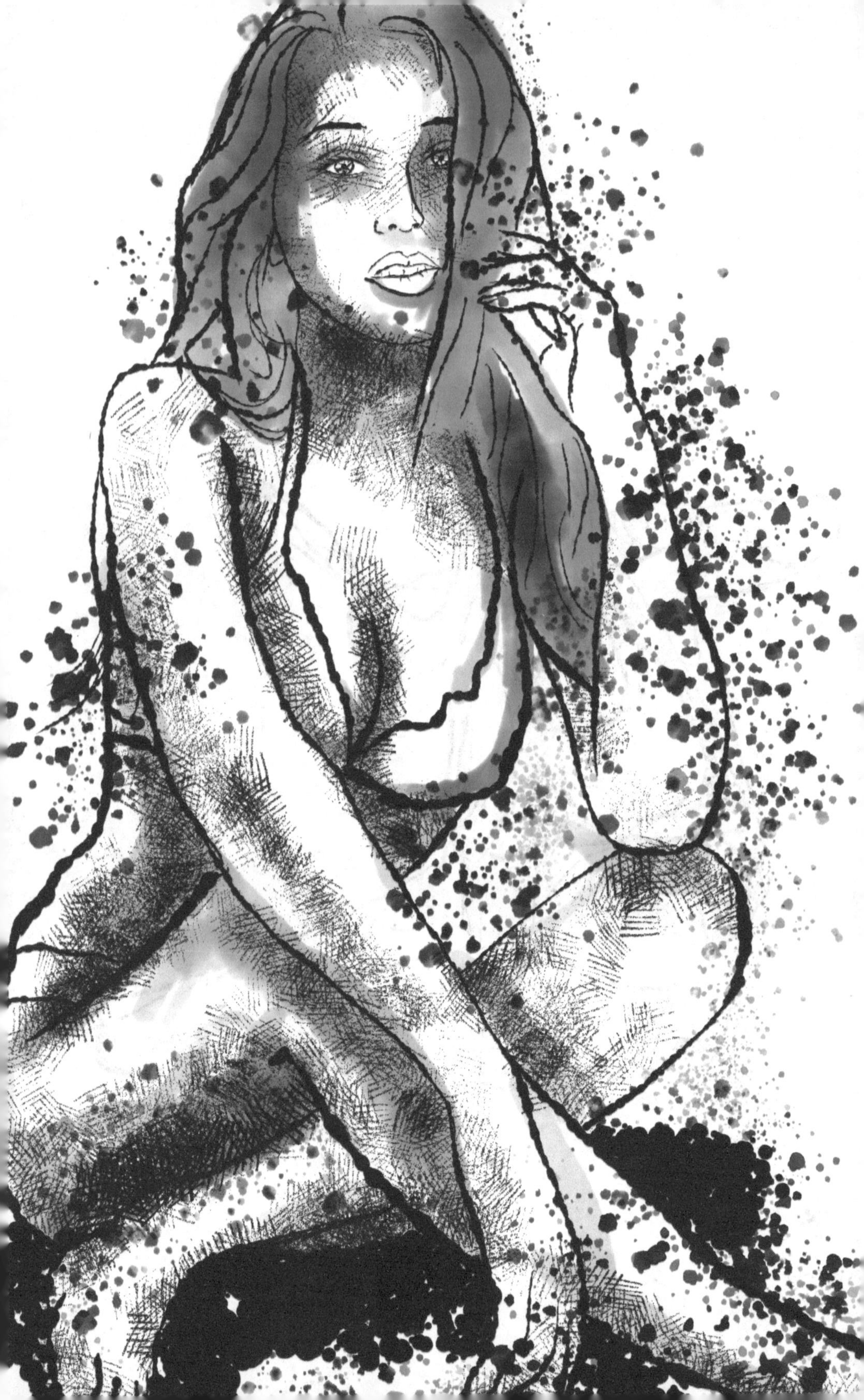

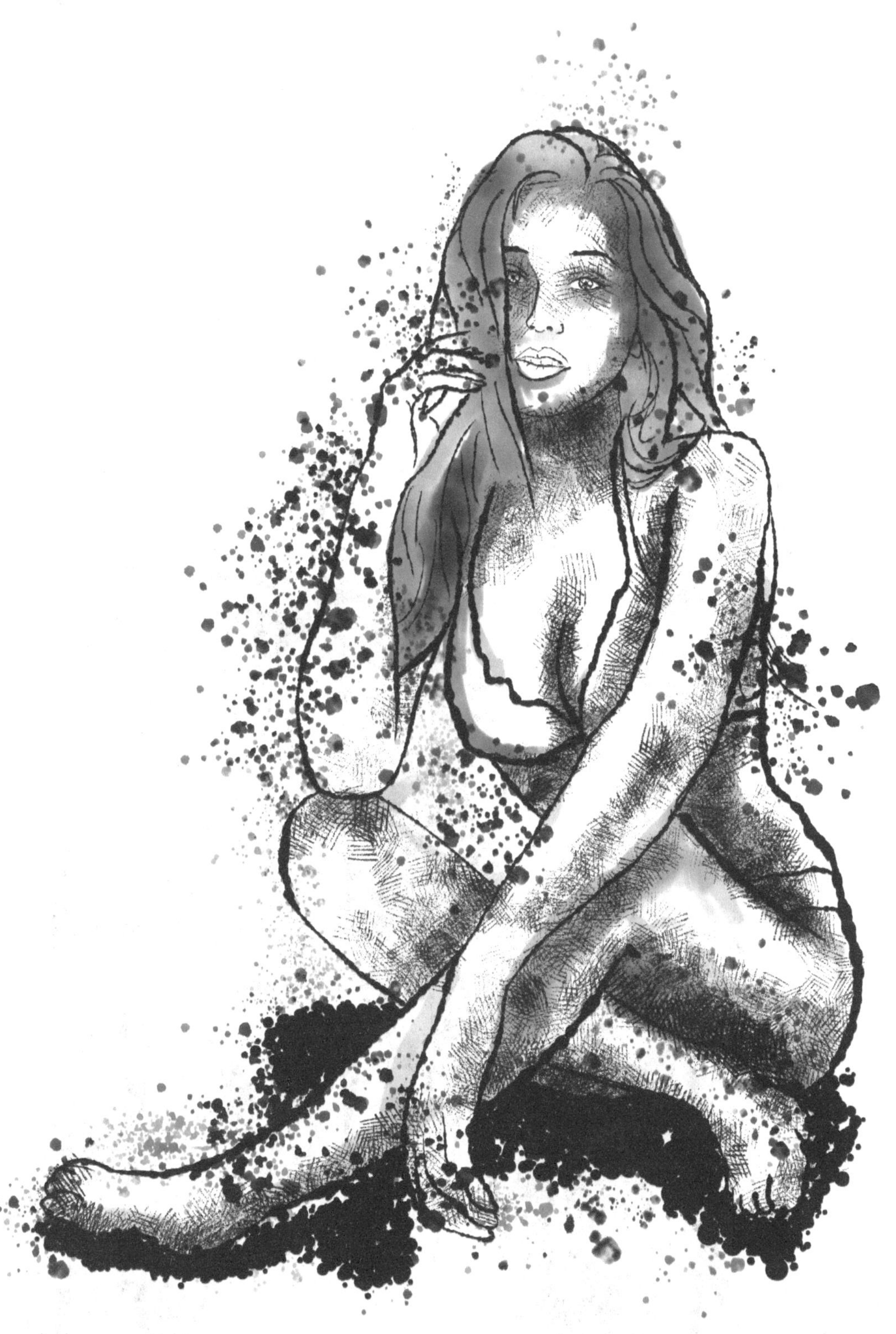

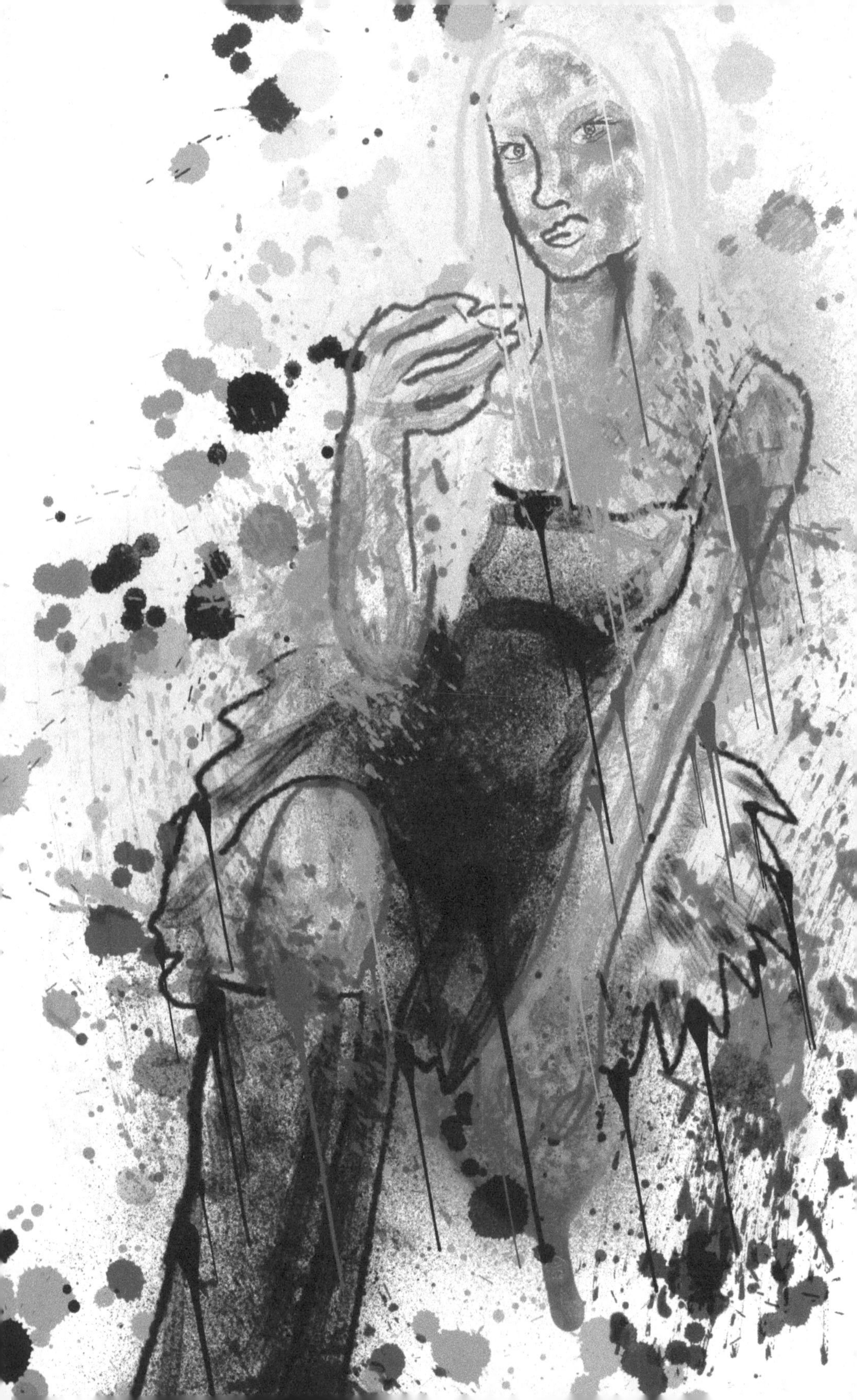

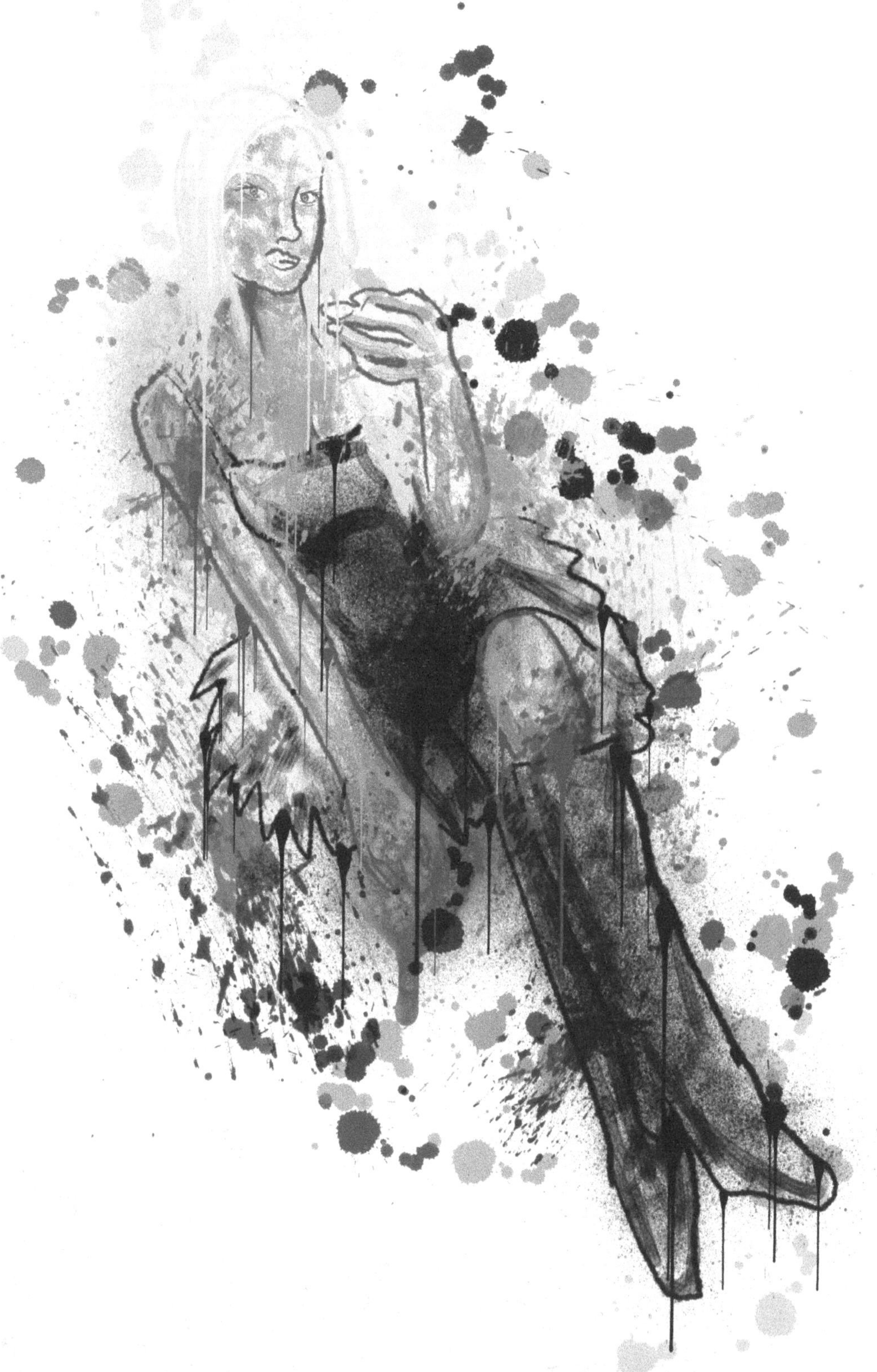

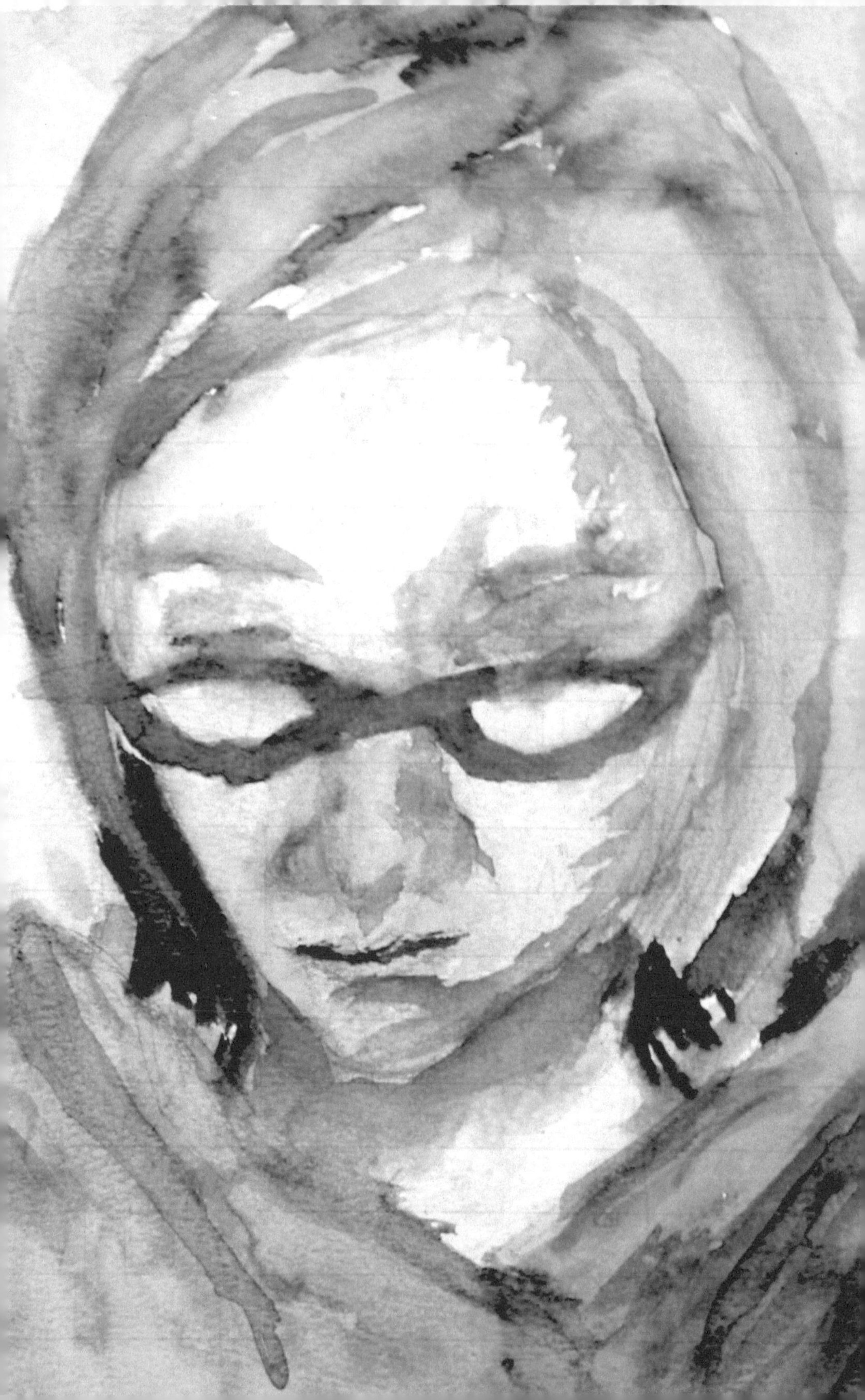

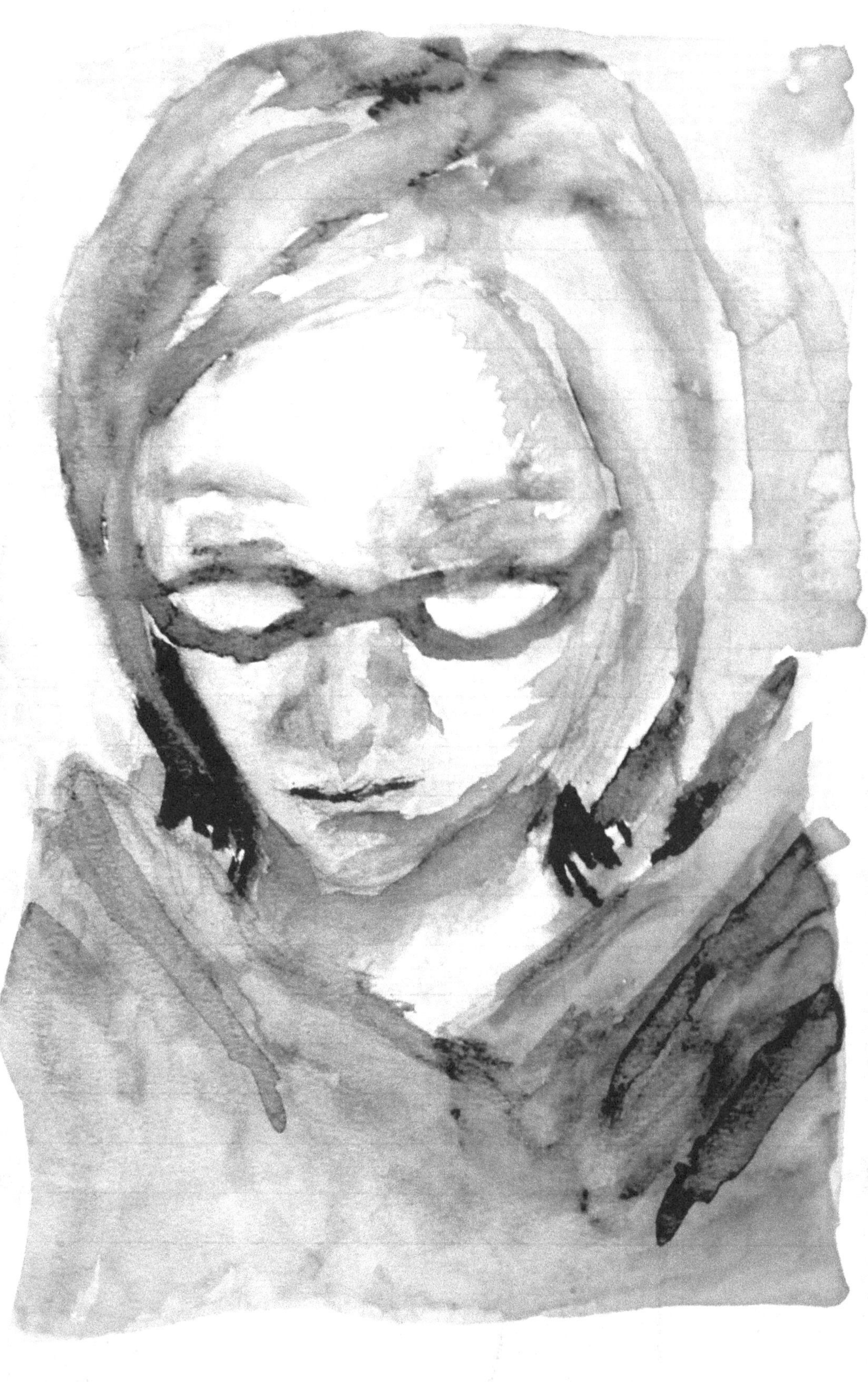

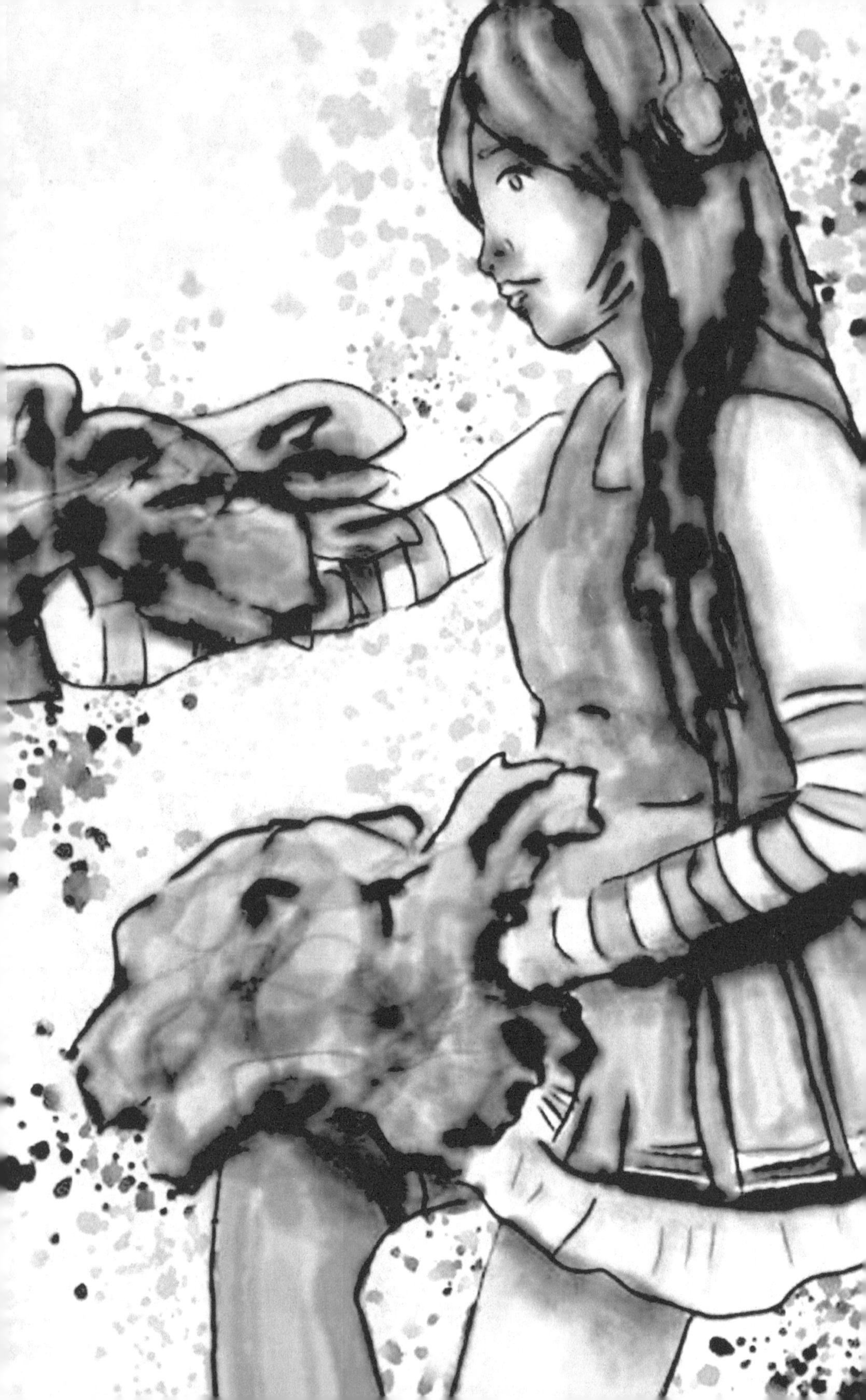

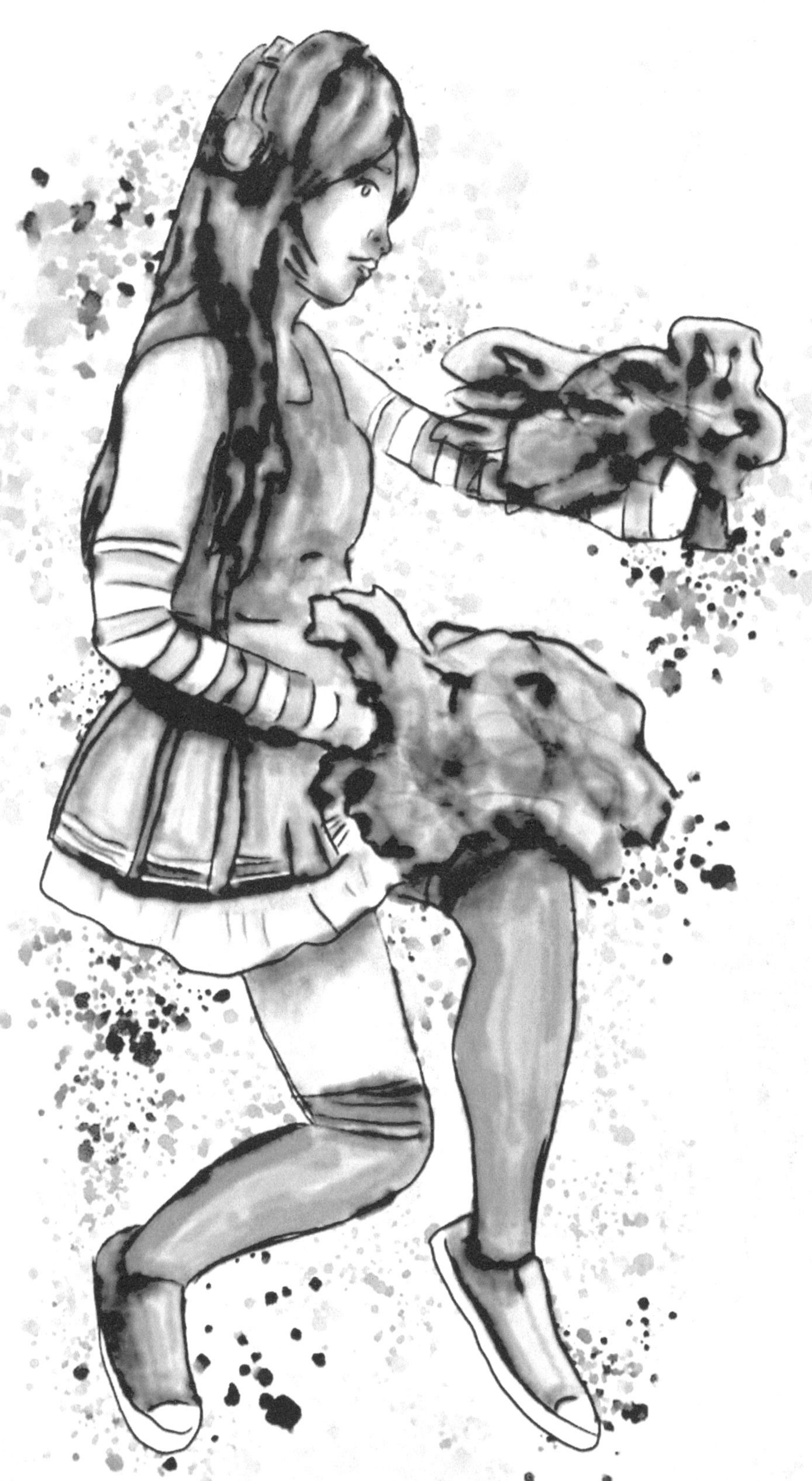

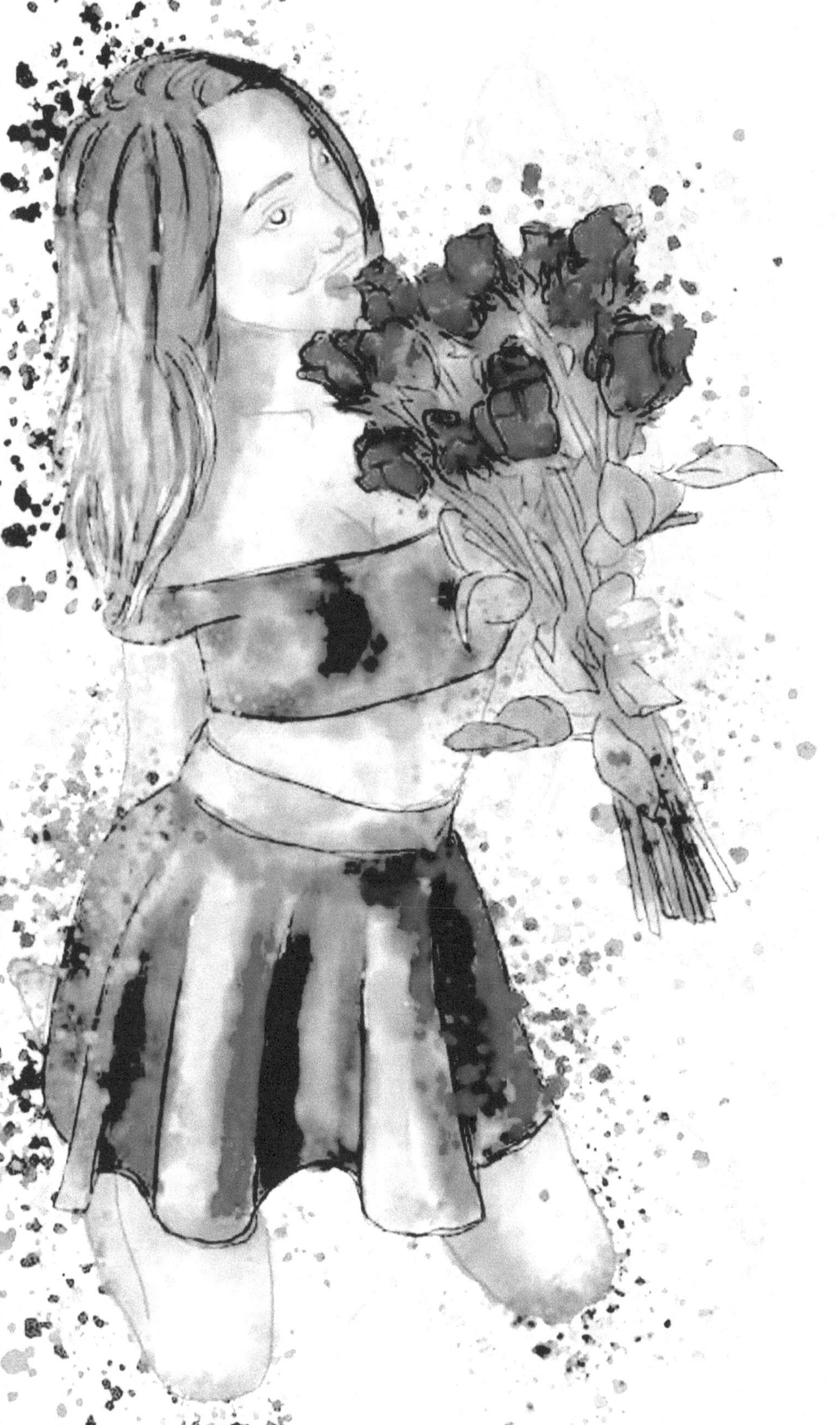

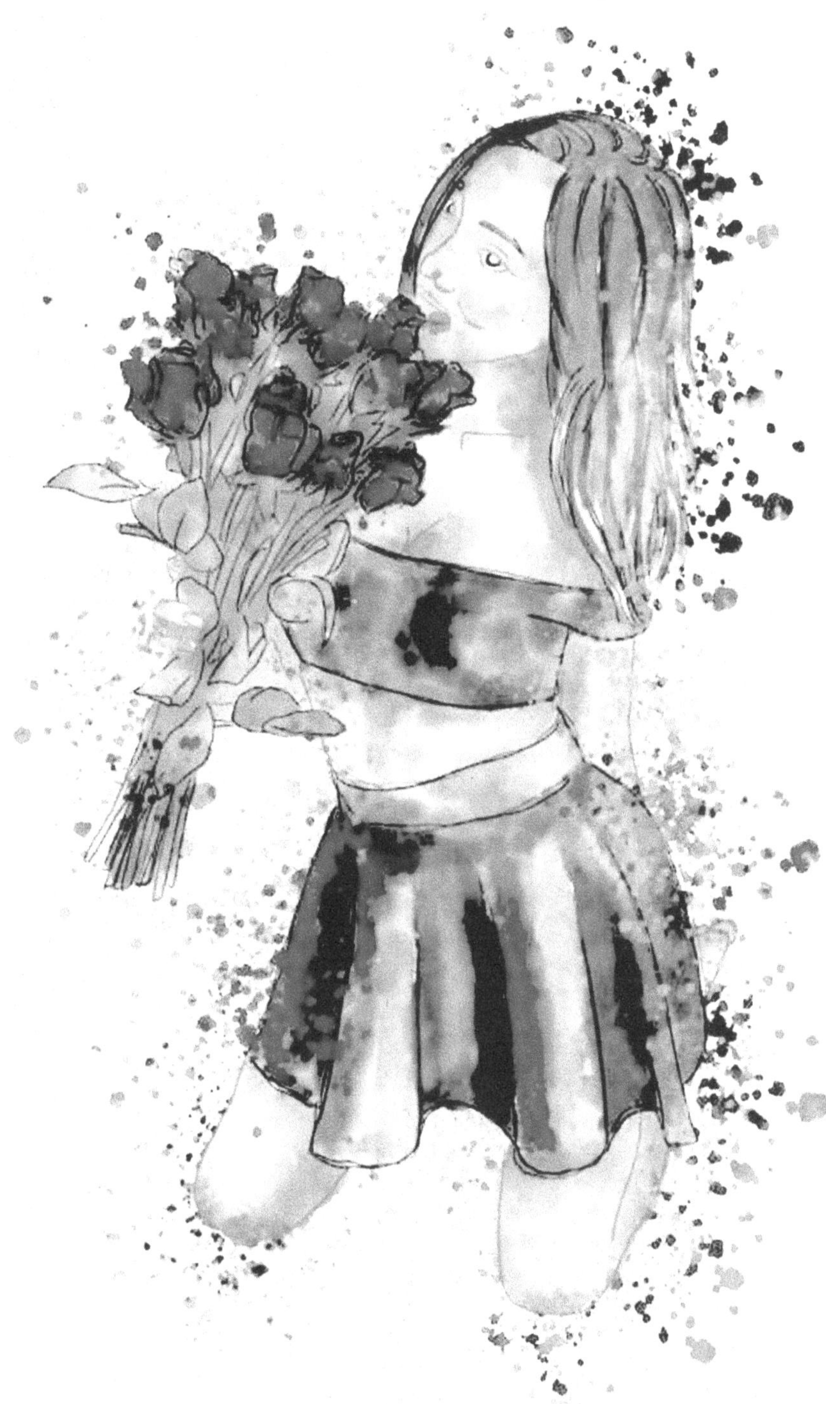

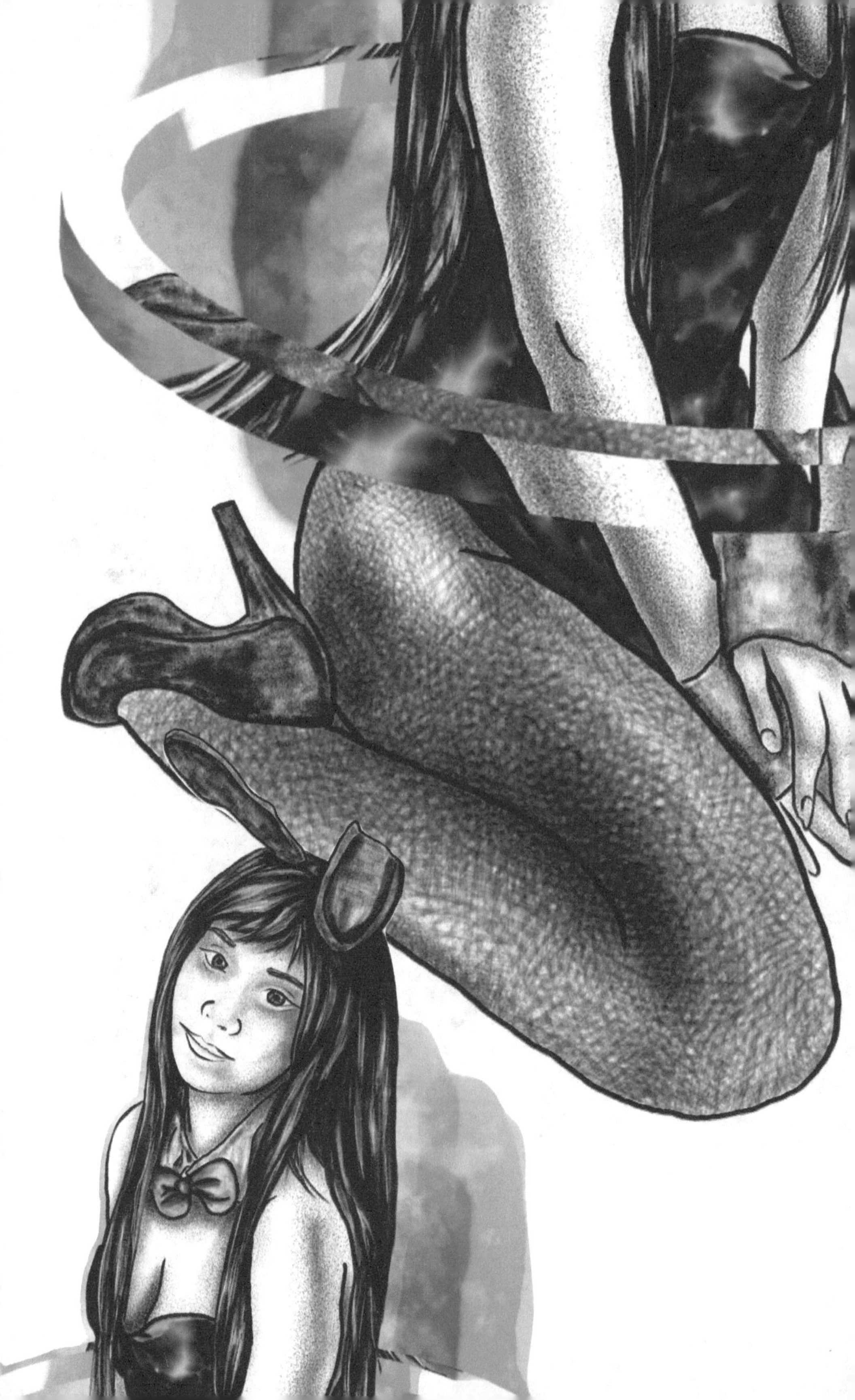

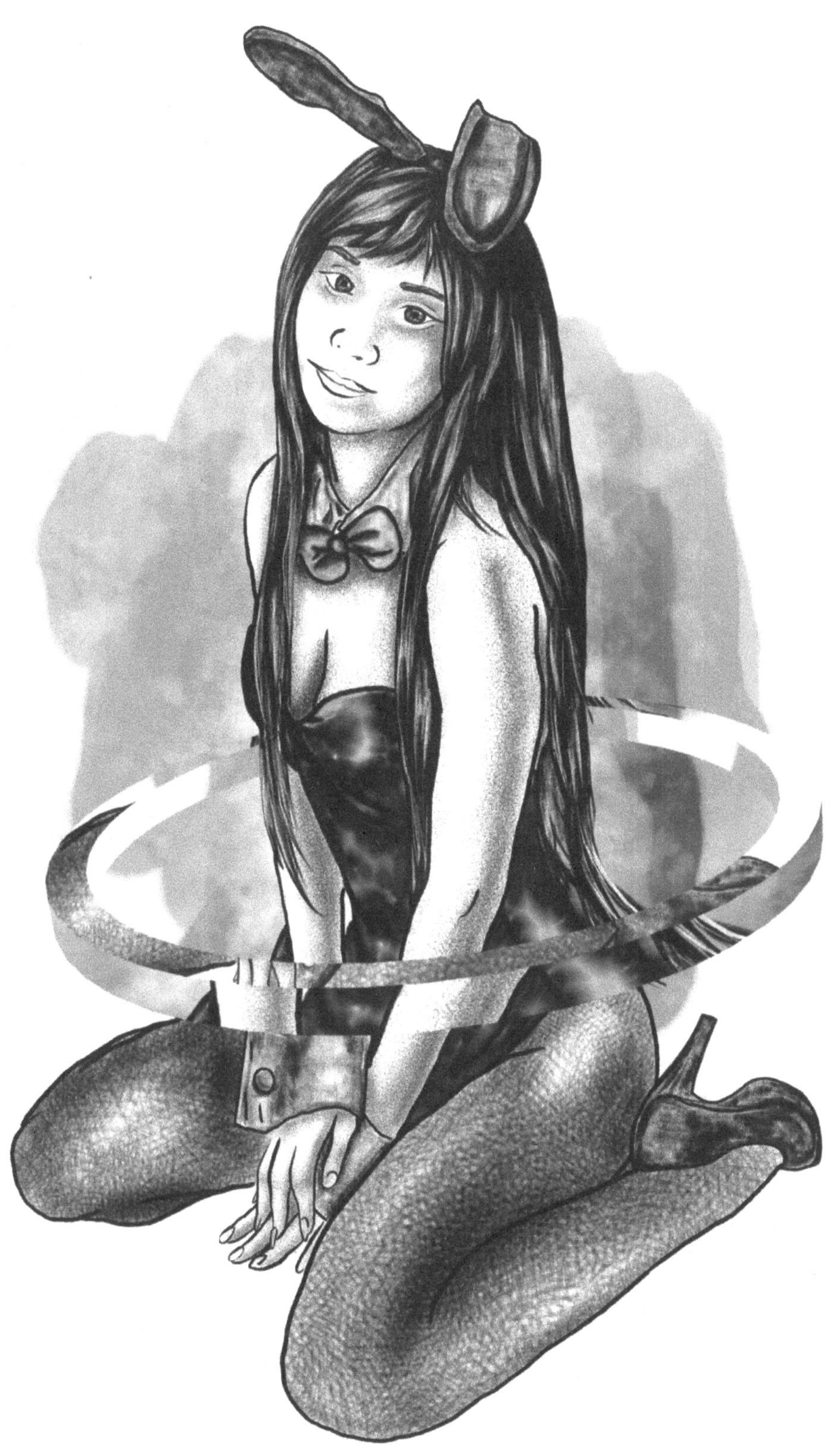

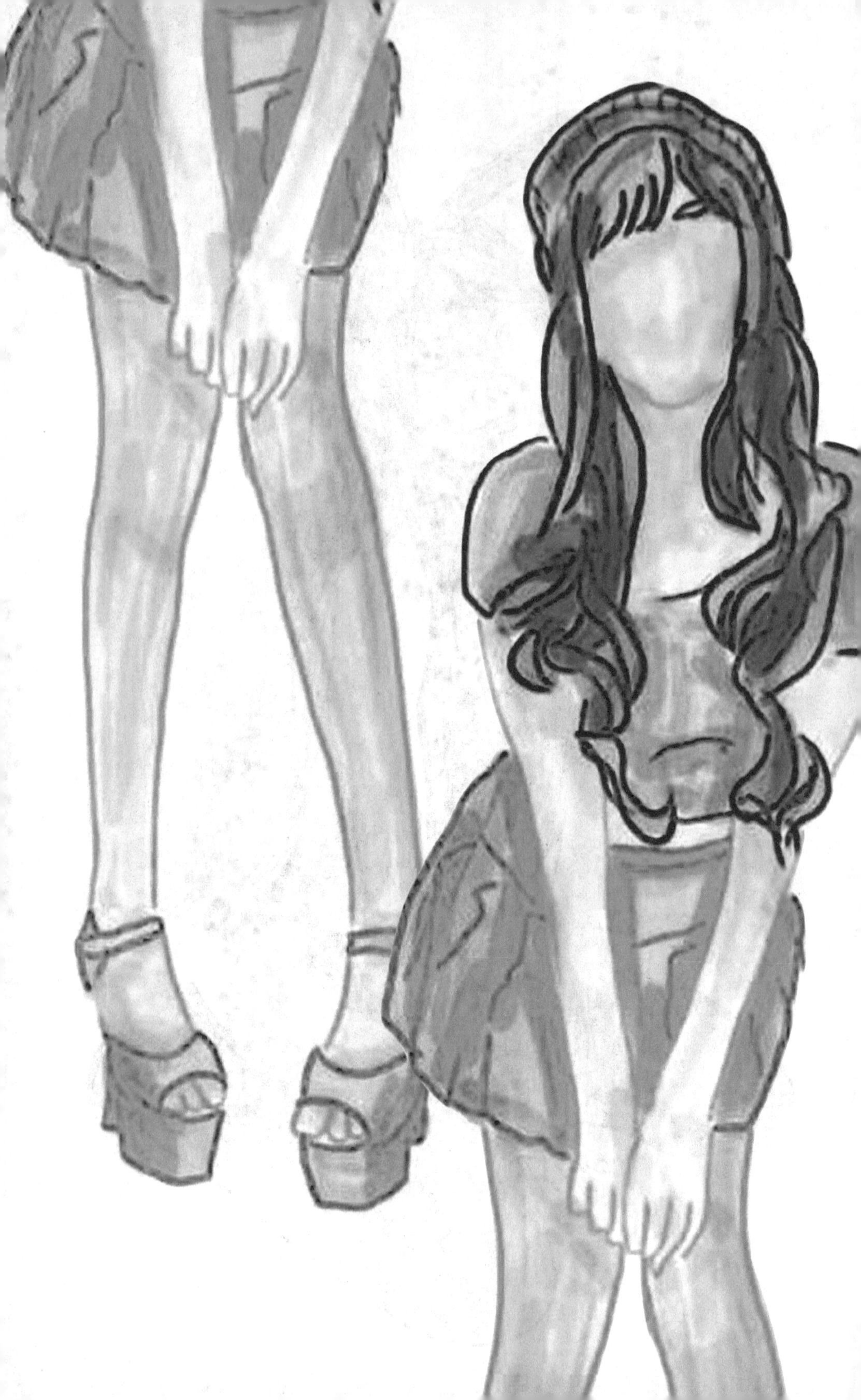

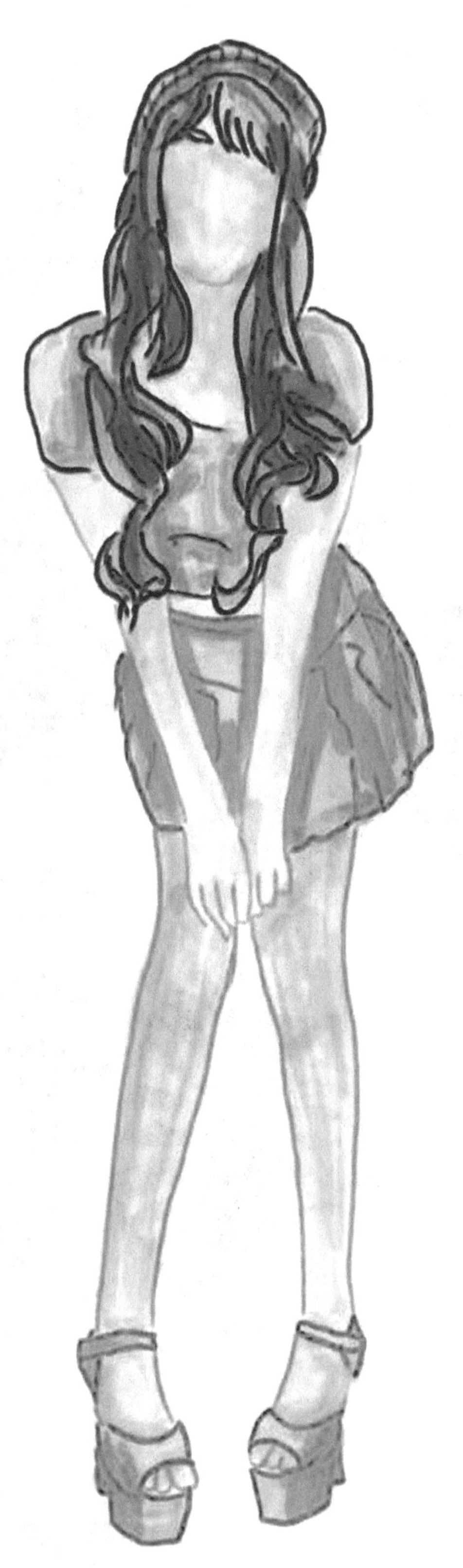

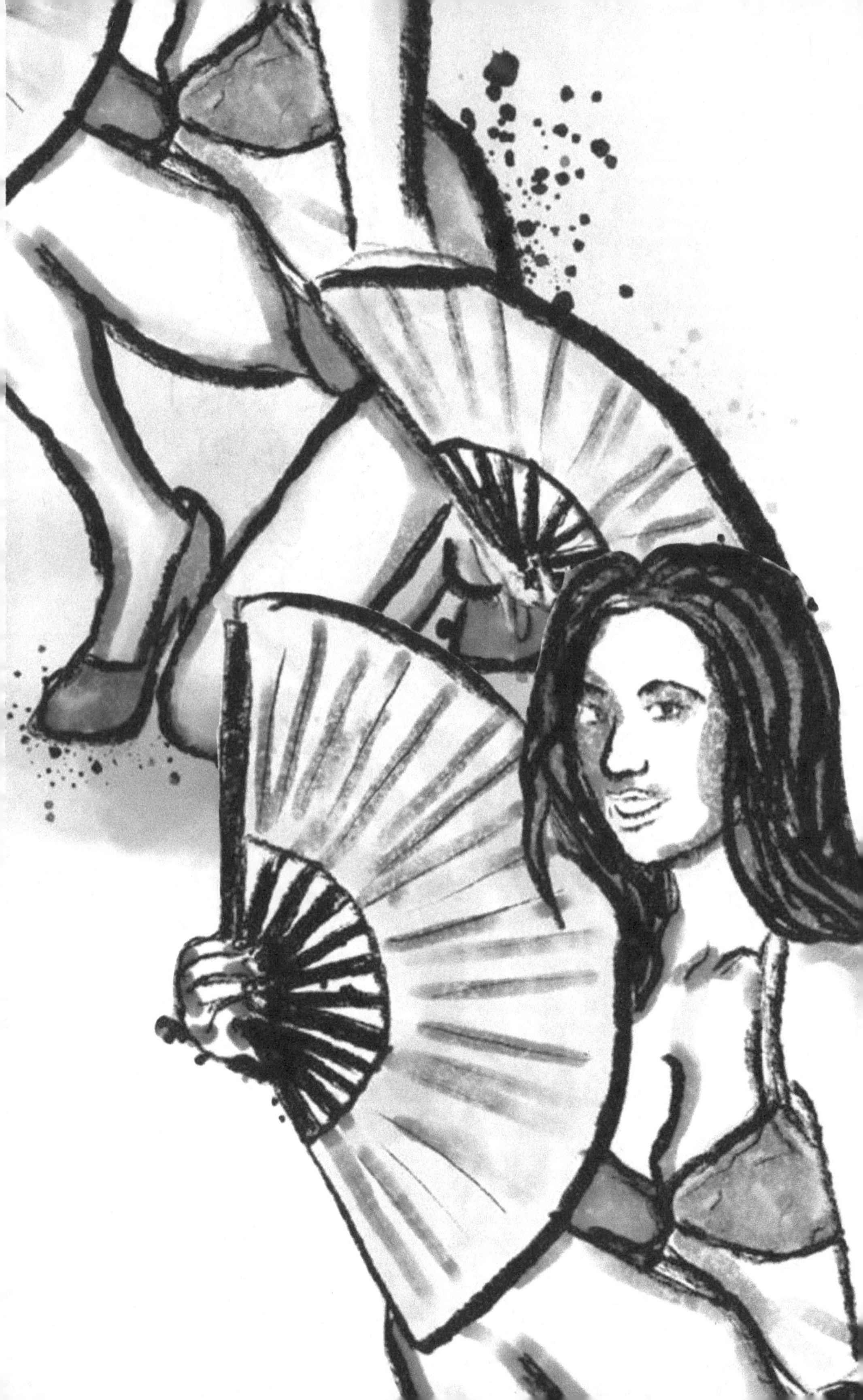

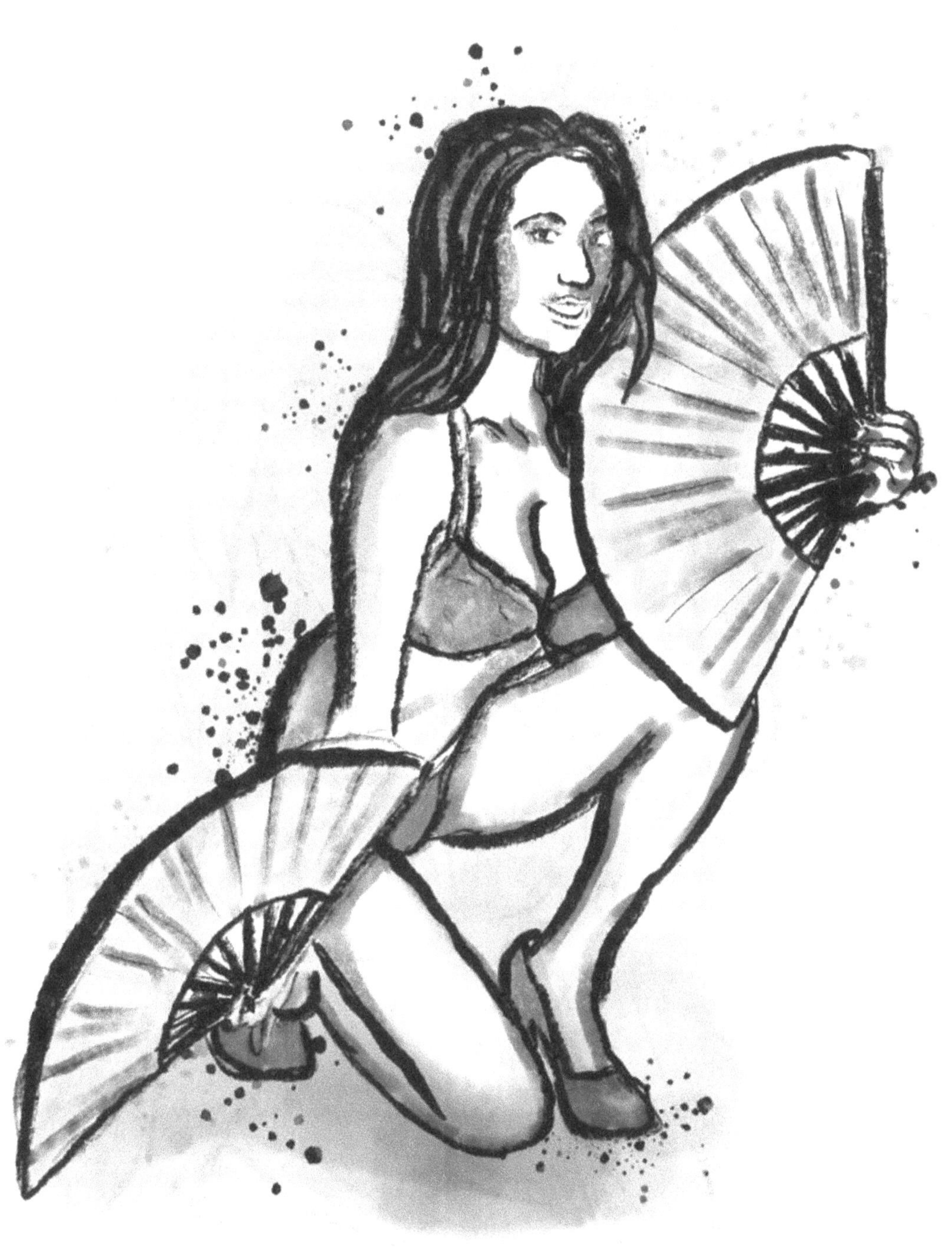

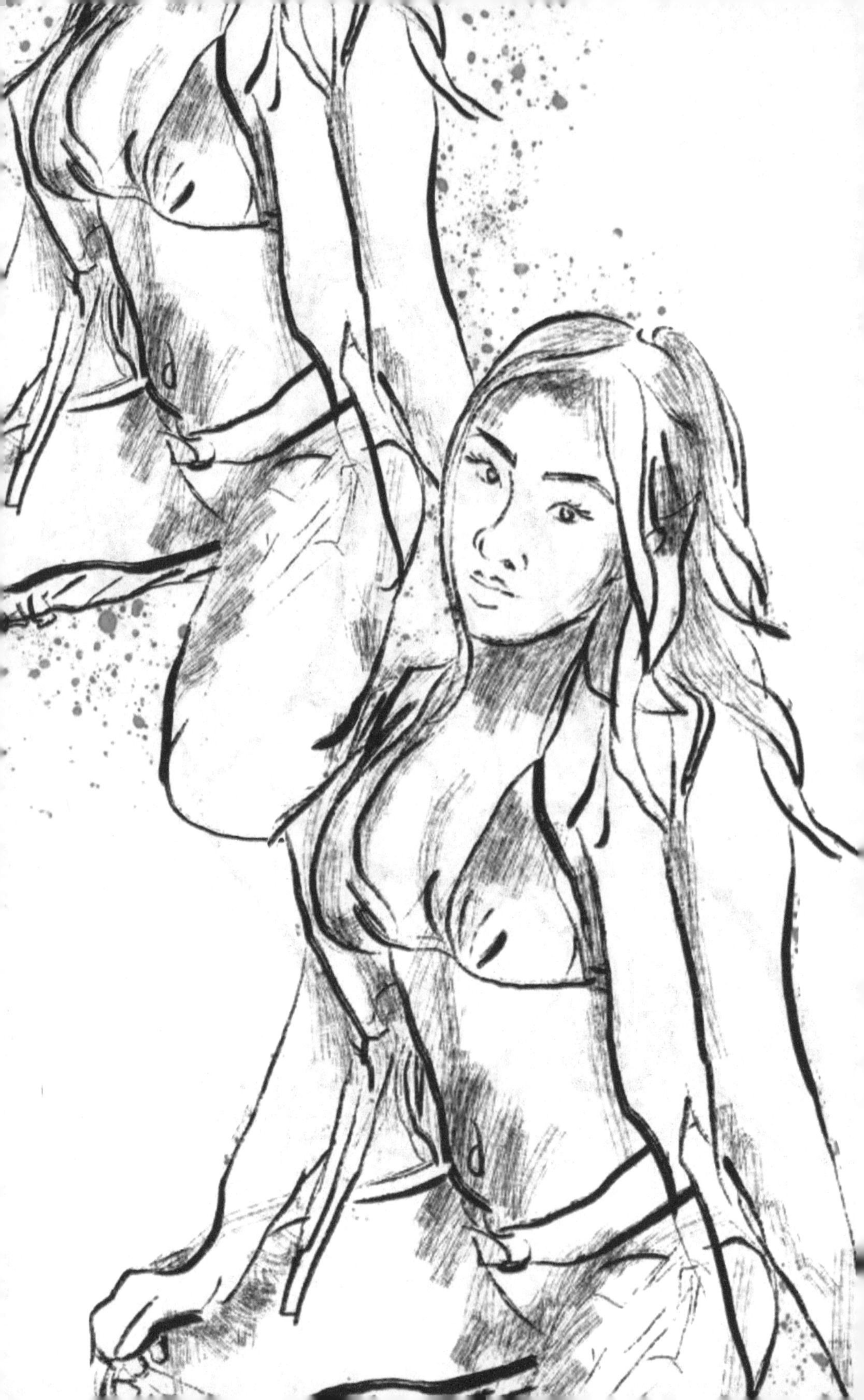

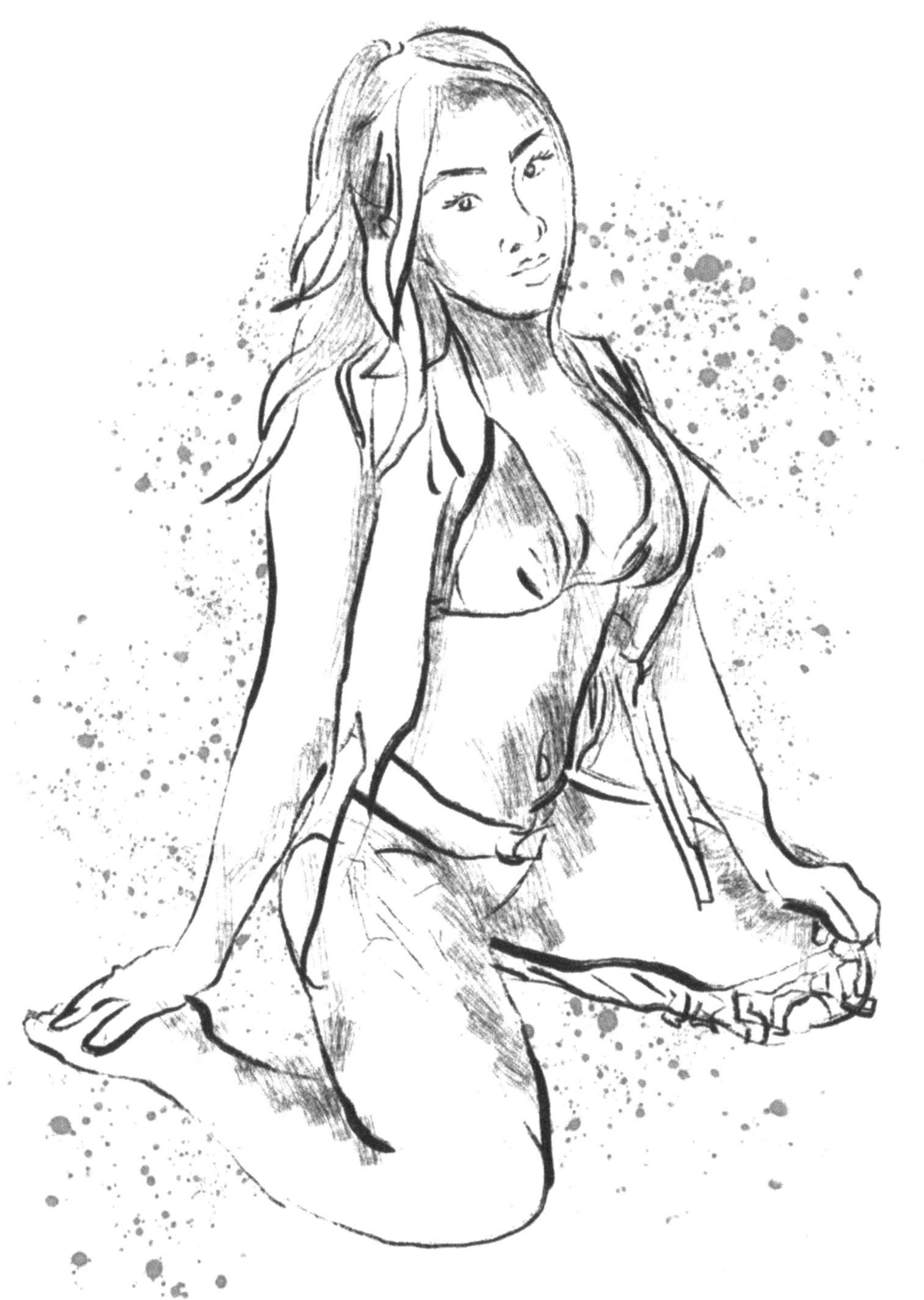

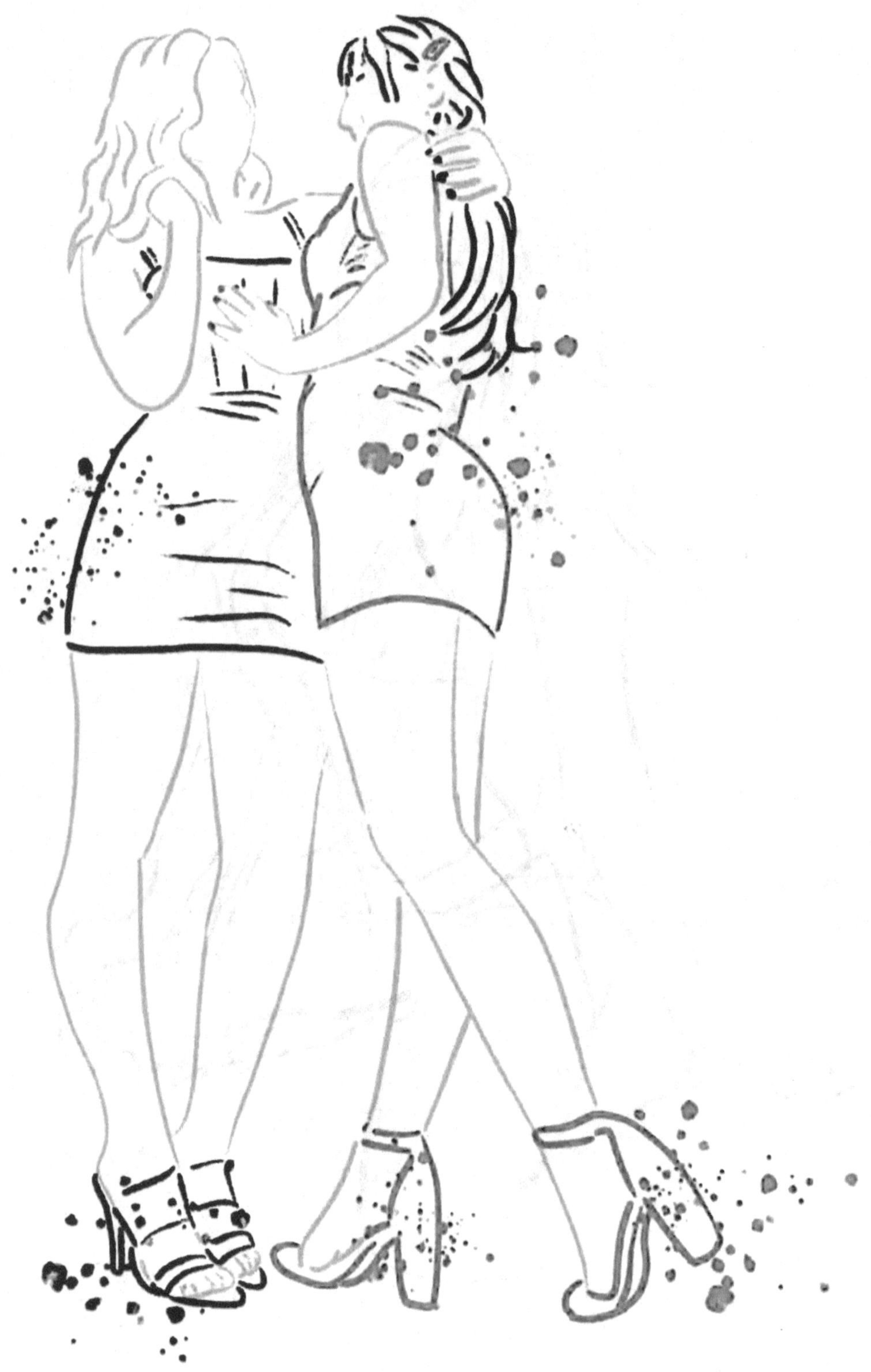

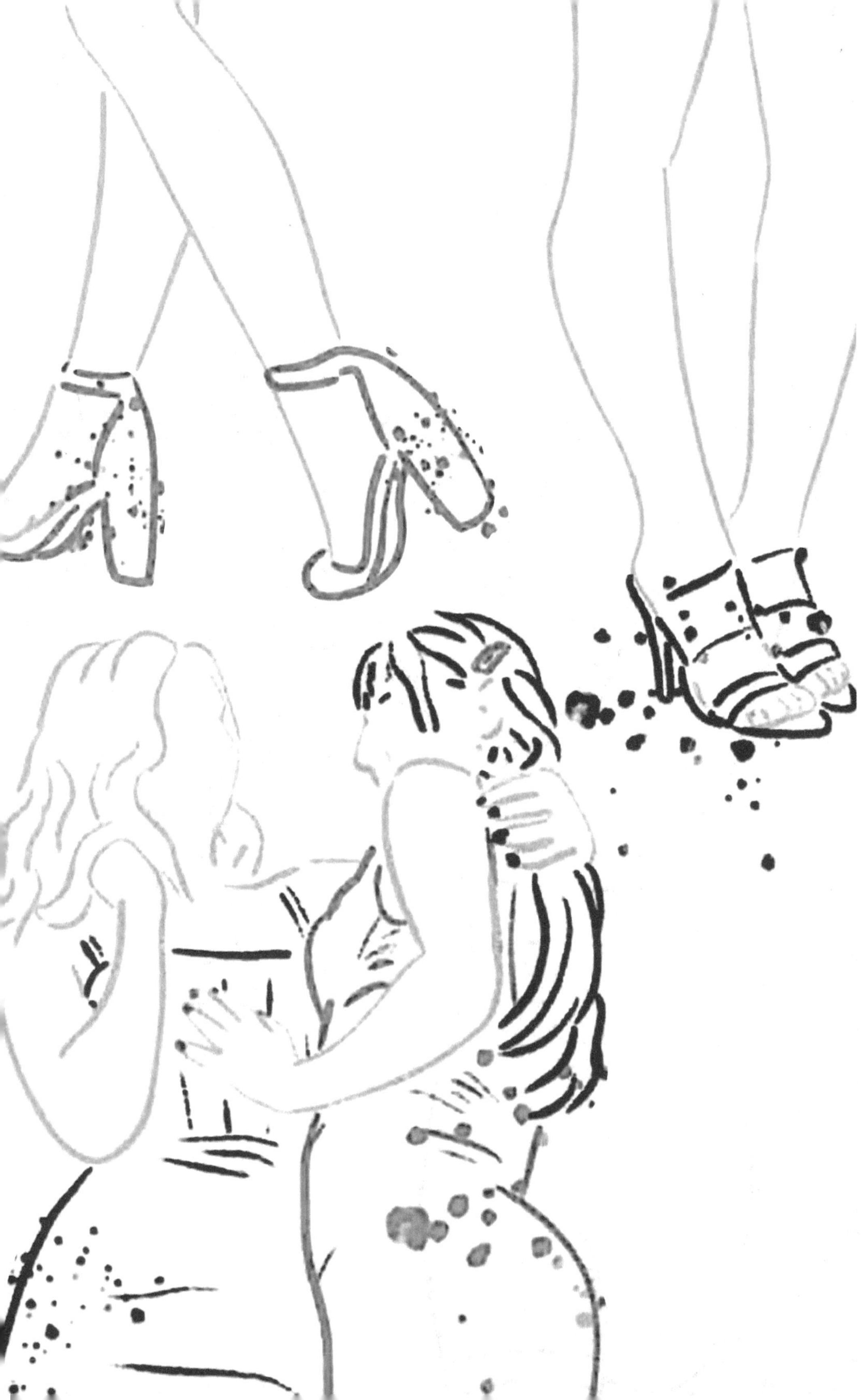

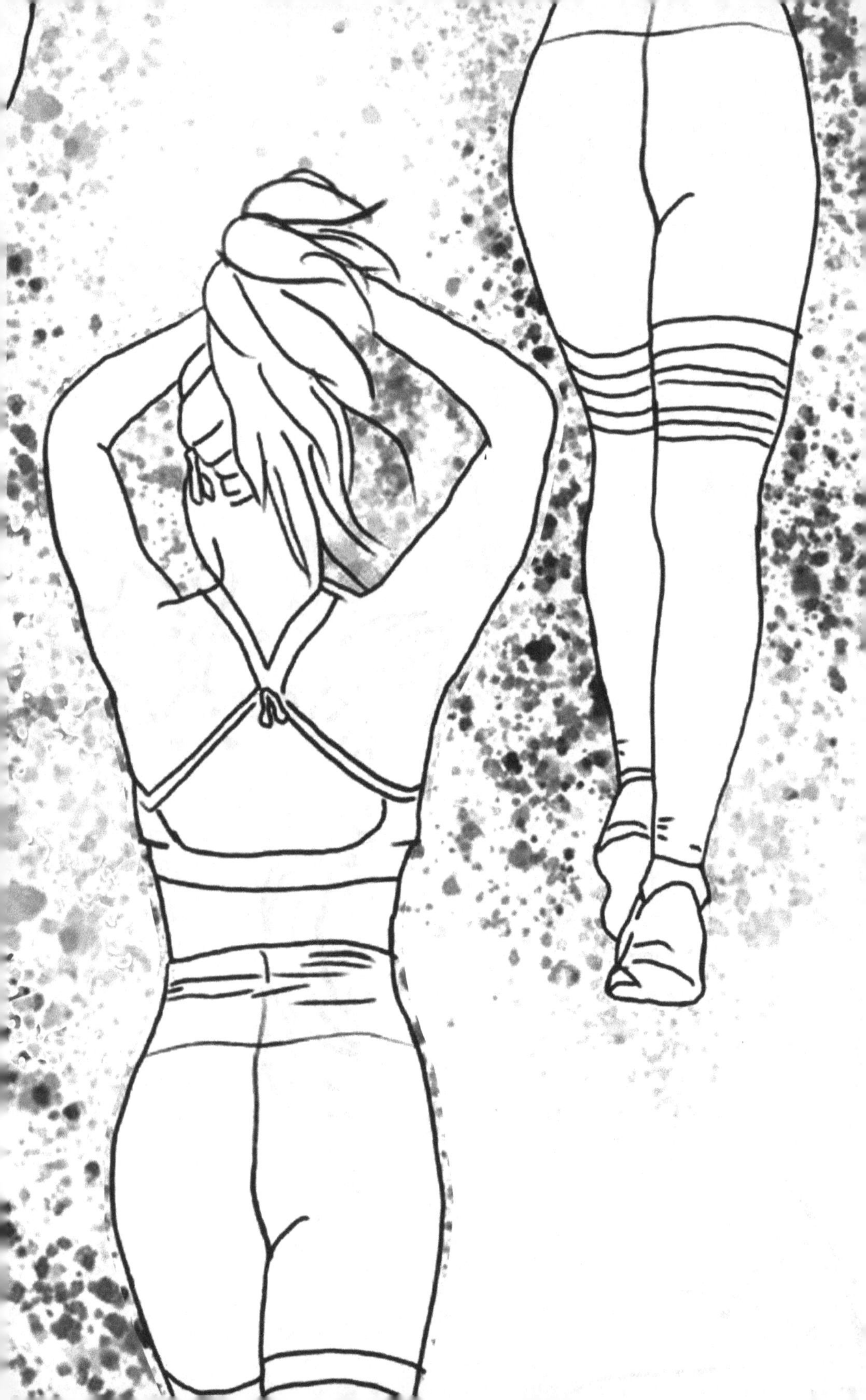

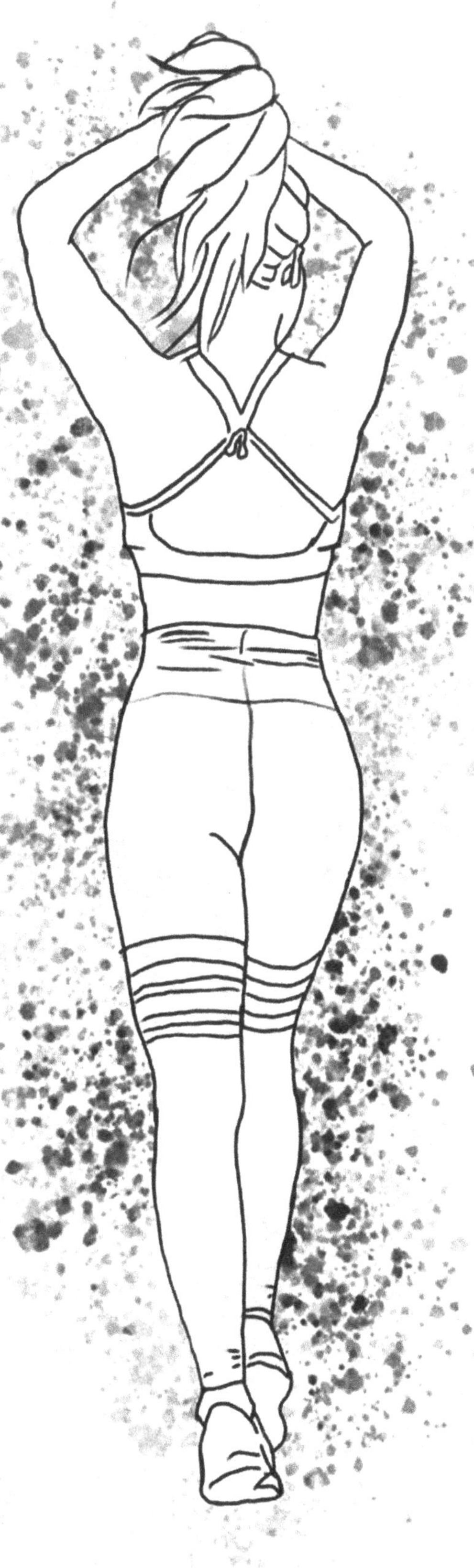

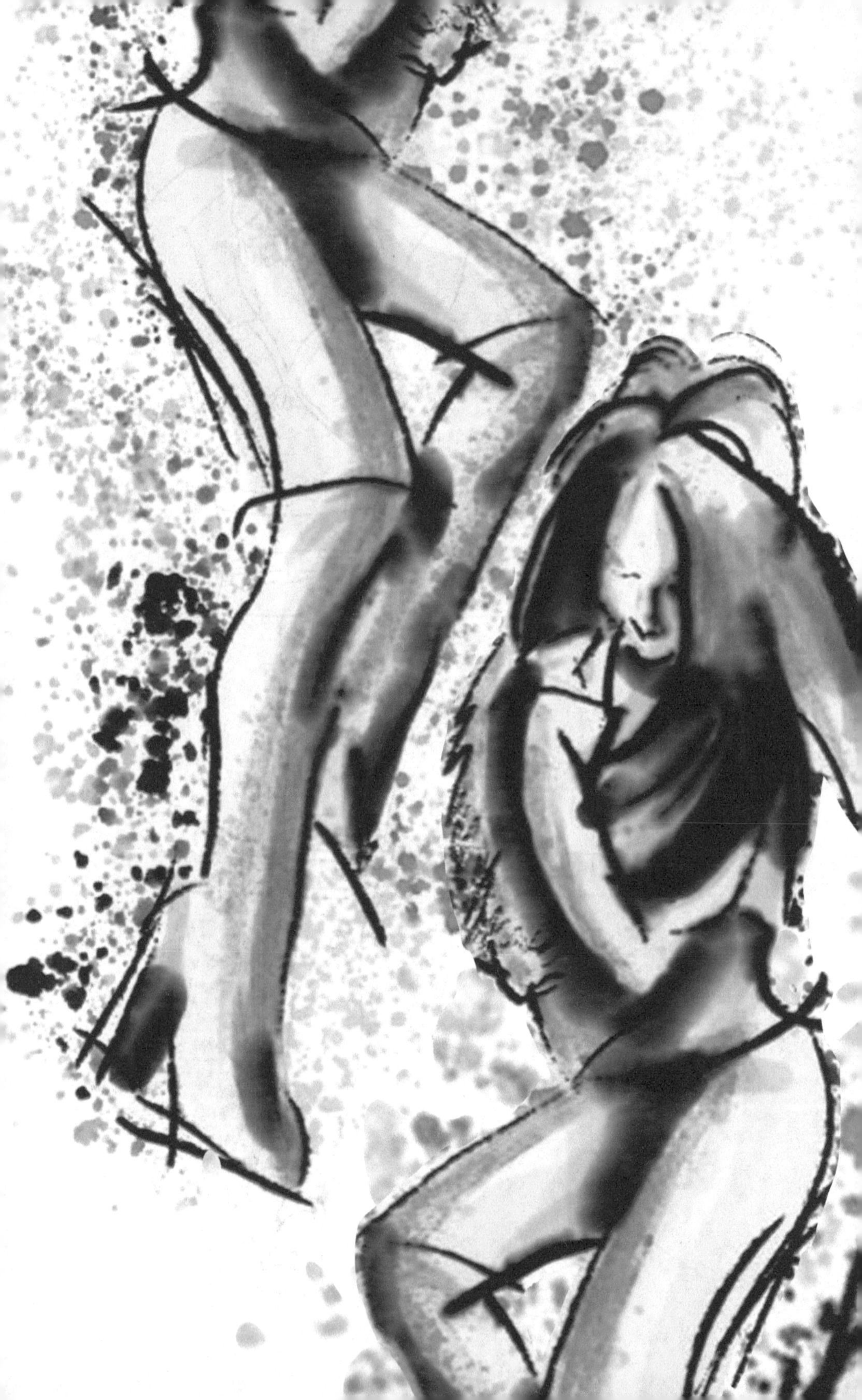

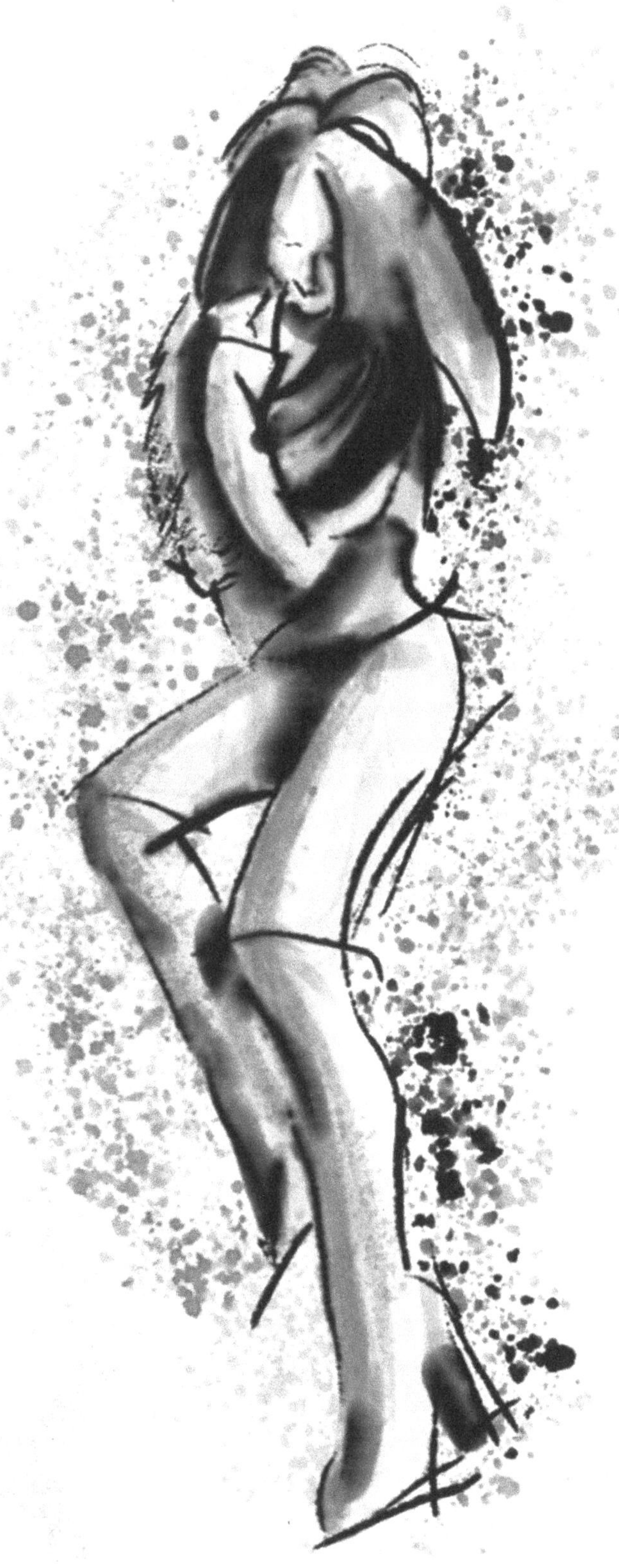

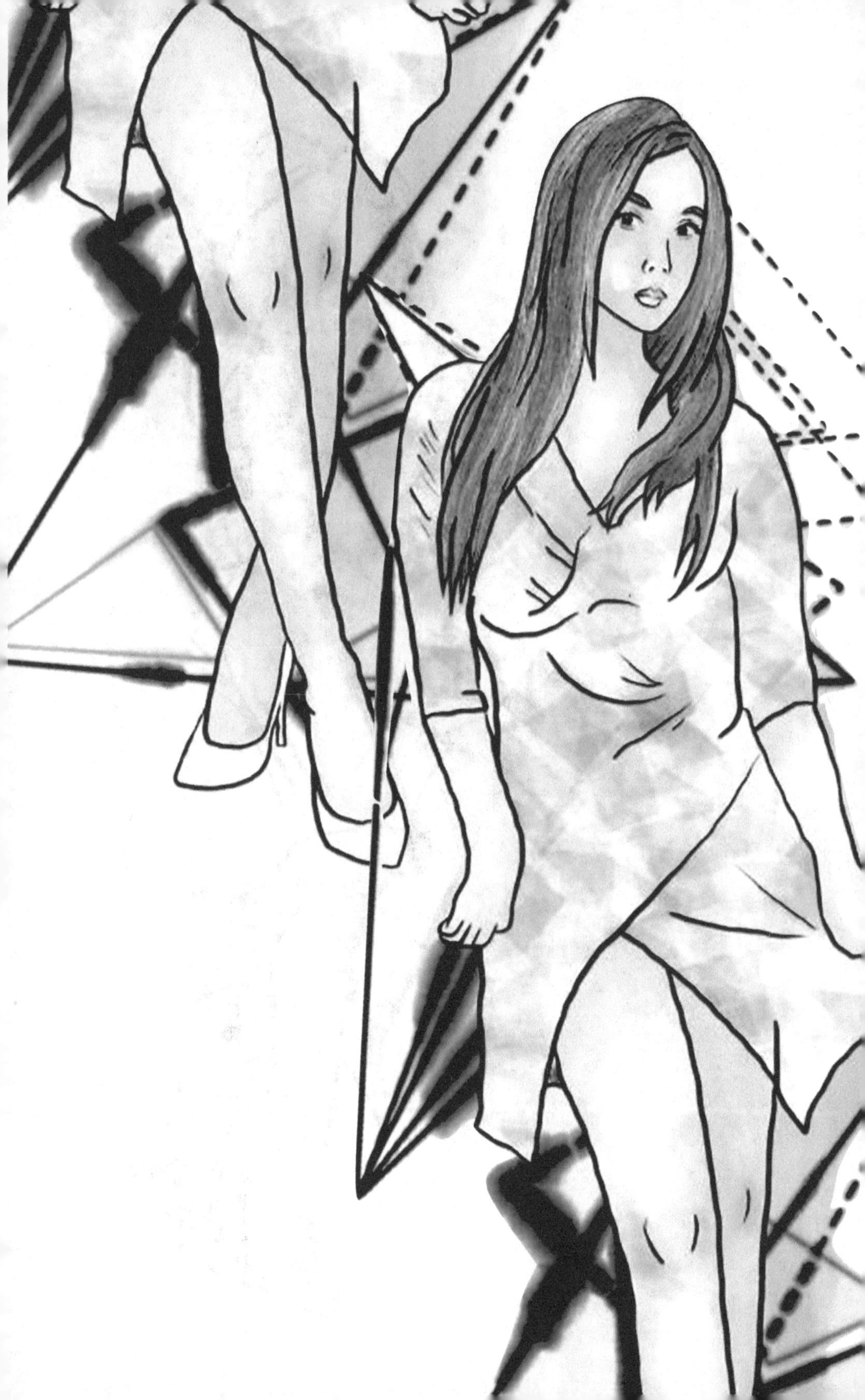

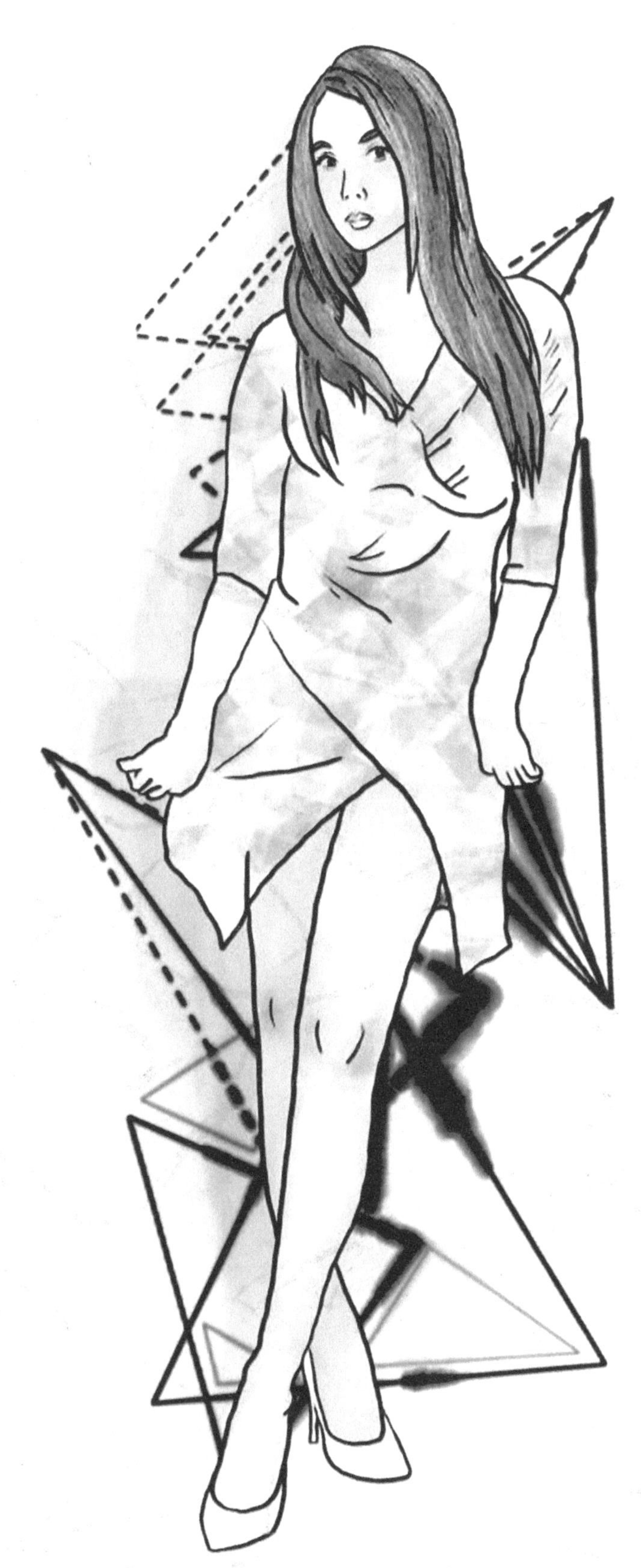

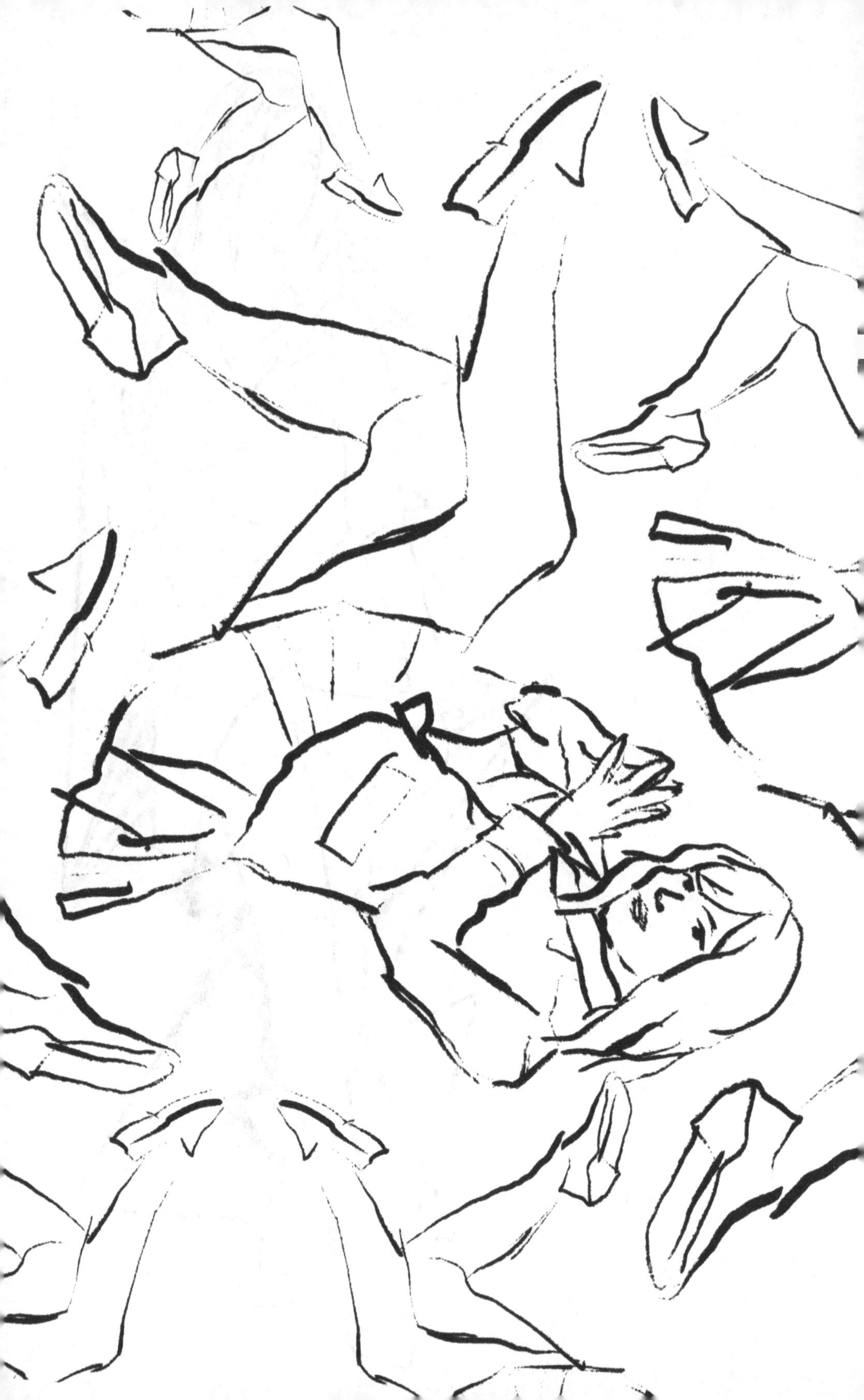

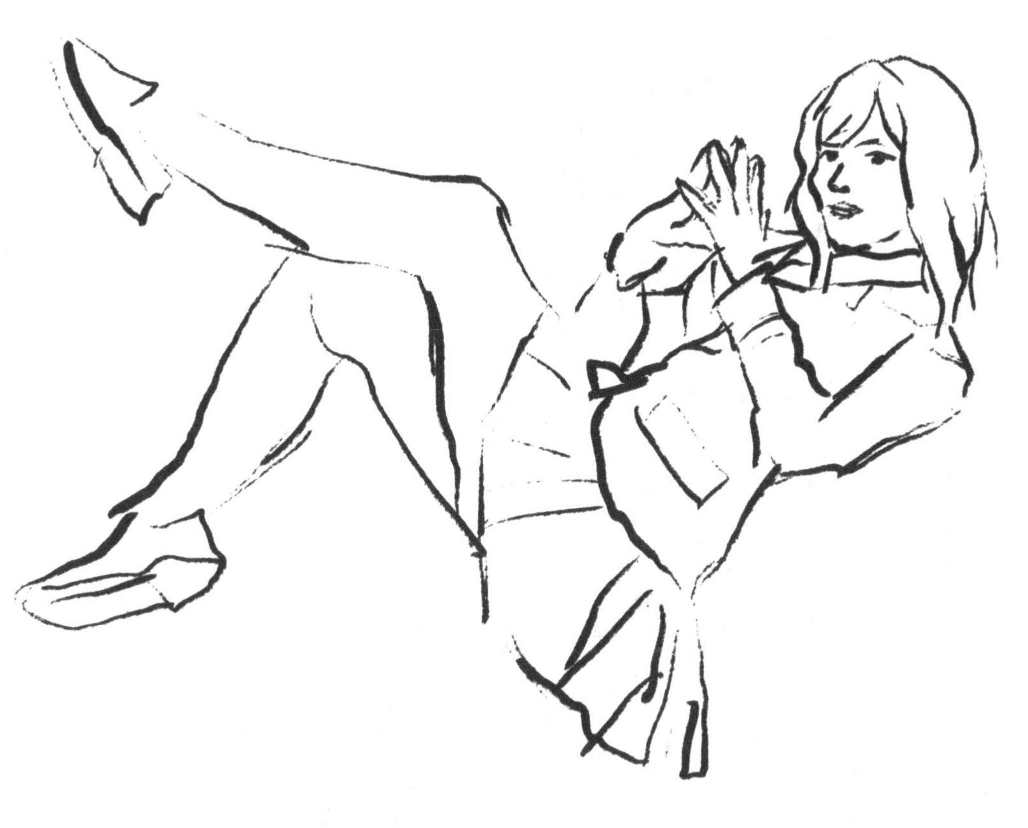

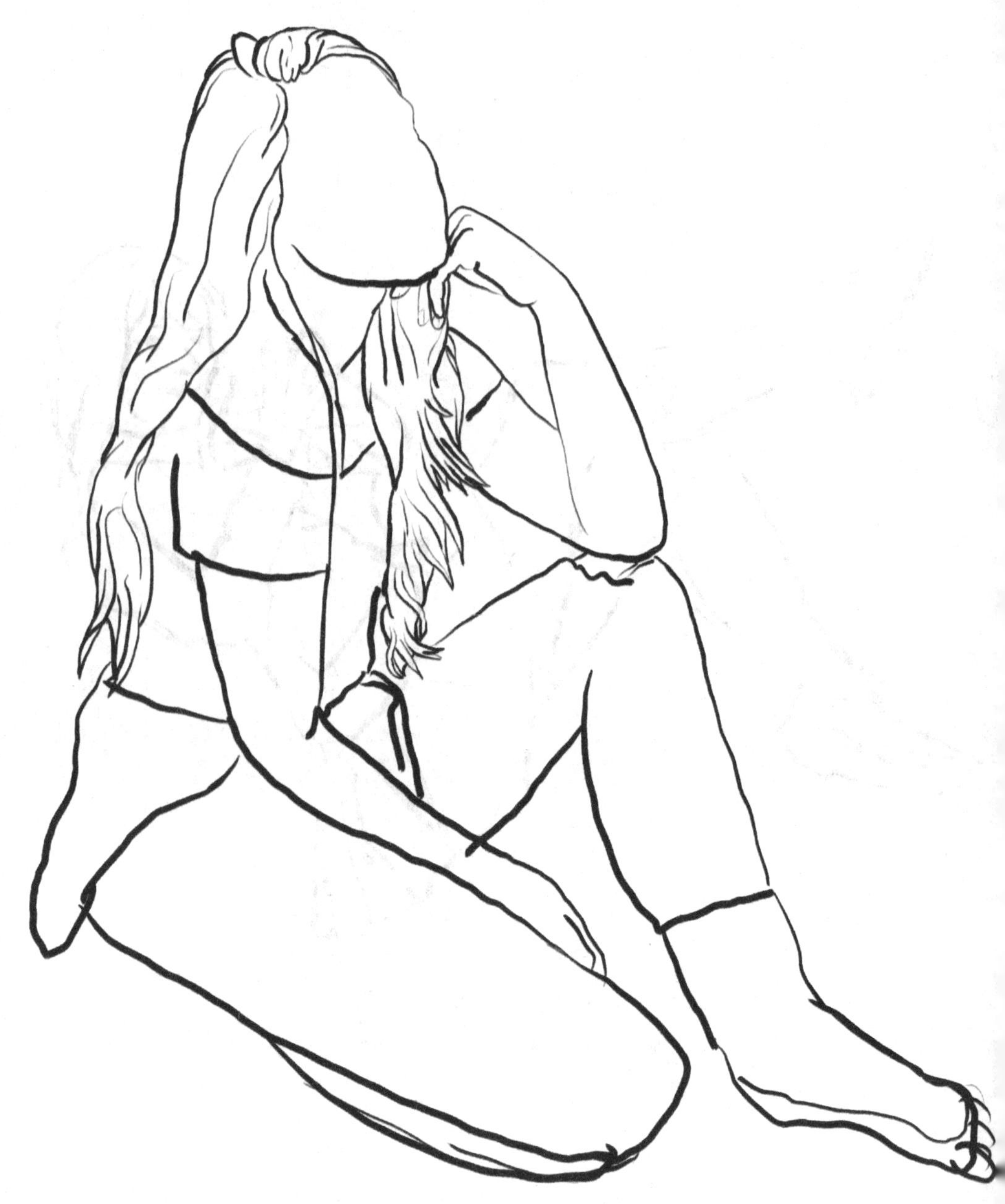

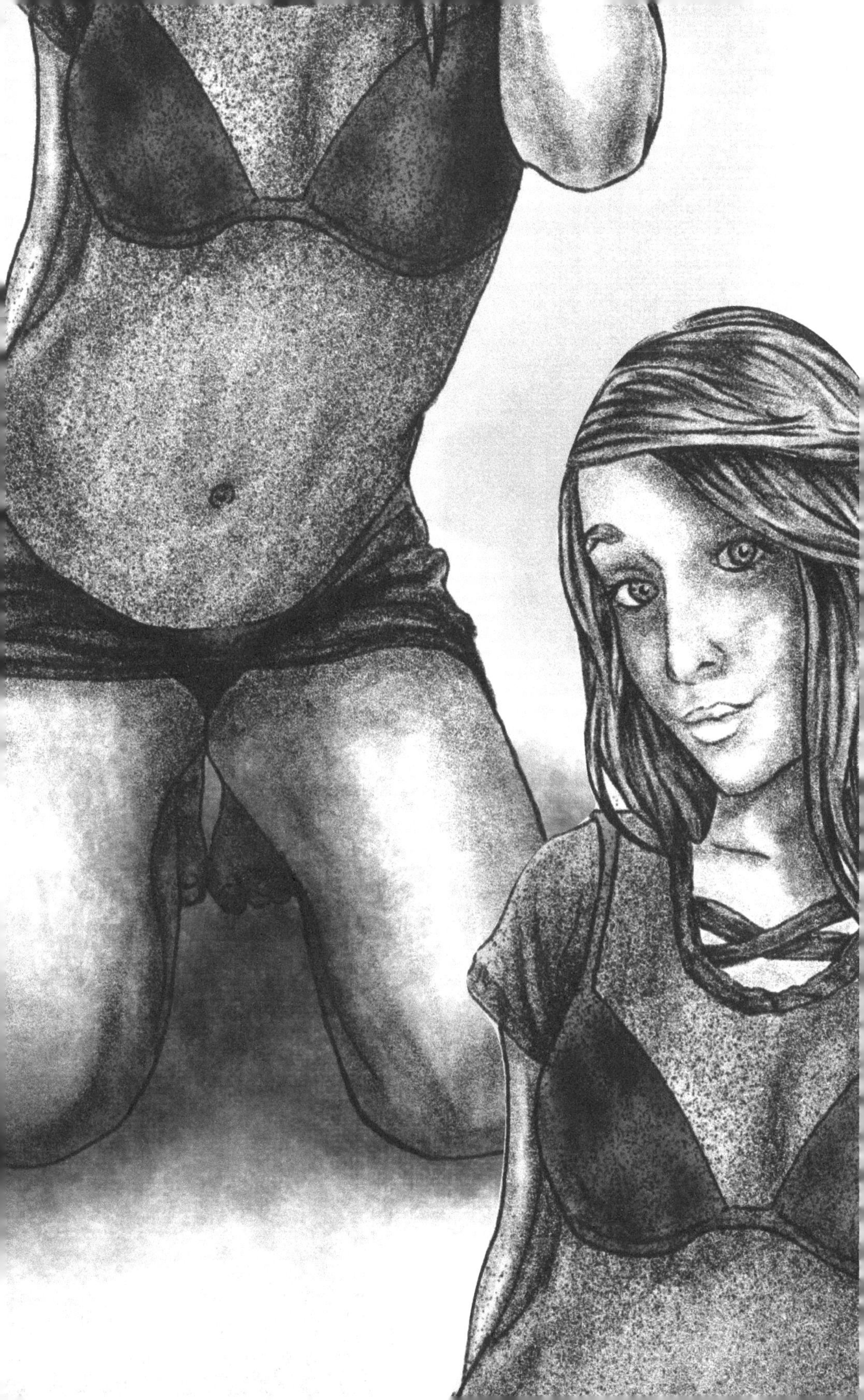

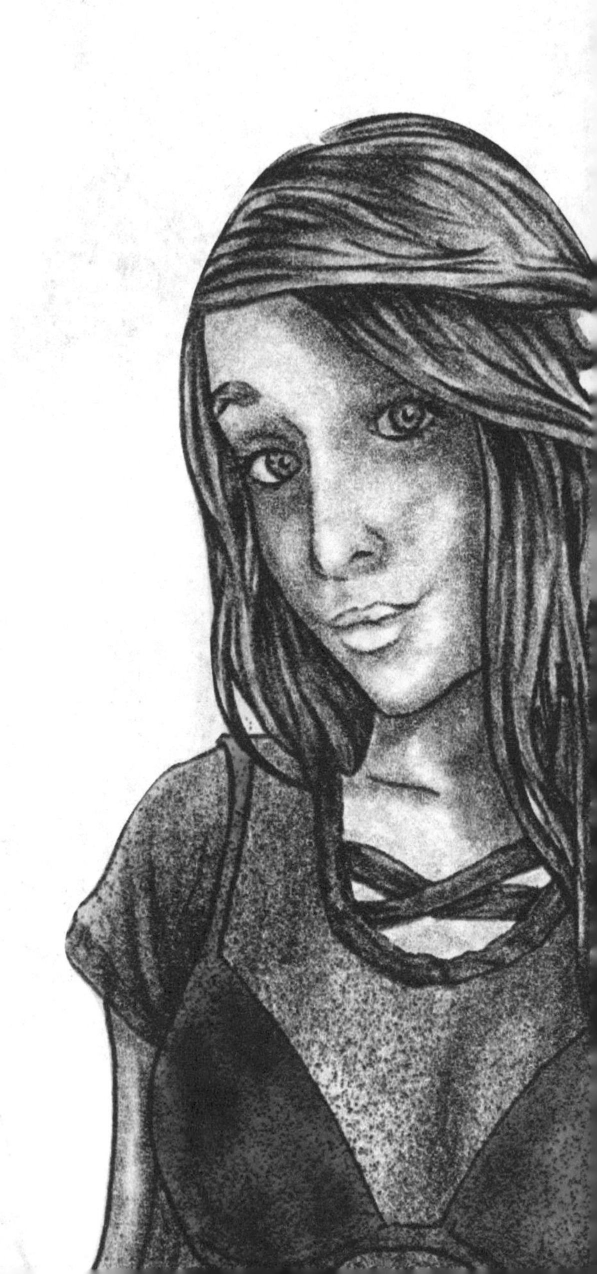

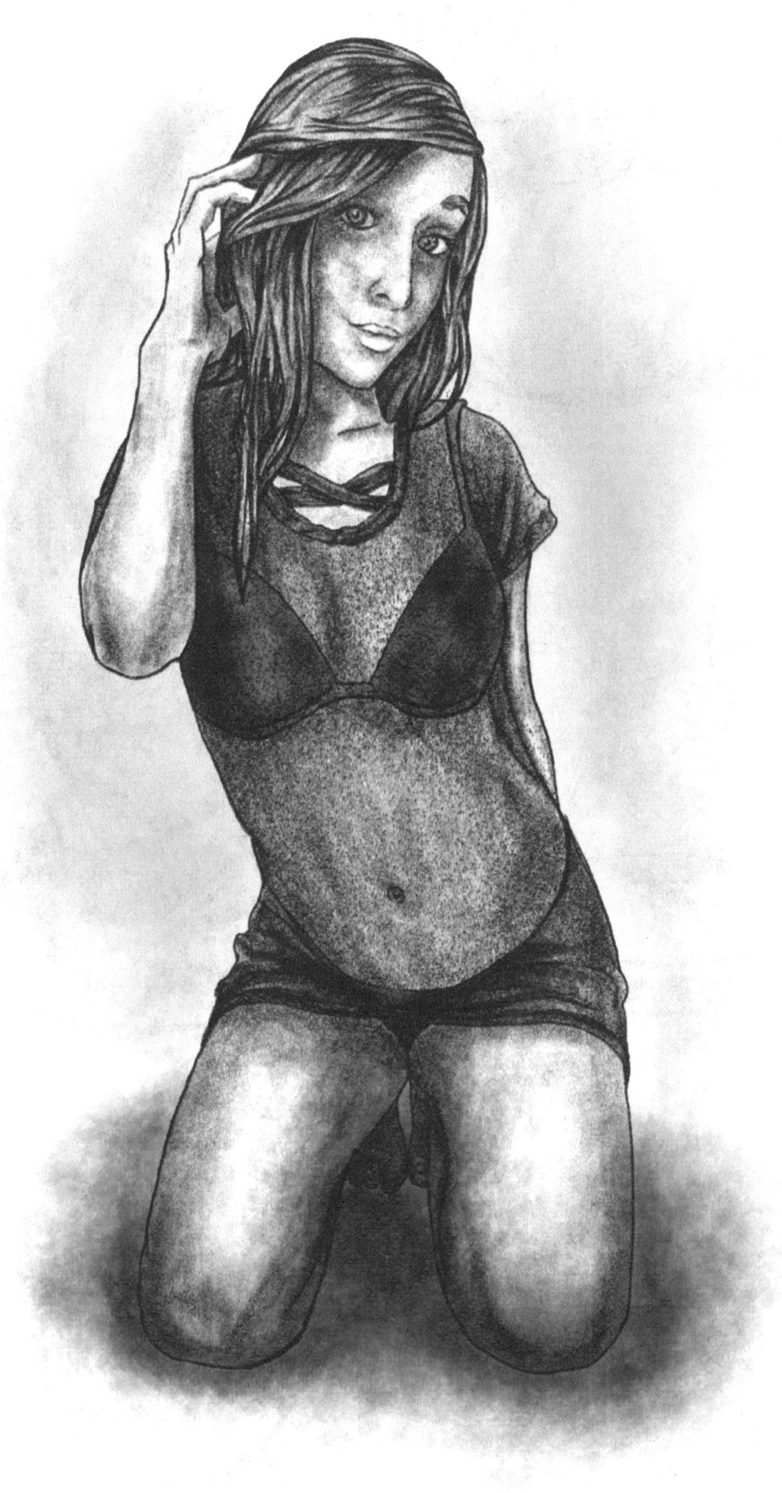

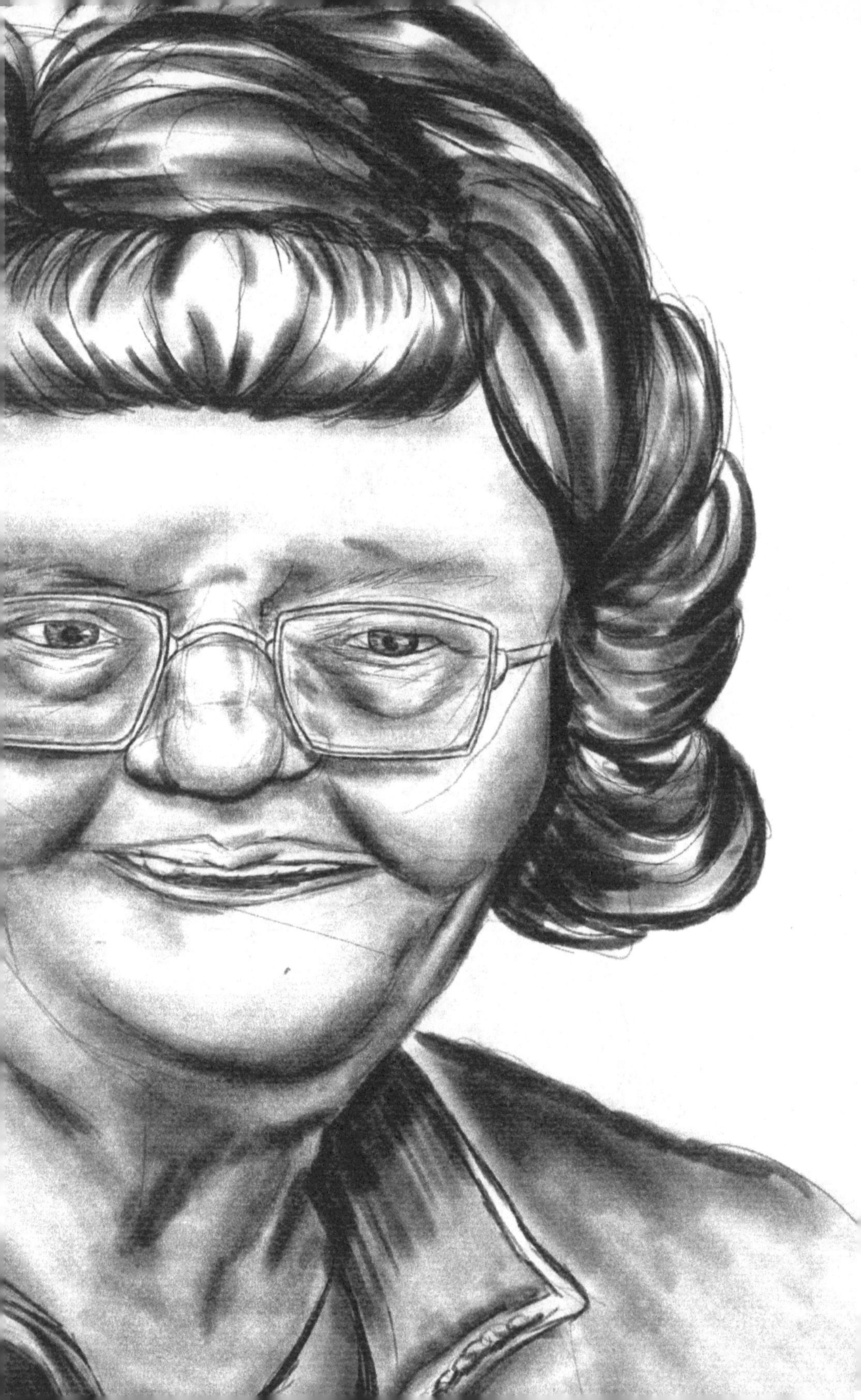

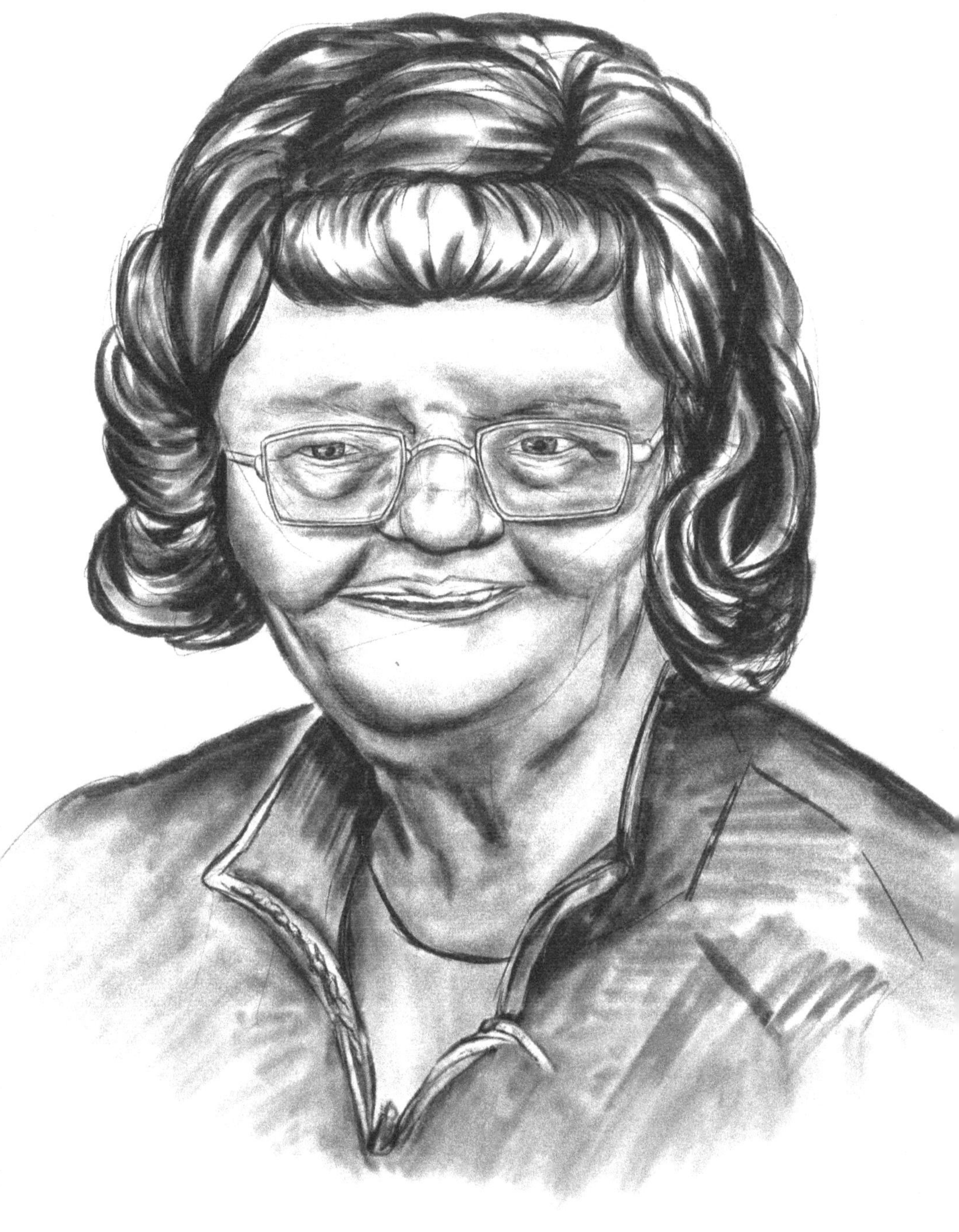

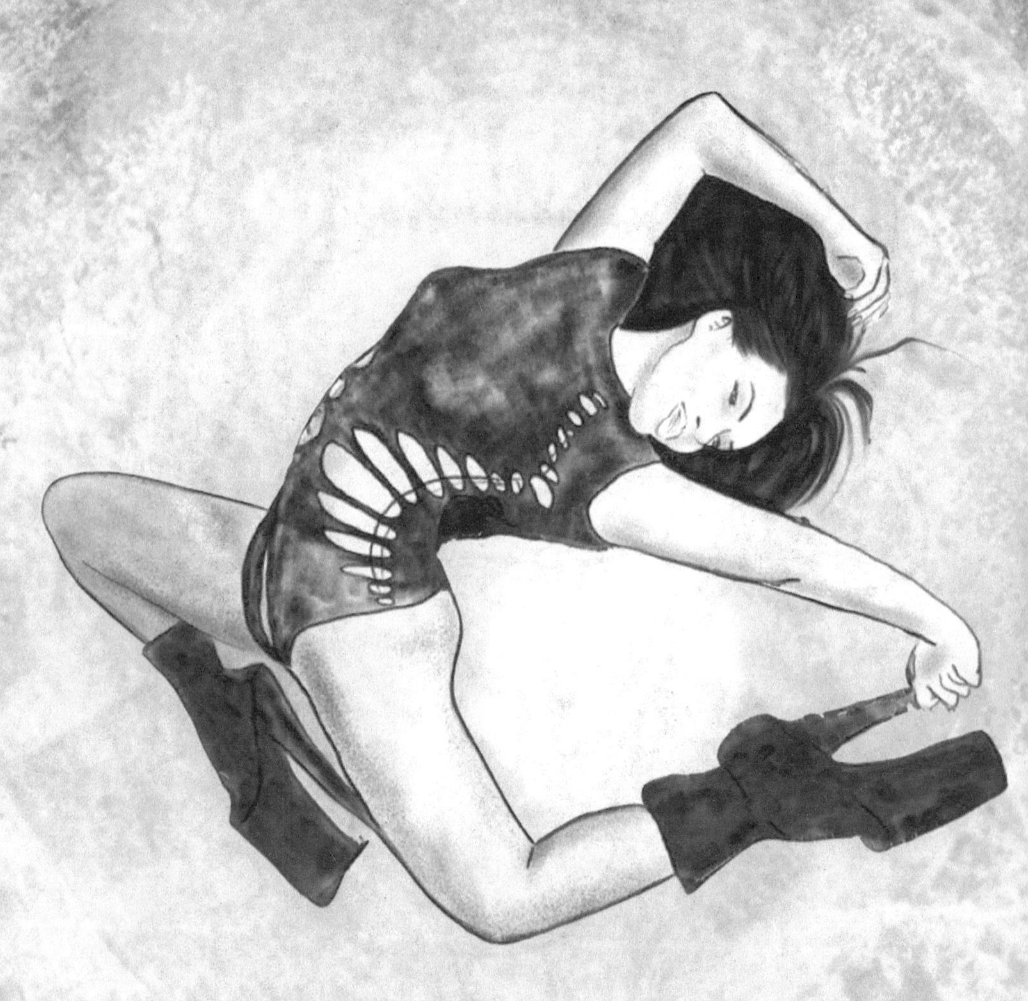

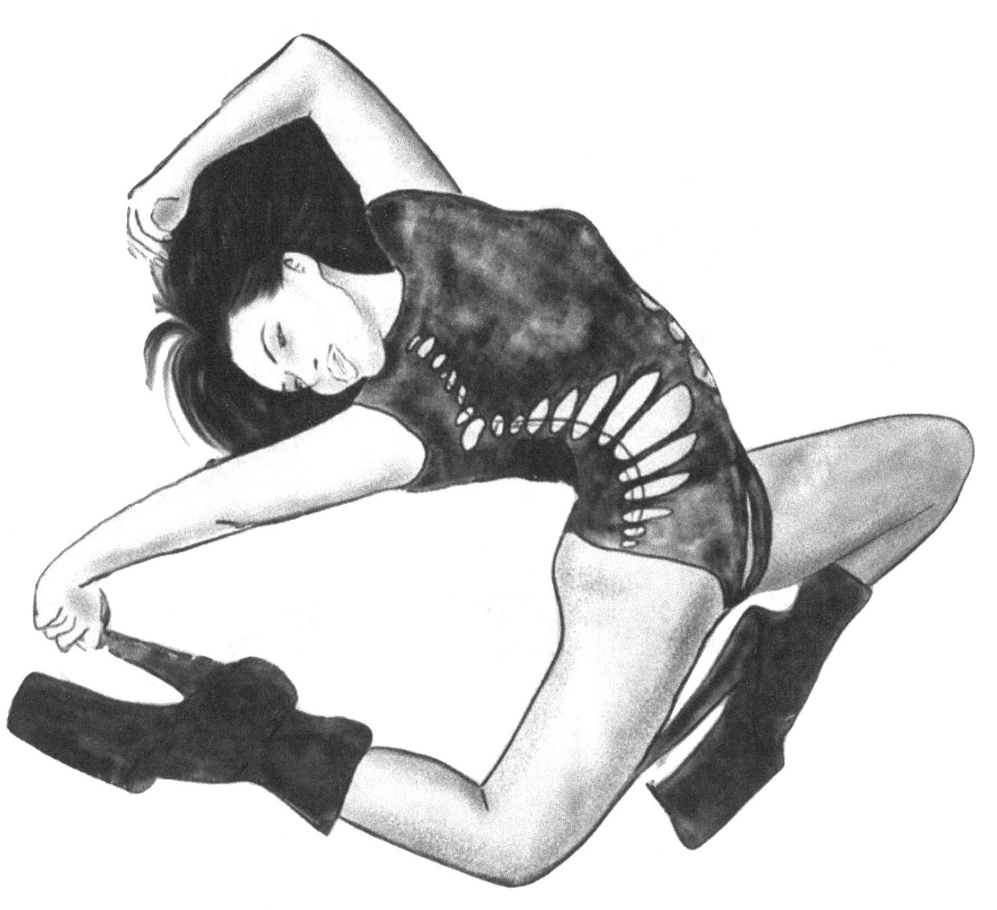

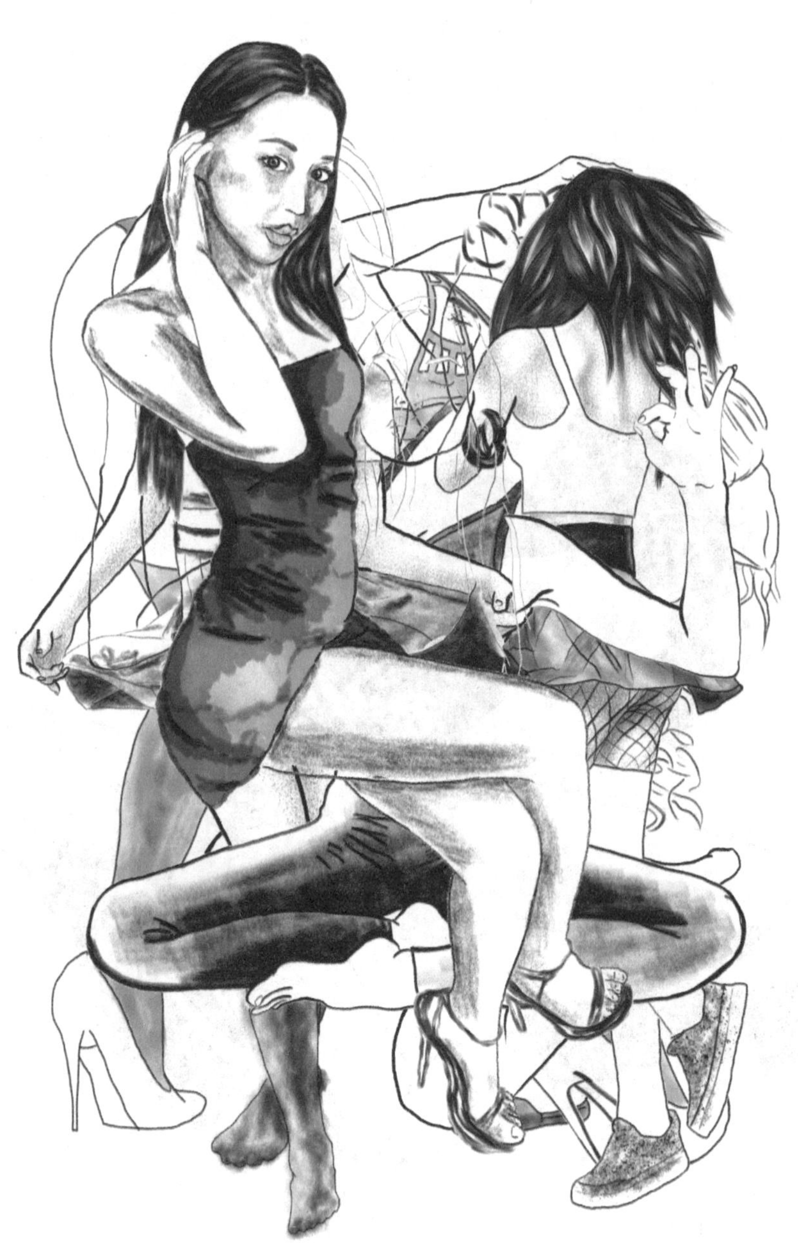

Epilogue

As we reach the conclusion of "Portraitography: Ink'd Artistry of the Female Form," I am profoundly grateful for the privilege of sharing this creative odyssey with you. To each reader who has journeyed through these pages, I extend my heartfelt thanks for your time, curiosity, and appreciation of art's power to captivate and inspire.

Behind every stroke of ink and every brush of paint lies a mosaic of influences and supporters whose contributions are invaluable. To my family, friends, and mentors, I owe a debt of gratitude for their unwavering encouragement and belief in my vision. Your presence in my life has been the cornerstone of my artistic journey.

I also wish to express profound gratitude to the countless women who have lent their strength, grace, and resilience to the creation of this collection. Your essence, captured in these portraits, serves as a tribute to the boundless beauty and power of the female form.

As we bid farewell to these ink'd impressions and monochrome muses, may their presence linger in your hearts, igniting a spark of creativity and appreciation for the artistry that surrounds us. May you continue to seek beauty, find inspiration, and embrace the richness of the human experience through the lens of art.

With deepest appreciation,

Michael Lambert Jr

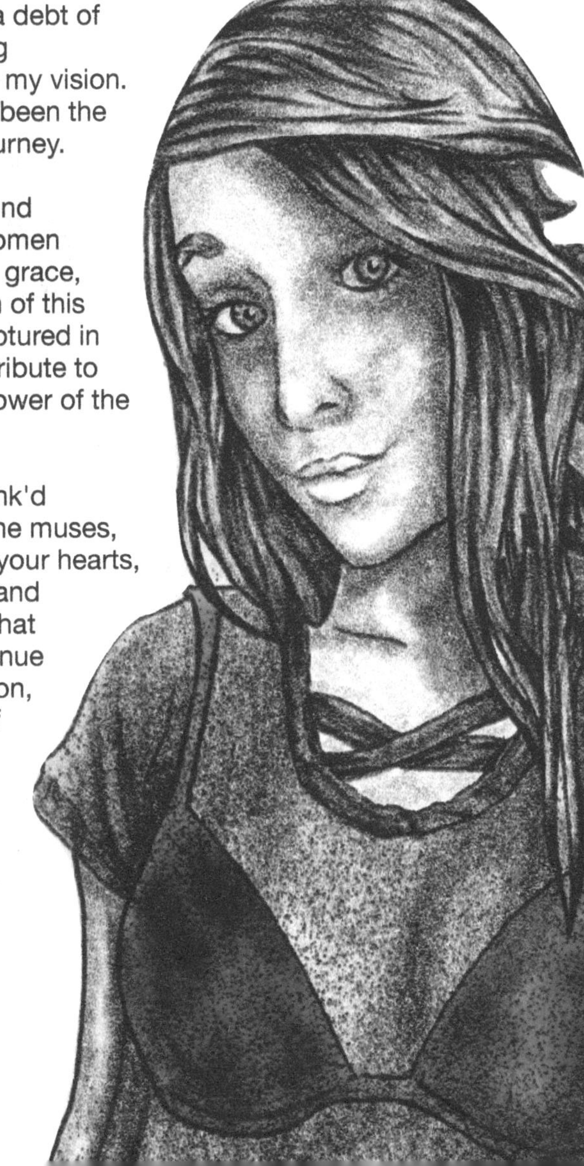

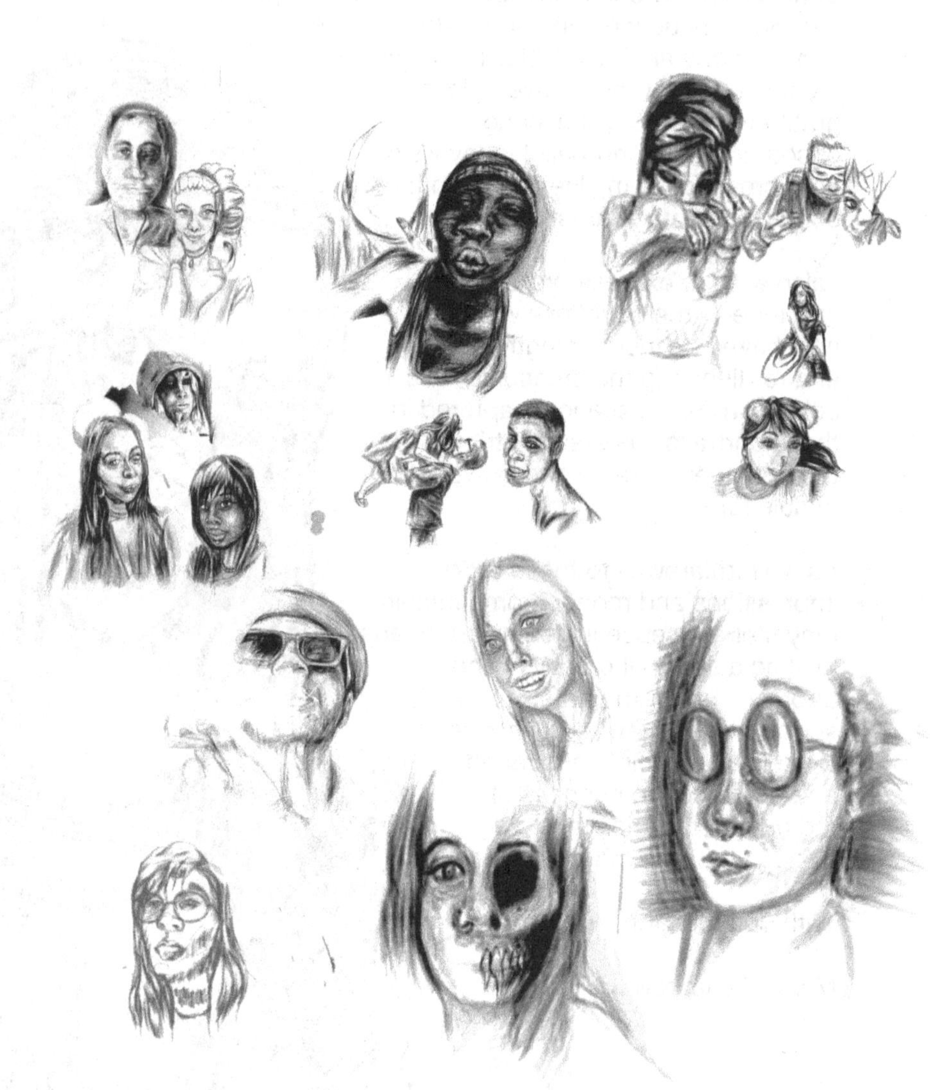